PERSPECTIVES ON PUNI
THE CONTOURS OF CC

Perspectives on Punishment

The Contours of Control

Edited by
SARAH ARMSTRONG
and
LESLEY McARA

OXFORD
UNIVERSITY PRESS

OXFORD
UNIVERSITY PRESS

Great Clarendon Street, Oxford OX2 6DP

Oxford University Press is a department of the University of Oxford.
It furthers the University's objective of excellence in research, scholarship,
and education by publishing worldwide in

Oxford New York

Auckland Cape Town Dar es Salaam Hong Kong Karachi
Kuala Lumpur Madrid Melbourne Mexico City Nairobi
New Delhi Shanghai Taipei Toronto

With offices in

Argentina Austria Brazil Chile Czech Republic France Greece
Guatemala Hungary Italy Japan Poland Portugal Singapore
South Korea Switzerland Thailand Turkey Ukraine Vietnam

Oxford is a registered trade mark of Oxford University Press
in the UK and in certain other Countries

Published in the United States
by Oxford University Press Inc., New York

British Library Cataloguing in Publication Data

Data available

Library of Congress Cataloging in Publication Data

Scottish Criminology Conference (2003 : Edinburgh, Scotland)
Perspectives on punishment : the contours of control / edited by Sarah Armstrong and Lesley McAra.
p. cm.
Revisions of papers originally presented at the Scottish Criminology Conference held Sept. 2003 in Edinburgh.
Includes bibliographical references and index.
ISBN-13: 978–0–19–927876–3
ISBN-10: 0–19–927876–8
1. Punishment–Congresses. 2. Punishment–Europe–Congresses. 3. Social control–Congresses. 4. Criminal
justice, Administration of–Congresses. I. Armstrong, Sarah. II. McAra, Lesley. III. Title.
HV7243.S25 2006
364.6—dc22   2006016669

Typeset by Newgen Imaging Systems (P) Ltd., Chennai, India
Printed in Great Britain
on acid-free paper by
Biddles Ltd., King's Lynn

ISBN 0–19–927876–8 (Hbk.)   978–0–19–927876–3 (Hbk.)
ISBN 0–19–927877–6 (Pbk.)   978–0–19–927877–0 (Pbk.)

1 3 5 7 9 10 8 6 4 2

For L.F.—S.A.
For R., C., and M.—L.M.

Acknowledgements

A few years ago, Lesley McAra suggested that it would be an interesting exercise to bring together, on its twentieth anniversary, the contributors to *The Power to Punish* (1983), a book that, along with several others appearing around the same time, has had a huge influence on the study of punishment. As well as most of the book's contributors, several other scholars whose work has been important to the field joined us in Edinburgh in September 2003 at the Scottish Criminology Conference. We had asked everyone involved to prepare a paper that somehow took stock of where we are in the study of punishment, and to apply this thinking to their main research area. Coordinating the logistics of this large workshop relied on the support and efforts of numerous people and goups. We would like to thank the British Academy and School of Law at Edinburgh University for financial assistance that made this project possible in the first place. We would also like to thank Margaret Beechey, head of the Research Office at the Law School, for her complete commitment in planning and running the conference.

As we developed the papers into a manuscript, we have been grateful for the intellectual stimulation and time we have received from colleagues. In particular, we appreciated the enthusiastic environment of Edinburgh's Centre for Law and Society, and especially discussions with Niamh Nic Shuibhne, and Peter Young. Victor Tadros Sarah also benefited from a sabbatical at the Center for the Study of Law and Society at the University of California, Berkeley, during the spring and summer of 2005, which supplied intellectual stimulation and overflowing research support. We would also like to thank Tony Bunyan at *Statewatch* and Spokesman Books for their permission to include in the chapter by Thomas Mathiesen several paragraphs published under their auspices as part of the launch of the European Civil Liberties Network (http://www.ecln.org/) in October 2005.

Part of Mathiesen's chapter will also be published in *Essays in Defence of Civil Liberties* (forthcoming 2006, Spokesman Books), reproduced here by kind permission.

As anyone who has edited a collection of essays will know, research assistance is essential and we were lucky to have the able skills of two doctoral students, James MacLean and George Papanicolaou. We relied towards the end especially on George, who was able to offer both substantive and technical guidance, and we thank him for taking time away from his own work to see this project through.

Sarah Armstrong
Lesley McAra

Edinburgh University
February 2006

Contents

List of Tables and Figures

List of Abbreviations

ACPO	Association of Chief Police Officers (UK)
ASBO	Anti-Social Behaviour Order (UK)
CPS	Crown Prosecution Service (UK)
ECHR	European Convention on Human Rights
EDCAP	European anti-death penalty organization
EDPS	European Data Protection Supervisor
ESRC	Economic and Social Research Council
EU	European Union
GDP	Gross domestic product
GUIN	central prison authority (Moscow)
ICCPR	International Covenant on Civil and Political Rights
ILO	International Labour Organisation
MCPR	Moscow Centre for Prison Reform
MPC	Model Penal Code (US)
NAPSA	National Association of Pretrial Services Agencies (US)
NGO	Non-governmental organization
OECD	Organization for Economic Co-operation and Development
PRI	Penal Reform International
SIRENE	Supplementary Information Request at the National Entries
SIS	Schengen Information System
TACIS	Technical Aid to the Commonwealth of Independent States
TECS	Europol Computer Systems
WCADP	World Coalition against the Death Penalty
WTO	World Trade Organization

List of Contributors

Sarah Armstrong (co-editor) is a lecturer in criminology and a member of the Centre for Law and Society, University of Edinburgh. Her current research is in the sociology of punishment and focuses on developing a sociology of accountability, analysing privatization in justice and punishment, and contributing to social and cultural scholarship on risk. Recent work has been published in *Punishment and Society*, *The Buffalo Criminal Law Review*, and *Sociology of Health and Illness*. She has recently organized, through a research grant from the Economic and Social Research Council, a number of workshops on law, probability, and risk in penal justice (http://www.lprseminars.org/).

Lesley McAra (co-editor) is a senior lecturer in criminology and a member of the Centre for Law and Society, University of Edinburgh. She writes and teaches in the following fields: the sociology of punishment; youth crime and justice; and gender, crime and criminal justice. Currently she is a co-director of a major programme of research (funded by the ESRC, the Scottish Executive and the Nuffield Foundation) on youth transitions and crime. She has also recently acted as a specialist adviser on youth justice to the Justice 2 Committee of the Scottish Parliament. Recent publications include an article in *Punishment and Society* (2005), developing a systems analytical framework for the study of cross-national transformations in the penal realm; an article in the *Cambrian Law Review* (2004) exploring convergent trends in youth justice in Scotland and England/ Wales; and a chapter on the 'de-tartanization' of the Scottish youth justice system in B. Goldson and J. Muncie (eds) (2006) *Comparative Youth Justice*. London: Sage.

David Downes is professor emeritus of social policy at the London School of Economics. His research interests include comparative sentencing and penal policy, crime and the labour market, and theories of crime and delinquency. He has published widely in these fields with articles in the major criminology journals. He co-authored (with Rod Morgan) 'The Skeletons in the Cupboard: The Politics of Law and Order at the Turn of the Millennium' for the *Oxford Handbook of Criminology* (3rd edn, 2002). The fourth edition of his book (co-authored with Paul Rock), *Understanding Deviance*, was published in 2004. His study of post-war penal policy in the Netherlands and England, *Contrasts in Tolerance*, was published in 1988 (and re-issued in paperback in 1993).

Lindsay Farmer is professor of law at the University of Glasgow. He is the author of *Criminal Law, Tradition and Legal Order* (1997) and editor (with A. Duff, S.E. Marshall, and V. Tadros) of *The Trial on Trial I: Truth and Due Process* (2004) and *The Trial on Trial II: Judgment and Calling to Account* (2006). He has written a number of articles on the history and theory of criminal law, and is currently working on a history of the criminal trial and criminal law in the late nineteenth century.

Malcolm Feeley holds the Claire Sanders Clements Dean's Chair of Law at the University of California, Berkeley. He has written numerous articles in social science journals and law reviews and is the author of several books, including *The Process is the Punishment* (1992), which received the American Bar Association's Silver Gavel Award and the American Sociology Association's Citation of Merit, *Court Reform on Trial* (1989), which received the ABA's Certificate of Merit, and *The Policy Dilemma* (1981). He is the co-author (with Jerome Skolnick and Candace McCoy) of *Criminal Justice* (2004) and (with Ed Rubin) of *Judicial Policy Making and the Modern State* (1998). Recent publications include, 'Crime, social order and the rise of neo-Conservative politics' in *Theoretical Criminology* (2003), and 'Entrepreneurs of punishment: The legacy of privatization' in *Punishment and Society* (2002). He is currently serving as president of the Law and Society Association (until 2007).

Evi Girling is a lecturer in criminology at the University of Keele. Her research interests include fear of crime; place and identity; oral history; children, young people, and punishment; death penalty and global penal politics. She is the co-author (with Ian Loader and Richard Sparks) of *Crime and Social Change in Middle England* (2000), and her recent work on abolition of the death penalty has been published in the journal *Punishment and Society* (2004) and in two collections, *The Cultural Lives of the Death Penalty* (2005, edited by A. Sarat and C. Boulanger) and *Zur Aktualitaet der Todesstrafe. Interdisziplinaere und globale Perspektiven* (2002, edited by C. Boulanger, V. Heyes, and P. Hanfling).

Kirstine Hansen is Research Director of the Millennium Cohort Study at the Centre for Longitudinal Studies at the Institute of Education. Her current research interests include: crime and labour markets and life course trajectories of disadvantaged children. Recent publications include: 'Education and the Crime-Age Profile' in the *British Journal of Criminology* (2003), 'Spatial Crime Patterns and the Introduction of the UK Minimum Wage', *Oxford Bulletin of Economics and Statistics* (2003), and 'Crime and the Minimum Wage', forthcoming in the *Journal of Quantitative Criminology*.

Neil Hutton is professor and co-Director of the Centre for Sentencing Research at the School of Law, Strathclyde University, and currently serving as Dean of the Faculty of Law, Arts and Social Sciences. He is a leading member of the team which has developed and implemented a Sentencing Information System for the High Court of Justiciary. His research focuses on sentencing and the sociology of punishment. Recent publications include: 'Beyond Populist Punitiveness?' in *Punishment and Society* (2005), 'Sentencing Guidelines' in *Confronting Crime* (2003, edited by Michael Tonry), and (with C. Tata) 'The Judicial Role in the Balance between Two Visions of Justice in Sentencing' in *The Judicial Role in Criminal Proceedings* (2000, edited by Sean Doran and John Jackson). He has also co-edited (with C. Tata) two books, *Sentencing and Society* (2002) and (with P. Duff), *Criminal Justice in Scotland* (1999).

Richard Jones is a lecturer in criminology at the University of Edinburgh. His research interests are in the areas of the sociology of punishment, technologies of social control, cybercrime, and the politics of criminal justice.

Thomas Mathiesen is professor of sociology of law at the University of Oslo, Norway. He is the author of a number of books in English and other languages on sociology of law, criminology, the sociology of power and counter-power, and media sociology. He is also a co-founder of the Norwegian prisoners' movement. He is currently engaged in research on the regional and global surveillance systems which are now developing in Europe, and has written extensively on them in English as well as Norwegian. His most recent books in English are *Silently Silenced – Essays on the Creation of Acquiescence in Modern Society* (2004), and *Prison on Trial* (3rd edn, 2006).

Laura Piacentini is a lecturer in criminology at the University of Stirling in Scotland. Her main interest and publication profile focuses on a critical and cultural engagement with penal policy in transition, with the present-day Russian prison system occupying the main focus of her research. Laura has advised international organizations on prisoners' work having recently been appointed as adviser to the Scottish Parliament on an inquiry into rehabilitation in Scottish prisons. She is the co-investigator, along with colleagues at Birmingham and Oxford Universities, of a project looking at the geography of punishment as it relates to Russian women prisoners. Laura's first book, *Surviving Russian Prisons: Punishment, Economy and Politics in Transition*, was awarded the British Society of Criminology book of the year award in 2005 and was nominated for the Distinguished Book Award of the Division of International Criminology of the American Society of Criminology also in 2005.

Andrew Scull is Distinguished Professor of Sociology and Science Studies at the University of California, San Diego. He has written extensively on social control, including work on law, policing, and the history of prisons, but has primarily focused on the historical sociology of psychiatry. His two most recent books are: *Madhouse: A Tragic Tale of Megalomania and Modern Medicine* (2005), and *The Insanity of Place/The Place of Insanity* (2006).

Richard Sparks holds the Chair in Criminology at the University of Edinburgh. His main research interests lie in the sociology of punishment (especially imprisonment); penal politics; and public responses to crime and punishment. Recent and current research projects have included an account (with Marion Smith and Evi Girling) of nine-year-old children's conversations about justice and punishment and (with Elaine Crawley) a study of older men in English prisons. He is the author of *Television and the Drama of Crime* (1992), co-author (with Tony Bottoms and Will Hay) of *Prisons and the Problem of Order* (1996), and (with Evi Girling and Ian Loader) of *Crime and Social Change in Middle England* (2000). He has also co-edited a number of books of which the most recent (with Tim Newburn) is *Criminal Justice and Political Cultures* (2004).

Loïc Wacquant is Professor of Sociology at the University of California, Berkeley, and Researcher at the Centre de sociologie Européenne, Paris. A MacArthur Foundation Fellow, he is cofounder and editor of the interdisciplinary journal *Ethnography*. His interests include comparative urban marginality, ethnoracial domination, the penal state, embodiment, and social theory and the politics of reason. His recent books include *Body and Soul: Notebooks of an Apprentice Boxer* (2004), *The Mystery of Ministry: Pierre Bourdieu and Democratic Politics* (2005), *Parias Urbains, Ghetto, banlieues, État* (2006), *Deadly Symbiosis: Race and the Rise of Neoliberal Penality* (2006), and *Punishing the Poor: The New Government of Social Insecurity* (forthcoming in 2007).

Table of Cases

1

Audiences, Borders, Architecture: the Contours of Control

Sarah Armstrong and Lesley McAra

Perspectives on Punishment

This book has three inter-related aims: to take stock of current thinking on punishment, regulation, and control in the early years of a new century and in the wake of a number of critical junctures (including 9/11), which have transformed the social, political, and cultural environment within which regimes of punishment are situated; to present a selection of the diverse epistemological and methodological frameworks which inform current research on punishment; and, finally, to set out some fruitful directions for the future study of punishment.

The contributions to this collection cover some of the most exciting and challenging areas of current research including: terrorism and the politics of fear; post-soviet penality; abolitionism and the search for a new European penal identity; the impact of digital culture on modes of compliance; the emergent hegemony of information and surveillance systems; and the evolving politics of victimhood. Taken together, they draw connections between local problems of crime control, transnational forms of governance, and the ways in which certain political and jurisprudential discourses have come to dominate policy and practice in Western penal systems.

In this chapter we map out the evolving terrains within which punishment and its study are located; highlight three inter-related themes which capture key aspects of contemporary developments—audience, borders, architecture; and explore the ways in which the contributions by our individual authors illuminate these themes.

A central claim will be that punishment has had an increasingly important role to play in building political capacity at all levels of the contemporary regulatory order (from the global to the local): it lies at the heart of contemporary debates on the liminalities of citizenship and the nature of inclusion; it is a mechanism through which political identities are constituted, ascribed, and sometimes resisted; it is a context within which the paradox of governance in late modernity is played out; and it forms the underbelly of efforts to construct new forms of community and political connection, to establish territorial and spatial integrity.

We begin the chapter with a background section on the 'sociological turn' in penology; we then trace some of the key transformations of the past twenty years which form the backdrop to the book, before setting out in more detail our three overarching themes.

Background

Prior to the late 1970s and early 1980s, there had been relatively little *systematic* application of social or political theory and method to the analysis of punishment. Aside from a number of seminal works such as Durkheim's (1964) functionalist analysis of the role of punishment in maintaining social solidarity and Rusche and Kirchheimer's (1934) application of Marxist materialism to the nature and function of particular forms of penal sanction, penology as a discipline tended to be empiricist in approach, descriptive and, on occasions, theoretically flat in execution (see Garland 1994).

From the mid-1980s onwards, however, the social analysis of punishment gained considerable momentum. This has been variously attributed to: the impact of Foucault's work in the late 1970s, linking punishment to power and social structures through his genealogical analysis (see Foucault 1979); the paradigm shift within criminology in the late 1960s and early 1970s (brought about by the increasing influence of labelling theory and critical criminological perspectives) which had the effect of focusing attention on the political dimension of crime control and penal process; and the looming sense of crisis within certain penal systems, in the wake of prison overcrowding, lack of confidence in prevailing penal ideologies, and increasing fiscal vulnerability (see Allen 1981; Bottoms 1980, 1995).

A number of key works published during the 1980s and early 1990s aimed to set an academic as well as a political agenda by critically engaging with social theory (as the principal lens through which to 'read' contemporary penal systems) and identifying the preconditions necessary for the development of a grounded praxis (Garland and Young 1983, Cohen and Scull 1984, Scull 1984, Cohen 1985, Lowman *et al* 1987, Blomberg and Cohen 1995). By restyling punishment as 'penality', Garland and Young (1983), in particular, attempted to show how punishment both reflects (indeed is 'over-determined' by) a range of social, economic, political, and cultural processes, and has a significant role in the construction of such processes.

Evolving Terrain of the New Millennium

In the twenty years since the 'sociological turn' in penology, there have been seismic shifts in the social, political, and cultural environments of penal regimes, coupled with transformations in the context of knowledge production.

These transformations present a number of epistemological and metho-dological challenges for an evolving discipline that is attempting to straddle both normative and descriptive sociology and whose *sine qua non* is the inter-dependency between punishment and the environment within which it is located.

Restructuring of conflict and global tensions

A dramatic shift in the dynamics of global conflict is a major part of this changing context. The political map of Europe has, of course, been transformed with the collapse of the former Soviet Union and the emergence of fledgling (and in some cases still fragile) parliamentary democracies formed out of former eastern bloc states. While older Cold-War ideologies (east versus west; capitalism versus communism) have now diminished in significance, these have been supplanted across Europe and Asia by pockets of aggressive identity politics, as, for example in Armenia and Azerbaijan or the former Yugoslavia. They have also been supplanted by the so-called north/south divide (between the rich northern nations including the United States and European countries, and poorer southern nations as, for example, in Africa and Central and South America). According to Sachs (2001), this divide has led to the emergence of a global consumer class which coexists with, and triumphs over, a socially marginalized majority (who subsist out-with global circuits). The gap between these classes is widening with deleterious consequences for climate and biodiversity, as well as economic development (Sachs 2001).

Tensions within the Middle East have also spilled over into a more global-level conflict precipitated by an intensification of radical Islamic politics against (what is perceived as) a more secular west. Jihad is hydra-headed, pro-secuted (for the most part) by a loose range of complex cross-cutting groups and manifested in (sometimes 'spectacular') acts of terrorism across different countries (Lesser *et al* 1999, Mythen and Walklate 2005). The so-called new forms of terrorism complement the emergence of, what some commentators have termed, 'new wars' (see Kaldor 1999) whose strategic goals are: population expulsion or ethnic cleansing through mass killings; forcible resettlement; as well as rape, mutilations, and other forms of intimidation (for example in the con-flicts in Bosnia and Rwanda during the 1990s). New wars are fought by a disparate and often highly decentralized set of groups, such as paramilitary units, criminal gangs, police forces, sometimes regular armies, sometimes breakaway units of these regular armies. They are conducted according to, what Bauman (2000) would term, a paradigm of exclusion where other identities require to be destroyed or expelled. Fear has become a primary mechanism of social solidarity among the protagonists of such conflicts, expressed in the terrorization, humiliation, and mortification of excluded groups.

Multi-level governance

Over the past twenty years law and legal regulation in advanced liberal societies have become, paradoxically, both more remote *and* more immediate as power and control leech away from the nation-state to the trans/supra-national and sub-state levels. At the transnational level, a range of sometimes competing and cross-cutting economic and political dynamics are at work – examples include efforts to ensure positive integration within the European Union, the development of the International Criminal Court and transnational police cooperation. At the sub-state level, a myriad of more soft forms of governance have emerged – underscored by new conceptualizations of territory, community, and family (for example social inclusion partnerships, neighbourhood watch, parenting programmes) (see Cole 2005, Carter and Smith 2004). In Europe, these processes have led to significant transformations in the nature of citizenship, repositioning citizens as functionaries of the more localized mechanisms of governance, as global consumers of emergent transnational security provisions, and as members of newly constituted supra-national communities. They have also led to changes in the scope and function of indigenous political institutions at the nation-state level, as they seek to rearticulate national identity and grapple with the fall-out from their loss of sovereignty (see Prokhovnik 1999, Jackson 1999, Pattie *et al* 2003, Major 2005).

Emergent narratives

The shifting modes of governance and global tensions have contributed to the increased dominance of a range of (often) competing and multi-textured narratives which frame the political discourse of late modernity.

Risk is one such narrative. All pervasive, it shapes institutional practices and social interactions in ways which are at one level rational and calculating (as exemplified by the use of 'scientific' risk assessment tools), but which too often are underpinned by darker sensibilities and a desire to exclude (with social solidarity stemming from the fear of 'the other', 'the outsider', 'the dangerous group') (see Beck 1992, Giddens 1991, Douglas 1992).

At the same time, a rights discourse has also increasingly leeched into normative political language in the wake of the collapse of Cold-War ideologies (S. Cohen 1993). There has been a rapid growth in the number of national and international pressure and campaign groups over the past twenty years (covering a range of issues from ecology and animal rights to copyright and genetic privacy), with a concomitant surge in international protocols and conventions (linked in particular to the rights of the child and to the administration of justice). In contrast to narratives associated with risk, rights discourse serves to situate the citizen both as a rights bearer and rights claimant in a contractual relationship with the state.

The emergence of such movements as 'third way' politics within the United Kingdom (see Giddens 1998, Gamble and Wright 1999) has developed out of the failure of neo-liberalism to provide a market solution to older perceived welfare dependency, and represents an attempt to navigate risk and rights discourses. Such movements mark a significant shift away from the crude individualism which had characterized neo-liberal administrations (both in the United States and the United Kingdom during the 1980s), whilst at the same time aiming to transcend older style social democracy. Third way politics has been accompanied by a renewed faith in scientific rationalism, with evidence-based policy and managerialist imperatives together forming a cornerstone of its narrative frame.

A concomitant development, however, has been the increased purchase which identity politics has come to hold on the contemporary psyche, manifested in a complex layering of narratives which cut across more traditional social divisions in respect of gender, class, and nationality. 'Women of colour', the 'fourth world' (as per its original meaning of indigenous and displaced peoples) and the pre-eminence of other religious and cultural groupings, are testimony to the range of multiple and sometimes contested identities which frame debates on inclusion and citizenship.

Communication and technological development

As has been well documented elsewhere (Bogard 1996, Garland 2001, Lianos 2000), one of the most profound transformations during the past twenty years has been the rise of mass information technologies and systems of communication. Advances in digital and microchip technology, the widespread availability of e-mail and mobile phones, and the nature and function of the internet have brought greater facility and immediacy to social interaction. These advances have undergirded evolving global networks and provide the hardware required for the construction of so-called information superhighways.

The paradox of many of these advances is that, while they provide opportunities for greater control (through increased electronic surveillance and information gathering), they also function to liberate, principally by creating a space in which counter-narratives of resistance can flourish (see Bogard 1996, Lyon 1994, Jones Chapter 10). The internet (via blogs, chatrooms, dedicated websites, etc) enables us to hear the voices of oppressed minorities, of political freedom fighters, of victims and survivors, and of ordinary individuals. In the electronic domain, social class/status becomes determined both by level of access and by the number of 'hits', whilst extreme social marginalization comes in the form of the electronically dispossessed (those with no access to the relevant hardware).

Ecology and urban dynamics

Urban architecture and the structure and usage of public space in advanced liberal societies have all experienced huge transformations as well. New terminologies have come to frame the post-industrial landscape, each eloquent testimony to the localized impact of macro (sometimes global) economic forces, for example: 'rust-belt' (industrial decline, economic marginalization, structurally redundant populations); and 'brown-belt' (development opportunity, economic regeneration, structurally upwardly-mobile populations).

Contemporary urban architecture is diverse, flexible, ironic (see in particular Coates 1992). It controls the flows of populations over time and space; it reconstructs urban communities and shapes lifestyle; it attempts to reconnect the individual with their particular locale through features as diverse as pedestrianization, the proliferation of public artworks, the reframing of older industrial architecture under the auspices of heritage. Such architectural change has been accompanied by the construction of digitized sanctuaries within the new forms of urban space (the gated community, the shopping mall, new-build offices, etc), colonization of which is controlled by forms of electronic surveillance – for example identity cards, biotechnological recognition systems, CCTV cameras (Norris *et al* 1998, Ditton and Short 1999).

Changes in the context of knowledge production

There have also been major changes in the context of knowledge production. Within the social sciences, there has been increasing recognition on the part of some scholars that the tropes and epistemic framework of the modernist scientific project fail to capture the shifting and fluid nature of contemporary social relations. Grand narratives such as Marxism, second wave feminism, various versions of systems theory have been 'outed' as too essentialist, too deterministic, too structuralist (see Giddens 1991, Morrison 1994, Gelsthorpe 1997). In their place a raft of post-structuralist, postmodernist theorizing has emerged, reframing the relationship between agency and structure in terms of immanence (rather than privileging structure over agency or vice versa) and embracing deconstruction as the principal methodological tool (see Deleuze 2001, Baudrillard 1993, Naffine 1995).

At the same time, however, there has been a concomitant trend towards a more scientific rationalist approach to knowledge production within policy discourse, as the mantra of evidence-led, or 'best practice', policy has come to dominate political thinking. The re-embracing of the 'scientific' paradigm in contemporary criminal justice and social policy differs from earlier periods in which science dominated (as, for example, in the 1950s and early 1960s). Then, policy makers were in thrall to the mystique of science, and the expert opinion of the psychiatrist or educationalist held sway. By contrast the new scientism is aimed at micro-managing professionals and rendering more transparent their operational practices (see S. Armstrong 2003; Scull, Chapter 11). One of the results of this has been a massive increase in government-funded research committed to evaluation and a concomitant expansion of contract researchers within the academy, whose longer-term career prospects are dependent on the creation of sustainable income streams from their individual institutions. Increased political input to the formulation of research strategies favours the short-term, quick and dirty project over more strategic/'blue-skies' research; and, specific outcome-driven design over more abstract theoretical development.

Shifting Modes of Analysing Punishment

Against the backdrop just described, the turn in the sociology of punishment has particularly encouraged two contrasting analytical approaches to the study of punishment and penal control. The first of these gives primacy to macro-level structural factors, with regimes of punishment being understood as shaped, more or less directly, by the evolving structural context within which they are situated. One consequence is that this approach tends to focus on convergence and uniformity in terms of western penal trends (a culture of control – Garland 2001; a new penology – Feeley and Simon 1994; punitive populism – Bottoms 1995). The second approach, by contrast, gives primacy to cultural factors, with analysis centring on the mediating processes through which broader structural factors are translated/transformed or resisted in particular jurisdictions and particular contexts. This approach tends to focus on divergence and difference and emphasizes a more localized interrogation of the power to punish (see Melossi 2001, on the differential impact of protestant and catholic national cultures on modes of punishment and control; Downes 1988, on contrasts in tolerance between England and the Netherlands; McAra 2005, on the ways in which Scottish civic culture has mediated structural impulsions for penal change).

These differences aside, the structural and the cultural approaches exhibit two similar tendencies: first, a tendency to analyse political power against the backdrop of the state (thus new regulatory forms which are distinct from the nation-state continue to be understood as 'other to state' – defined by what they are not); and secondly, a tendency to analyse penal regimes against the backdrop of the prison (thus new modes of punishment are understood principally as being 'other to prison').

We argue that the macro/micro, structure/culture dualisms, together with the state and prison-centric tendencies just described, limit an understanding of current penal forms. Indeed the dynamics of the evolving terrain highlight the need for a looser more multi-textured analytical frame. In particular, the transformations in the nature of citizenship and the nature of social inclusion/exclusion in advanced liberal societies, indicate that penal policy and practice are being increasingly directed towards responding to the needs and demands of a wide and multi-faceted set of *audiences*. The significance of multi-level governance (which has destabilized the state as a central analytical category) suggests that explanations of penal practice need to be located beyond and beneath the *borders* of contemporary nation-states. Similarly, the evolving technologies and narratives associated with punishment provide an increasingly complex *architecture* that is distinctive from the prison (both in terms of its physical and spatial dimensions, as well as its symbolic and discursive qualities).

The core challenge for contemporary scholars, then, is to develop an analytical framework which decentres both the state and the prison but without dismissing them. We would suggest that the themes of audience, borders, and architecture go some way to providing the building blocks for a reinvigorated epistemological and methodological agenda, and we use the rest of this chapter to elaborate on what we mean by these themes and how they are raised in current work.

Audience

The theme of audience raises descriptive questions (mapping the ways in which audience is constituted as a discrete object of knowledge, including who or what drives this process; and tracking modes of signification, namely the conduits through which punishment 'speaks'); critical questions (assessing the implications of particular invocations of audience for the nature and function of punishment); as well as normative questions (who the audience of punishment ought to be and how its needs, or even demands, should be satisfied).

Privileging audience as an analytical category requires the commentator to unpick the various discourses relating to personhood and individual/group identity which underpin contemporary modes of punishment and opens up to enquiry how these discourses are received and responded to by their various publics. In doing so it also opens up to investigation the ways in which individuals and groups encounter the regulatory domains within which they are situated and negotiate strategic pathways through them (through absorption of or resistance to their dominant imperatives). The theme of audience also reconnects with debates regarding the emotions and sensibilities involved in punishment and how these shape its manifest or latent functioning.

Audience is certainly not a new theme within penology. Indeed commentators have long acknowledged that punishment has a powerful communicative dimension. Punishment and penal process have been variously described as: involving the ritual degradation and public denunciation of the offender (Garfinkel 1956); a mechanism through which our passionate reaction to crime can be conveyed and which in turn reinforces social solidarity (Durkheim 1964); a process through which social meaning and culture is produced and reproduced (Garland 1990); and a way of educating the working classes to know, or become locked into, their 'place' (see discussion in Bottoms 1995, Wacquant 2000).

However, as this section aims to demonstrate, the evolving terrains within which penal policy and process are situated have contributed to the construction of a far more complex set of penal narratives relating to audience. These

narratives serve to position subjectivities through the attribution of insider/
outsider status to individuals, particular social groups, and even certain countries, in a manner akin to the circuits which, Rose (2000) argues, maintain social
inclusion and exclusion. Attribution of status is not purely the province of the
state, or of particular governments, or even of state-regulated penal institutions
(such as the prison or asylum), but is also a feature of the more micro and macro
regulatory domains which our authors collectively identify as shaping the penal
enterprise (such as neighbourhoods or community level institutions, supra or
transnational political entities, globalized information and surveillance systems).
Conferred status/identity/citizenship are all rather 'leaky' categories: multi-
textured; selectively applied (shaped in part by the cultural practices of key
institutions at different stages and levels of regulatory bureaucracies); and
sometimes resisted (see Farmer, Chapter 3; Piacentini, Chapter 6; Sparks,
Chapter 2; McAra and McVie 2005; Bosworth 1999; Carlen 1985).

Victims as audience

Victims of crime form a key audience of penal policy and practice. The victim
focus initially gained purchase (along with crime prevention) in the 1980s as
one, predominantly state-led, response to the collapse of the rehabilitative ideal
(see Garland 2001). However, victim strategies have expanded exponentially in
recent years, particularly through the incorporation of restorative principles into
criminal justice frameworks, across a range of Western jurisdictions.

The ostensible aims of victim strategies are to enhance victim satisfaction with
criminal justice and penal process, to reduce fear, and to ensure that victims feel
that they have had some sort of redress for the harm that has been done to them.
These strategies are, in part, aimed at facilitating the social inclusion of both the
victim and the offender, through the creation of partnership between the victim
and the community in tackling offending and, on occasions (dependent on the
type of restorative programme in operation), through the reintegrative shaming
of the offender. However, they can also be read as reflecting a trend towards
greater marketization in punishment, with the victim being constructed as a core
consumer in the penal process (see especially Miers 2004; Zauberman 2000;
Farmer, Chapter 3).

The sensibilities associated with victim strategies are rather complex. One
reading is that they tap into the increased desire for connectedness and intimacy,
which forms the obverse of contemporary narratives of risk (see Giddens 1991,
Taylor 1997, Jamieson 1998). The ontological insecurities which, Giddens has
argued, go hand in hand with late modernity result in an increased obsession
with inwardness and feeling, as the recent mushrooming of academic literature
on the 'sociology of emotions' attests (Bailey 2000, Brennan 2001). Family
group conferencing, reintegrative shaming, and other restorative strategies reach
out to victims but also provide an arena in which victims themselves reach out to

offenders: in contrast to the formal processes of the criminal trial, emotions here take centre stage, with the aim of reconnection, of rescue, and of forgiveness (see Brookes 2004 for an overview).

However, victimhood also touches deeper, more visceral public sentiments, as exemplified in public (and often media-orchestrated) responses to child murder victims, the victims of paedophiles, and to the survivors of terrorist atrocities. Victims in this context become iconic, signifying themes of lost innocence, or new found heroism – the victim as bulwark against those who would destroy 'our way of life'. While the often heart-wrenching images of victims instil empathy, at the same time they also whip up anger and hate-speech, directed at the perpetrators themselves or at those who have come to signify a 'perpetrator-class' in the, sometimes warped, imagination of the 'public' (as indicated by recent increased levels of 'islamophobia' in some European jurisdictions) (see Sparks, Chapter 2 and Wacquant, Chapter 5).

Other visions of victimhood are more troubling: the 'jumpers' from the twin towers; the prostitutes who are murdered; the drug dealers who are addicts. In very different ways these victims invoke both pity and fear and the tragic quality of their victimhood is often silenced. The latter two examples, in particular, are problematic because they cut across popular concepts as to what a 'real victim' is – as such they bring into sharp focus the limits of our capacity to forgive.

Victim strategies, in general, conceptualize victims and offenders as discrete categories, with the former comprising a more 'morally deserving' group. However, evidence from a range of sources suggests that this may be an inaccurate portrayal, principally because it is offenders who are most likely to be the victims of crime (see Miers 2000, Hayward and Sharp 2005, Smith 2004). The close relationship means that when the penal system is addressing victims it is more often than not speaking to offenders (and vice versa). This, of course, highlights how victimhood is in practice a rather 'leaky' category and muddies the principles upon which many restorative programmes, in particular, are based.

The construction of victimhood is a theme which is taken forward in Farmer's chapter. Focused on a discussion of the case involving Tony Martin, in which the victim of a burglary was prosecuted as the murderer of the burglars, he highlights the extraordinarily fluid ways in which victimhood is deployed in popular and legal discourses. Farmer argues that there is a need for commentators to re-engage with the role of rights in both the exercise of, and justifications for, the power to punish. Indeed, through his reading of the *Martin* case, Farmer highlights a rights claim *not* to be a victim (which transcends the victim/offender distinction and obviates the need to search for the illusory category of the 'real' victim), a claim that is made *against* and not from the state.

Taken together, victim strategies highlight the novel path-dependencies which can sometimes occur when new audiences emerge. By giving victims a voice, by providing a space within which they could mobilize and engage (as indicated now by the expanded number of victim support groups – both formal and informal), early state-led strategies eventually became colonized and driven by the audience (sometimes the victims themselves, sometimes an angry wider public 'on behalf' of the victim). The end point of this pathway may well be the transformative moment to which Farmer alludes, when the identity of 'victimhood' is uncoupled from the victim. More importantly, the ways in which victim strategies work on two levels to reinforce solidarities (emblematic of both a positive desire for intimacy and a negative desire to exclude), is suggestive of the powers that can sometimes be invested in the oppressed.

Offenders as audience

The construction of the offender in contemporary regulatory practice is also undergirded by both exclusionary and inclusionary dynamics. Again these dynamics can be read as stemming, in part, from the complex sensibilities mobilized in response to the evolving terrain of penality.

As a number of our contributors indicate, there has been a massive growth in the use of exclusionary modes of punishment across many Western jurisdictions (see Downes and Hansen, Chapter 8; Sparks, Chapter 2; Wacquant, Chapter 5). Such punishments include: the supermax prison; curfews and electronic monitoring; certain forms of risk management as exemplified by orders for lifelong restriction in Scotland, 'three strikes' in California, and new public protection sentences in England. These modes of punishment at best signify that the offender is someone who needs to be controlled or managed, at worst someone who is incapable of reintegration and who is doomed to social and political marginalization (see Wacquant, Chapter 5; Feeley and Simon 1994; Hannah-Moffitt 2005; McAra 2005).

The 'othering' of offenders also results from the raft of surveillance and information systems which have developed in recent years at both the local and global level (see Mathiesen, Chapter 7). These systems create risk profiles of groups and categorize the individuals who come within their purview as 'presumed' threats. According to Mathiesen, the new globalized information systems are lacking in accountability, floating somewhat adrift of national parliaments and peoples. Individuals may not be aware of data that is held about them and, even if aware, will have little (or no) power to challenge or alter it. As a consequence, those designated as high risk may be doomed to permanent outsider status with limited capacity for resistance.

A common theme within contemporary sociological penology is to read these developments as being impelled by the macro social and economic transformations of late modernity, which together have created a new set of 'folk devils': the structurally redundant (as a consequence of the global flows of capital); asylum seekers and migrant workers (as a result of globalized population flows), non-white foreign nationals as well as Asian and north African men (due to the global war on terror). However, the fears and insecurities associated with the risk narrative (mentioned earlier) mean that there is now a *convergence* of moral panics (Hier 2003). Accordingly fears regarding globally constructed outsiders, morph into popular fears about more 'traditional' and localized targets, such as youths, gypsies and traveller populations, the mentally ill or wayward; resulting in an exclusionary continuum from the global to the local. This forms a central theme of Chapter 2, in which Sparks highlights the elision that has occurred between discourse on low level forms of disorder (such as vandalism, graffiti, and other aspects of anti-social behaviour) and discourse on more spectacular terrorist atrocities, which results in an exponential ratcheting up of collective fears. His chapter charts the pivotal role played by the media in both communicating and shaping popular fears on crime and disorder, enhancing suspiciousness, and sloganizing; at times working in tandem with politicians, at other times working against them.

Although exclusionary dynamics are often undergirded by fear and vitriol, a more chilling aspect is the distancing, non-emotional qualities which can also inhere in contemporary modes of penal control (Bauman 2000, Christie 2000). The power of information and surveillance systems, for example, lies partly in the bureaucratic and routinized manner in which they function. Routinization masks the casual injustices and sometimes tragic consequences which modes of control can have for the dispossessed and outsider groups (see Wacquant, Chapter 5). The non-emotional component of these forms of control is part of the reason why exclusionary dynamics can somehow seem acceptable and 'non-contaminating' to a wider public, resulting in a degree of moral indifference (Christie 2000).

Somewhat paradoxically, over the same time frame that exclusionary punishments and surveillance systems have expanded, a more inclusionary dynamic in relation to offenders has also flourished. Indeed there has been a gradual elision between social inclusion and penal policy, as exemplified by early intervention initiatives to support at risk children and families, youth inclusion schemes, and prisoner 'throughcare' or resettlement programmes. Such policies are aimed at protecting individuals from sliding (further) into outsider status, re-embedding intermediate institutions such as the family into the community, and re-admitting offenders to the moral status of citizen (see Rose 2000).

A somewhat different aspect of the inclusionary dynamic links to the 'what works agenda', the cornerstone of so-called effective practice (see Gendreau and Ross 1980, Muncie 2002). What works programmes, with their emphasis on cognitive behavioural therapy, construct the offender as a rational and responsible individual – one who is capable of making choices, of developing and sticking to relapse prevention strategies, of making positive decisions to change (McGuire 1995). More particularly, the offender is perceived as a consumer of punishment, around whose individual characteristics particular programmes are tailored. This trend has been given further impetus with the increasing incursion of rights discourse into modes of punishment; this has served to situate the offender both as a rights bearer and a rights claimant (see Farmer, Chapter 3).

As consumer and rights bearer, the offender shares many of the characteristics of 'normal' citizens, and as such retains the imprimatur of insider status. However, the very use of punishment to underpin the inclusionary dynamic points to the heavily conditional nature of inclusion itself. Insider status turns on revamped conceptions of the deserving and the undeserving: those who have taken advantage of opportunities presented or made positive choices versus the wastrels. The boundaries drawn between insider and outsider status are, as a consequence, somewhat thin and permeable: indeed it is often the same groups who are subject to both inclusionary and exclusionary forms of control. Thus, in the United Kingdom, youth inclusion programmes go hand in hand with dispersal and anti-social behaviour orders; in Scotland the children of asylum seekers, along with their families, are swooped upon in dawn raids and placed in detention, in a country whose flagship juvenile justice policy is called 'Getting it Right for Every Child' (see McAra 2005); and ethnic minority groups are over-represented at all stages of the penal system in France, the United States, and the United Kingdom (see Smith 1997; Wacquant, Chapter 5). It is in these ways that both the exclusionary and inclusionary aspects of punishment function to signify and police the boundaries of citizenship.

Neighbourhoods and local communities as audience

An important trend in recent years has been the reconnection of penal policy with more localized community concerns. Indeed, in many Western jurisdictions there has been a gradual fusion between the criminal justice, community safety, and social crime prevention agendas, with the expectation that communities will police themselves and act, more generally, as a mode and site of penal control (Clarke 2002).

Local community policies replicate the exclusive/inclusive dynamics of offender and victim construction just described. Many policies oriented towards the local community have the potential to promote, what Crawford (1998) terms, a defended exclusivity (for example anti-social behaviour orders, dispersal orders, curfews), whereas others aim to promote inclusivity and more democratic forms of participation, with a number of interventions aimed at reintegration, for example restorative initiatives or volunteering and mentoring schemes.

Importantly, the definitions of local community which underpin current initiatives are somewhat complex and confused, predicated as they are on both a spatial and affective dynamic. Communities defined by geographical space are often highly fragmented and diverse, bundled together by accident of location. Communities defined by some form of identity/emotional attachment may transcend local boundaries and appear to be more cohesive but these can also be riven with internal fractions, and problems remain in respect of which groups or individuals constitute their 'usable and legitimate representatives' (Hughes 2004: 13).

The contributions to this book indicate that there is a high degree of reflexivity at play in terms of neighbourhood identity construction and that ascribed definitions of community (in terms of policy) may only have a small part to play in local perception of space and place. Sparks (Chapter 2: 36), for example, argues that awareness of place is now 'relational, comparative, and reflexive', a theme developed more fully in his various writings with Girling and Loader (see Girling *et al* 2000, Sparks *et al* 2001). According to Sparks, individuals make sense of locale through 'parables and warnings' of distant others (the 'dens of thieves' elsewhere), as a consequence, spatial integrity requires such 'dangerous mobilities' to be 'still' (Sparks, Chapter 2: 36).

Trans/supra-national communities as audience

A concomitant trend to that of local communities has been the role of punishment in exposing the liminalities of transnational or supra-national communities. Again, such processes are underpinned by an exclusionary/inclusionary dynamic.

According to Girling (Chapter 4), penal policy has had a key role to play in the construction of a European 'community of sentiment', centred on the EU campaign for the abolition of the death penalty. Abolitionism is conceived as a marker of taste, a civilized and cosmopolitan response to violent crime. This contrasts with, and bestrides, the more localized penal cultures of individual member states, which, Girling claims, are more ambivalent or punitive in orientation. As part of the process of community construction, inmates on death row in the United States have been extended cultural citizenship – consequently 'distant others', as Girling terms them, are reconceptualized as honorary EU citizens. Importantly, Girling's work points to a core paradox underpinning some contemporary modes of political capacity building – by speaking to an 'imagined' European community of sentiment, the very speech acts associated with the abolitionist campaign, help to bring such a community/audience into being.

The cosmopolitan theme in Girling's work finds echoes in Piacentini's chapter on the incursion of human rights discourse into post-Soviet penality and Russia's quest for penal 'respectability'. The requirement to recognize human rights (and in particular prisoner rights) has become a key test for countries aspiring to join supra-national organizations such as the European Union. Aspirant members' policies and practices are carefully scrutinized and policed, and countries divided into the respectable/unrespectable; those which are deserving of support from those which are not. Conferring pariah status (a process which Piacentini argues is a form of 'carceral disgrace') has important consequences in terms of economic aid and support as well as consequences for the aspirant member's self identity.

In contrast to Girling's and Piacentini's civilizing processes, Wacquant argues that the punitive treatment of migrant workers and non-white foreigners across the European Union (either through expulsion or 'internal extirpation' via incarceration) has had an important role to play in the building of a European state and society and in 'germinating the transnational personhood of the European'. Unlike Girling, Wacquant identifies strong commonalities between local and EU penal practices in this regard. The exclusion and demonizing of certain groups, sends powerful messages regarding the core membership of both national and supra-national communities, defining the boundaries of these by what they are not (a point we return to later in this chapter).

Modes of resistance

At the beginning of this section we noted that the theme of audience opened up to enquiry the subjective experiences of individuals and social groups as they encounter the complex regulatory orders of late modernity. This reintroduces the concept of agency into analysis, highlighting the possibilities for resistance.

Resistance to penal strategies was once isolated to studies of prisoner conduct – riots, women's rejection of female stereotypes, academic critique – but now might be accompanied as well by open displays of resistance among other groups. The increasing regulation and direction of probation officers in England and Wales, culminating in the merger of this function into the country's corrections agency, may yet see disaffected union members locking arms in public protest with the offenders they oversee. The parents of young offenders who have committed suicide in penal institutions are increasingly waging media wars, implicitly claiming their entitlement to the designation of 'victim'. And the endless avail-ability of information about public agencies, the result of a public accountability dogma that prizes transparency, may allow as yet unformed citizen groups to hone their ability to take the battle to the government's own ground, presenting evidence of fiscal irrationality and lack of results.

The topic of resistance threads its way through a number of our chapters. Scull (Chapter 11) argues that psychiatry functions more effectively than punishment in terms of social control, principally because its scientific/medical quality lends it an aura of objectivity and thus protects it from political attack. Nonetheless, he claims that the subjects of these forms of control do retain a degree of autonomy and agency, and space has now been opened up to hear their voices. The capacity to resist psychiatric forms of control, however, is heavily circumscribed, given the disparities in power between the controllers and the controlled. This echoes work by feminist scholars who highlight the ways in which female offenders struggle to resist identities (assigned both by penal agents and scholars) and negotiate a pathway through the mechanisms of control which enmesh all aspects of their lives (see Bosworth 1999, Howe 1994).

In Chapter 9, Hutton focuses on judges as a penal audience that has persis-tently resisted not only attempts to circumscribe their power and bring it into alignment with managerial goals, but also attempts by scholars to overlay some theory of coherence in the nature of their sentencing. Hutton deploys the tools of Bourdieu (1977), particularly his notion of *habitus*, to explain the efforts of this group to evade subordination to an overall criminal justice *system*. Discretion is the consummate power of the bench, and resistance to the harnessing of this power to determine sentencing systems or government-produced management systems is perennial. Judges in the common law systems have consistently rejected the notion that fiscal concerns can or should affect their decision making. Hutton suggests that if we look upon the judicial realm as a field, a cultural environment with its own rituals, traditions, and hierarchies, sentencing practices become sensible displays of juridical capital (Bourdieu 1987). He opens up a space between functionalist accounts of state power and cultural explanations that focus on national legal systems, within which we can develop more nuanced accounts of justice at work.

In a rather different vein, Sparks (Chapter 2) highlights how the ratcheting up of popular fears on crime and disorder (mentioned earlier) and the normalizing of the so-called 'politics of fear' have been accompanied by a greater degree of scepticism on the part of the public. According to Sparks, the public has become increasingly mistrustful of the messages purveyed by government on its capacity to tackle perceived threats from disorder and terrorism, and cynicism and conspiracy theories have become all pervasive. This process is facilitated by the nature of information flows in contemporary mediascapes. Jock Young (1971) once described the media as providing a universe of discourse in an increasingly fragmented and dislocated social world. However, this media role has changed in the context of the sheer weight of information that is now available, particularly through the internet. There is no editorial control across the internet, eyewitnesses speak to us directly, outsider groups campaign, individuals are murdered before our eyes, alternative takes on official information abound. The media, in this context, provides a multiplicity of discourse, one that enables the various audiences of punishment (including the wider public) to question and fight back.

In this section on audiences we have mapped the ways in which contemporary networks of regulation form the backdrop *against* and through which the formation of insider and outsider identities takes place. In later sections of the chapter we return to the theme of resistance, to explore in more detail how the new and diverse architecture of penality shapes and circumscribes the capacity of audiences to assert agency. The exclusionary and inclusionary dynamics which construct the audiences of punishment, of course draw attention to boundaries and borders, and it is to this theme the chapter now turns.

Borders

The theme of punishment's borders arises in some form in all of the writings selected for this volume, and in the diversity of its invocations underlines how contested are the contours of control. The perception of penality as a well-bounded field, comprising a particular set of actors and practices, or, in other words, amounting simply to the state's response within its territorial borders to the violation of criminal laws by domestic subjects, is coming under attack. We have already elaborated on the liminal boundaries of identity and citizenship. Even the border that seems to provide a clear separation of local crime problems and global ones seems ever more hazy in the context of globalization. The disproportionate representation of ethnic minorities in prison, to take but one example, in the 1980s and 1990s was addressed in the literature primarily through a (domestic) politics of race relations. This persistent imbalance must be recognized also as a consequence of transnational flows of people and commodities: the large proportion of Afro-Caribbean women in English prisons and South and Central Americans in US prisons, provides the evidence of such illicit global markets.

This section traces two more ways in which the borders of punishment have blurred and evolved. First, a geographical concept of borders provides the opportunity to think about how porous the boundary separating the local and the global is, allowing for dynamic interactions that affect both how people understand and experience punishment, and how agendas for control are developed and play out in spatially diffuse and, sometimes, unpredictable places. Secondly, the border inside which punishment is treated as a distinctive realm of action, one in which the state displays its power of life and death, comes under scrutiny. Earlier, we claimed that a managerialist mode of signification (a new scienticism) is a dominant part of the evolving terrain of penality. It is an ethos that has permeated many areas of governance, and the pervasiveness of this rationality works, we argue, to level distinctions between realms of social action, submitting all to identical standards of validation, and neutralizing particular strategies of resistance, while enabling others.

Interaction and convergence across local, national, and global borders

It is convenient to treat problems of punishment as domestic, limited in cause and effect to national or sub-national territories. This reflects neither historical accident nor intellectual lapse since the right to punish is conceptually linked to the legitimacy of a sovereign whose jurisdiction was defined by geographical borders. The power to punish terminates at the spatial limits of the sovereign's power, and so the arc of penality's trajectory has often remained isolated – in both scholarly analysis and empirical occurrence – from geographically or topically distant demands on state power. For instance, the American Model Penal Code (MPC), published in 1962 (American Law Institute), fundamentally reformed and restated the purposes of punishment for US legal audiences, but the formulation of this restatement and the influence it had on state and national powers, occurred in a vacuum from surrounding political developments, including the intensification of the Cold War after the failed invasion of Cuba, the use of federal troops to enforce racial desegregation policies in the southern states, and the full-scale involvement of the United States in the Vietnam War (see also Dubber 2003). All of these events raised important questions about the nature and legitimacy of state power and yet had no clear influence on penal policy or practice. We are most familiar with examples from our own American and British contexts, but this phenomenon certainly may be observed elsewhere: the criminal law of South Africa under apartheid, with the exception of the death penalty, remains largely intact today, and the claim that it operated as a political and racist tool continues to be contested, to the extent that the issue is raised at all (Gready and Kagalema 2003). What now seems obvious in retrospect was invisible at the time, since few scholars connected penal policies with other policies, domestic and international, which, together, operated *de facto* as a single strategy of control, that had systematic and disproportionate effects on particular groups, notably 'ethno-racial', 'ethno-national' (Wacquant, Chapter 5), and economic outsiders.

The radical criminologists broke the silence in the 1970s; Sparks' chapter in this volume revives the early work of Stuart Hall, who, along with many others, revealed how penality is exploited for the general maintenance of power, and used to neutralize and entrench the oppression of particular sectors of society. While the success of this work in revealing the relationship of power to law means that we now take for granted the claim that states are centrally concerned about securing their stability, this critical stance relied on an assumption that the state operated an unchallenged monopoly on legitimized control (or violence, Weber 1968). Hall's more recent work seeks to correct this assumption, and reflects the position of the chapters in this volume, by recognizing the current 'corruption and decline of state governance' (although we are warned that the tendency to accept this process as complete is dangerously unfounded, Hall and Winlow 2003). It is natural, then, that penological scholarship is finally drawing connections between local, national, and global problems of control. Jock Young again argues that by rejecting the oppositions of 'spatial, social and moral . . . boundaries' we will be able to see the common 'aetiology and phenomenology of crime and punishment, . . . crimes occurring in war . . . , in terrorism and the response to it, and genocide' (2003: 392). Describing the response to crime in the language of war is now leading us to consider the possibility of a literal connection: Sparks (Chapter 2) notes that the UK government's proposed control orders on terrorist suspects, are modelled on domestic anti-social behaviour orders.

What may be drawing these two levels of control ever closer together is the emergence of *security* as an overarching interest. It is a concept that cuts across all kinds of borders, something we seek at an ontological level (J. Young 1999, Giddens 1990), a community and cultural level (Sparks, Chapter 2; Girling *et al* 2000), and a political level (Zedner 2003b, Runciman 2004). That security from crime is conflated with security from terrorism is evinced in the fact that, in the UK, the New Labour government has ramped up campaigns against both, using pressure in one policy area to justify expansion in the other. Sparks (*ibid*) wonders what the destiny of these developments will be, warning against the simple and reductive default characterization of all this in terms of a 'politics of fear'. The question is whether the border between global and local anxieties has been breached permanently or represents only a predictable set of responses to an exceptional (and partially state-generated) period of emergency. The different paths lead to distinct consequences.

The removal of traditional borders between domestic problems of crime and transnational problems of war and terrorism necessarily produces new borders – 'bordering rejects as well as erects othering' (Van Houtoum and Van Naerssen 2002: 126). These new boundaries emerge out of the war for security, making use of, but also transcending, national and other geo-political markers. Wacquant (Chapter 5) exposes one cut of this new border, exposing the process by which the political status of refugees is transformed into the disposable criminal status of individuals (over-staying visas or failing in applications for asylum). This transformation allows their forcible and sometimes deadly removal from Europe and thus from the resource of European human rights laws. The territorial border between 'Fortress Europe' and 'out there' constructs a conceptual border of insiders and outsiders, reinforcing other strategies of inclusion and exclusion. Some of these strategies we laid out in our earlier discussion of penal audiences, noting that inclusion policies simultaneously pursue tactics of exclusion: not only does the blurring of spatial borders flow from a *negative* reaction to our fears and consequent need for security, but may also be a *positive* strategy, for creating a sense of community, at either a local or supra-national level (Girling, Chapter 4).

So far, this attention to blurred spatial borders has focused mostly on the impulse to define and control the *inside* of political spaces, pushing out the unwanted and cultivating a communal identity for the insiders. Strategies and methods of control flow out as well, though, and it is this globalized flow – of capital, information, and people – that reminds us of the relative autonomy of global processes. Franko Aas (2005) has looked at how penal technologies, dominated by the need to present information in non-narrative and, therefore, ostensibly objective ways, introduce into the global slipstream a new, universalized, form of culture, one that affects the nature of identity and which displays a great deal of mobility. Criminal records, insurance history, credit ratings, and risk assessment scores, are the disembodied binary codes of which we are now made, and unite in a shared language of control among groups as diverse as Canadian psychologists, Scottish prison officers, Spanish insurance companies, and Australian family therapists.

Flattened distinctions between modes and areas of governance

Practitioners and policy makers are also uniting across borders of professional expertise and organizational culture reaching beyond those fields directly concerned with control. Although the realm of punishment seems to feature quite clear borders around its institutions, actors, and practices, its separation from other policy areas depends on the strength of arguments about its distinctiveness. Political philosophers based a claim of distinctiveness on the fact that punishment by the sovereign is the power of life and death, and this requires a set of special institutional practices, such as a rule of law that conferred especially heavy burdens on the state before this power could be executed (standard of proof, rights of due process and against self-incrimination, etc). Criminology for the most part remains committed to these original principles of separateness, organizing its work around the traditional agencies involved in the public delivery of justice: police, courts, prisons, and probation. Even the turn in the sociology of punishment towards critical analysis of institutions tended to re-emphasize penal boundaries, claiming penality as an especially significant and specific site of social control (for example Garland and Young 1983).

Recently, however, globalized trends in governance, have led some in criminology to challenge the penal realm's uniqueness as a field that can, or should, be studied in isolation from other sectors of public or private activity (Braithwaite 2000). This line of argument flows from claims about the changed nature, or hollowing out, of the state and the consequent alteration in the operation not just of punishment but of multiple areas of governance. Trends in penal policy in the jurisdictions of the United States, the United Kingdom, Canada, and Australia, such as privatization, quantification of goals and results, business models, and pro-entrepreneurial practices are the same trends governing the direction of policies in health, education, transport, and any number of other areas. These are the traits of the so-called regulatory state, in which a government's job is 'steering, not rowing', where audit provides a universal technique of evaluation, and the business world is the source of all models. Hence, the managerial entrepreneurialism that we flagged up as an important part of penality's evolving terrain, forms an equally influential part of the landscapes in countless other fields as well.

This must lead us to question whether the influence of this rationality on punishment raises new sociological or political questions about the nature of control. The fact that punishment has not been singled out to endure the pressure of economistic rationalism suggests that we ought to cast our questions more widely: what are the social and political implications of treating punishment as just another field of governance? How can specific normative and critical debates about punishment be raised in this new, levelled field? Public administration writers observe that the broader implications of a New Public Management agenda (part of third way politics in the United Kingdom), or a 'reinventing government' movement (in the United States), is that 'reinventors do not appear to attach much importance to broad social and political ideas ... As they see it, their principles are applicable "regardless of party, regardless of ideology"' (Spicer 2004: 357, quoting former Vice-President

Gore). This redrawing of the political landscape marginalizes normative and political dispute, and precludes full consideration of the issues conventionally raised about punishment, treating them as quasi-pathological: normative and political questions are unhelpful and obstructive because they distract from a focus on the core goals of efficiency and effectiveness (Mathiesen, Chapter 7). Challenging core values – reflecting on the contemporary basis of the legitimacy of punishment or penal institutions – are rendered irrelevant by these new analytical borders (S. Armstrong 2003; Piacentini, Chapter 6). McKibbin warns that this 'destruction of the public sphere' surreptitiously and ironically promotes a particular ideological politics under an anti-ideology banner:

Despite assurances that the political elite is interested only in what works, this is the most intensely ideological period of government we have known in more than a hundred years. The model of market-managerialism has largely destroyed all alternatives, traditional and untraditional . . . Our students are now clients, our patients and passengers customers. It is a language which was first devised in business schools, then broke into government and now infests all institutions. It has no real historical predecessor . . . and is peculiarly seductive. It purports to be neutral: thus all procedures must be 'transparent' and 'robust', everyone 'accountable'. It is hard-nosed but successful because the private sector on which it is based is hard-nosed and successful. It is efficient; it abhors waste; it provides all the answers (McKibbin 2006: 6).

Zizek characterizes this ideological non-ideology as 'post-politics' (cited in Van Houtoum and Van Naerssen 2001: 128) 'in which economics is politicised and politics is economised.' Hiding underneath this economization of social life and governance, though, problems of control still matter and are taking on new forms. Scull (Chapter 11) revisits his own career and that domineering concept of 1980s penological study – social control – to correct some of the expansive uses to which it was put, arguing for its continued salience as an analytic label. While more recent historical work on control of mental health populations requires us to revise our image of the mental patient as passive vessel of control techniques, we should not make the opposite mistake of assuming total empowerment either. Scull focuses on the pervasiveness of a scientized language in which problems are presented – limning the border-levelling qualities of economistic technocratic languages – that allows for the lowering of barriers of control between the seriously mentally ill and the 'wayward', or those whose mental health issues can be neither ignored nor coercively controlled through formal social control institutions. This common form of talk can 'reduce or eliminate problems of morality, guilt, and blame, and suggest the existence of technical remedies for life's troubles' (*ibid.*: 216.).

Scull's ultimate aim in his chapter is to fight for the importance of attending to the dynamics of specific institutional contexts, to argue that prisons and mental hospitals are not interchangeable sites of control, and yet common frames of analysis can reveal important cross-institutional patterns. The levelling of borders across fields of government, rendered from above by globalized movements especially of capital, and from below by the increasing reliance on sub-government agencies and entities, does not negate the need to ferret out distinctions. It does provide a more nuanced agenda for research, one that asks us to describe and explain more phenomena at the organizational level, 'it is the organized power of the state that captures most of the attention of social scientists. However, we must also address the potential for the abuse of organized power by large corporate structures' (Sjoberg, Gill, and Williams 2001: 28), and equally, we should take into account the role of other organizational actors – non-governmental organizations (NGOs), consultants, the United Nations, and the World Trade Organization (WTO) – in shaping and delivering control policies.

The powerful role of particular rationalities and organizational forms described by Scull, links together the arguments raised in the previous section on the narratives of audiences, and leads us onwards to the theme of architecture, in which we consider the construction of the space in which punishment is conceptualized and carried out.

Architecture

As we have noted, the turn in the sociology of punishment towards the 'social analysis of penality' (Garland and Young 1983) transformed scholarship about the response to crime into a field that entertained fundamental questions about state power and the nature of social control in modern times. While opening up entirely new possibilities for the study of punishment, these theoretical explorations had in common the fact that they were tethered to, even when leading to criticisms about over-emphasis on, a single institutional practice – *imprisonment*. Moreover, an eclectic and inspired collection of contributions on which this new way of working was built, one that used the methods and knowledge of history (Rothman 1971), social theory (Foucault 1979), literature and sociology (for example Goffman 1961), psychology and psychiatry (Scull 1984), feminism (for example Carlen 1983a, 1983b), and Marxist theory (for example Ignatieff 1980, and also Garland 1990, in reviving the work of Rusche and Kirchheimer and Pashukanis) produced a *particular construction of the prison's social function and cultural importance*. In this sense, architecture provides not a new lens for filtering the salient aspects of punishment at the turn of the millennium, but has been the signature analytic for designing critical criminologies of state power since the 1970s.

The theses emerging from this work on the prison have given us some well-worn ideas about its role. The prison represented the distinctive form of social power in modernity, because it: is the panoptic setting in which all – the guards and the guarded – can be watched; displays through its monolithic design the exemplary form of modern power as social control, which conditions and constructs subjects as, for example, good workers or obedient women; manifests the flawed and persistent consequences of reformers' good intentions; casts, symbolically, the shadow in which other punitive measures are imagined, enacted, and enforced; and, reflects a general cultural tendency away from welfarism and towards punitiveness. At some point, the prison's status as dependent or independent variable, in relation to the larger social world, has blurred. By reaching up to the grand theorists – Marx, Durkheim, Weber, and so on – to explain a very particular practice, the critical literature has come to treat punishment, and therefore imprisonment, as a privileged site from which to access the secrets of power. The study of prison has become the study of society; punishment both reflects and constitutes the social (Garland 1990).

We hope to readjust the picture somewhat by identifying the prison as but one of many realms in which the fascinating, disturbing, and transformative developments of late modernity might be glimpsed. To further this argument, however, we must de-centre the prison without dismissing it. The theme of architecture focuses on the importance of space, on the way in which objects and things are arranged to achieve control. Prison thus constitutes a uniquely important form of penal architecture, creating the historically unprecedented ability to contain thousands – even millions – of human beings, and to target and define unwanted groups. Generalizing penal space from the prison into a concept of architecture, however, allows us to think about, first, other sorts of spaces where penality works, and secondly, spaces of the prison that have either been neglected in earlier periods of study or which have only become visible under current conditions. Finally, the theme of architecture can be deployed at the metaphorical level, offering us a framework for arranging the conceptual building blocks of penal discourse and analysis.

The architecture of the spectacular and the mundane

It has been thirty years since Foucault (1979) juxtaposed the spectacle of the scaffold and the mundane routine of the penal timetable. His purpose was to display a succession in forms of power as modernity evolved. Durkheim, Garland, and others have reminded us, though, that, at its core, the effectiveness of punishment relies on making an impression, thus demonstrating in spectacular ways the authority of the ruler. The prison simultaneously works both by its power to impress through horror and its ability to degrade through tedium. American 'supermaxes', the secret terrorist suspect interrogation centres allegedly used by the United States, and prison films that invariably emphasize the worst brutalities of institutionalization, refute the possibility that punishment will ever be entirely removed from public view or characterized by a civilized notion of the humane.

Beyond the compellingly monumental imagery of the supermax are hidden the prison's small spaces. The places where anger management groups meet, the rooms where parole hearings are held, the corridors in which prisoners spend so much time on the move, and especially neglected in the conventional focus on cells and walls, the administrative spaces of offices, the places where workers and managers generate annual reports, business plans, and contracts. In the architecture of punishment, these elements of penal space are equally important for managing penal operations and defining the nature of the penal experience. They are the places where penality takes shape, containing and conferring meaning on the objects that are necessary to translate policy into practice: risk assessment forms (and other files), blood and urine samples, restraints, whiteboards and markers, projectors for PowerPoint displays, and flowcharts.

The spectacular mixes with the mundane in complicated ways. Piacentini's analysis of a human rights discourse in Chapter 6 tracks its route through Council of Europe offices, into NGO manuals, and onto Russian prison managers' desks. From here, human rights have begun to make their way into the prisoners' spaces. She identifies an irony in the progress of this rights agenda: the abominable conditions of Russian prisons, which made Russia particularly susceptible to outside pressure to adopt a Western view of enlightened punishment, have not been fully eradicated (TB and HIV/AIDS are still rife), and yet this agenda has also side-lined resourceful and creative local practices that served to take the edge off incarceration and which might have provided the basis for developing some culturally specific concept of penal legitimacy (such as local barter systems, Piacentini 2004c). So far, the main impact of this particular human rights model has been to increase a bureaucratic mindset among prison workers, and to encourage prisoners to identify their own problems in terms of Western-defined entitlements. Inmates frame their campaigns of resistance around newly conferred identities as European subjects.

Also working to elaborate the architectural elements of global control and surveillance, Mathiesen (Chapter 7) argues that formerly local regimes of supervision are now becoming, through the rapid development of record-keeping and surveillance technologies, globalized systems of control. The breakdown of the border between domestic crime control and global regulation of populations was the theme of the previous section; what matters at an architectural level are the ways in which Mathiesen shows that this convergence depends on mundane considerations of space and time. People may be held in local jails, immigration detention centres, and police stations, but maintaining the technology and agreeing the terms that allow for this incarceration is happening in, and to some extent being shaped by, spaces like meeting rooms. In one example, he shows that simple concerns about expediency, convenience, and efficiency led to the linking of a border control agreement (the Schengen Treaty), a transnational policing body (Europol), and a supra-governmental justice agency (the European Justice and Home Affairs Council). This happened when the various meetings required to coordinate operations of separate programmes involved the same people on different committees. Merging committees meant fewer meetings. However, the result of streamlining committee meetings has achieved more than convenience: Mathiesen shows that such attempts to minimize redundancy have also led to the substantive and transnational convergence of surveillance systems and goals (*ibid*). Discussing the Schengen Information System (SIS, a set of surveillance technologies originally justified by border control rather than crime control goals) at a meeting including representatives of Europol (a nascent law enforcement agency) has sped the use of the SIS as a quasi-crime control tool.

The architecture of this control system, both in terms of its technology and in terms of the hierarchy of its human managers, leads Mathiesen to develop some profound, if tentative, suggestions about the architecture of control more generally. To what extent do states direct control mechanisms if the development of far-reaching surveillance systems partly results from prosaic concerns by middle management staff about expediency? The access of crime control personnel to SIS information (the database of which contains comprehensive information about individuals who have never been convicted of a crime nor even necessarily suspected of one) resulted, in the first instance, from the fortuitous combining of committees rather than a political decision that such integration was justified or necessary. He concludes that:

> ... the various interlocking systems do not develop quite of their own accord, but with, what I would call, increasingly ... *diluted* ties to the institutions of the nation-states. While not global law fully without a state, a dilution of connections with the formal institutions of the nation-state is taking place. Most significantly, the institution of parliamentary sanction has become, at least in several European states, a perfunctory exercise with a silent public as a context. (Mathiesen, Chapter 7: 131, emphasis in original)

Mathiesen suggests that, as the architecture of control expands, there is no single architect, certainly not a democratic polity, overseeing it. Technologies of control can have lives of their own, working out their spread and direction in ordinary spaces and outside the radar of political accountability. The troubling implication is that democratic political institutions become weakened, acting only as fora for approval of such systems, and the *post facto* nature of these decisions minimizes the possibilities for, and effectiveness of, public debate. However, states are not passive observers of a global control network. The United States and the United Kingdom are examples of two nations with political regimes seeking to hasten the development of global surveillance networks.

Simultaneously, these nations have commandeered more and more *local* spaces in which to carry out domestic penal measures. State punishment now takes place in homes (electronic tagging, internet usage bans, curfew orders), neighbourhoods (where the United Kingdom's anti-social behaviour orders amount to local exile), civic offices (payment of fines), day reporting centres, and the street (through the use of on-the-spot fines and increased powers of police to disperse groups). How will the architecture of these spaces shape penal practices?

The case of situational crime prevention allows one to consider some possibilities. The 'design of public spaces express[es] civic values...encourag[ing] certain social activities' and 'discourag[ing] others' (Jones, Chapter 10: 177). Jones finds the metaphor and concept of architecture, as elaborated in scholarship on the internet, an untapped resource for thinking about crime and punishment. Returning once more to the theme of resistance, Jones' work suggests that the new possibilities for action created by architecture, are not easily anticipated. Bringing Lawrence Lessig's characterization of cyberspace architecture to bear on criminology, Jones argues that:

> ...situational crime prevention simultaneously constrains and enables; a situational crime prevention measure that overly constrains all activity is unlikely to be favoured by users in general, and hence may even be subverted by them – as in the case of overly noisy or laborious mechanical security doors which regular users simply leave unlocked or even permanently jammed ajar. (*ibid.*: 193)

This borrowing from eclectic theoretical sources is the sort of creative inspiration encouraged by the analytical turn in the sociology of punishment, and it enriches knowledge further by suggesting a new take on the old, and pessimistic, literature of unanticipated consequences (see Hayward 2004 for another, inspired perspective on how criminology can learn from sociologies of the city). While Cohen (1985) and others diagnosed all possible outcomes of state penal reform as dangerous, insidiously widening nets of control, new voices in the field like Jones suggest that some consequences open up equally unanticipated opportunities of resistance. In the example he uses to illustrate the argument, ostentatious or excessive attempts to control the use of space actually undermine the effectiveness of control goals. Such a possibility respects the significance of state-directed strategies of spatial control, and yet challenges the radical criminological tendency to assume the state is always and consciously the beneficiary of such strategies.

The architecture of penal imagination

Physical structures of control require conceptual bases of legitimacy, and so the architecture of policy space and the flow of penal discourse become critical topics for understanding penal development. Attempts to monopolize the architecture of penal discourse may also reveal a state's acknowledgement of its limited power to control disorder itself, whether this means crime in a domestic realm (Garland 1996) or terrorism in a global one (Sparks, Chapter 2). We employ a concept of architecture here to capture, in a metaphorical sense, the way in which both political and scholarly discourses can prioritize penal problems in the first place and thus enact particular visions of the social world (see Law and Urry 2004). The architecture concept is useful because it covers similar ground as, without bringing with it the baggage of, ideology. Resisting the label of ideology prevents an implicit attribution of state agency and control over the discourse itself, and thus avoids imputing coherence to the policy agenda under review. We are interested to explore the possibility that, as with the literal architecture of punishment, conceptual structures take on lives of their own, defining the space of the politically and scientifically acceptable. In addition, the emergent architecture of the penal imagination creates new path-dependencies, new possibilities for action, and new sites of resistance, which may not be readily anticipated by the actors and entities forming it.

We have already mentioned the language and science of risk as a dominant influence on contemporary penal narratives. Feeley (in Chapter 12) makes clear the power of such concepts to take on roles unimagined by their creators. Risk management, and its special designation as the 'new penology' by Feeley and Simon (1992), has come to provide not just, as Feeley says he and Simon originally intended, a descriptor of everyday penal practice, but a grand theoretical umbrella under which all manner of practices in diverse jurisdictions are compared and found to be similar.

What is the appeal of the risk narrative? By bringing together the unquantifiable problem of the dangerous offender on the loose with the entirely quantified science of probability, the tools of actuarialism have allowed for the proliferation both of a rationalistic logic of efficiency in justice and of irrational fears and expectations. That is, risk assessment, on the one hand, provides the comfort of 'scientific' decision making, and obscures the fact that subjective discretion is a quintessential quality of justice (Hutton, Chapter 9). On the other hand, the problem threatened by an extremely tiny minority – contorted into the image of the 'child sex predator' and such like – gets fallaciously translated into the logic of the precautionary principle: where the magnitude of a harm is severe and irreversible, all measures to avoid the harm are justified, even in the absence of evidence about the likelihood of its occurrence. Thus risk logic explains a paradox: the relative insulation of justice agencies (consider the lack of fiscal debate about prison building programmes) from the fiscal conservatism prevailing in public services more generally.

This development might also explain the stunning correlations Downes and Hansen (Chapter 8) observed between a country's commitment to welfarist social policies and its incarceration rates. They studied the incarceration rates of eighteen developed nations and found a significant inverse relationship between the amount of national wealth invested in welfare programmes and the rate of incarceration. They conclude that the higher incarceration rates consistently observed in those countries spending proportionately less on social support services may reflect tough on crime politics. This fits within a managerialist paradigm, one which relies on actuarial measurement but which has never quite managed to shake off its neo-liberal origins, and it might show also that governments committed to 'efficiency' drives and accountability through audit narrow their own flexibility, leaving only punishment as the arena in which cost-efficiency can be treated as both irrelevant (when it is a question of protecting our children) and achievable (when it is a question of measuring improvements in processing times, for example).

Managerialist imperatives form an ever more dominant mode of signification and provide the umbrella under which quantification and neutralization strategies are carried out. The capacity to demonstrate that elements of the penal system are meeting targets, to be able to show how money is being used with the system, to be able to track cases and measure inputs and outputs, to publish the results of evaluation research – all of these are now utilized by governments as a means of justifying their approach to crime and legitimizing themselves in the eyes of the public (Hughes 2004, Garland 2001, Nellis 2004). Indeed, as Hughes has argued, audit has become 'the new incarnation of public interest', and success has been reconstructed in terms of what can be easily measured and counted (Hughes 2004: 14). The emergence of evidence-based policy is of course closely connected to this process. By signifying objectivity, the evidence-based approach to programme development, purports to be scientific as well as politically neutral (Muncie 2001, Hope 2004).

At the transnational level, international conventions have also increasingly become an important conduit of communication – forming as they do, the principal measuring rod against which the moral status of penal systems is gauged (Piacentini, Chapter 6; Girling, Chapter 4). Penal agents and even nations thus form a core audience of this new public management, with many of its precepts being aimed at greater uniformity of practice through the micro-management of discretional space.

Downes and Hansen have shown us one result of the redesign of penal concepts as the old welfarist ideal is dismantled, perhaps forever mothballed, as a rhetoric of being tough on crime is erected in its place. Although such a rhetoric tends to produce, and often actively cultivates, an inflammatory and emotive basis of public discourse, at the same time, it strikes us that one of the most important continuing trends of penality is the simultaneous attempt to sanitize penal practice by employing a neutralized language to describe it. The irony of the supermax, or maximum security correctional facility in the official jargon, is that it wreaks its terror through unquestionably higher levels of cleanliness, safety, and legality. Cement moulded bed frames, 24-hour fluorescent lighting, and robotically controlled doors that minimize contact with other humans, reduce risk of suicide and assault but have been linked to inmates developing severe mental health problems including psychosis. Legal challenges to these conditions consistently fail (Feeley and Rubin 1998). The view of the American courts is that such prisons represent best practice and reflect the successful influence of reform efforts such as those to specify minimum square footage in cells, minimum calorie content of meals, and training for staff. The language of the courts' praise and the reality of torture by 'humane' practices, juxtaposes a positive, approving vision of penal professionalism with the persistence of a terrible form of brutality (S. Armstrong 2003).

For those caught up in the most extreme and brutalizing manifestations of the contemporary regulatory order, the neutralizing language of public management offers little comfort. However, by rendering transparent the contradictions inherent in dominant modes of puishment, the architecture of the penal imagination begins to open up a critical space in which to question, probe and fight back. In tracking the path dependencies created by discourse and practice, we are reminded that the legitimacy of penal regimes is fragile and contingent and that newly formed audiences (victims, neighbourhoods, trans and supranational communities of sentiment) may yet be mobilized to resist their most pernicious tendencies.

Conclusions

Our review of contemporary developments and the evolving terrain within which penal regimes are situated, indicates that punishment and penal control are multi-faceted and multi-level in both organization and function. Both the state and the prison have become destabilized as central analytical categories in the context of the globalized and localized dynamics of the regulatory frameworks of late modernity. By focusing analysis on the themes of audiences, borders, and architecture, we have aimed at constructing a holistic, multi-level, and textured conception of how punishment works, and the ways in which it is connected to debates about power and control in far flung fields. Despite their very different subject matter, the chapters in this book share a central interest in understanding on whose behalf, and with what consequences, particular control strategies are pursued; how punishment practices seep into or are increasingly shaped by practices in other social arenas and places; and, what the actual or conceptual spaces of control are like.

This book indicates that contemporary penal regimes are both exclusionary and inclusionary and underpinned by a complex range of, often, shifting sensibilities: at times punitive and emotive in orientation; at times technical and sanitized; at times emblematic of the need for connectedness and intimacy. Importantly there is no evidence that these varying sensibilities are the consequence of some *co-ordinated* plot or master-plan on the part of the state or other, more globalized entities to sustain oppression, or to recapture lost authority. Indeed the challenge for scholarship is to make sense of a field which exhibits limited logic and rationality. The state is both an actor and an audience within this field and the prison only one of a range of symbolic structures in a diverse and complex architecture. Boundaries between real and imagined communities, between insider and outsider groups, between the local, the national, and the global are porous and the categories which have come to frame popular conceptions of crime and criminals are leaky. Contemporary mediascapes and the literal and metaphorical spaces opened up by penal architecture, facilitate modes of resistance and open up the potential for new pathways and sometimes unanticipated path-dependencies.

Little did we anticipate, in reflecting on the common themes of the work in this book, that some optimistic note about opportunities of resistance would emerge. The picture of control at the dawn of a new century is in many ways dystopic, displaying as it does a manic and insatiable impulse, which has produced literal control over massive numbers of people and shaped cultural practice and values. We would not want to under-emphasize the significance of expanding global control networks. We merely hope to suggest in this brief reflection on the audiences, borders, and architecture of penality, that as these grow, metamorphose, and become interconnected so, too, do movements that question and challenge them.

2

Ordinary Anxieties and States of Emergency: Statecraft and Spectatorship in the New Politics of Insecurity[1]

Richard Sparks

A 'Politics of Fear'?

Once, perhaps, the allegation that we live in an environment of culturally produced anxieties that are sometimes politically serviceable, may have been the more or less exclusive province of radical criminologists and similar malcontents. It is an idea that has lengthy and respectable antecedents, of course, and would have been by no means astonishing to Machiavelli or to Hobbes. In its latter-day guise, however, this mistrustful and dubious notion was for quite some time a fringe idea. It had a certain heady appeal to students (like me) attracted to the more oppositional reaches of criminology and the sociology of deviance. It suggested a connection between crime control and Marxian theories of ideology, on the one hand, and accounts of the symbolic construction of social problems of interactionist inspiration on the other. In exploring these resources it became possible to argue that there was an intimate and important link between images of deviance, social control, and punishment, and politics properly so-called.

Over the last few decades a number of key contributions (and numerous lesser ones) have posited relationships between contention in public discourse about crime and punishment and shifts in the apparatus of control and the wider political culture. Cohen's notion of 'moral panic' (1972) is the most evocative and widely known of these. It is certainly one of the more successful examples of a 'double hermeneutic' (Giddens 1979) in having breached the bounds of academic exchange and become, even if often in barely recognizable form, a staple of journalism and general discussion. It is now part of the field that it also describes, in other words.

[1] The text of this chapter originated in a talk to the University of Glasgow Law School early in 2005. I am grateful to all present on that occasion, in particular Adam Tomkins and Sarah Armstrong, for comments and encouragement.

Among the contributions of Garland and Young (and other contributors) in *The Power to Punish* (1983) was that of establishing the social analysis of penality as equally the study of 'specific institutional sites' and as the interrogation of their cultural underpinnings. Garland's subsequent work is, of course, a key reference point in this discussion. *The Power to Punish* coincided in time, and to some extent in theme, with the emergence of new forms of media scholarship and cultural analysis, which offered a novel twist on the longstanding question of the relations between the instrumental and the ritual or demonstrative aspects of punishment and social control. Thus, for example, Wuthnow *et al*:

> While humans continually strive to maintain their sense of arrangement, this sense is continually threatened by the marginal situations endemic to human existence. Dreams, fantasy, sickness, injury, disaster, emergency, mistake, all reveal the unreliability of the social world; all present a menace of various degrees to the paramount reality of everyday life. (Wuthnow *et al* 1984: 37)

From various sources – interactionist sociology, structuralist and post-structuralist literary and social theory, new perspectives in social anthropology – the pressure was towards one or other version of constructionism. It became feasible, and eventually fashionable, to understand official discourses and dominant media scripts as rhetoric and claim, as tactics for imposing closure, erasing ambiguity, shutting down opposition, and sometimes for inciting the repression of minorities and outcasts.

No one, however, least of all the authors whom I have just invoked, imagines that these contributions in themselves provide a key motor of change in the wider public discourse. The 'hermeneutics of suspicion' (Ricoeur 1970) remained to a large extent the province of leftist intellectuals. Yet nowadays, in Britain at least, this kind of posture, often expressed using such terms as a 'politics of fear', seems quite widespread. It arises not just in academic contexts but in the columns and leading articles of newspapers, and in television documentaries. It is no longer a marginal idea; it is almost indeed a cliché. It is a coinage that seems simultaneously to suggest an increasing degree of uncertainty as to the proper scope, objects and intensity of fears or concerns and a thread of suspicion of the motives of those who would invoke fear in us; and these twin uncertainties seem to develop in tandem.

My aim in this chapter is neither that of tracing out the genealogy of the 'politics of fear', which is a much bigger project, nor that of adding yet another lamination to the seemingly pervasive commentary on the 'risk society', which may be increasingly redundant. Rather I want to begin to draw out some connections which I suspect may be quite important, but which seem to me relatively under-explored, between different current mobilizations of fear, risk, and insecurity. In particular I want to explore whatever relationship may exist between invocations of worry and concern about crime in its 'ordinary' or 'domestic' aspect (the crimes and incivilities of the street and neighbourhood, the usual stomping ground of criminologists) and those that have to do with the recent intensification of counter-terrorist activity and the controversies about the creation of new measures to deal with the sense of emergency that underpins this.

My hunch is that these issues are perhaps more tightly and more reciprocally linked than we might be inclined to think. Clearly, acting more robustly, as politicians of all stripes promise, against local crime and disorder on one hand or against the postulated threat of terrorist incursion on the other, may *both* involve the extension of powers of investigation or detention and, as such, may *both* involve controversial questions about civil liberties. Similarly they both generate pressures on political actors to demonstrate commitment, competence, and capacity, when these are placed severely in question. Beyond this I want to suggest that these levels of intervention have features in common on the level of cultural representation and pose related problems *and* opportunities for politicians. These features tend to promote an elision between them in current discourse on 'security', in ways that could prove consequential for how either is pursued and developed. Equally the overlap between the ways in which they are described and discussed may have a distinct bearing on the habitat in which we – as citizens, parents, voters, consumers – now live and the inventories of worries that attend our daily life. What kinds of connections arise between 'fears'[2] in these seemingly diverse contexts? What sorts of circulations of discourse about risk, threat, and blame take place? Against whom are allegations directed? What actions are postulated as necessary? What challenges arise for state capacity and sovereignty?

These are, at the risk of repetition, not in essence new questions. David Garland pointed out around a decade ago that some of the most vivid forms of state action against crime arise when the state's capacity to cope with a threat is most sharply in question. Garland (1996) has influentially argued that there are two distinct and contrary tendencies in the way that contemporary nation-states respond to crime under contemporary conditions. Chief among those conditions is that high volumes of crime have become chronic and are becoming normalized. A dominant response (which Garland terms the way of 'adaptation') is therefore to adopt various strategies for managing, coping, and ameliorating, including multiple varieties of delegation to, responsibilization of, and partnership with local authorities, individuals, voluntary bodies, and companies. A second response (which Garland styles 'denial' or 'hysterical' counter-reaction) is to engage in display, an 'archaic' show of punitive force which seeks to reassert the state's power to govern simply by displaying its power to punish: 'A show of

---

[2] *Fear* in this context means an invoked threat and not a mentalistic assumption about what any individual thinks or feels. It refers therefore to the ways in which the sense of threat is mobilized and directed within a particular political culture so as to provide warrants for new policies or interventions. It seems quite likely that this will have some bearing on what we as citizens, voters, and consumers of media do think and feel – but this is a distinct, empirical question and I try to avoid that slippage.

punitive force against individuals is used to repress any acknowledgement of the state's inability to control crime to acceptable levels' (1996: 460). In Garland's view, these 'schizoid' and 'ambivalent' tendencies are both now deeply entrenched – with predictably dismaying consequences for the demonization of 'othered' and outcast populations – those who are imprisoned, tagged, surveilled, ghettoized.

In arguing thus, Garland stands within a major current of contemporary social analysis which emphasizes the frailties, the 'hollowing out' of the nation-state by globalization. Thus, as strategically decisive economic decisions increasingly escape its influence; as flows of capital and information become uncontrollably mobile; as the great corporations come to rival or exceed it in scale and geo-political significance; so the state cleaves to such levers of influence and prestige as remain under its exclusive control. Moreover, facing a political culture that is marked by, in Bauman's phrase, 'ambient fear' (1998: 22), there is rich scope for media and political campaigns that are graphically emotive and charged with vicarious victimization, anxiety, and resentment.

It is only these criminologies 'of the other' that fully involve the mobilization of the collective passions – fear in the visceral sense; the sense of a lurking threat from without or from enemies within; mistrust, hostility, and ultimately warfare. In Garland's view, the limited success of contemporary states in restraining the growth of crime (and, as it has become more or less mandatory to add in the United Kingdom, 'disorder') calls into question their competence in pacifying their territory and by extension their ability to rule by sovereign command. The resulting sense of threat to the authority and credibility of the state is, on this view, what produces the 'hysterical counter-reaction' characteristic of some versions of recent penal politics. It has also been well argued that the use of the language of warfare in respect of crime control, most obviously in the so-called 'war on drugs' in the United States, has very particular escalatory effects (Beckett 1997).

I want to argue here that we should now attempt to rethink these connections somewhat. The wars and other campaigns against crime now share the stage with another war, the 'war on terror'. I suggest, tentatively and admittedly somewhat speculatively, that this coincidence or connection (and working out which of these it is seems to be central to the task at hand) may be quite consequential in grasping some of the more unnerving and confusing features of the present, and the elevated states of arousal and agitation now visible in our public discourse. As I will go on to discuss, the generation of a certain sense of threat can be significant in various ways, but it becomes particularly so – and stands particularly in need of analysis – when it operates in several of those ways *simultaneously*. Under such circumstances the whiff of danger, of diffuse and diverse dangers, becomes more pervasive. Whilst the sense of threat is highly likely to attach intensely to particular people, places, or issues, there is also perhaps at times a fuzzy sense of these dangers being somehow connected, an inchoate unease that is itself *additionally* unsettling and potentially corrosive of the authority and legitimate standing of institutions and their agents. Perhaps, then, there is a transfer or spill-over between one source of anxiety and another. Or perhaps our mundane concerns for safety and the larger worries about the security or capacity of the state and its institutions have a less readily identifiable common origin?

Yet, at the same time, the diction of 'the politics of fear' also connotes a degree of mistrust, verging on cynicism, as to the sincerity and motivations of politicians claiming the necessity of more stringent security measures. This seems to me to be an important aspect of the contemporary scene and one that also merits analysis. The 'limits of the sovereign state' to which Garland points, might seem more problematic still if the state also encounters recurrent difficulties in persuading a sceptical political culture (or at least a culture containing quite a few sceptics) of the veracity of its account of things. That seems to be an extra twist on the legitimation problems that Garland and others identify. But where does this idea take us? This is a problem to which I return shortly.

Ordinary Anxieties?

Amongst the particular contributions that students of crime and punishment can make here, are the ways in which larger contemporary concerns with state, boundaries, and powers, merge into the more local contexts of political struggles, scandals, and sensibilities. One of the ambitions that Evi Girling, Ian Loader, and I sought to pursue in our local study of fears and feelings about crime in one English town at the tail-end of the twentieth century (Girling *et al* 2000) was precisely that of *showing* and *tracing* these connections *in situ*. We tried to show that the study of citizens' 'crime-talk',[3] even though that talk itself is often profoundly local in character and peppered with anecdotes and allusions that tie it strongly to particular places and experiences, not only reveals much about popular beliefs about justice, welfare, inclusion and exclusion, or the proper role of government in social life which lie at the heart of contemporary debates about crime control (*ibid*: xii), and by extension 'the place that crime occupies in people's everyday lives and consciousness, but also in contemporary social relations more generally' (*ibid*). We took seriously the premise that the stories that people told us concerning their experiences of crime in their town, and about the changes that they had witnessed in their lifetimes, were also in some sense stories about globalization. We thought we could discern that when people spoke about crimes occurring in certain places then they were also commenting on their sense of their place, meaning both their own biography and the town's trajectory, in the light of their understanding of the changes wrought on each by

[3] The term 'crime-talk' was borrowed from Sasson's (1995) analysis of Boston residents' discussions of crime, policing, and punishment (and the ways in which social factors such as race, class, and gender shaped these).

convulsive economic, cultural, and technological change. Place has not ceased to matter under these altered conditions, and in some senses (not just the dull economic compulsion of property values, for example, but also the more interesting question about what 'values' *signify*) it matters extremely. But the awareness of place had become relational, comparative, and reflexive. Other places sometimes served as parables and warnings, or figured in people's discourse as containers of threats ('dens of thieves'), from which the predatory and ill-willed came calling (see Girling *et al* 2000, Sparks *et al* 2001). Our ways of picturing the threats of crime are thus pervaded by images of porous boundaries and never-quite-sufficiently-defensible spaces.

All of this seems to betoken a certain set of worries that circulate around motifs of *mobility*. There is mobility in the figurative sense of change – the town, the society, the world have all changed in ways that impinge too much and whose effects are felt in declining behaviour, increasing noise and rowdiness, and over-exposure to 'the outside'. And there is mobility in the concrete but no less metaphorically and associatively rich sense of travel and movement, but construed as a series of incursions, invasions, sorties, attacks. In the background of these worries there may lie a series of erosions of boundaries, expectations, and solidities, of the kind that Richard Sennett (1998) has discussed; and conceivably more broadly of a sense that there are institutions and social relations that are fit repositories for 'appropriate trust' (Baier 2001). Bauman reminds us here of Sartre's discussion of our fear and distaste – indeed disgust – for things that are indefinite yet difficult to shake off, and which therefore, in Sartre's terms, have the quality of *sliminess (le visceux)*: 'If I sink in the slimy I feel that I am going to be lost in it' (Bauman 2002: 152).

It might thus not be too outlandish to suggest that the resulting desire to make threatening others *be still*, to restrain their potentially illicit or disruptive mobility, is an indicative contemporary preoccupation. It is something that the discourses of 'ordinary' crime control, on the one hand, and the newer kinds of security-talk concerning counter-terrorism, border controls, and immigration detention have increasingly in common. Such commonalities on the level of representation may help to explain how it comes about that very different kinds of threat could come to be, to some extent, conflated or elided in contemporary political discourse and with what consequences. These would both be part-and-parcel of the 'anxieties that press in on everyone' (Giddens 1991: 126) in late-modern societies.

It might also turn out, thereby, that an anxiety, that stems at least in part from uncertainty concerning sovereignty and security in their proper, political senses, issues in a more fretful preoccupation with order in its mundane, local, domestic sense; or in a preference on the part of politicians that we direct our attention there. Conversely it might be the case that a state whose public discourse was already intensely focused on crime (and disorder) would also be one primed to respond vigorously, and perhaps belligerently, to external threats too. As Garland grasped early on, the relations between the criminologies of 'self' and 'other', of adaptation and hysterical counter-reaction (or, Garland again in another context (1999), between 'the commonplace' and 'the catastrophic') need to be understood as a dynamic, not just an opposition – a duality rather than a dualism as someone once put it (Giddens 1984).

'Specific Threats'

Emergencies are special moments. They are times when the rules and proprieties of normal conduct may be varied or suspended, and when the demand for immediate and vigorous action stands centre-stage.

There is nothing particularly revelatory *per se* about noting that the discourse of counter-terrorism and the discourse of mundane crime control seem to have certain features in common. The diction of the 'politics of fear' itself seems to indicate a high level of reflexivity about this in at least some sections of the media. Likewise the suggestion that these latest twists in the discourse could be highly illiberal in their consequences has been widespread. It has arisen in the pages of the *Daily Mail* and *Financial Times*, for example, as well as in the more obvious contexts of *The Guardian, The Independent,* or *The Observer.* Nor will this chapter be the place for a developed narrative account of the debates in Parliament, the resulting legislation, or its implementation. A small number of examples will suffice to give the tone. I then turn to the somewhat more slippery and evasive problem (trickier to state and certainly more difficult to evidence) of theorizing the points of connection between the different insecurities brought into play in current security-talk, including the stylistic aspects of their concurrent invocation.[4]

A convenient starting-point for the recent controversies in the United Kingdom is the Queen's Speech, setting out the Government's proposed legislative programme at the state opening of Parliament, on 22 November 2004. The term 'The Politics of Fear' was used as a front-page headline by *The Independent* the following morning. In the Queen's Speech – at the outset of the last session of Parliament before a general election – a series of diverse 'safety and security' measures were proposed. These ranged from new anti-terrorism legislation, via the creation of the new Serious Organized Crime Agency, through proposals for the introduction of civil identity cards, to measures designed to curb anti-social

---

[4] The paragraphs below on populism return to a theme that I have addressed a number of times before, especially in my 'Bringin' it all back home: populism, media coverage and the dynamics of locality and globality in the politics of crime control' (Sparks 2000); this chapter develops and updates that account. Naturally enough I worry about repeating myself and apologize to that very small number of readers who may know any of my other writing well enough to know when I do so. More broadly it just seems that the relationship between anxiety, crime, and politics is the recurrent preoccupation of my work: thus, eg, Sparks 1992; Sparks 2000; Girling *et al* 2000; Sparks *et al* 2001; Sparks 2003.

behaviour by empowering local authorities to act against 'dog-fouling, littering, vandalism, making excessive night-time noise, fly-posting and throwing fireworks'. Over the course of the next several months this expansive and varied programme continued to be sharply controversial. Although in general terms more congenial to the political Right, the Government's proposals, and perhaps especially the introduction of 'control orders' for persons suspected of involvement in terrorism, were also extensively criticized by Conservatives on grounds of their incompatibility with common law principles. The House of Lords debate on the Prevention of Terrorism Bill on 1 March 2005 was a particular case in point. Critiques of the Government position of the 'politics of fear' variety seem also to have reached a peak in the early months of 2005, with the election immediately in prospect. Thus *The Independent*'s leading article of 10 March 2005 announced: 'Terror scares, deadlines and election fever make for the worst kind of law-making.' Martin Samuel's column in *The Times* on 8 March provided an elegant crystallization of the dubious and sceptical position favoured by many journalists:

The *Prevention of Terrorism Bill*, or the Blair Witch Project as it should be called, is motivated by fear. For it to become palatable, you must be scared. After all the Government is scared. But what you fear and what it fears are very different. You fear a repeat of the atrocity in Madrid; it fears a repeat of the election in Madrid. You fear the bomb; it fears the blame . . .

This was a particularly pithy example of what had by this time emerged as a distinct genre – see similarly, for example, Andreas Whittam Smith in *The Independent* on 7 February: 'Avoidance of blame is key to Blair's anti-terror strategy.'

Unsurprisingly there were somewhat fewer such pieces immediately following the enormity of the 7 July attacks in London and the no less frightening attempted bombings of 21 July. Nevertheless, any attempt by the Government to claim vindication was severely undermined by the shooting of an unarmed Brazilian commuter, John Charles de Menezes, on 22 July 2005. In the aftermath of that killing allegations of incompetence, excessive and inappropriate use of lethal force, and lack of accountability were rife. A number of newspapers in fact claimed that the use of firearms seemed likely to become more extensive rather than less. For example, *The Independent*, on 25 October 2005, summarizing a Metropolitan Police review of its policies on the issue, declared: 'Police are given shoot-to-kill powers in domestic violence and stalking cases.'

The danger of conflation or confusion between the anti-terror strategy and crime control measures in general certainly continued to worry some, though most obviously, but not exclusively, the liberal press. There was no small concern over the seeming instability in this respect within the controversial proposals for civil identity cards (for example *The Independent*, 25 June 2005). Critical observations by the human rights commissioner for the Council of Europe,

Alvaro Gil-Robles, were relatively widely reported (for example *The Guardian,* 9 June 2005). Mr Gil-Robles was among a number who raised questions about the proliferation during this period of Anti-Social Behaviour Orders (ASBOs), especially their application to the under-sixteens. The fact that new control orders for terrorist suspects (themselves introduced following rejection by the House of Lords of extended detention in prison without trial) were in several respects modelled on ASBOs attracted some, though by no means widespread, comment. Their common features – curfew, tagging, restrictions on association, and communications – refer again to the need to limit dangerous mobilities.

To no one's great surprise the antisocial behaviour agenda gathered momentum throughout 2004 and 2005, with a very significant year-on-year increase in the number of ASBOs (together with the first use late in 2005 of a 'dispersal order' to prohibit gatherings of young people entirely within a specified area in the comparatively unlikely setting of Mid-Calder in West Lothian: 'Quiet village curbs its noisy youths' *The Guardian,* 12 December 2005).

States of Emergency

What are we to make of these sightings? The current conjuncture seems particular, but not perhaps entirely without precedent. We should not forget that studies of crime, punishment, and control (criminology, for want of a better term) have made their own earlier contributions to accounts of state exceptionalism. For example, Stuart Hall and his collaborators in their landmark work *Policing the Crisis* (1978) – an acknowledged landmark yet oddly sparsely referenced now – observe that moments of particular alarm and their associated calls for action (crises, in a word) do not 'emerge from nowhere' but rather arise out of a pre-existing field of 'tension, hostility and suspicion' (Hall *et al* 1978: 181). They also take the view that 'moments of "more than usual alarm" followed by the exercise of "more than normal control"' tend to be associated with significant historical upheavals and social-political transition (1978: 186). The context has undoubtedly shifted since Hall *et al* wrote. Nonetheless, certain of their remarks seem both prescient and still pertinent, even if we will also need to revise or extend them. One question that animated Hall and colleagues was what might happen when circumstances conspired to bring political leadership and cultural authority into particular question. They conceived this as a moment of crisis in hegemony:

Such moments signal, not necessarily a revolutionary conjuncture nor the collapse of the state, but rather the coming of 'iron times' . . . domination will be exercised, in such moments, through a modification in the modes of hegemony; and one of the ways in which this is registered is through a tilt in the operation of the state away from consent and towards the pole of coercion. It is important to note that this does not involve a suspension of the 'normal' exercise of state power – it is not a move towards a fully exceptional form of the state. It is better understood as – to put it paradoxically – an *exceptional moment* in the *normal* form of the late capitalist state. (Hall *et al* 1978: 217)

The kinds of accretions of anxiety contemplated here will not have the discrete and somewhat arbitrary character sometimes associated with the idea of 'moral panic'. Indeed, Hall *et al* suggest that one of their concerns is to re-imagine 'moral panic' as 'one of the forms of appearance of a more deep-seated historical crisis' and as one of the means by which the 'silent majority' is won over to the need for greater stringency and coercion (Hall *et al* 1978: 221). Thus, they suggest, one can sometimes observe (as they claimed to observe of Britain in the 1970s) a tendency for a 'succession' of panics around topics of controversial public concern to give way to a 'mapping together of moral panics into a general panic about social order', one in which there is a 'jumpy and alerted control culture' standing ready to react to signs of trouble. In such conditions, they further suggest, our predominant way of grasping troubling events is through a signification spiral that imputes *connections between* otherwise disparate threats as part-and-parcel of the process of preparing the way for firmer action against them (Hall *et al* 1978: 223).[5] Emergencies may differ from 'moral panics' in a number of other respects too. They need not, in any case, be primarily *moral* in character – a threat to the integrity of the state and the safety of citizens may be quite enough to constitute an emergency – the more so when the incumbent regime has staked a high quotient of legitimacy precisely on the point of its strength, determination, and competence in protecting citizens and sustaining security, and this appears compulsory for politicians at present, even if much more plainly so in the United States and United Kingdom than in some other places.

The barometric pressure of law and order politics in the United Kingdom has risen and fallen at various times since Hall *et al* wrote. The sense of a crisis has not been uniform; neither has it simply intensified without interruption. There have been moments of seemingly greater confidence, when a return to a less sharply politicized scene has seemed feasible. There has been no small amount of business-almost-as-usual pragmatism in many areas of policy. And there has been a fairly serious and sustained interest in questions of 'inclusion'. There are

---

[5] The new political dispensation after 1979 claimed to be better able, as Giddens puts it, to 'ride the juggernaut' (1990: 151) of social change and economic volatility by stripping down the role of the state to its essentials, ie superintending the operation of a dynamic free market and restoring, in Margaret Thatcher's words 'freedom under law'. There was thus no contradiction between a 'minimal' state and one that was to be more vigorous and effective in pursuit of its proper tasks, including a renewed and more robust emphasis on crime control. This novel 'state regime' with its potent confluence of neo-liberalism in economic affairs and its techniques of governing and neo-conservatism in social and cultural matters thus came to dominance by representing the accumulation of problems of the Keynesian welfare state as a twin crisis of 'ungovernability' and uncompetitiveness. This in part explains why governments on both sides of the Atlantic since the 1970s have staked much of their claim to legitimacy on tough-mindedness in crime control.

good reasons, therefore, to be cautious of the language of watersheds, endings, turning points, and so on, as Garland (2001: 22) observes, and as Loader and I have quite strongly asserted (2004). However, if the spiky political moment that Hall *et al* addressed feels somewhat *less* exceptional in retrospect, this is at least partly because the succession of panics and controversies has really never ceased, and the 'jumpy and alerted' culture of which they spoke has never stood down from a state of alert for very long. A somewhat heightened level of arousal and activity has become to this extent a chronic condition, and one that seems less and less likely to go into remission for very long. There can be both larger and more local reasons for this state of affairs; and even now some people are much more exposed, or simply more sensitive, to it than others. Many of us find ways of ignoring the world's troubles, or distracting ourselves from them, much of the time. But they form our habitat nonetheless.

For these reasons we would be unwise to proceed with the social analysis of crime control and punishment, even in their mundane, domestic aspects, without thinking about the ways in which these too might be affected by the defensive-aggressive character of the surrounding political-cultural climate. The implications of 'globalized insecurities' for current conceptions of state sovereignty and territoriality have become a major preoccupation for scholars of political theory and international relations (see further <http://www.libertysecurity.org>; Agamben 2005) concerned with the emergence of a new 'state of exception'. It is an important corollary in this literature that the *site* or *sites* of 'the exception' may turn out to be more slippery and more culturally invasive than is apparent at first sight (see Walker 1997). The effects of exceptionalism would seem to reach quite far down into 'domestic' affairs, and indeed ordinary popular sensibilities. This is most evident in the convergence, already noted above, between the languages of crime control and of warfare (see, for example, Bigo 2005). They might similarly be registered, however, in a convergence between the concerns of crime control and those of social policy generally (Boutellier 2001).[6]

As I have commented elsewhere (Sparks 2003), it is no doubt possible both to overstate and to oversimplify this relation. The place of the politics of crime and insecurity in the public life of nation-states varies in intensity and texture from time to time and place to place. It comes in flurries as major stories break and scandals and *causes célèbres* are played out, focusing our collective attention (Fine 1997) and engaging our sympathies and enmities around their 'heroes, villains and fools' (Klapp 1954). It is in the nature of contemporary politics, given the global reach of mass media and the extent of their infiltration of

---

[6] In other words, convergence between these areas, which is presumably inevitable in some degree, only becomes a special problem when it occurs on terms dominated by a surrounding sense of insecurity or *ressentiment* such that the dictates of crime control tend to overwhelm those of other policy considerations. This would give rise to the posture nicely described by Jonathan Simon as 'governing through crime' (1997: 173), see also Simon 2002.

everyday life, that these questions come at us in the form of discrete stories or episodes. There is a certain pattern in the frequency and regularity with which we are exposed to such stories and the ways in which they speak to our fears and feelings. These days when we want to suggest that an issue is politically significant we often say that it is 'sensitive' or 'emotive'. In so saying we seem to imply that whatever is political (in the sense that it engenders discourse, highlights contention, or provides a motivation for collective action) is so in virtue of its capacity to pluck the nerve of our anxieties, to destabilize our confidence in the reliability or orderliness of things, or to menace our faith in the future.

The endless multiplication of media of communication produces in some ways far greater mutual awareness (the consciousness of living amongst a multitude of diverse lives and fortunes) but this by no means signals a general enhancement of the sense of amity or intimacy across social boundaries. Indeed, what comes at us through our multi-channel, multi-media encounters is just as likely to be a series of disconcerting reminders of, as the great anthropologist and anatomist of cultural responses to risk Mary Douglas (1992) puts it, 'danger on the borders'. Yet in an ever more globally inter-connected world the sense of just exactly where our borders lie and how they can feasibly be defended and by whom is increasingly unclear. One consequence can be an anxious re-focusing on our *personal* boundaries – on the safety and integrity of our bodies and possessions and those of our intimates, on the inviolability of the home, street, and neighbourhood against incursion from others whom we mistrust and who seem to carry with them the dangers and contagions of an endemically uncertain world. This is primarily the domain that Girling, Loader, and I have sought to document in the work to which I alluded above (Girling *et al* 2000, Sparks *et al* 2001). Another effect, felt especially acutely lately, may be a renewed concern over our leaky and dubious political and territorial borders. Nation-states can look decidedly defensive and beleaguered in the face of historical shifts that escape their planning and control. Moreover they face new problems. The drastic arrival of the 'war on terror' is one obvious ratchet to the insecurities of the times. Similarly, the recent intensification of controversies over mass migration and asylum-seeking further menaces the credibility of states' claims to sovereign potency. A third and closely related dimension therefore would often seem to be an embedded scepticism as to the capacities of those 'Leviathans that stand guard over us' (Baier 2001) actually to do all that they are required to claim – and hence about whether they claim to do so in good faith. This diminished trust seems to be what produces the trope that I have termed 'the politics of fear'.

This of course is exactly the conclusion that much recent social theory urges. Consider for a moment what is entailed in this regard by recent arguments about globalization. For example, Manuel Castells (1997) suggests that we live in a world which is shaped by conflicting trends of globalization and identity. In this world, Castells says, power (in the sense of 'strategically decisive economic decisions') moves more fluidly and more freely than ever before, yet the locus of our political attachments and demands remains firmly stuck at the traditional level of the nation-state. That state, Castells argues, still 'looks very nice in its shiny buttons' (1997: 303) but is structurally incapable of vindicating its claims to sovereign authority and hence of meeting the demands for cohesion and security that we repose in it. Power therefore moves in 'the space of flows' but we are fated to inhabit the 'space of places', and for most of us those places become one form or another of 'defensive trench'.

Zygmunt Bauman explores a similar thesis with more express reference to the fear of crime and the politics of punishment. In his view there is an intrinsic potentiality for the unholy meeting of media hyperbole, the 'ambient insecurity' under which we the audience live and the willingness of political actors and moral entrepreneurs to promise the kind of strong medicine that will palliate our symptoms:

In an ever more insecure and uncertain world the withdrawal into the safe-haven of territoriality is an intense temptation; and so the defence of the territory – the 'safe home' – becomes the pass-key to all doors which one feels must be locked to stave off the ... threat to spiritual and material comfort ... It is perhaps a happy coincidence for political operators and hopefuls that the genuine problems of insecurity and uncertainty have condensed into the anxiety about safety; politicians can be supposed to be doing something about the first two just because being seen to be vociferous and vigorous about the third. (Bauman 1998: 117)

One of the difficulties here, as Bauman has argued, is that the prospects for meaningful and effective political action, certainly for any purportedly 'sovereign' nation-state acting alone, are not very encouraging. Yet the pull towards display is very strong. As Bauman comments, states may on occasion be drawn back towards the primitive principles of sovereignty where:

The true defining feature of sovereignty is not so much the right to determine the law but the right to exempt from the law; it is the capacity to denude its subjects of the repressive/ protective envelope of the law that makes power fully and truly sovereign. 'Sovereignty', we may say, means the right to issue 'Wanted – dead or alive' posters that designate easy prey for bounty hunters (Bauman 2002: 5).

One consequence, according to Bauman, is that displays of patriotic fervour, anger, or outrage come in spasmodic bursts. They proceed, he suggests, 'after the pattern of a swarm – a massively copied style of individual behaviour – rather than that of the coordinated conduct of a stable community' (*ibid*: 7). One implication of Bauman's account of globalization thus appears to be that our need, individual as well as collective, to push seemingly threatening others back, or else to see them fixed-in-place, is itself an effect of 'the endemic porosity and frailty of all boundaries' (*ibid*: 13).

Populism and Spectatorship

We need hardly labour the point that nowadays the process of politics, and all the assertions of authority, attributions of blame, and play of claim and counter-claim that this implies, is inseparable from the characteristic forms and formats of the mass media. As Hall *et al* put it, now so long ago, in a complex, plural, mobile, and mutually anonymous society the 'networks that connect' are crucial.

In *Policing the Crisis* it was the mobilization of the respectable, law-abiding nation against the alien intrusion of 'mugging' that such 'connections' made possible. Now the questions concern, among an almost endless array of possible dangers, the extent and nature of the threats posed to our way of life by 'terror', on the one hand, and, on the other, the corrosions of the possibilities of a peaceful and ordered existence by 'anti-social behaviour'. They also include, I have suggested above, some persistent questions as to the ability of politicians to address these issues as effectively as they seem compelled to claim *and*, at least in some quarters, a worm of doubt as to their sincerity and good faith in so claiming.

It seems important at this juncture to return to the question of the media's role in sustaining our apprehensions (in both senses) of crime in a properly contemporary way – ie one attuned both to the kind of 'mediascape' that now exists and to the kinds of consumers, listeners, and viewers that we now are; and hence that can provide some degree of insight into the particular varieties of attention, commitment, and emotional engagement in terms of which we can read and respond to them. Among the issues that might arise here would be the particular kinds of emotionality that now characterize some of our engagements with crime and punishment – the 'new expressiveness' as David Anderson (1995) nicely has it in the course of his insightful discussion of the impact of the Willie Horton case on American political culture – the brittleness of some of our social relations and, as I have suggested above following Bauman, the fragility of our physical and figurative boundaries. In Anderson's view, the rise of 'the new expressiveness' in American penal politics had something to do with 'helping an angry and anxious public manage its feelings' (see further Garland 2000: 349).

Ericson *et al* have convincingly shown that the usual business of mass media in focusing discussion on 'what is out of place: the deviant, equivocal and unpre-dictable' (1991: 4) is intrinsically concerned with the question of 'order' – where order is conceived in terms of 'morality, procedural form and social hierarchy' (1991: 1) – and in turn that the activity of representing order in the news takes the domain of law as paradigmatic of authority and legitimacy (1991: 7–10). For Ericson *et al* this makes the media not merely the receptacles, bearers, or channels of reports but rather 'an active *agency* of social control, stability and change', and part-and-parcel of the unceasing processes of social exchange that constitute the 'symbolic politics of order' in our kind of society. We should add now that, given the proliferation of media and channels in recent years (and their market segmentation and niche targeting), and the corresponding attenuation in the capacity of the media to function in some sense as a 'public sphere', only certain topics will be potent enough, graspable enough, emotive enough, 'visualizable' enough, to make *connections across* publics, markets, and sectors.

Some at least (perhaps a disproportionate number) of such connections are likely to be made through the representation of crime, terrorism, and the threats they carry to our safety and security. Thus the temptation upon politicians to reach for the common, connecting theme (to make 'the war on drugs' into 'the nation's number one priority', for example: Beckett 1997) is intense, and is structurally provided for. Meanwhile, whilst it is in no sense any longer the case that we are all watching, reading, or listening to the same media at the same time, nevertheless, certain names and their emotional associations (William Horton, O.J. Simpson, Louise Woodward, Jamie Bulger, and so on) are known to all, at least for a time. Even in heatedly dividing us they give us something to talk about; they prompt discourse; they engender that form of social communion that *only* mass media can provide, what Thompson in *The Media and Modernity* calls 'despatialized commonality' (1996: 231).

It is now quite commonplace to refer to some of the characteristic ways of presenting crime and security issues in our culture as 'populist'. Quite often it is not completely clear what is meant by this. We tend to apply this term in a general way to many things that we dislike – demagogic gestures, alarmism, 'punitiveness'. Used in this way the notion of populism contains a series of unflattering attributions – the cynicism, opportunism, and short-termism of politicians who 'play to the gallery'; the irrationalism, prejudices, and deep-dyed conservatism of the public. And, of course, the battlefields of penal politics are littered with examples that seem to lend themselves to this kind of commentary. More thoughtful accounts distinguish the element of populism from other contemporary tendencies with which it coexists (Bottoms 1995). Other scholars suggest that among the defining features of populism in its contemporary sense are certain ways or techniques of communicating. In this vein Canovan (2000) argues that populism is one of the inevitable modes of contemporary politics. In her view, the very complexity and hence 'opacity' of the 'backstage' practices of governance is itself one of the conditions that favours politicians' recurrent tendency to resort to populist gestures. In place of a candid admission of the often tedious, arcane, and unsatisfactory realities of contemporary political and administrative life, we find a preference for 'sound-bites', 'spin', and slogans. Populism is thus a way of talking about politics designed for people who are essentially onlookers and spectators:

Ideology, which reduces the complexity of politics to dogmatic simplicity, is ill-fitted to deal adequately with [these] intricacies,[7] and yet ideology is indispensable in mass

---

[7] ie the intricacies that flow from a 'crowded and dynamic political arena' in which many interests and opinions exert 'some small influence on policies' (Canovan 2000: *loc cit*).

politics... [But] the ideology of democracy is full of populist themes that belie the current trend of democratic politics, stressing sovereignty and will against compromise and accommodation, popular unity against multiplicity, majority against minorities, directness and transparency against complex and intricate procedures. The paradox in other words, is that while democracy (more than any other political system) *needs* to be comprehensible to the masses, the ideology that seeks to bridge the gap between people and politics misrepresents (and cannot avoid misrepresenting) the way that democratic politics necessarily works. This contradiction between ideology and practice is a standing invitation to raise the cry of democracy betrayed, and to mobilise the discontented behind the banner of restoring politics to the people. (Canovan 2000)

This observation seems highly redolent of some observed features of the penal realm in recent times – colonized by 'managerialist' systems and 'actuarial' procedures of opaque sophistication yet quite unable to break free for long from the pull of emotivism and sloganizing.

There is another twist on this issue, once more noted by the ever-watchful Bauman. This is the frequent sense of helplessness that goes with our awareness of the intractability and complexity of the issues (which no amount of populist simplification erases altogether) and of their increasingly global character, scope, and extent. Yet, Bauman argues, it is not just we as ordinary citizens who are thus positioned in the uncomfortable role of bystanders. Politicians are, for many purposes, bystanders too. They too are, in his view, 'unprepared and confused... finding all trusted routines singularly unfit for the fast changing conditions and desperately seeking new and hopefully more effective stratagems' (2002: 16). The disconcerting prospect is feeling oneself to live in a world where 'everything may happen, yet nothing can be done' (*ibid*: 17). This seems to me to be as pithy an account as possible for the seemingly overwhelming temptation on political actors to simplify and to over-bid in respect of crime and security questions and, simultaneously, for the perhaps increasing tendency to mistrust them for doing so.

The frequent irruption through the media of certain powerfully emotive themes and images associated with crime and punishment into political culture, and the tactical uses to which they can then be put, works powerfully to the advantage of certain political positions and the detriment of others. It is tempting to see this as a peculiarly American, or to some extent Anglo-American, problem. The exceptional nature of the American prison population encourages this view, as does the disparity between the recent criminal justice histories of, say, America and Canada. Conversely one might discover that the hyping of the penal was a temptation to which all advanced capitalist countries were subject and that they differed only in degree or in the particular targets to which their anxieties and enmities attached. But if that were so it would mean that the media politics of punishment were implicated in a set of transformations that were being felt in some way *everywhere*, as Castells, Bauman, and others indeed suggest.

None of this should be read simply as repeating the loose but not infrequently made assertion that fear and anger about crime are just inventions got up by the wicked media to bamboozle and exploit us. Yet the recurrent invocation through the media of an interlocking array of anxieties and passions makes these a theme in political culture whose significance is hard to overstate. What is really at issue here is how in our kind of society, in which political process and media discourse can hardly meaningfully be separated, certain especially resonant themes and images address, channel, and give form to otherwise inchoate concerns, around which discussion and action congregate. What kind of people are we being encouraged to be by these discourses? What sorts of governance are we persuaded to accept?[8]

[8] I am aware that this is a downbeat way to finish. There is much that can and should be said of more encouraging sorts, but the very end of an essay is not the place to embark on them. Working out a position which is adequate to the complexities involved and not content to reiterate the cynicisms of the 'politics of fear' style of journalism is a major challenge, and one that cannot be postponed for long.

3

Tony Martin and the Nightbreakers: Criminal Law, Victims, and the Power to Punish[1]

Lindsay Farmer

Introduction

On the night of 20 August 1999 two men, Fred Barras (aged 16) and Brendon Fearon (aged 30), broke into Bleak House, a remote Norfolk farmhouse. They were carrying holdall bags and torches and wearing gloves. As they moved around one of the ground floor rooms in the dark they were disturbed as the homeowner, Tony Martin, appeared on the staircase and began firing a shotgun at them. Three shots were fired, one hitting Barras in the back and killing him, and one causing serious injuries to Fearon's legs as he made his escape. Martin was arrested and charged with murder and wounding with intent, while Fearon was charged with conspiracy to burgle. Although Martin claimed to have been acting in defence of his person and property, the court took the view that the force used was excessive and without justification. He had given no warning, had fired not one but three shots, and had used an illegally obtained, unlicenced, pump-action shotgun.[2] He was found guilty and sentenced to life imprisonment, though this was reduced on appeal to five years' imprisonment on the substitution of a conviction for manslaughter by reason of diminished responsibility. Fearon was sentenced to three years' imprisonment for his part in the burglary. Martin was released from prison in the summer of 2003, having served two-thirds of his sentence.

The events in this case more than any other in recent history have given rise to particular controversy about crime, policing and punishment in contemporary Britain. Other recent cases, such as the murders of Stephen Lawrence or Damilola Taylor in England or Surjit Singh Chhokar in Scotland, have been traumatic, forcing the institutions of police and prosecution into periods of

---

[1] I would like to thank Sarah Armstrong, Gerry Johnstone, and Victor Tadros for their comments.

[2] He had previously been disqualified from holding a firearm licence following an incident in 1994 when he shot at a man taking apples from his orchard.

prolonged self-examination and reform. However, in these cases the reaction of professionals, media, and public has been largely, and remarkably, consensual. All have agreed by and large that the killer should be found and prosecuted, that procedures should be reformed, that the evil of institutional racism should be rooted out – notwithstanding procedural difficulties or differences over the extent of reform required. The cases can be safely located within a narrative of reform, stages (albeit difficult ones) in the journeys of police and community towards the recognition of multiculturalism and the understanding of diversity. The case of Tony Martin, by contrast, has divided professional, media, and public opinion, with each new development in the case apparently reopening old wounds rather than leading towards any form of resolution. The threat of legal action between Martin and Fearon continued into early 2004, accompanied by media outrage over the potential availability of legal aid for Fearon. More significant have been the continuing attempts to promote a so-called 'Tony Martin' law to protect householders threatened by intruders. At the end of 2003 a popular poll on BBC Radio 4 to choose the subject matter of a private members' Bill was won by the 'Tony Martin Bill'.[3] The issue was then taken up in late 2004, initially by Conservative MP Patrick Mercer, who published a private members Bill on the subject, and later by the then Conservative Party leader, Michael Howard, who sought to make the protection of householders an issue in the 2005 general election, arguing that householders should be able to use all but 'grossly disproportionate force' in the defence of their homes.[4]

There does not, on the face of it, seem to be any particular reason why this case should have given rise to such a prolonged and intense debate. The legal issues are settled: force may be used in the defence of property or person provided that it is necessary, reasonable in the circumstances, and not excessive. The way that force was used and the absence of a warning meant that this point was quickly settled at Martin's trial. His successful appeal was readily resolved by the acceptance of medical evidence about his state of mind that was not available at the original trial.[5] And though there were differences in the views of the doctors who assessed his psychological health, these were largely matters of degree as all agreed that Martin was an eccentric loner, who suffered from a paranoid personality disorder and periodic bouts of depression. In other circumstances, with another defendant, the right to use force in defence of property would readily

[3] The Labour MP who had undertaken to promote the Bill refused to do so. It was taken up by a Conservative MP, but was blocked by government ministers on the grounds that it had 'something of the Wild West about it' (*The Guardian*, 30 April 2004).

[4] The government has argued that the existing law is adequate, if not properly understood by the general public. This led to them taking the unusual step of publishing a leaflet in February 2005 explaining exactly how much force might be used against intruders. *Householders and the Use of Force Against Intruders* (Crown Prosecution Service and Association of Chief Police Officers, 1 February 2005).

[5] The ruling on appeal does raise a minor question about the extent to which a jury might use psychiatric evidence to assess the defendant's perception of the threat (*R v Martin (Anthony)* 2001, Lacey *et al* 2003: 797–8).

(if reluctantly) be conceded by the law. Indeed, in this and similar cases we seem to be drawn into a world of cranks and obsessives who seek to fortify their homes, to arm themselves against the real or imaginary terrors of the outside world. Yet it is this case over which debate has raged, led by commentators and politicians on the political right, leading to calls for changes in the criminal law, in policing, in the sentencing and imprisonment of certain classes of offenders, and in the rights of victims.[6]

The controversy turns on two particular aspects of the case, where our normal understandings of right and wrong and of offender and victim, and thus of crime and punishment and law and order, seem to turn in on themselves. The first concerns the status of right in the case. What is the right that obtains on the commission of a wrong? How do we deal with the wrong that is committed in defence of a right? What kind of right to life can demand death as its price? Is there, indeed, any clear sense of right or wrong that can ground the law in this type of case? The second aspect concerns the status of the category 'victim', which is destabilized in this case where there is an offender who becomes a victim, and a victim who becomes an offender.[7] Both men are then, arguably, 'victimized' once more in the criminal process: Martin through the medicalizing discourse that presents him as psychologically abnormal; both through the continuing and intrusive attentions of the media. Problems arise here from both the fluidity of the content of the category and from uncertainty around the question of what flows from membership of this category. Who is the victim of this crime? What 'rights' does a victim have, and which victims should have such rights? And how are the rights of the victim to be measured against those of the accused person? The fundamental nature of these controversies shows that this is, in an important sense, a limit case, revealing the contradictions which occur when trends in criminal law and penal practice come into conflict with each other, and it is for these reasons that the controversy is unlikely just to fade away.

What I want to do in this chapter is to begin the process of drawing out these contradictions in more detail, to show why the case is important – and why this is not necessarily for the reasons fastened on by rightwing politicians in Britain who have sought to exploit the controversy to promote an agenda of house-holder's rights and increased punitiveness. I shall do this by examining the case in the light of what I see as being the more general underlying tension here, that between questions concerning the right to punish – under what conditions the use of force can be justified – and those concerning the power to punish – how penal powers are actually organized and used. I shall argue that these questions of right – the juridical – occupy a central position in contemporary penal politics, and that they have been somewhat neglected in contemporary analyses of

---

[6] It is also worth noting that although the issue is clearly a matter of popular concern there has been little academic comment (but see, now, Getzler 2006).

[7] We might note in passing the similarity of the logic here to that applied in the cases of battered women who kill their abusers: our response to the 'vigilante justice' in each case might be different.

penality. In other words, the resurgence of questions concerning the right to punish (both in practice and in theory) raises important issues for the understanding of the criminal law in contemporary (or late modern) society.

Private Defence and the Sovereign State

The most important legal issues raised by the case concerned the doctrine of self-, or private, defence. There were two main questions. First were those of the circumstances in which a victim of crime is entitled to use force in defence of their person or property, and, second, the consequences that should follow in the case of an unsuccessful plea of private defence. The first issue was raised explicitly by Martin's defence team, and has subsequently been raised by a number of politicians and other commentators on the case who have argued that there should be an expanded right of self-defence to allow the 'responsible' property owner greater powers to defend their property.[8] It has also been argued that the law should acknowledge a new category of voluntary manslaughter, death resulting from the use of excessive force in self-defence. This would mean holding that the actions of the accused were not justified in the circumstances, but that they should nonetheless be (partially) excused. This would cover intentional killings falling short of murder, thus allowing the courts to avoid the imposition of the mandatory life sentence which follows from a conviction for murder, a rule which has long been unpopular with the courts.

In legal terms, the right to so-called private defence can be broken down into a number of distinct issues. Under section 3 of the Criminal Law Act 1967 a person may use 'such force as is reasonable in the circumstances' in defence of property.[9] This question of what is reasonable in the circumstances is regarded as one to be determined by the jury, though the accused person is to be judged on the basis of the facts as they believed them to be.[10] English law also requires that the use of force should be necessary, and that it should be proportionate to the threat (Simester and Sullivan 2003: 620). There is no duty on the householder to retreat, and they may even use pre-emptive force if they believe that an attack is imminent. It can be seen from this that the law of private defence is already quite broad,

---

[8] William Hague, then leader of the Conservative Party, argued that the law should be changed to create a strong presumption in favour of those protecting their homes and families (*The Guardian*, 26 April 2000). Recent proposals from the Conservative Party have suggested reforming the law so that the householder can use all but 'grossly disproportionate force'.

[9] For a general discussion of the English position, see Lanham (1966). Scots law takes a slightly more restrictive approach, requiring that the threat be imminent, the response be proportional and necessary, and that the accused should use any means of escape available (Jones and Christie 2003: 168–72).

[10] *R v Williams* [1987] 3 All ER 411; *Beckford v R* [1998] 3 All ER 425; Owino (1996) 2 Cr App R 128. See also the gloss on the meaning of reasonableness in the leaflet published by the CPS and ACPO: *Householders and the Use of Force Against Intruders* (February 2005). In Scots law an honest belief in a threat must none the less be based on reasonable grounds (*Jones v HM Advocate* 1990 JC 160).

notwithstanding that what is reasonable falls to be determined on a case-by-case basis. However, the courts are uneasy about giving the property owner too great a licence when acting in defence of their property, and in recent times have generally favoured the view that the law should be applied restrictively since it would be unreasonable to kill or cause grievous bodily harm merely to protect property. This has not prevented critics of the law in the Martin case from arguing that the law should be changed to create the presumption that the property owner was acting reasonably, arguing in effect that if the state fails to secure individuals and their homes against violence, then the state monopoly of force should give way to an individual right to self-protection (for example Fletcher 1988). The rights of the householder, in other words, should override the power to punish that is vested in the state. The claim of the critics might be defended on various normative or prudential grounds: as a moral claim about the respective value of life and property; as a right to protect personal autonomy; as an argument that the aggressor/intruder forfeits his own right to life; or as a right to resist any unlawful aggression (Uniacke 1994, Green 1999). However, in this chapter I wish to leave aside a discussion of the merits of these claims to analyse the case within the context of the changing nature of the state and police in 'late modern' or 'advanced liberal' societies, for these abstract normative justifications take on a particular character when analysed in this specific context. In order to make this point it is necessary to set out some of the history of the right to private defence.

The rule that a householder was entitled to kill an intruder or thief in the night can be traced back to both biblical and Roman law, and was a conception that was influential in shaping the early development of the common law, which stressed the importance of private defence against manifestly dangerous or threatening actions, and specifically night-time intrusions.[11] The property owner exercised dominion over their household, conceived as a combination of possessions and persons, and could exclude (even to the extent of a power over life and death) those who threatened their security and enjoyment of that property (Dubber 2004). In English law this found a characteristic expression in the idea that the Englishman's home is his castle – or more properly that the lord of the castle possessed a power or jurisdiction over his household, offering protection against internal and external threats to those who swore fealty to him.[12] The defence of property was conceived as a form of private justice, on the basis that the thief or intruder deserved to be executed as a criminal for the threat that they posed to the peace of the household. Even as Royal jurisdiction developed, incorporating lesser jurisdictions, this power survived in a limited form as an important element of the criminal law. Thus, for example, for Blackstone (1966 [1765–9]): 'If any person . . . attempts to break

---

[11] Exodus 22: 1–3; Twelve Tables, VIII.3. For a discussion of the origins of this rule see Fletcher (1978: 855–75).

[12] Dubber (2004: 15–18) argues that the King's peace was merely the extension of this dominium, with the realm conceived as the King's household. For the assertion that the home is a castle, see *Semayne's Case* 77 Eng Rep, 194 (KB 1604); (1604) 5 Co Rep 91a.

open a house *in the night time,* (which extends also to an attempt to burn it) and shall be killed in such attempt, the slayer shall be acquitted and discharged' (iv, 180). Yet he was also careful to note (against Locke who supported an absolute right to defend property)[13] that the exercise of this right was not unrestricted, depending on a conformity with public standards established by law; the laws of a well-regulated and civilized country, such as England, must attend to the public peace and the lives of the subjects such that it will not 'suffer with impunity any crime to be *prevented* by death, unless the same, if committed, would also be *punished* by death' (*ibid*: iv, 182, emphasis in original). In other words, killing in private defence was justified if the crime against which the killer was defending him or herself was a felony (ie capital) – a law that might be rather difficult to enforce as it seems to require the erstwhile victim to make an instant and finely-tuned judgement about the precise legal nature of the attack.[14]

The efficacy of the rule permitting private defence can readily be seen in the absence of an effective central state authority or regular police force. In these circumstances the right to act as judge and executioner in defence of one's property against manifest danger had been important to the maintenance of security and order. However, as the state grew in strength, and property and order became more settled, the traditional form of private justice was overlaid by a system of state rules and sanctions. This was part of a wider transformation in the relationship between sovereignty and security in which the state took on the role of the primary guarantor of security. In these circumstances the legal basis and justification of the rule were transformed. The question of defence of property was incorporated within a broader right to self-defence, restating the question of self-preservation as a matter of law rather than power, and posing the question of the boundaries between individual right and sovereign power.

The most celebrated expression of this classic modern form of sovereignty and its relation to private defence is in the work of Thomas Hobbes, who based his theory of the state on the natural right of each individual to preserve his own life: 'The finall Cause, End, or Designe of men (who naturally love Liberty, and Dominion over others,) in the introduction of that restraint upon themselves, (in which wee see them live in Common-wealths,) is the foresight of their own preservation, and of a more contented life thereby' (Hobbes 1968 [1651]: 223). Although Hobbes concedes that the right to self-preservation will always ulti-mately lie with each individual, the more important point is that the respons-ibility for preserving security is vested in the state, which becomes the source of law. Legal authority, and the monopoly of force, displaces any natural right and, as a corollary, vigilantism and acts of revenge are to be outlawed.[15] The

---

[13] The Tony Martin Supporters website explicitly invokes Locke, defending the property right in these terms.

[14] This formulation of the law is still retained in some US jurisdictions. See Green (1999: 14–16).

[15] Hobbes distinguishes between right and law: 'Right, consisteth in liberty to do or forbeare; Whereas Law, determineth, and bindeth one of them' (1968 [1651]: 189).

formation of Leviathan does not end the war of all against all, but makes the state responsible for the prosecution of this war – whether against internal or external threats.[16] This leads to an important shift in the understanding of private defence. The individual might resort to violence in the protection of their interests – for the interest of the property owner or person under attack will always outweigh that of the aggressor – but only as a last resort and subject to conditions established by law. The natural right is thus constrained by law, and legal (even human) rights are derived from state power. This is thus a fundamental shift from the individualist Lockean position (of pure private defence), and establishes the structure of the modern law of self-defence as an exception to liability for a more broadly defined crime of homicide.[17]

There is a further element of this shift that we should note. The modern law distinguishes between, and ranks, certain values. Thus, the right to security or integrity of property is generally of a lesser degree than the maintenance of life. We see this not only in the particular rule limiting the defence of property, but also in the more general subsumption of the right within the law of homicide, a law that is broadly aimed at the protection or preservation of the lives of the subjects of the Crown. The emphasis on the right to life (in a broader sense than simply the right not to be killed) is such that it has recently been argued that the English law of self-defence may be incompatible with Article 2 of the European Convention on Human Rights because there may be a failure on the part of the state to protect the lives of its citizens (Leverick 2002a, Smith 2002, Leverick 2002b; and see, originally, Ashworth 1975).[18] This underlines the extent to which such rights do not have an absolute character but must be limited by law. We see here, then, not only how the right of private defence lies at the origins of modern forms of sovereignty, but also how the rule has been shaped by modern law so as to cut away the original justification for the rule. The modern right of private defence is, thus, characteristic of the 'phase of juridical regression' described by Foucault; the juridical power has not been eclipsed, but has taken on a new, less absolute, character (1978: 144). There has been a move from private violence to public power, from a right to kill to the preservation and administration of life; and from an absolute right to security to one that is moderated and regulated through legal norms.[19]

This is of significance for the analysis of the power to punish in the modern state. On the Hobbesian view, the power of the state to punish must always, at

---

[16] M. Foucault (2003, lecture 5) argues for a different interpretation of significance of war in Hobbes.

[17] It is arguable that this leads to self-defence being classified as an excuse, placing an increasing emphasis on subjective aspects of self-defence, ie the perception of the threat, rather than as a justification.

[18] Art 2: 'No one shall be deprived of his life intentionally save in the execution of a sentence of a court.' Where the person acting in self-defence makes an honest, but unreasonable, mistake that they are being attacked, the person who is mistaken for an attacker dies through no fault of their own.

[19] Foucault argues that the right to life was a new kind of right that was linked to the emergence of the juridical being, the sovereign (1978: 135–6).

least in theory, be derived from the pre-existing individual natural right. However, this analysis of private defence shows how the right has been withdrawn from the individual to become the exclusive domain of the state. The state, in turn, possesses not the right to punish but a power – a police power – which must be used in such a way as to secure the welfare and prosperity of its subjects.[20] This understanding of sovereignty thus drives a wedge between the right and the power to punish – as noted by Garland and Young in their critique of modern penal discourse (1983: 10–13). These are no longer seen as two parts of a single practice, but as separate realms whose precise relationship need only ever be contingent. In modernity the questions of the justification or legitimacy of punishment have an external relationship to the practices of punishment; thus while legitimacy or the structuring of penal interventions through law might be desirable, it is not essential or internal to the practice (Weber 1968). The problem, indeed, for a post-Hobbesian philosophy of punishment may be the failure to come to terms with this foundational schism.

Crime and State in Late-Modern Society

Thus far I have told the familiar story – if from a slightly unfamiliar legal perspective – of the development of the modern 'governmental' state. This background is, however, essential if we are to understand the features that give the *Martin* case a special resonance. One of the special features of Martin's argument was the claim that the police had failed to provide adequate protection. Martin claimed that his house had been repeatedly burgled, because of its remote situation, and that the police had failed to investigate these previous incidents properly. He claimed that he was being victimized by gypsies, who would prey on houses in remote parts of the countryside (the two burglars in the case were, in fact, gypsies). As a consequence he had taken steps to improve his security – ranging from cutting away parts of the floor as a booby trap, to sleeping fully clothed, pump-action shotgun by his side. These features of the case tap into a particular set of fault-lines in the terrain of policing and security in contemporary Britain: urban versus rural policing; the policing and punishment of certain target populations like repeat offenders; and into a longer-standing cultural anxiety about the threat posed by gypsies or those who do not belong to particular local communities. In more abstract terms these can be described as failures in the distribution of security, in the management of dangerous populations, and in the policing of excluded populations (Feeley and Simon 1994, Rose 2000, Garland 2001). In all these areas it is argued that there is a failure of policing, and that the state is failing in its duty to protect its subjects.

---

[20] This is the broad structure of the contemporary philosophy of punishment which sees deterrence as a general justifying aim, limited by individual right (Hart 1968).

Various commentators have argued that these failures are an inevitable feature of contemporary criminal justice. Resources are finite, hard choices have to be made about how they are distributed, and risks may be managed but cannot be eradicated. The demand for security is one that can never be fully met, and in this growing realization that the state can neither afford the costs of policing nor, ultimately, deliver on the provision of complete security, we are asked to see the limits of the sovereign state (Garland 1996).[21] It is thus argued that a defining characteristic of the late-modern state is that it has redistributed some of its responsibilities to private individuals or organizations, who are increasingly being required to take greater responsibility for their own security (facilitated by the state), through insurance, crime prevention, or the use of private security firms (Zedner 2003a, 2003b; Ericson and Haggerty 1997). The responsibility of government increasingly becomes that of managing the pervasive sense of insecurity.

It is tempting to read the *Martin* case as a response to these trends in contemporary penality, and a number of different possible interpretations along these lines suggest themselves. On one reading we could argue that the problem here is precisely that Martin dramatically misread the message coming to him from government. Householders must take responsibility for the protection of their homes, but they must do so in a way that respects the law, and may not resort to the illegitimate use of private force. This would show the boundaries of this limited form of sovereignty, for the state shows that it remains the ultimate guarantor of security through the reassertion of its power to punish. Alternatively, the case can be seen as a working out or negotiation of the boundaries between private right and public responsibility – a boundary that might be significantly moved (against the trajectory of protecting the right to life) if the proposed category of manslaughter by use of excessive force in self-defence were to be legislated.[22] There is scope for some reform of the law of self-defence, redistributing responsibilities along the lines of some US state laws, to authorize greater powers for the 'responsible' home owner that would mirror the shifting boundaries of responsibility for crime control (Green 1999). In both of these instances it is clear that the primary issue is that of legitimacy – whether the particular government policies and the criminal law more generally can continue to command sufficient public support both in relation to short-term issues and the broader trends. This is primarily a political question, concerning the mobilization of support around particular issues, such as policing and the fear of crime, to reduce the sense of insecurity.

However, there is another possible reading of the case that goes beyond these issues of legitimacy to raise more fundamental questions about legal and

---

[21] This argument parallels similar arguments about juridification and the limits of the welfare state (Habermas 1987) or globalization (Sousa Santos 2002).

[22] Though both Leverick (2002a, 2002b) and Smith (2002) are of the view that a new category of manslaughter need not breach Art 2 of the ECHR.

political right. This account would argue that the case demonstrates the limits of the Hobbesian state: where the state fails to protect its citizens against mortal threats there is a reversion to the natural right of self-preservation. The victim of an attack is justified in the use of lethal violence to protect themselves where the state has failed to do so. This reading is troubling in a number of different respects. It seems to authorize private vengeance or vigilantism, a rudimentary kind of punishment. There is a fear that this licences direct action, is too hard to regulate, is too close to the 'war of all against all' – that it has something of the 'Wild West' about it (Green 1999). The fear of vigilantism plays explicitly on anxieties in the criminal law about premeditated actions, as opposed to the spontaneous response to violence.[23] Indeed, on this reading the case gains its power from the fact it reveals a deep anxiety within the criminal law, and especially the law of self-defence, which has been carefully constructed over the years precisely so as to reduce the scope for premeditation or private action.

In addition, this kind of vigilantism has a normative quality that gives it a complex relation to the normative order that it challenges, for it 'arises when some established order is perceived to be under threat from the transgression of institutionalized norms' (Johnston 1996: 229). It does not necessarily seek to undermine the established order, but may try to enforce existing norms by offering an assurance of security where the formal systems of control seem to be ineffective[24] – even though the effect of the actions (the mode of enforcement) might be further to undermine those norms. Here, our unease is related to the fact that it is not only an attack on the state, for failing to guarantee security, but also on the distinction between right and wrong that is founded on the institution of the state. Indeed, an unrestricted claim of private defence undermines the logic of sovereignty precisely because it is the attempt to claim for the individual the right to declare their own state of exception – their own conditions of security and life (Agamben 1998). The claim is not based on a right to life – or at least not that which is guaranteed by the state, for this, as we have seen, is already included within the legal order and therefore cannot sanction its own suspension. It is based on a prior right to survival, in Agamben's terms the assertion of 'bare life', that which is both excluded from and included within the realm of politics and sovereignty.[25] It is a form of resistance to the totalizing

---

[23] Premeditated killing was considered the most serious form of murder, and this was the original meaning of 'malice aforethought' (see Fletcher 1978, cf the requirement in the law of provocation that the response be immediate (Horder 1992). Self-defence requires retreat and an immediate and real threat to life.

[24] It understands that order is based on the appearance or representation of security. It is not the case that the government must literally protect us from fear or offer its citizens freedom from crime. but that modern government is founded on the promise or representation of security. It misreads this order to the extent that it moves from the expression of will ('people will take the law into their own hands!') into action. Cf Foucault's (1978) reading of Hobbes.

[25] Excluded as a condition of political life; yet included with the regulation of the body of the population with the emergence of bio-politics (Agamben 1998).

power of the modern state. The demand for life that requires death thus goes beyond a misreading of individual responsibility to challenge the nature of modern sovereign power. In this sense, then, it refers not to an actual legal right, but to the symbolic right to self-preservation which is the foundation of the state.

These readings of the case are troubling, then, because they are formulated not only as a challenge to the legitimacy of the state but also as a claim of right against the state. As such, they are not only framed within political discourse, an appeal to the themes of fear and insecurity that shape much contemporary penal policy, but also as a juridical claim which rejects the promises of life and security made by the modern state. The important question concerns the type of right that is being claimed here, and the basis for this claim, and this is something that we can begin to explore through an examination of the other set of contradictions in the case.

Victims and Rights

I want now to turn to the second aspect of the *Martin* case, that of the meaning of the category 'victim', for this offers further and related insights into the problematic nature of the case. In the *Martin* case the distinctions between victim and offender collapse in on each other, and this has legal consequences as the rights of the victim become confused. The original offenders, Fearon and Barras, become the victims of the attack by Martin, just as Martin, the original victim of the burglary (and of prior burglaries), becomes the offender. Then, in the course of the criminal process, Martin was once again placed in the position of victim as his case was medicalized, with professional psychiatrists stressing his dependency, or lack of subjectivity, in order to establish his legal defence. In a final twist, Fearon, the survivor of the attack, sought to bring a legal action against Martin, supported by the state in the form of legal aid, claiming compensation for injuries inflicted by Martin. The irony here is that the closure that the victim is said to achieve by the reinstitution of the legal order in the criminal process is impossible here, as each move reopens the trauma for the other party. Much of the media and popular outrage and political commentary has indeed taken the form of a dispute over who is the 'real' victim in this case – whether it be one of the protagonists, the taxpayer, the ordinary citizen, or the British people as a whole – and who is doing the victimizing. The difficulty, however, lies precisely in the impossibility of identifying the 'real' victim (A. Young 1996). Victimhood is not a category that pre-exists the various discourses that deploy it, and therefore it is futile to search for some end point, or grounding sense of the 'real' victim. What is more interesting, I would argue, is the use of the category 'victim' in these disputes as if it were real and could provide a solid foundation for the dispute. Indeed, I would go so far as to argue that one of the major weaknesses of the field of 'victimology' in general is its failure to reflect on the meaning of this supposedly foundational category.

Though we might expect to find a definition of the 'victim' in the criminal law, this is usually presented in terms that are more implicit than explicit. Criminal lawyers commonly seek the normative core of the criminal law in a distinction between offences which are autonomy-infringing and those which are merely harm-preventing or regulatory.[26] 'Real' crimes are seen as those where there are actual victims, where the actions of an aggressor have infringed the autonomy of an individual victim; regulatory crimes by contrast are victimless, serving the purposes of social coordination or the promotion of a collective welfare. The former, where crime is reduced to a (state-mediated) exchange between victim and offender, are seen as both the historical and theoretical foundation of the criminal law (for example Kames 1792). The latter, based on collective interests in public welfare, are frequently depicted as more recent developments which threaten to destabilize the criminal law through over-criminalization, the displacement of the value of autonomy, or the 'theft' of the conflict from its real owner, the victim (Husak 2002, Brudner 1993, Christie 1977). These illustrate a powerful individualist ideology that animates much contemporary academic writing in the field of criminal law, which seeks to locate the right to punish in an individual right of the victim which is both logically and historically prior to the state. In these terms, then, there would seem to be a direct connection between victims' rights and the right to self-defence. However, despite these connections, it is not clear either that the modern criminal law can be founded on such a simple category of victimhood or that the character of contemporary victims' rights is consistent with such a model. Indeed, going further, I shall argue that it is the difference between these different models of rights that lies at the heart of the tensions in the *Martin* case.

The rise of the victim in contemporary penal politics cuts against this understanding of the criminal law, so that it is not clear that there is a readily identifiable 'real' victim at the heart of the criminal law (Zedner 2002, Newburn 2003). Collective and individual interests are not easily disentangled. Most crimes do not fall easily into a model where there is one offender and one victim, and it can even be argued that these crimes are the exception rather than the rule in modern criminal law. Crimes can be defined in such a way that there might seem to be either many or no victims (for example preventive or possession offences), or so that the focus is on the conduct rather than the outcome.[27] Even

---

[26] This is also often seen as the distinction between *mala in se* (things which are wrong in themselves), and *mala prohibita* (things which are wrong only because made so by statute) see eg Wilson (2002). Dubber (2002) has a more complex account that locates the legitimate core of the law in offences of inter-personal violence, and the symbolic importance of the identification of the victim as a person.

[27] ie penalizing actions which create a risk of harm rather than the harm itself.

in 'real' crimes such as burglary, it may be difficult to identify a single victim, as a burglary might affect both the tenant and the owner of property, the immediate neighbourhood, not to mention the insurance company or their customers who pay higher premiums in future (R. Young 2000). While it may be argued that the 'real' victims are those who suffer an immediate physical or psychological harm, even here the instability of the category is revealed as the concept of harm allows for the almost infinite expansion of the category of victim. After all, if a person claims to have been harmed physically or emotionally by the commission of a crime, who is to say that he is not a victim.[28] In addition, victim advocates argue that individuals may suffer 'secondary victimization' in the way that they are treated by the criminal justice system.

This flexibility may be the great political strength of the concept, allowing different individuals or groups to express their sense of victimhood – giving a privileged position from which to express the truth of their suffering – but it is also a substantial weakness. If we adopt these wider understandings of victimhood, then it is undoubtedly the case that we are all the victims of crime, either through raised taxes and insurance premiums or through our loss of a sense of security, but at this point the concept becomes so general that it begins to lose any critical purchase. If we are all victims, then it is hard to criticize existing penal practices from the victim perspective or to justify any claim for special treatment.

Notwithstanding (or perhaps because of) this, the contemporary power to punish is increasingly organized around the figure of the victim, in a manner which suggests that the rise of the victim movement reflects a broader change in our culture. Particular individual victims, or groups of victims are used as a means of mobilizing crime control initiatives (Dubber 2002). The best known instances of this are the high profile campaigns for the monitoring of sexual offenders that have followed the commission of crimes against young children.[29] In this context it is striking that even six years after the events in Bleak House there are still calls for a 'Tony Martin' law to protect householders – though in this case Martin is not the victim of a dangerous sexual predator but, his supporters claim, of a dangerously insensitive and inflexible legal system. What is important about these campaigns is the way in which the symbol of the individualized victim is made to stand for the (actual and potential) harm to the community. That the politics of crime control is frequently ordered around responses to high profile crimes, as a means of giving focus to a more general anxiety or fear of crime, suggests that there is an

---

[28] A position that is also reflected in the recording of racially motivated crimes, where the perception of the victim is the determining factor in the official classification of the crime. This position has also recently been adopted in the recording of crime statistics, see Adams and McLaughlin (2004).

[29] Notably the unsuccessful campaign for a 'Sarah's Law' that followed the murder of Sarah Payne in July 2000. For details see <http://www.sarahpayne.com/>. These campaigns mimic the enactment of 'Megan's Law' in the US. On Megan's Law and similar campaigns, see Dubber (2002).

increased recognition that the impact of crime goes beyond the purely physical to allow emotional identification as well.[30]

At the same time, the status of victimhood offers a form of recognition and a means of making a political or legal claim. This basic insight lies behind the success of victim advocacy or victims' rights movements, which are founded on the idea that the victim has a special status because of their unique (and generalizable) vulnerability, and that this should be recognized through a series of measures ranging from monetary compensation to therapeutic care and counselling to a special legal status. This makes the status of victim desirable as a means of expressing a perceived injustice or pressing a claim for compensation. Indeed, it is often asserted that we live in a 'victim culture' in which those found guilty of committing crimes are increasingly ready to declare their own status as victims (of biology, circumstance, society). There is the invocation of the cycle that turns some victims into offenders – the abused who becomes the abuser, the victim who becomes the aggressor (Furedi 2004: 117–26). From this perspective the criminal process is often seen as a therapeutic opportunity, where the trauma of the crime can be healed through confrontation with, or involvement in the punishment of, the offender. Individual victims are granted ever greater opportunities to relate their experiences to a legal or political audience, to the extent even that victim advocates argue that the denial of this opportunity, where there is no forum in which the story can be told or where no one can be held accountable, is a further instance of victimization. However, what is significant about these developments is that rather than empowering the victim, the taking on of the status of victim presses individuals or groups of individuals into a situation of dependency. The victim is helpless, in need of professional assistance in the identification and healing of their needs and traumas (Furedi 2004). The paradox of victim recognition is thus that rather than ending victim status, it reaffirms and reinforces the dependency of the victim. It is a mechanism of inclusion and differentiation, bringing about a sense of belonging or community, while educating individuals in how to behave as a citizen (A. Young 1996). In these ways, the figure of the (actual or potential) victim makes possible strategies of risk management and control. This brings us, then, to the question of victims' rights, which in a certain sense can be seen as the most characteristic form of contemporary rights, combining the special position of the victim with the right form – the most effective way of making a claim of the state.

Although claims about victims' rights have a strong political, rhetorical, and, perhaps, ethical force, they do not, in legal terms amount to much. There are some consumer type rights: to be informed about decisions at different stages in the criminal process, to receive proper service from the courts, and, in some

---

[30] See generally Furedi (2004). It is important to note that this does not automatically lead to a more punitive response – witness the effectiveness of the Stephen Lawrence campaign in leading to reforms of police practices.

cases, to be able to put their side of the story. These are based on the grounds that the victim should be recognized by the state for their role in the pro-secution of crime, while remaining essentially passive in the state-run system (Zauberman 2000). Victim advocates have been successful in securing reforms in these areas, but these are about accommodating the victim within existing procedures. The victim has no right to demand trial or punishment or to participate in that process. The victim, as we have seen, has only a limited right to respond to personal violence. A second type of claim of right is based on the welfare principle: that the victim should be compensated for the wrong that has been committed against them, to be left no worse off than they were before the commission of the crime. This led initially to access to limited compensation from the state, or even reparation from the offender, and subsequently to the provision of counselling as the emotional and psychological impact of crime was recognized.[31] There is also some legal recognition of different classes of victims in the creation of special offences (or aggravations) that give special protection to 'victimized' groups of the population. Here the victim assists the system of state prosecution, aiding in the development of a more repressive and interventionist penal law. In both these instances the victim is dependent, and qualification for compensation might depend on being the 'right' sort of victim (passive, helpless, vulnerable) (Dubber, 2002). And though these are frequently described as victims' 'rights', they are essentially about improving the service that victims receive from the state.[32] A third type of claim is that the victim be accorded some procedural rights: to legal protections in the courtroom and, more controversially, to have some involvement in the process of sentencing through the use of Victim Impact Statements.[33] In this context it is often argued that the accused has been granted rights at the expense of the victim and that this balance should be redressed. Though many lawyers are sceptical about giving rights to victims because of the challenge to legal authority and threat they present to general standards in the legal order, victims' rights can largely be accommodated within this order, notwithstanding that they can give rise to local problems in the ordering of priorities (see Ashworth 2000a). Once again, though, we see that the claim to special legal protection or recognition is based primarily on the argument that the victim has special needs or vulnerabilities that should be accommodated within the legal process.

---

[31] This type of development would also include the use of restorative justice schemes, though there is not space here to analyse fully the significance of restorative justice.

[32] See, eg, *New Rights for Victims of Crime in Europe*, Council Framework Decision on the Standing of Victims in Criminal Proceedings (European Council of Ministers 2001/220/JHA), which aims to establish minimum standards of treatment.

[33] There is a wide range of protections for the 'vulnerable' witness. See Ellison (2001). Victim Impact Statements have been introduced in a limited form in Scotland. See Criminal Justice (Scotland) Act 2003, s 14. These initiatives have generally been more influential in the US. For a review, see Dubber (2002: 163–73); Fletcher (1992).

In an important sense, then, the modern governmental state and the victim are a 'sociological and historical couple' (Zauberman 2000: 39). While historically state formation may have required the exclusion of the victim (or private) interest as a precondition for the establishment of a centralized criminal justice system, the centrality of criminal justice to the legitimacy of the state project has led to ever greater concessions to victims. There are two important aspects of this that we should note. First, the recognition of the victim is intrinsically linked to the right to life, the development of which in relation to the law of self-defence we traced in the last section. If the primary function of the modern state is to secure the welfare and prosperity of its subjects, this obviously extends to their protection from crime, for crime shows 'a lack of respect for humanity and fundamental human decency' (Lea and Young 1984). More recently this connection is made in the formulation of international human rights instruments where the victim is identified, emotionally and psychologically, with the victim of the abuse of state power.[34] Secondly, the increasing recognition and integration of the victim is central to the continued legitimacy of state justice. However, as criminal justice becomes just one of a number of services provided by the state in the public interest, and individuals evaluate the service they receive as consumers, this legitimacy comes to depend on the quality and breadth of the service (Zauberman 2000). It is not based on any fundamental principles, but the comparative evaluation of the treatment of other individuals or groups, or even the availability of alternative service providers. The form of the rights thus does not challenge the state, but is simply a claim to more and better special treatment.

How, then, are we to understand the type of claim being made in the *Martin* case? Once again this could be understood in a number of different ways. First, in its weakest form, it could be seen as a claim that the status of the victim in this type of case should be legalized. This could readily be achieved if the proposed reform of the law to create a category of manslaughter by excessive force in self defence were created. This sort of partial excuse (as opposed to justification) works precisely on the basis of allocating the legal status of 'victim' to the putative offender (Dubber 2002). Here there is legal recognition, but on the basis of dependency. Secondly, it might be seen as a challenge to the legitimacy of the system. It is the claim that the rights of *this* victim – whether the responsible or vulnerable property owner or the injured burglar – are not being respected, and a demand for a remedy. It is a clash over the distribution of welfare, status, and security within the legal and political system. Here the argument invokes not the sensibilities of victims in general, but rather the sensibilities of a particular class of victims with respect to offenders or other classes of victims as consumers of criminal justice. For Martin and his supporters

---

[34] This connection has become much more explicit in recent international human rights instruments. For a survey, see Doak (2003: 5–6).

it might be read as a demand for a kind of physical and emotional security that the criminal justice system cannot provide to the prospective victims of crime, with true security resting only on the knowledge that one can resort to lethal force in the defence of your property. Happiness may indeed be a warm gun.

In both of these readings what is being proposed is a reordering of priorities within the existing order, however, it seems to me that once again there is a third, and potentially more challenging, reading available. This would be to argue that the claim of private defence is significant because it invokes the claim to a right not to *be* a victim. This should not be understood in the sense of the right to be free of crime, but in the more specific sense of not having to occupy the position of 'victim'.[35] This reading rejects the paradoxical definition of victimhood that ties recognition to dependency, to argue that the function of the criminal process should be understood as that of vindicating autonomy rather than restoring it (which places the victim in a position of helplessness and dependency).[36] Here there is no categorical distinction between victim and offender, there are only persons who are sometimes wronged by the actions of others, and the function of the criminal process should be no more or less than the vindication of the rights of the former and the protection of the rights of the latter.

If there is a solid core to victims' rights, this is surely where it is to be found, but it is important to be clear about the type of claim that is being made here and why it is significant. This kind of claim implies a radical retrenchment of the idea of victims' rights and a rejection of the victim culture that was outlined above. It is a rights claim *against* the state, running counter to the logic of contemporary sovereignty, rather than being a claim for rights *from* the state. However, the right not to be a victim in this sense does not entail a reclaiming of the power to punish from the state, for it is not possible to fall back on a pre-existing state of nature (there is no natural state of victimhood or subjectivity). It is instead a new kind of juridical claim, that the exercise of the criminal law be justified, where self-government is turned back against sovereignty. It is a symbolic claim to autonomy, a refusal of the proliferation of strategies and policies that are developed in the name of victim but in the interests of the state.

Conclusion: Rights and the Power to Punish

Over the last twenty years there has been a huge explosion of academic and practical interest in questions surrounding the right to punish and rights in the criminal process more generally. Evidence of this can be seen in a variety of

---

[35] cf feminist strategies in the cases of battered women who kill.

[36] Just as it should also vindicate the autonomy of the accused person through a respect for their rights, including the right to be punished. This position has been most systematically developed in the work of Dubber (2002).

different sources, from academic writings on the philosophy of punishment to the growth of the field of victims' rights to human rights litigation concerning prisoners or the criminal process. Yet it is striking that this transformation has not really been reflected in academic analyses of the power to punish – a discipline which has also grown dramatically over the same period – and many of the leading texts in this area make little or no mention of this 'rights revolution'. This, I think,. can be traced back to a deep ambivalence about rights within the social theory of punishment. Foundational texts such as *The Power to Punish* (Garland and Young 1983), which have been extremely influential in shaping the field, were properly concerned to shift the focus of the analysis of penality from questions of the justification of punishment to a concern with how that power was exercised. This shift was also implicit in an argument about governmentality that saw disciplinary forms of penal practice/ power replacing the juridical.[37] And there was a tendency in much of the literature around the time that *The Power to Punish* was published to view a concern with rights as anachronistic or conservative. While the faint-hearted or reactionary wanted to go 'back to justice', progressive thought must move forward, fixing its sights clearly on the realities of power underlying systems of rights. Characteristic of this position is Carlen's essay (1983a) in *The Power to Punish*, in which she argued that debates about rights should be subjected to the language of political powers.[38] The consequence of this is that contemporary writing about penality has failed to come to terms with the growing significance of rights, not only in terms of their function in relation to the development of particular penal strategies, but also in terms of their importance in legitimizing state action or justifying the use of power. To this extent it seems to me that one of the major challenges for a social theory of punishment is precisely that of accounting for the role of law and rights in the exercise and justification of penal powers.

This examination of the controversies around the case involving Tony Martin is a first step towards developing such an analysis. It has sought to show how the case raises a series of important questions about responsibility, rights, and sovereignty, and to develop an analysis of some of the different ways in which rights are of significance to the contemporary power to punish. In its most basic terms, I have shown how, on the one hand, the power to punish is exercised through law and, on the other, how political claims are formulated in terms of the demand for rights. More important, I have tried to distinguish between different types of rights and their functions, principally, those rights which entrench individualization and dependency and those which potentially

---

[37] An argument that has been further developed in Garland's work on the limits of the sovereign state and the culture of control (2001), although one might question how it is possible to talk about sovereignty and responsibilization without engaging with questions of rights.

[38] Carlen's position ends by collapsing the law into politics, because there can be no foundation for rights (either in essentialism or proceduralism).

present a challenge to the logic of modern sovereignty by drawing on values of autonomy and responsibility. The significance of the case, then, does not lie in the, undoubtedly important, questions about when the use of force should be permitted in the defence of property, but in what it reveals about the nature and importance of the criminal law in contemporary society.

4

European Identity, Penal Sensibilities, and Communities of Sentiment

Evi Girling

Introduction

In the latter years of the twentieth century, the European Union and the Council of Europe campaigned actively for the worldwide abolition of the death penalty. This chapter examines these campaigns as an instance of the translocalization of penal sensibilities, an instance that elucidates some of the seemingly intractable and unpredictable global future(s) of penal sensibilities. *Penal sensibilities* as 'structures of affect' and 'emotional configurations' (Garland 1990: 195) contour our sense of what is tolerable, appropriate, or permissible in the practice of punishment. Penal sensibilities and their attendant penal cultures have, in the main, been apprehended as 'local' in nature and mostly circumscribed by national boundaries. However, the intricate repertoire of images and narratives of punishment for worldwide audiences invites us to reconsider the 'local' character of such ensembles. We need to consider the extent to which penal politics is now part of what Tomlinson called 'proximity politics', a distinct order of political issues caused by structural (complex institutional interconnections) and phenomenological (time-space bridging technologies) proximity (2000: 403). What are the implications and consequences of the flow of images of punishment through 'global communications spaces' (Schlesinger 1999) or, what Appadurai (1990) has called mediascapes, for penal sensibilities? These mediascapes foster new collectives, 'communities of sentiment', groups which imagine and feel things together (*ibid*), collectives that inhabit shared worlds beyond the traditional boundaries of the nation-state. The spectacle of the death penalty and its place in the mediascape and ideoscape of European identity politics provides a case in point.

Somewhat ironically, transnational campaigns against the death penalty have emerged in the face of strong support for the death penalty in particular localities. It has been argued elsewhere that under conditions of proximity, punitiveness and inclusion prove themselves to be volatile and unpredictable; punitiveness is fractured, and inclusionary motives become more urgent and apparent (Girling *et al* 2000). In the case in point, what were the conditions in these discussions and spectacles of the death penalty that effectively silenced support for the death penalty? 'Place' continues to matter in sensibilities towards crime and, indeed, a sense of here/there, us/them may intensify under globalizing conditions (Girling *et al* 2000, Loader and Sparks 2002). The inclusive nature of global penal politics, described below, stands as a counterpoint to the angry politics of revenge and exclusion that permeate crime discourse at the local level. Once again (this time under conditions of distance) punitiveness is fractured and inclusionary motives find a new language in which to speak. In a climate of volatile criminal justice politics fuelled by a readily deployable cruelty discourse (Simon 2001: 140), such silencing merits further exploration. Yet the implications of these counter-narratives of punitiveness and penal exchange for the formation, development, and dynamics of penal sensibilities have not been fully explored in criminology. This chapter seeks to map the 'emergent landscapes of crime, order, and control' (Loader and Sparks 2002) and to engage with the global as culture (Urry 1998) and its consequences for everyday life in transforming the ways in which people conceive their relationships to 'others' across the globe (*ibid*). How others under such conditions become objects of identification, pity, or compassion (see Boltanski 1999, Cohen 2001) is a question central to apprehending the fate of the death penalty in particular and possible futures of penal sensibilities in general.

This is an emergent landscape in which 'values and judgments are . . . formed in a complex web of national, international and global cultural exchange' (Held *et al* 1999: 19). The juxtaposition of local lives and global cultures and cultural experiences which lie at the heart of debates on globalization (see Tomlinson 1999: 181) is also a juxtaposition central to our understanding of developments in penal politics and penal sensibilities. What Robertson (1992) described as 'different orders of human life' (individual human beings, national societies, the world system of societies, and the overarching collectivity of humankind) are set up in sometimes uneasy and unpredictable relationships. Understanding the fortunes and prospects of the death penalty in a globalized world does not mean eschewing consideration of local sensibilities but requires an understanding of both global flows *and* local lives of penal communications.

Arjun Appadurai's work seems apposite to our attempts to set out a framework through which we may begin to apprehend the impact of these global-local relationships for penal politics in general and the European penal politics of abolition in particular. Two aspects of Appadurai's work specially challenge the 'apparently stable structures' (Appadurai 1996) of the nation-state – his account of translocal cultures and his discussion of the role and nature of imagination in the production of communities of sentiment. It is often stated that we live in a world of flows: flows of people, discourses, and images, all of which have replaced traditional fixed landscapes. Appadurai describes the world of flows in terms of a set of 'scapes': ethnoscapes (the movement of groups of people), mediascapes (electronic capabilities for disseminating information), technoscapes (the distribution of technology), financescapes (the transnational exchanges of economy and finance) and ideoscapes (the interaction of ideologies) (Appadurai 1996: 33–36). These flows travel at different velocities, have varied points of origin and termination and (significantly for our purposes here) stand in varied and unpredictable relationships to local institutional practices and cultures (*ibid*: 5) resulting in what Appadurai has called disjunctures, where the production and subsequent manifestation of problems in local forms 'have contexts that are anything but local' (Appadurai 2001: 6). According to him, one of the effects of these scapes is the creation of 'communities of sentiment', groups which inhabit new shared worlds and imagine and feel things together (1990).[1] For Appadurai, this *imagination* is a key component for the emerging global orders, creating alternative prescriptions for identity, agency, and solidarity (1990: 31). These alternative prescriptions for identity, agency, and solidarity can have momentous implications for penal sensibilities.[2]

The juxtaposition of the translocal production and local manifestation of predicaments engenders what we may call penal disjunctures in which the practice of the death penalty on distant shores becomes an urgent issue, over-riding its contentiousness and ambivalence in local penal politics and consti-tuting 'communities of sentiment' which construct translocal penal identities, forms of agency, and solidarity.

Abolitionism and the European Penal Imaginary

The *imagining* of the nation-state, the subject of much debate in history and sociology (see, for example, B. Anderson 1983, Hobsbawm 1990, Gellner 1983, Smith 1998, Hastings 1997), has left little doubt that Europe as a political and cultural space encapsulated by the European Union would be imagined and that this imagining would have 'real consequences' (Eder 2000: 222, cited in Delanty 2002). One of these consequences is that a penal imaginary proffers a counter-narrative that challenges the intellectual and political reign of penal populism

---

[1] These communities of sentiment and the identities as the entities that define them are what Bauman (following Kracauer) has called 'communities welded by ideas', for whom the question of identity arises urgently and frequently because 'there are many such ideas and principles around which "communities of believers" grow that one has to compare, to make choices, to make them repeatedly to revise choices made on another occasion, to try to reconcile contradictory and often incompatible demands' (Bauman 2004: 11)

[2] One such alternative prescription key to our understanding of the translocalization of penal sensibilities is cosmopolitanism. Cosmopolitanism as a disposition is in Hannerz's words a ' per-spective, a state of mind' (1990: 238). It is an attitude of 'openness' towards other cultures that involves an ethical orientation to universalist values and ideas. This ethical orientation is a central motif of discourses of European identity – an identity based on what Habermas described as constitutional patriotism or akin to what Walzer described as 'thin identity', an identity based on civic values (see Delanty 2005).

and punitivism.[3] The death penalty seems to be one of the last bastions of criminal justice where governments lead by example. It is an area that stands in counterpoint to the creation of a 'fortress Europe' and national and EU-wide debates on immigration in which 'populist punitiveness' is discernible (see Wacquant, Chapter 5). Abolitionist narratives have become a salient feature in EU foreign and domestic politics and project an implicit call to restrain populist punitive impulses. In the drive for the abolition of the death penalty the call has been for politicians to be brave enough to lead so that public opinion may follow. In contrast to predictions of ostentatious and emotive punishments (Garland 2001, Pratt 2002), what we are witnessing is ostentatious restraint and sympathy for the offender.

Such developments at least begin to question the dystopian futures predicted by criminologies of catastrophe (see O'Malley 2003). Our criminological imagination has been saturated by anxieties about ontological security: a key theme around which we have built our understandings of responses to crime. The penal communities of sentiment with which criminologists have acquainted us tend to be communities of anxiety and fear. The question of penal identity has become a central one in the engineering of the European soul and the apparent humanist solidarity against judicial execution, presents us with a unique opportunity to explore communities of sentiment from beyond the spectre of fear and anxiety. The elusive and fragile European identity is partly a penal *community of sentiment* – imagining and feeling things about how and whom we punish or redeem. The 'convenient fables' (Ignatieff 1998: 18) worldwide of the European identity project speak of an abhorrence of the death penalty and ostentatiously pursue a missionary project to set the 'moral limits' of punishment (Piacentini, Chapter 6).

The European politics of abolition provide a cautionary tale for the presumed resilience, omnipresence, and omnipotence of populist punitivism beyond national politics.[4] From beyond the nation-state a cosmopolitan European imaginary recasts the plight of distant others as significant for Europe. Those distant others are, in this case, offenders facing the death penalty. Penal cosmopolitanism is to be found in European residents' everyday experiences and communications – opening up what Clifford (1998: 362) has described in another context as 'worldly, productive sites of crossing' between the global and local, the near and the distant. In these crossings the death-row inmate is a

---

[3] Recent commentators have described convincingly and at length a shift in penal policy making (at least in the UK and the US) from an elitist to a more populist style (Johnstone 2000, Windlesham 1998, Garland 2001) resting on assumptions of what Bottoms has called 'populist punitiveness' (1995: 39). It has already been acknowledged that despite the prevalence of populist punitivism in different Western contexts its effects remain 'widely divergent' (Tonry 2001: 530).

[4] The events and aftermath of the attacks on the World Trade Center in New York on 11 September 2001 may have been expected to provide fertile ground for the public re-emergence of pro-death penalty support. Still, the anti-death penalty position has turned out to be a permanent feature of European foreign politics and has withstood the conflicts with the US brought about by Europe's refusal to extradite those suspected of terrorism to the US unless guarantees that the death penalty would not be imposed were given.

distant friend worth defending. Such 'sites of crossing' have become central to sensibilities about punishment that have been promoted as quintessentially 'European'. In the rest of this chapter I propose to explore the cultural presence of the death penalty in the lifeworlds of the EU citizen.

Acts of Imagining I: Foreign Policy and the Europeanization of Penal Sentiments

The European anti-death penalty campaign has important consequences in at least two aspects. First, it has taken pride of place in the European Union's pursuit of an international role as promoter of norms. As Manners (2002) observes, the aspiration to abolish the death penalty now passes for normal in world politics and opposition to abolition has been pathologized. Secondly, it circulates narratives of a shared set of European values and, as I argue in this section, goes some way towards creating a European consciousness, a European *community of sentiment*. Policy makers have seen European identity as instrumental in achieving the legitimacy of EU institutions and especially in remedying the democratic deficit which seems to plague discussions of EU policies and institutions in individual member states (Strath 2000a, 2000b). Despite an explicit political objective of promoting the 'European idea', enshrining these narratives of common heritage and a 'European consciousness' has remained a difficult task (Delanty 1995; Strath 2000a, 2000b; Shore 2000). The pursuit of a world free of the death penalty provides narratives of European self-understanding that give focus both to ideological and policy development (Fontaine 1993, Manners 2002, Manners and Whitman 2003).

The turn of the new millennium provided a focus for this pursuit of a death penalty-free Europe. The year 2000 marked the fiftieth anniversary of the European Convention on Human Rights and it was decided that the European Union and the Council of Europe member states should celebrate this event by clearly demarcating Europe as a death penalty-free continent. (Council of Europe 1999: 1). The last two decades of the twentieth century had seen a marked change in the politics of the death penalty in Europe, a change which seemed to be reaching its peak in the late 1990s. The death penalty was brought to the forefront of the European Union's foreign policy agenda and news of anti-death penalty activism became a regular feature in the European media. At the start of the new millennium the quiet work that characterized the abolition of the death penalty in individual EU states in the latter half of the twentieth century gave way to a frenzy of activity on a transnational level (see Zimring 2003, Girling 2002). In 1998 the General Affairs Council of the European Union issued 'Guidelines to EU policy towards third countries on the death penalty'. In those guidelines member states were invited to 'work towards universal abolition of the death penalty as *a strongly held* policy view agreed by all EU member states' (emphasis added). In each instance in which the death penalty was practised the guidelines asked member states to 'call for its use to be progressively restricted and to insist that it will be carried out to the minimum standards'. Throughout the campaign that followed, Europe was defined and promoted by its 'abhorrence' of the death penalty.

Following this 'new millennium' resolution the Council of Europe put renewed effort into persuading both aspiring member states and 'rogue states' with observer status (US and Japan) to abandon the death penalty. From the beginning of January 2000 the European Union and the Council of Europe began a series of much publicized pleas, lobbying the then Clinton administration and individual state governors to abolish capital punishment or, at the very least, to limit its application. There was political activity on two levels. First, there were diplomatic attempts to effect an overall change in US death penalty policy that would lead to the abolition/restriction of the practice. Secondly, the most intense lobbying involved widely publicized individual cases of death row prisoners either facing imminent execution or claiming innocence. In February 2000, the European Union launched a series of pleas to the United States specifically for the withdrawal of its reservation on Article 6 of the International Covenant on Civil and Political Rights (ICCPR), which prohibits the death penalty for juvenile offenders, and more generally for respect to be shown for international instruments which seek to curtail the use of the death penalty. To this effect the European Union submitted a Memorandum at both federal and state level in which it provided an overview of the experiences, principles and policies that have made possible a death penalty-free continent.

The most frequent form of foreign policy communication regarding the European Union's campaign against the death penalty has come in the form of *démarches*. *Démarches* are communications from the European Union to third countries and, on the issue of the death penalty *démarches*, they were attempts at persuading third countries to limit or abolish the death penalty according to the EU guidelines (1998). A plethora of *démarches* (especially to the United States) reiterated the road to abolition that the European Union had taken and encouraged America to follow its lead. The official *démarche* process was supplemented by direct interventions from the Presidents of the European Parliament, the Council of Europe, the heads of EU states (during periods of their country's EU presidency) and other personalities from the European political arena (such as Forni and Badinter), heads of state and government of member states, and ambassadors.

Since 2001 the level of intervention in US death row cases has risen. Rather than *démarches* and general pleas, the European Union has been submitting *amicus curiae* (friends of the court) briefs to the US Supreme Court, providing information on legal matters and attempting to lobby the Supreme Court in key cases. The European Parliament's and the Council of Europe's joined up and concerted attack, with relentless repetition of a 'European' position on the death penalty, seem to have enshrined it in both domestic and foreign policy.

A range of non-governmental organizations (NGOs) also used the turn of the millennium as a symbolic moment to launch their campaigns for abolition of the death penalty. These efforts both claimed and constituted a distinctive European identity such as 'Hands off Cain', 'Ensemble contre le peine du mort' (Together Against the Death Penalty), and the pan-European anti-death penalty organization (EDCAP), which enjoys close links with the Council of Europe and the European Parliament. In recent years these organizations, with their extensive European and global networks, have introduced a number of very successful initiatives such as the Moratorium 2000 campaign (and subsequent 'moratoria' campaigns). A host of religious and secular groups have also emerged, ranging from regional activist groups campaigning for specific prisoners to pen-friend organizations for those on death row. Their range of activities varies from visits to death rows, and petitions for reprieve of particular prisoners, to organizing mass mobilization in the form of demonstrations, vigils, and other civic rituals.

In June 2001 the First World Congress on the death penalty (organized by 'Ensemble contre la peine du mort') was held in Strasbourg at the home of the Council of Europe – the symbolic heart of the European political ideological project. The congress brought together activists from around Europe, along with representatives from the United States, Japan, Russia, and other 'target' states. It received the full backing of both the Council of Europe Parliamentary Assembly and the European Union. A special session of heads of member states was convened to 'solemnly call for a moratorium on the death penalty'. The European Union and the Council of Europe put their publicity machinery behind the conference to call on the world to abolish the death penalty. On the final day, 5,000 activists and ordinary people from all over Europe marched through the streets of Strasbourg protesting against the death penalty, and the city awarded Mumia Abu-Jamal (an African American on death row) the keys to the city. The events received wide publicity across Europe. By bringing together the Council of Europe (which has been called the 'conscience' of Europe) with its executive and democratically accountable branch, the conference served to affirm abolitionism in the *ideoscape* of European civil society and the importance of NGOs and smaller ad hoc groups in the mainstream of European sentiment.[5]

Van Ham has described how 'the EU depends for its existence upon a multitude of collective acts of imagining (as well as forgetting)' in the media and culture, as well as in politics (Van Ham 2000: 25). One forum in which this imagining of Europe has taken place has been in the pursuit of the anti-death penalty stance. This imagining has occurred on two levels. First, it

---

[5] This is in keeping with emerging patterns in European policy making where we can see a range of public, private, community, and voluntary organizations mobilizing around a specific issue (Bennington 1994: 3; Piacentini, Chapter 6).

is unsurprising that the foreign policy cooperation between EU member states has set in motion a process through which individual EU states perceive themselves as a 'we', delineating, through the European Union's morally superior abolitionist commitment, the unique features setting 'us' apart from 'them' (Europeans and non-Europeans) (Manners 2002). After all, the forging of a foreign policy agenda is, as Manners argues, a symbol of both sovereignty and statehood (*ibid*). European foreign policy narratives are consequently narratives of a community of people with shared values, 'doing good'. An abolitionist penal identity thus serves to construct a community of sentiment among European citizens based on a positive and inclusive sense of social solidarity (rather than one mobilized around more negative and punitive emotions, stemming from fear of the other). Through this community of sentiment, distant others (death row inmates) become symbolically significant and, as I will now argue, experientially near (Girling 2004, 2005).

Secondly, local and regional anti-death penalty initiatives ensure the local cultural life of such narratives. The European anti-death penalty campaign relies on the Europeanization of penal sensibilities and appeals to 'European' penal sentiments. Through the very processes of doing so it creates a kind of public sphere that, otherwise, has been difficult to conceptualize on a European level (Schlesinger 1999).[6] The intense media interest, official pronouncements, and the level of public participation in the anti-death penalty movement provide us with such a public sphere, a public sphere in which a reformist voice (unlike the voices of penal populism) dominates the discourse of European media and political culture.

Accusations of a democratic deficit in this aspect of penal policy-making taint European trajectories towards abolition. EU interventions on the death penalty are often the subject of accusations of elitism from US politicians and journalists. It is, they argue, not so much a case of European versus American values but a division of elite values (see, for example, Gedmin cited in Harnden 2001). This is because abolition occurred in most European jurisdictions despite existing support for the death penalty (Zimring 2003, Hood and Koralev 2001). Opinion polls (albeit with all their methodological inadequacies) seem to suggest that there is substantial minority support for the death penalty in individual EU countries, which increases at times of crisis (Marshall 2000, Moravcsik 2001). The apparent residual level of support for the death penalty in European jurisdictions has become one of the key defences against EU interventions in US penal policy. The pursuance of such a high profile foreign policy agenda on the death penalty despite this residual level of support was attributed to the alleged 'democratic deficit' of the European Union (Marshall 2000).

---

[6] Van de Steg has provided us with a more open definition of the public sphere as 'a group of actors who debate in public a topic which they consider to be in the public interest i.e. of concern to the polity . . . who are [in some way] in contact with each other [and] who are aware that they are observed by a public . . . [and] in principle anyone from the public can come on stage and take an active part' (2002: 507).

In some ways it was expected that the style of European governance would develop buffers against direct engagement with penal populism. What was less predictable was the ostentatious missionary zeal with which abolition of the death penalty has filled European public discourse since. The substantial minority of death penalty supporters in individual countries was in that way permissive, conceding – at face value – its exclusion from a European penal community of sentiment. Yet the spectre of a bloodthirsty European public lurks on the edges of abolitionist discussions, showing the case of the 'death penalty' (as most of the discourse that accompanies this penalty) to be exceptional, divorced from the processes and emotions of national penal politics.

Acts of Imagining II: Distant Others as Honorary Europeans

Discussions of global penal politics belong to the realm of 'human rights' and are divorced from the messy world of penal populism (see also Piacentini, Chapter 6). Such a conceptual divorce, however apt, overlooks one important factor, namely that international policy interventions on the issue of the death penalty on the basis of human rights, are still interventions and appeals in the penal realm. As such they necessarily take a stance on the relationship between the offender and the viewer – a relationship that goes to the very heart of the spectacle of punishment.

The European case for abolition is made using a set of convergent arguments pointing to the moral and political necessity of abolition (see Lerch and Schwellnus (2006)). On an international level they appeal to established international human rights law. In trying to persuade states that aspire to admission to the EU fold they appeal to shared cultural values (*ibid*). Appeals to the United States focus not only on international human rights law but also on the cultural affinity that the European Union and the United States share (Girling 2005). EU arguments also focus on the breach of human rights other than the right to life, such as 'cruel and unusual treatment or punishment' and the potential dangers of executing innocent persons. It is the latter two arguments that are taken up by the activists as issues around which to mobilize. Issues of legality in that context can be turned into campaigns about 'saving' a criminal 'other'.

In the process of campaigning to save a criminal 'other' there is a narrative elaboration of the links between various localities or groups in Europe and those on death row. For activists around Europe, saving the other from death row involves extending ideas of citizenship and belonging by adopting individuals on death row as 'honorary' Europeans. These high-profile individual cases have captured the imagination of residents of one or other of the member states. Through them 'Europe' lives on death row, through them 'Europe' articulates its right to intervene – the 'other' finds himself/herself metaphorically in the territory of Europe. The old rationale of protecting all those who find themselves in the literal territory of Europe (see 1950 European Convention on Human Rights) has resonance here and is extending cultural citizenship beyond legal definitions to include a set of more informal definitions and rules of membership (Stevenson 1999).

There have been a number of campaigns that seek to help EU citizens who have found themselves on death row (for example the LaGrand brothers and Kenny Richey). But in some ways more seminal are two examples in which cultural citizenship was extended to US citizens: the cases of Derek Rocco Barnabei and Joseph O'Dell.

Barnabei was an American citizen. His father (an Italian citizen) emigrated to the United States, where Barnabei was born and raised. Barnabei's cause was taken up by European, and specifically Italian, anti-death penalty organizations and prompted protests by the Italian Olympic team during the opening ceremonies of the Sydney Games in 2000, mass demonstrations in Italian towns against the death penalty, and web pages dedicated to saving his life. In the region of Tuscany the case of Barnabei was taken up with particular fervour and public involvement went much beyond the activist circles to include school-children, ordinary citizens, and the local church. This 'disjuncture' did not go unnoticed, both politicians and the press tried to make sense of this mobilization behind Barnabei's case. The then president of the European Parliamentary Assembly explained that Barnabei's case 'had given rise to particularly strong reactions in Europe because there were doubts about his guilt and because, while he is an American citizen, his family originally came from Italy' (cited in Fleishman 2000). The *Philadelphia Inquirer* pondered the absurdity that all this took place while Barnabei's execution only got a passing mention in the US press: 'Whereas 6,000 miles away in Italy, Barnabei had become a *cause célèbre*, portrayed as a martyr trapped in an American court system bent more on vengeance than compassion' (Fleishman 2000). At the time of writing (five years after his execution), the case of Barnabei still arouses interest in Italy. Plays about his life have been staged in Florence, and his mother was an invited guest at the meeting of the World Coalition Against the Death Penalty in spring 2005.

Unlike Barnabei, Joseph O'Dell had no family links (however distant) with Italy and yet he too became the focus of a high profile and passionate local campaign. On the day of his execution, Italy observed a minute's silence and flags were lowered in the town of Palermo. After his execution, his body was flown to Palermo and he was buried in what the press described as a local dignitaries' cemetery. On his tombstone he was described as an honorary citizen of Palermo: 'Joseph R. O'Dell 3rd, beloved husband of Lori Urs O'Dell, honorary citizen of Palermo, killed by Virginia, U.S.A., in a merciless and brutal justice system' (Fleishman 2000).

Acts of Imagining III: Global Witnessing, Local Rituals, and Taste Judgements

The global spectacles (and spectators) of punishment that the practice of the death penalty in the United States has provided invite us to ponder the implications of globalization in the constitution of sensibilities about punishment. In the next few paragraphs I set out some of these webs of cultural exchange in which penal sensibilities are now formed.

The European Union pursues the abolition of the death penalty wherever it happens in the world, but the issue of the practice of the death penalty in the United States is of particular political and moral poignancy (Girling 2002, 2005) since it is perceived to be carried out by what Nils Christie called 'cultural relatives'. Even though death penalty news gets media coverage around Europe, in certain countries, such as France and Italy, the reporting is both detailed and intense. In the French press, for example, executions have often been front-page news. The life stories of some American death-row inmates such as Karla Faye Tucker, Gary Graham, Odell Barnes, and Mumia Abu-Jamal would be familiar to readers of French newspapers (Dudziac 2000). In Tuscany local media continue to give extensive coverage to Bainabei's case.

The relentless denunciation of the death penalty in the United States by European media (Lacorne 2001) highlights the role of the global media in the public staging of shaming – a shaming from which, as Urry (1998) pointed out, no one can be exempt. This public staging of shaming gained new momentum during the campaign and early presidency of George W. Bush around 2000. As the Governor of Texas – a governor who presided over more executions than any other in recent years – he increased the pace and the stakes of this media spectacle. George W. Bush was described as world champion executioner and, in the words of former Justice minister Robert Badinter, 'a horrible symbol of your mania for the death penalty' (*Washington Post*, 18 December 2000). Executions in Texas came under intense scrutiny during the presidential campaign and during President Bush's first visits to Europe in the early summer of 2001. Protesters, the press, and politicians alike, raised the issue of the death penalty. Since 11 September 2001, the war against terror has provided new opportunities for the chasm between the views of the United States and the European Union to be widely reported. Following the Charter of Fundamental Rights agreed in Nice in late 2000, EU member states have refused to extradite terrorist suspects to the United States if they risked facing the death penalty. Such an extradition would be against Article 19(2) of the Chapter, which declares that 'no one may be removed, expelled or extradited to a state where there is a serious risk that he or she would be subjected to the death penalty, torture or other inhuman or degrading treatment'. Certain states, such as France and Germany, have extended the interpretation of this article to refusal to release evidence that may lead to a death sentence (as in the case of Massaui). In the days after the invasions of Afghanistan and Iraq, the European media raised a range of hypothetical questions and tried to predict what would happen if 'allied', rather than American, troops captured Bin Laden or Saddam Hussein.

America's death row and the twists and turns of its 'war against terror' are not the only sites of this global spectacle. Executions are brought to and fought on European soil. The Colosseum in Rome is one such symbolic location of both state killing and the abolitionist cause. The Colosseum has become a site in which executions in far away places are 'repatriated'. It gets bathed in light every time a death sentence is commuted anywhere in the world or when a country abolishes the death penalty. The first ever World Day against the Death Penalty, a pan-European event, took place in November 2002 and was followed by a series of events under the banner of Cities for Life, in which landmarks in European towns and cities (mostly in Italy, Austria, Belgium, France, Ireland, the Netherlands, Denmark, Spain, and Switzerland) were chosen as key locations for vigils, readings, and illuminations. The driving force behind the launching of the World days against the death penalty was the Italian organization *Comunità di Sant' Egidio*, with the endorsement of the World Coalition against the Death Penalty (WCADP).

The Benetton campaign against the death penalty in the United States also gave rise to a much publicized clash between American and European sensibilities (Girling 2004) and encapsulated both the increasing questioning of the death penalty by 'European sensibilities' and the unpredictable juxtapositions set up by the global spectacles of punishment. Benetton used images of death row prisoners on posters and in magazine advertizing campaigns.

As I argue elsewhere (Girling 2005), for Europeans the 'revealing' of the faces of those condemned in the campaign was not a surprise, the death row inmates had names, families, and histories. However incongruous the posters may have looked in the United States, they did not look out of place in European cities because the newspapers were often adorned with the faces and names of those facing death. Europeans were already witnessing this particular scene of punishment. Like most Benetton campaigns in the genre of shock advertising, it did cause a storm of controversy, but unlike other campaigns the level of controversy and flurry of lawsuits was such that Benetton had to apologize and withdraw the images from the campaign. The campaign invited Americans to share in a community of sentiment – in Appadurai's terms, to feel and imagine things together (Appadurai 1996). In the end, US citizens refused to look at those faces under the condemning eye of the Europeans (Girling 2004). The campaign sought to locate the 'death penalty' in the realm of advertising and to establish a dual identity of the citizen as both consumer and penal commentator. The position against the death penalty was thus set up as a taste judgement, a mark of distinction (Bourdieu 1984, see also Hoechsmann 1997). This was a taste judgement which, as I describe above, is central to European abolitionist narratives, a mark of distinction through which the global spectacles of punishment are apprehended.

Conclusions

The convergence of the two projects of identity (the penal and the 'European') provides an opportunity to recast the cultural project of punishment beyond the boundaries of the nation-state. In Appadurai's terms, the imagining of Europe as a death penalty-free zone and its self-determination in spearheading the mission for a death penalty-free world takes the form of many collective acts of imagining and witnessing, a 'multitude of collective acts of imagining' that are the first steps towards an imagined community. Since 1973 the European Union and the Council of Europe have introduced state symbols of Europe's identity (the flag, the European anthem, etc). There has been a concerted effort to inscribe a consciousness of the European Union in public practice as well as in the everyday life of its citizens. This routinized inscription, which Michael Billig (1995) called 'banal nationalism', would then be achieved for Europe. The position of 'anti-death penalty' has become a potent agent in such inscribing of a European consciousness.

The mediascape and ideoscape (Appadurai 1997) of European identity have thus created a space and time for 'work' against the death penalty. One of the least examined consequences of 'global cultures' has been the ways in which people in their everyday lives apprehend their relationship to distant 'others'. In this chapter I have explored some of the ways in which the 'other' (especially the other as offender, and the other as death row inmate) become objects of identification, pity, and compassion (Boltanski 1999, Cohen 2000). The implications of this aesthetic and intellectual openness (Hannerz 1998, Tomlinson 2002) towards others demanded by cosmopolitanism for our apprehension of the relationship to criminal others should be an ongoing project for criminologists and students of penality.[7]

The translocal production and local manifestation of penal sentiments around the ultimate penal predicament, engenders a disjuncture in which the practice of the death penalty on distant shores becomes an urgent issue that overrides its contentiousness and ambivalence in local penal politics. In a somewhat different context, Loader, Sparks, and myself (Girling *et al* 2000) have argued that there

---

[7] The crossings between attachment and detachment inherent in the cosmopolitan disposition are seen by even the most pessimistic of commentators as offering possibilities and in some ways the only possibility for postmodern ethics:

'As far as the prospects of safeguarding human lives against cruelty . . . are concerned, it does not matter much who is in charge of social spacing and whose charts are proclaimed obligatory; it does not matter either whether it is the cognitive or the aesthetic spacing which structures the human habitat. If anything does matter, it is the redemption of moral capacity and in effect the re-moralization of human space' (Bauman 1993: 239–40).

are limits to what action is desirable or even imaginable if we are to continue to lead lives in places in which we think life is worth living. The polls may return time and again a level of support for the death penalty and, at times of crises, even a majority of support. But as the affluent residents of Prestbury, in our Macclesfield study, kept pointing out (at least in the case of crime prevention), certain responses are not appropriate for the times and places we live in, restraint becomes a taste judgement, a mark of distinction. The appropriateness or inappropriateness of responses is something that abolitionism embeds into EU citizens' everyday lives. The public rituals associated with the abolitionist stance in Europe ensure that it is inscribed into individual life stories. The emerging challenge for criminology would be to assess the impact of this banal aboli-tionism for penal sensibilities in general. The abolition of the death penalty has been heralded as an unqualified success – eradicating the death penalty from European jurisdictions, creating a European public sphere, and encouraging a much sought after participation in European politics. Indeed, it is held up as a lesson for other abolitionists across the globe (see Zimring 2003). However, the consequences of the acts of imagining described above that have enabled this political success may have more seminal and long-term implications that go beyond the European political project. In this chapter I have sketched the new kinds of penal engagement, taking place on a transnational stage, that may shape the global futures of penal sensibilities. The interface between a European identity project and penal identity (about who we are when we punish) has produced an ostentatious reformist position that strikes a dissonant note in penal politics, but its significance may lie in the banal abolitionism that has disabled re-imagining the death penalty in Europe. This banal abolitionism may not only hold important lessons for abolitionists across the globe but may also lead us to at least question the inevitability of dystopian visions of penal futures or criminologies of catastrophe.

5

Penalization, Depoliticization, Racialization: On the Over-incarceration of Immigrants in the European Union[1]

Loïc Wacquant

Introduction

In 1989, for the first time in history, the population entering state prisons in the United States turned majority black. As a result of the crumbling of the urban ghetto and of the 'War on Drugs' launched by the federal government as part of a broad law-and-order policy designed to restabilize racial boundaries in the city and reassert state power against the backdrop of rapid economic restructuring and steep welfare retrenchment,[2] the incarceration rate of African Americans doubled in just ten years, jumping from 3,544 inmates per 100,000 adults in 1985 to a staggering 6,926 per 100,000 in 1995, nearly eight times the figure for their white compatriots (919 per 100,000) and over twenty times the rates posted by the larger countries of continental Europe. If individuals held in jail, sentenced to probation, or released on parole are taken into account, it turns out that more than one of every three young black men aged 18 to 35 (and upwards of two in three at the core of the big cities in the deindustrializing Rust Belt) find themselves under supervision of the criminal justice system.

If blacks have become the favoured 'clients' of the carceral system of the United States, it is not on account of some special propensity that this community would have for deviance and crime; nor is it due to a sudden increase in

---

[1] This chapter is an extended version of a shorter piece circulated *in absentia* at the session on 'The Power to Punish' at the Scottish Criminology Conference, held in Edinburgh, Scotland, on 11–12 September 2003, based on chapter 6 of my book *Deadly Symbiosis* (2006), and is reproduced here with the kind permission of Polity Press. I am thankful to the participants and colleagues who reacted to it via e-mail afterwards and otherwise stimulated me to enter this debate (with special mention to David Garland and Richard Sparks), as well as to Sarah Armstrong and Lesley McAra for their patience and persistence in getting me to revise it for this volume.

[2] For an analysis of the dimensions, causes, and functions of the rise of the US penal state after the mid-1970s, see Wacquant (2005b).

their share of the nation's offences against the law. It is because they stand at the point of intersection of the three nexî of forces that, together, determine and feed the unprecedented regime of carceral hyperinflation that America has experienced for the past quarter-century after discarding the Fordist-Keynesian social compact and the frontal attack on the caste regime by the US Civil Rights movement and its urban offshoots:

(1) the dualization of the labour market and the generalization of precarious employment and un(der)employment at its lower pole;

(2) the gradual dismantlement of public assistance for the most vulnerable members of society (itself necessitated by the spread of desocialized wage-labour) and its eventual replacement by disciplinary programmes designed to push them into the substandard jobs of the deregulated service economy; and,

(3) the crisis of the ghetto as instrument of control and confinement of a stigmatized population deemed unassimilable to the national body and turned supernumerary on both economic and political counts: their labour power is no longer needed, given their lack of skills and replenished reserves of pliant immigrant workers; their ballots can be ignored in the wake of the dealignment of party voting, the tightening stranglehold of corporate interests on policy-making, and the shift of the country's electoral epicenter from city to suburb (Wacquant 2006).

Extreme though it has been in scale, slope, and velocity, the carceral trajectory of African Americans in the post-Civil Rights era may be less idiosyncratic than the woolly notion of 'American exceptionalism' would lead one to believe. One can hypothesize that the advanced societies of Western Europe will generate *analogous*, albeit less sudden and pronounced, situations of lopsided incarceration to the extent that they, too, embrace neo-liberal penality and embark on the path of the punitive management of urban inequality and marginality, deploying their prison system not only to curb crime but also to regulate the lower segments of the employment market, to warehouse labour turned redundant, and to hold at bay populations judged disreputable, derelict, and dangerous. From this point of view, *Third World foreigners and quasi-foreigners would be 'the blacks' of Europe at the fin de siècle* inasmuch as they occupy a homologous position at the confluence of the system of forces polarizing the occupational structure, fraying the social safety net, and eroding the established ethno-national boundaries and make-up of the countries of the Old World.

With the closing of state-sponsored schemes of foreign labour import in the 1970s, the immigrant 'guest worker' from the colonial periphery has mutated into the immigrant *tout court* whose persistent presence at the core is increasingly perceived at once as an occupational threat (he displaces and undercuts native labour), an economic burden (he is unemployed and drains scarce public services), and a social menace (having failed to 'integrate', he and his offspring are vectors of corrosive cultural alterity, criminal deviance, and urban violence). With the acceleration of supranational integration after the Maastricht Treaty and the Schengen Agreements (see Mathiesen, Chapter 7), the visible presence of non-white foreigners has become doubly anomalous since the very drawing of the outer boundaries of the European Union is predicated on a clear-cut opposition between 'us' Europeans and 'them' the Third-World migrants who are no longer welcome – even as they continue to be needed (Sayad 1999: esp. 417–26, Geddes 2000, Santel 1995, Stolcke 1995).

As we shall see in this chapter, the building of 'fortress Europe' in the age of labour flexibility and generalized social insecurity has indeed accelerated a twofold movement of ostracization of unwanted *Gastarbeiter* turned *Ausländer*, through *external removal* via expulsion and *internal extirpation* via expanded incarceration directly aimed at those populations embodying the social and symbolic 'exterior' of the emergent postnational Europe. In the process, the penal arm of the state has assumed a pivotal role in articulating the discursive and organizational construction of internal and external insecurity to the point where they have been fused, projecting the darker-skinned illegal or criminal alien – the two adjectives have become virtual synonyms – as the living antithesis of the New European in the making.

Sizing up Ethno-national Disproportionality

Over the past three decades, nearly all the countries of the European Union have experienced significant and steady increases, and in several cases explosive growth, in their prison population, coinciding with the onset of mass unemployment, the casualization of wage work, and the official curtailment of labour migration. Between 1983 and 2001, these increases reached one-third to one-half in several of the larger countries, with the number of inmates (including those in remand detention) rising from 43,400 to 67,100 in England, from 41,400 to 55,200 in Italy, and from 39,100 to 54,000 in France. Carceral inflation has been even more spectacular in smaller countries and alongside the Mediterranean, with Portugal (6,100 to 13,500), Greece (3,700 to 8,300), and Ireland (1,400 to 3,000) sporting a doubling and Spain (14,700 to 46,900) and the Netherlands (4,000 to 15,300) more than a tripling of their carceral stock (Tournier 2002).[3] Despite periodic recourse to mass pardons (for example in France on Bastille Day every year since 1991) and waves of early releases that have become commonplace (in Italy, Spain, Belgium, and Portugal), the continent's store of inmates has swollen relentlessly and penitentiaries everywhere are full to overflowing (Kuhn *et al* 2000: 136–7).

[3] It should be noted that the larger increases affect countries that have small correctional populations and started from inordinately low rates of incarceration. For a more nuanced analysis of trends by country, see Kuhn (1998) and Snacken *et al* (1995: 18–53); also, the data periodically compiled by the International Centre for Prison Studies at King's College in London.

But, above all, throughout Europe foreigners, migrants, and so-called 'second-generation' immigrants of non-Western extraction, and persons of colour, who figure among the most vulnerable categories both on the labour market and *vis-à-vis* the social welfare sector of the state, owing to their lower class distribution, paucity of credentials, and the multiple forms of discrimination they endure (Wrench *et al* 1999), are massively over-represented within the confined population, and this to a degree comparable, nay in most places superior, to the 'racial disproportionality' afflicting blacks in the United States.

As a first approximation of 'ethno-national disproportionality' in the European Union, one may use the percentage of foreigners behind bars weighed by the share of aliens in the country's population. Admittedly, this is an imperfect indicator that should be manipulated with caution since both numerator and denominator are fraught with problems of accuracy, reliability, and consistency across time and national boundaries. It lumps together, in different proportions, immigrants from the global periphery and foreigners from other countries of the Euro-American sphere. Notwithstanding these limitations, this indicator is revealing of striking transatlantic parallels. Table 5.1 shows that the presence of foreigners inside European houses of detention far exceeds their weight in the general population in every single nation-state of the continent. And that, in nine of fourteen members of the European Union, the disproportionate

Table 5.1. Foreigners in the carceral population of the European Union, 1997

Country	Foreign inmates	Proportion of carceral population (%)	Proportion of foreigners in total population (%)	Ratio
Spain	7,700	18	1.6	11.2
Italy	10,900	22	2.1	10.5
Greece	2,200	39	4.7	8.3
Netherlands	3,700	32	4.3	7.4
Portugal	1,600	11	1.8	6.1
France	14,200	26	5.6	4.6
Belgium	3,200	38	8.9	4.3
Sweden	1,100	26*	6.0	4.3
Norway	339	15	3.6	4.1
US blacks	**816,600**	47	12	3.9
Germany	25,000	34*	9.0	3.8
Austria	1,900	27	9.1	3.0
Denmark	450	14	4.7	3.0
Finland	127	4.5	1.6	2.8
Ireland	203	8	3.1	2.6
England	4,800	7.8*	3.6	2.2

* Estimates

Source: *Statistique pénale annuelle du Conseil de l'Europe, Enquête 1997* (Strasbourg, Editions du Conseil de l'Europe, 1999: 17), for European prison figures; OECD, *OECD Social Indicators 2002* (Paris: OECD, 2003), table G3, for the percentage of foreigners; Bureau of Justice Statistics, Correctional Populations of the United States 1997 (Washington: Government Printing Office, 2000: 2), for blacks in the United States.

Table 5.2. Evolution of the share of foreigners (%) in the carceral population of selected European countries, 1985–95

Country	1985	1995	Increase (%)
Belgium	27.6	41.0	48
Germany	14.5	29.4	103
France	26.4	28.5	8
Italy	8.9	17.4	95
Spain	10.6	15.5	46
England-Wales	1.3	7.8	500
Ireland	1.8	6.4	255

Source: André Kuhn, Pierre Tournier and Roger Walmsley, *Le Surpeuplement des prisons et l'inflation carcérale* (Strasbourg: Editions du Conseil de l'Europe, 2000: 37).

incarceration of foreigners is superior to the demographic over-representation of blacks in American jails and prisons.[4]

Even more striking than their sheer over-representation behind bars is the fact that, during the very period when rates of black incarceration were sky-rocketing in the United States as the policy of penal management of poverty and inequality was going into full swing, there was a uniform and often spectacular increase, in nearly all European countries, of the share of foreigners in the population under lock and key, as indicated in Table 5.2. In the decade 1985–95, the proportion of aliens confined in jails and prisons rose consistently by five percentage points in Spain, England, and Ireland, and by ten to fifteen points in Belgium, Italy, and Germany; the European record for 1995 was held by quiet Switzerland with 57.6 per cent (for a foreign population approaching 20 per cent, resulting in a comparatively low disproportionality – due to their recent Malthusian policy as regards both political asylum and labour import in spite of the country's long tradition of mass migration and continued need for foreign workers). While the documented and undocumented foreign population grew during this period in most of the countries concerned, this growth was limited and cannot possibly account for, say, the doubling of the share of non-nationals among the confined in Italy and Germany.

Part of the disproportionate incarceration of European foreigners is presumably caused by their higher overall rates of offending – although this is a contentious issue that cannot be adjudicated empirically in most cases owing to the lack of adequate statistical data – which can itself stem from their skewed class, age, and spatial distribution as well as from the different opportunity structure for life strategies they face (Engbersen and van der Leun 1999). Part of

[4] This directly refutes the notion, accepted as a matter of common sense among most European and North American criminologists, that 'the extraordinary overrepresentation of African Americans in the population incarcerated or under criminal justice supervision is not found on the same scale in European countries' in the case of foreigners (Landreville 2002: 429).

it is likely to be due, as with blacks in the United States, to the preferential targeting of aliens by the police and their differential processing in the courts, as well as to the application of neutral criteria (such as holding a legal job as a condition for release on bail) that systematically handicap aliens in the administration of punishment. Finally, a fraction of the excess confinement of foreigners derives from offences such as unlawful entry and residence that by definition cannot be committed by nationals (or only as accomplices), or germane infractions such as the fraudulent fabrication and manipulation of official documents (identity cards, marriage certificates, residence permits, etc).

While it does not allow one to consistently weigh these various factors, a methodical mining of available studies of bias in the penal treatment of aliens and related ethnic categories among nationals, bears out both the prevalence and the deepening of the over-incarceration of foreigners and immigrants in the European Union. And it confirms that, with the onset of neo-liberal hegemony, penal segmentation has become a key modality of the drawing and enforcing of salient social boundaries in the Old World as in the New World.

Selective Targeting and Preferential Confinement

In England, following the urban riots of the early 1980s, officially diagnosed as in part 'racial' by the government report of the Scarman Commission, the question of street crime, often reduced to the sole offence of 'mugging' has been confounded, in public perception as well as in the routine practices of the police, with the presence and demands of subjects of the Empire who come from the Caribbean. Whereas British blacks had been viewed as a low-offending group until the mid-1970s, by the mid-1980s 'crime, in the form of both street disorder and robbery, was gradually identified as *an expression of black culture*'; and 'the populist potential of the black crime theme' enabled the conflation of supposed black crime and black ethnicity to cross the divisions of the political field and suffuse the media (Gilroy 1987: 109, see also Cashmore and McLaughlin 1997). The shift towards authoritarian forms of social regulation, multi-agency policing, and intensified surveillance of 'criminal areas' closely overlapping with inner-city neighbourhoods of Afro-Caribbean concentration correlates with the fact that blacks are seven times more likely to be incarcerated than their white or Asian counterparts (and West-Indian women ten times more likely).

This wide ethno-racial gap can be explained in part by the differential propensity of blacks and whites to commit offences. Much like their American counterparts, blacks in Britain are more likely to engage in street crime due to the fact that they are of lower class provenance and poorer, more likely to suffer high unemployment, and to reside in distressed and declining neighbourhoods (Modood *et al* 1997) where illegal activities in public space are more common and thus easier to engage in, detect, and repress. But their grossly bloated presence in prison also stems from the cumulative effect of the selective targeting and differential treatment of Afro-Caribbeans by law enforcement agencies: they are more prone than white Britons to be stopped and arrested on general suspicion by the police, to be prosecuted rather than cautioned in the case of juveniles, and to be tried in Crown Courts rather than before magistrates as well as to be remanded in custody, both of which, *ceteris paribus*, result in a higher rate of prison sentences (Walker 1989, Hood 1993).

A similar phenomenon can be observed in Germany where the question of *Ausländerkriminalität* has become a staple of political and even criminological debate, as the media and parties across the ideological spectrum have fastened on the increased presence of foreigners as the putative cause for urban crime and disorder (Walter and Kubink 1993). The over-imprisonment of foreigners and visible non-national ethnics has increased dramatically over the past two decades, reaching astronomical levels in many regions, even as the overall use of incarceration declined due to a deliberate Malthusian penal policy that reduced the national population behind bars for much of that period. In North-Rhine-Westphalia, for example, Sinti and Roma Gypsies originating from Romania sport incarceration rates more than twenty times that of native citizens; for Moroccans the figure is eight times, and for Turks between three and four times. And, the proportion of foreigners among those awaiting trial in detention rose from one-third in 1989 to one-half five years later. In Germany too, differential rates of offending cannot possibly account for the breadth of such ethnic disparities in incarceration and for their speedy growth in recent years. The widely held belief that teenage foreigners are more prone to delinquency than their German counterparts, for instance, does not withstand a methodical examination of police investigations and court processing (Geissler and Marissen 1990).

In the Netherlands (whose carceral population has quadrupled over the past twenty years, as successive governments consciously sought to align Dutch penal policy on the more punitive European mean, and comprised a hefty 43 percent foreigners in 1993) the probability of being sanctioned with an unsuspended prison sentence is systematically higher for the same first offence when the person convicted is of Surinamese or Moroccan origin (Junger-Tas 1997). Studies using quasi-experimental and field observation methods have shown that, although the incidence of police arrest is not biased by the ethnicity of suspects, once arrested non-whites have a greater likelihood of being convicted and of receiving a custodial sanction. In line with the American pattern, in which authorities have historically displayed pronounced indulgence for offences committed within black neighbourhoods, punishment in Dutch society also turns out to be less likely and less severe when the crime victim is a member of a subordinate ethnic category (Junger 1998, Engbersen 1995).

After plummeting from 50,000 at the close of the Second World War to 10,500 in 1968, the prison population of Spain has doubled every ten years since 1975 to return to 55,000 today along with the rise in recorded crime accompanying the democratization of society following Franco's death and the deregulation of the economy. The growth of casual wage employment and the wide tolerance, even encouragement, of undocumented labour inflow from Morocco, against the backdrop of an official policy of rationing of immigration, have combined to push growing numbers of African migrants into a legal limbo at the margins of society. Together with xenophobic media campaigns and periodic police sweeps intended to reaffirm state power and stem mounting social anxiety caused by accelerating economic and demographic trends, changes in the criminal code that have hardened sentences for petty crimes against property and narcotics offences and penal procedures that deny foreigners the benefit of alternatives to short prison sentences (such as weekend custody and day fines) have translated into a doubling of the share of foreigners behind bars since 1985 (Serrano 1993, Cid and Larrauri 1998, Rivera Beiras 1999). Among Spanish nationals, a similar process of differential penal targeting and preferential confinement impacts on the Gypsies: one of every four Spanish female inmates in the Iberian peninsula is a *gitana*, even though Gypsies comprise only 1.6 per cent of the country's population (Hernández *et al* 2001).

In France, the share of non-nationals in jails and prisons has ballooned from 18 per cent in 1975 to 29 per cent twenty years later, even though foreigners account for only 6 per cent of the country's population and about 15 per cent of police suspects throughout that period. And this figure does not register the pronounced carceral 'over-consumption' of French citizens perceived and treated as foreigners by the police and judicial apparatus, such as youths born in France to Maghrebine immigrants (*beurs*) or who come from the predominantly black French overseas dominions and territories.[5] Suffice it to say that the cells of France have grown distinctly 'coloured' these past years, since two-thirds of the 15,000-odd foreign prisoners officially recorded in 1995 originated from North Africa (53 per cent) and Sub-Saharan Africa (16 per cent). That year the jails and prisons of Greater Paris, which hold a quarter of the country's inmates, harboured a population 44 per cent foreigner and thus *majority non-white*, if one includes French inmates of colour (Gailliègue 2000). Aside from their higher unemployment and poverty rates, the 'ethno-national disproportionality' that afflicts residents from France's former colonial empire arises from the fact that, for the same offence, the courts resort to confinement more readily when the condemned does not possess French citizenship. Suspended sentences and non-custodial sanctions are practically monopolized by nationals, on grounds that they offer better social and legal guarantees of 'community attachment'. Thus foreigners make up 10 per cent of offenders punished with community service (*travail d'intérêt général*) and 13 per cent of those receiving a fine, but one-third

---

[5] '*Beur*', a street slang (*verlan*) term for '*arabe*', designates so-called second-generation North Africans, the French offspring of Algerian, Moroccan, and Tunisian immigrants drawn to France during the 'thirty glorious years' of post-war economic growth.

of persons sanctioned by an unsuspended prison term and over one-half of convicts sent behind bars for more than five years. Demographer Pierre Tournier has shown that, depending on the charges, the probability of being sentenced to prison is 1.8 to 2.4 times higher for a foreigner than for a Frenchman (all persons tried taken together, without regard to prior record) (Tournier 1996).

Far from resulting from an alleged increase in their criminality, as the ambiant xenophobic discourses of elected officials, police experts, and the media would have it, the growing share of foreigners in the confined population of France turns out to be due *exclusively* to the tripling in twenty years of incarcerations for violations of immigration statutes. If inmates sentenced for this charge are excluded from correctional statistics, the ratio of over-incarceration of aliens to citizens drops from six to three. As with blacks in the United States, then, the disproportionate share of foreigners in French custodial institutions expresses not simply their lower class composition but also the greater severity of the penal institution towards them, as well as the 'deliberate choice to repress illegal immigration by means of imprisonment' (Tournier 1996: 158) instead of a gamut of non-custodial sanctions, as in earlier decades.

This confirms that we are dealing here with penal captivity that is first and foremost a *confinement of differentiation* or segregation, aiming to keep a definite group separate and to prevent its amalgamation into, or to facilitate its subtraction from, the societal body – as distinct from 'confinement of authority', intended to reassert the legitimate power of the state, or 'confinement of safety', aimed at neutralizing dangerous individuals.[6] This is why such confinement results more and more frequently in deportation and banishment from the national territories that compose the European Union.

The Penal Management of Foreign Intrusion and Extrusion

To the foreigners and quasi-foreigners held in jails and prisons, often in tiers segregated according to ethno-national origin (as in the jail of La Santé, at the heart of Paris, where inmates are distributed into four separate and hostile wards, 'white', 'African', 'Arab', and 'rest of the world'), one must thus add the tens of thousands of migrants without papers arrested at border-crossings or awaiting deportation, especially owing to the generalization of 'double sentencing' procedures that attach a decree of expulsion to a penal sanction.[7] This floating

[6] This ideal-typical distinction between three forms of confinement is elaborated by Faugeron (1994).

[7] Under penal law in France, as in several other European countries, foreigners can be subjected to '*double peine*': they are sanctioned, first, by imprisonment for the offence they committed (including illegal entry and sojourn) and, secondly, by expulsion from European territory after they have served their sentence in the case of undocumented immigrants or legal aliens deemed to 'pose a threat to public order' (a clause routinely invoked by the authorities to deport repeat offenders).

population is corralled and detained in those *state-sponsored enclaves of juridical limbo that are the 'waiting areas' and 'retention centres'* which have proliferated across the European Union over the past dozen years.

A 1999 parliamentary commission on France's retention centres likened entering them to 'entering another country, in another epoch, far away from the Republic', and forthrightly deplored the appalling conditions of overcrowding and lack of hygiene, the rampant violation of rights, and the multifarious administrative irregularities committed in them (Mermaz 2001). A concurrent report by the Cimade, a non-governmental agency charged by the French government with assisting the populations passing through these facilities (where length of stay averages four to five days), reveals the common reliance by the authorities on improper documents, the theft of the personal papers and belongings of detainees, the near total absence of legal counselling, and repeated instances of expulsion of single adolescents as well as children born in France and sick persons under medical treatment (including detainees suffering from full-blown AIDS). This is all an effort to accelerate procedures, disengorge the establishments, and increase the yearly count of the deported.

In Belgium, where the number of aliens held in the custody of the *Bureau des Étrangers* increased nine-fold between 1974 and 1994, persons consigned in the detention centres for foreigners *'en situation irrégulière'* fall under the authority of the Interior Ministry (in charge of public order) and not of the Justice Ministry, and they are thus omitted from the statistics of the correctional system. Conditions in these centres evince the same routine denial of rights, services, and dignity as in their French counterparts. Five so-called closed centres, surrounded by a double row of barbed-wired fences and under permanent video surveillance, serve as launching pad for the deportation of 15,000 foreigners each year: this is the official government target number given as express proof of the 'realistic' immigration policy implemented with the professed aim of cutting the ground out from under the far right, which meanwhile has continued to prosper as never before (Vanpaeschen *et al* 1998, Brion 1996). In Italy, deportation orders quintupled in only four years to peak at 57,000 in 1994, even though there are ample indications that illegal immigration subsided during that period and that the vast majority of foreigners who do not have proper papers enter the country legally to fill 'black market' jobs disdained by the natives (Pallida 1996) – as the government of Massimo D'Alema implicitly recognized when it increased by a factor of six the number of residence and work permits initially granted as part of the 'regularization' programme launched in winter 1998.

Under the provisions of the Schengen and Maastricht treaties (aimed at accelerating juridical integration so as to ensure the effective 'free circulation' of citizens of the Union), immigration has been redefined by the signatory countries as a continental and, by implication, national matter of *security*, under the same heading as organized crime and terrorism, onto which it has been grafted at the level of both discourse and administrative regulation (Bigo 1992, see also

Mathiesen, Chapter 7).[8] Throughout Europe, police, judicial, and prison practices and policies have converged in that they are applied with special diligence and severity to persons of non-European phenotype, who are easily spotted and made to bend to penal injunctions, to the point that one may speak of a process of criminalization of immigrants that tends, through its destructuring and criminogenic effects, to (co)produce the very phenomenon it is supposed to combat, in accord with the well-known mechanism of the 'self-fulfilling prophecy' (Merton 1968). Its main impact, indeed, is to push its target populations deeper into clandestinity and illegality, to feed their fear of authorities, and to foster the durable structuring of specific networks of sociability and mutual help, as well as of a parallel economy that escapes state regulation, an outcome well-suited to justifying in return the special attention given to them by law enforcement agencies (Dal Lago 1998; on the Dutch case, Engbersen 1997; and on Germany, Kubink 1993). Managing immigration with the penal wing of the state transmutes bureaucratic violations into criminal acts and fosters the selective police targeting and differential treatment by the courts that amplify initial differences between natives and aliens in the composition and incidence of offending. It also forces foreigners to live in a submerged world in the shadow of legality, setting off a *fatal dialectic of criminality and criminalization* that becomes self-sustaining, with the added pressing demands of the journalistic and political field for dramatic displays of the state's capacity to tame this insidious threat to national cohesion and European integrity.

With the redefinition of peregrination from outside the European compact as a problem of 'security' synecdochically linked to crime, the expulsion of undocumented foreigners and alien convicts sentenced to territorial banishment has turned into a media theatre onto whose brightly-lit stage elected officials vie to step up and display their professed resolve to 'stop clandestine immigration', and thus symbolically stem the tide of unemployment, delinquency, dependency, and assorted cultural maladies commonly attributed to it. In France, for nearly two decades successive Ministers of the Interior of both the right and the left have boasted of boosting the number of deported migrants yearly and have eagerly sought public credit for forcible mass deportation via specially chartered aircraft. By the late 1990s, various European countries were cooperating with France to pool their deportees onto jointly commissioned planes and then unload them in Senegal, Mali, Ivory Coast, Zaire, Romania, and China. One night in late September 1996, for instance, 43 Zairians and 23 Senegalese, 18 of them embarked in the Netherlands and three brought in from Germany, were forcibly heaved onto a Euralair jet for the sixth European 'exilee' charter flight to Kinshasa from Roissy-Charles-de-Gaulle that year. These operations have become frequent and large enough to foster the creation and ensure the

---

[8] The officially stated goal of the Schengen treaty was to establish a transnational legal and administrative framework to reduce crime while encouraging open borders (Kapteyn 1991).

prosperity of airlines specializing in the transport on-demand of expelled aliens –
some estimates put the total number of foreigners thus banished from 'Fortress
Europe' at 200,000 annually (De Stoop 1996: 26).

These operations effect a *reductio ad absurdum* of immigration policy to
pure penal ceremony and brute bureaucratic myth. They are not rites of passage, marking a temporal transition from a 'before' to an 'after', but *rites of
institution* drawing a clear-cut frontier separating those whom the rite concerns
– unwanted aliens, undocumented or delinquent, thus amalgamated together –
from those who cannot and will not undergo it – members of the community
of European nationals, which is thereby set apart and solidified.[9] They purport
to dramatize the capacity of the state to police its internal boundaries and to
protect its external borders through penal means, just as both are coming
unglued under the press of global economic restructuring, on the side of the
market, and European integration, on the side of political sovereignty. Yet
upon close scrutiny they evince little more than the derisory character of such
pretension.

Penal expulsions are intended to reaffirm legality, yet they induce a multiplication of administrative irregularities (the deported often have not exhausted
their legal recourses and appeals or they are later found to be ineligible for
eviction) and a routinization of illegalities and state-sanctioned violence that can
escalate to homicidal proportions. Of the 23,100 individuals placed in France's
'waiting zones' in 2001, some 14,000 were ejected abroad, including 1,733
under close police escort following their refusal to board flights back to their
presumed home country – the refusal rate among convicted aliens deported
under 'double sentencing' is considerably higher, nearing one-third. In such
cases, the exilees must be pushed, pulled, and dragged aboard the plane and then
physically suppressed throughout the journey. They are commonly injected with
sedatives in blatant violation of French law, their hands and feet bound with
manacles and chains, their mouths taped shut with duct tape, their torsos
immobilized with belts or blankets. They are forcibly manhandled, with physical
commotion frequently causing trauma, injury, and in several instances death.
These 'charters of aliens' further undermine the rule of law in that they appear to
violate both Protocol 4 of the European Convention on Human Rights and
Article 19 of the Charter of Fundamental Rights of the European Union, which
stipulates that 'collective expulsions are forbidden' and that 'no one can be sent
away, expelled or extradited to a state where there exists a serious risk that he [sic]
will be subjected to the death penalty, tortured, or receive other inhumane or

---

[9] 'To speak of rite of institution is to indicate that all rites tend to consecrate or legitimate an
arbitrary boundary, that is, to cause it to be misrecognized as arbitrary and recognized as legitimate,
natural. . . . By solemnly marking the passage over a line that establishes a fundamental division of
the social order, the rite draws the attention of the observer to the passing (whence the expression
'rite of passage') when what matters is the line' (Bourdieu 1991: 118, author's translation).

degrading sanctions and treatments'.[10] Officials of the European Union have defended the legality of the policy by arguing that these are not 'collective expulsions' but 'grouped expulsions' of persons, each of whom has been served an individual decree of eviction.

Penalization, Depoliticization, Racialization

In many respects, the spread of the ritualized mass expulsion of illegal or con-victed aliens in the European Union as penal spectacle stands as the structural analogue to the reintroduction of chain gangs, striped uniforms, and assorted shaming punishments harking back to a bygone era of social cruelty towards black convicts in the United States.[11] First, it fulfils the same function, namely to convey to the witnessing public the resurgent *penal fortitude of the authorities* by staging their commitment to act in an openly retributive manner towards categories that conspicuously disrupt the (supra)national symbolic order. Sec-ondly, it offers an expressive vehicle for the social amplification and cultural *legitimation of collective feelings of resentment* towards these same categories.

In his path-breaking studies of Algerian peregrinations to and through France, Adbelmalek Sayad (1991: 305–6) has shown how 'emigration-immigration always engages two political orders, two nations and two nationalities, and not simply two countries, two societies, or two economies as we are accustomed to consider'. This implies that migration expresses 'a relation of domination between different socioeconomic formations' and thus between the governments that rule them; it is the precipitate of an *interstate nexus* that is eminently political also, in that it necessarily entails 'the transfer of citizens and thus of nationals, and in the final analysis of political subjects'. Yet, magically as it were, through such penal rituals as collective expulsion, the doublet emigration-immigration is reduced to the singleton of immigration, itself shrunk to the illicit and intol-erable presence of postcolonial foreigners. Through such state ceremonies, 'the relation of state to state that is at the very foundation of immigration [is] negated' so that the phenomenon 'becomes a domestic matter, pertaining to the sole competency of the receiving state' (Sayad 1991: 267 and 304; see also Portes and Böröcz 1987). That state can then (pretend to) act to extirpate and rid itself of unwanted persons, who are thereby obliterated as nationals and political subjects, much as convicts are erased from the civic map of the United States through extensive and expansive disenfranchisement laws.

---

[10] See *Chartes des droits fondamentaux de l'Union européenne*, available on line at the site of the *Ligue des droits de l'homme*: <http://www.ldh-france.asso.fr>. Mass expulsions of aliens have been chronically denounced by Amnesty International, the International Observatory of Prisons, and other human rights organizations in the major countries of Europe.

[11] The racial tenor of public chain gangs comes from the fact that the last inmates to be visibly punished in this fashion in the interwar South were African Americans (Lichtenstein 1996: 160).

Next, 'charter deportations' turn out to be just as financially ruinous, organizationally wasteful, and penologically pointless – if not counterproductive – as contemporary chain gangs. The latter were reinstituted with much fanfare in August of 1995 by the state of Alabama (and later by Florida, Arizona, Wisconsin, and Iowa), whose Department of Corrections took the trouble to organize media visits and bus tours for tourists to come and witness the shackling of inmates made to break rocks inside Livermore penitentiary. But a short four years later this experiment in vengeful punishment had to be aborted as it turned out to be legally intractable, practically troublesome, and excessively costly in that it required too many guards for too few inmates (Allen and Abril 1997, Ozimek 1997). Similarly, expulsion under 'double sentencing' is a labour-intensive operation that absorbs a growing share of the resources of the border police, derails the normal processing of inmates, and aggravates prison overcrowding. Many foreign convicts facing a decree of deportation choose to serve their sentence in full rather than opt for an early release, since they will be transferred from the prison straight into a remote detention centre; they then often commit additional crimes, physically resist, self-mutilate, or attempt suicide (for example by swallowing razor blades on the day of their deportation) to avoid eviction thousands of miles away, which leads them to serve additional time behind bars for 'refusal to comply' with a banishment order. And they generate vitriolic controversy and intense public and legal scrutiny that make for fast diminishing political and journalistic returns when an incident, such as the death of a deportee, breaks into the top of the news (thanks to video footage) or leads to years of litigation embroiling leading political figures.

Much like the stylized reassertion of retribution for retribution's sake that temporarily obviates the need to face the absence of an operant philosophy of incarceration in the United States, the fixation on the politics of the intrusion and extrusion of extracommunitarian aliens serves as a substitute and subterfuge for the *lack of a policy of incorporation* of immigrants and assimilated categories. The hysterical obsession with the former contrasts sharply with, and indeed serves as mask for, the 'vertiginous void of public action' as regards the latter (Faber 2000).[12] And, just as rolling out the carceral system to restrain and contain the troublesome segments of the African American community in the remnants of the historic Black Belts allows the United States to continue to avoid addressing the threefold legacy of slavery, Jim Crow, and the urban ghetto, as well as the persistently peculiar position of blacks in America's social and symbolic space (as expressed by their inordinately high levels of residential

---

[12] Faber goes on to write: 'France no longer knows what to do with its immigrants. It has laboured relentlessly to regulate their entry and exit, with all the more ferocity as it was fleeing the question, otherwise more important, of what to do with those who remain with us' (2000: 15–16). Jean Faber is the pseudonym of a high-ranking state official formerly in charge of immigrant 'integration policy' in the French government, a domain he contends is a political and bureaucratic wasteland.

segregation, near-total ethnic endogamy, and the subtle undercurrent of denigration in public perception), the deployment of the penal apparatus to deal with immigration enables Europe to shun facing its deep-seated entanglement in the fate of the postcolonial societies of its former empires as well as the multifarious forms of social and state ostracization that continue to derail the path of non-European migrants in national life even as they gain legal status.

On both sides of the Atlantic, penalization operates as a *conduit for the depoliticization of problems*, ethno-racial division, and immigrant incorporation, that are quintessentially political in that they engage the definition of core 'membership' in the national or supranational community (Benhabib 1999, Walzer 1983). This transmutation of political issues – inclusion-exclusion from the civic compact and state-to-state relations – into technical questions of order maintenance along the country's internal or external borders, liable to receive a penal solution through the targeted activation of the police, courts, and carceral apparatus, whereby established or putative members of the civic compact are made over into deviant bodies to be marked, neutralized, and removed, is emblematic of neo-liberal penality. So is the paradoxical articulation of high technology – jet aircraft, advanced video surveillance systems, massive electronic databases that can be consulted from countless locations to determine instantly the juridical status of any individual – and antiquated imagery: in the United States, public chain gangs are meant to evoke a bygone epoch of racially inflected penal punitiveness directly descended from the days of Southern slavery; in Europe, aircraft expulsions reactivate the cultural logic and long dormant representations of transportation and penal relegation as practised by Britain and major continental countries from the seventeenth to the nineteenth century. It is no happenstance, then, if mass deportation by charter flights and chain gangs share a profoundly archaic quality (Oshinsky 1996, Ekirch 1987, Balibar *et al* 1999).

Finally, the generalization of 'double sentencing' laws in Europe not only helps to *produce* the very criminality that such laws are meant to suppress via the geographical 'neutralization' of would-be offenders, in that they force an ever-growing and self-centred population of undocumented aliens and returning deportees into a submerged life made of illicit employment, administrative subterfuge, unstable residence, identity manipulation, and avoidance of the authorities, all of which normalize and intensify delinquent activities. It also *institutes a bifurcated and asymmetric juridical space*: the nationals are sanctioned once, for the criminal offence they have perpetrated; the foreigner on the other hand, even when legally established and socially integrated, is struck twice, once for the acts (s)he has committed and a second time for who (s)he is. His or her very being triggers an extra dose of punishment, sending the unmistakable signal that (s)he is not part of the emerging European civic community. This differential treatment partakes of the racialization of foreigners insofar as it *treats foreignness as an inherently criminal property* that automatically warrants an aggravation of retribution. Being an extra-communitarian alien thus functions as a permanent and indelible penal handicap much in the manner that convict status (and blackness) does in the United States (Wacquant 2005a).

Now, anti-immigrant sentiments in European countries have a long and lush history. Foreigners and visible 'ethnics' throughout the continent have been recurrently associated with the gamut of disorders ranging from public health threats and political dissidence to sexual degeneracy and street crime since the onset of the urban industrial era. The trajectory of transborder migration across the Old World is stamped by the contrapuntal interplay of ascending nationalism and gusting xenophobia (Miles 1993). But, if anti-foreign animus is a relative constant, or at least a regularly recurring factor, the configuration crystallizing at the turn of the millennium differs from previous iterations of capitalist transformation and ethno-national conflict in at least three important respects:

(1) Old World nationals presently face, as it were, a double menace: the one arises *from below* through the consolidation of unwanted 'foreign intrusion' in the nether regions of social space made more palpable by the gradual conversion of labour migration into settlement migration; the other comes *from above*, in the guise of a juridical and bureaucratic process of European integration that converges with the global neo-liberal revolution to strip from the nation-state its capacity to penetrate and protect the social body. This pincer movement exacerbates the sense of group vulnerability and rivalry at the bottom of the social structure and intensifies the quest for collective scapegoats as well as the urge to exclude rather than absorb them (Bourdieu *et al* 1999: 23–36, 106–22, 317–20).[13]

(2) The deployment of the police, courts, and prisons to tackle extra-communitarian foreigners partakes of a broader, epochal shift from the social-welfare to the penal treatment of problem categories and territories in the dualizing metropolis (see Downes and Hansen, Chapter 8). To be more precise, the 'extrusion' of immigrants from both declining lower-class neighbourhoods (via disproportionate arrest, prosecution, and incarceration) and from the national territory (via criminal expulsion and administrative banishment) serves as a *spearhead* to implement the penalization of urban poverty designed to complement economic deregulation and welfare retrenchment insofar as it elicits less resistance and even generates support for such punitive policy from among the precarious fractions of the native working class that constitute its main foil.

---

[13] There are partial historical precedents: xenophobic stereotyping and hostility towards foreigners in south-eastern France in the 1930s was intensified by the sense of vulnerability of the country's borders to foreign powers during that decade, as argued by Lawrence (2000).

(3) Penalization strikes at vulnerable and stigmatized categories against the backdrop of the *decomposition of the working class and its historic territories*, such that no centripetal forces of solidarity can effectively counteract it. In previous eras of economic transformation, industrial conflict and union mobilization supplied both an operant organizational vehicle and a potent idiom to unify the disparate segments of the labour force issued from various countries, to fuse issues of work and community, and to convert 'foreigners into nationals'. By swamping nationality with class in and around the workplace, unions and assorted labourers' associations joined with left parties to fashion a compact bloc presenting collective claims to the state that cut across and even erased putative ethnic lines in the public sphere. Nowadays, the fragmentation of the working class into atomized households facing a structural crisis of reproduction simultaneously on the labour market, in the neighbourhood, and in the school system, just as they are being deprived of a voice in the political field by the rightward shift of socialist parties, has stripped unskilled immigrants from the institutional and cultural buffer they enjoyed in the previous era of class consolidation anchored by the Keynesian-Fordist compact (Tripier 1990, Beaud and Pialoux 1999).

It is not hostility against foreigners that is novel, then, nor the degree of cultural alterity or phenotypical distinctiveness of the latest wave of migrants that explains the sharp spike in the salience of foreigners on the criminal scene and their massive presence in the prisons of Europe. Rather, it is the vastly *greater capacity and propensity of the state to deploy its penal resources* at both the national and the supranational levels to 'resolve' the problems they pose or embody, whether real or imagined, connected to transborder perigrination or displaced from the broader broiling arenas of work, place, and identity.[14] Indeed, exclusionary impulses and punitive formulas have dominated the media construction and bureaucratic management of extracommunitarian migration throughout Europe, with limited legalization schemes, expanded border control, and mass deportation the three most prevalent responses given throughout the continent to the continuation of transnational movement, family reunification, and irregular labour import. The extensive discursive cum organizational linkage between the 'domestic side' of the criminal justice system and its 'foreign side', fostered by the accelerating construction of a European-level system of penal measures to check the intrusion and amplify the extrusion of unwanted aliens, is a novel phenomenon.

Darker skinned, uneducated, unattached and uncouth, prone to crime and violence: undocumented immigrants are not so much 'non-persons' leading an invisible existence in the shadowy zones of the city, as Alessandro Dal Lago

[14] The acceleration of the top-down creation of a European penal space after the 1992 Maastricht Treaty and the 1997 Amsterdam Treaty is tracked by Tulkens (2002).

(1999) has suggested, as *anti-persons*, negative tokens whose conspicuousness enables the germinating transnational personhood of Europeans to be delineated and affirmed via sociosymbolic contraposition, much like African slaves operated as anti-citizens in the early decades of the American Republic. On this account, the police targeting, court treatment, and correctional weight of postcolonial foreigners, immigrants, and assimilated categories – Maghrebines and *beurs* in France, West Indians in England, Turks and Roma in Germany, Tunisians and Yugoslavs in Italy, Moroccans and Gypsies in Spain, Africans in Belgium, Surinamese in the Netherlands, Angolans in Portugal, and Albanians in Greece – constitute a veritable litmus test, a shibboleth for Europe (Bourdieu 1998: 15–18). Their evolution allows us to assess the degree to which the European Union resists or, on the contrary, conforms to the American policy of criminalization of urban poverty and marginality as a complement to the generalization of social insecurity and the destabilization of ethnic hierarchy in the metropolis. Like the carceral fate of blacks in the United States, it gives us a precious and prescient indication of the type of city and state that Europe is in the midst of building onto the scaffolds of triumphant neo-liberalism.

6

Prisons During Transition: Promoting a Common Penal Identity through International Norms[1]

Laura Piacentini

Introduction

This chapter considers how human rights are experienced in Russian prisons and the mechanisms through which they deliver new priorities in the administration of imprisonment. Not only does the chapter attempt to help correct the woeful neglect of Russian prisons in criminological scholarship, it also aims to inform debate on how fundamental social, political, and economic transitions enable prison systems to take new directions, precisely because such systems may exhibit a kind of porosity in their penal peripheries. It is my contention that Russia has followed a path of human rights because of their directive force in a global context, a force that is conceived from a symbolic politics that fuses global conformism with morality. This force found a particularly receptive penal environment in Russia, a state in transition that has lost its overarching (Soviet) ideology. As useful for filling a void in penal ideology as the human rights model may have been, however, they are a *received* ideology. The effect is that a Western-designed, universalized model of human rights imposed on the Russian context has produced a rhetoric of *carceral disgrace*. Human rights discourse is used as a mechanism to shame. These developments reconstitute ideological and political boundaries between societies according to westernized mandates of 'good' or 'bad' punishments. Ironically, despite the emphasis on such concepts, the normative basis of punishment has become lost from its point of origin as debates about, and interpretations of, the reasons to punish are subverted and, to a degree, silenced.

The chapter draws on research conducted in 1999 and 2003 in fifteen penal establishments of varying categories across western and eastern Russia. The research identifies two periods of Russian penal reform. The first period begins in

[1] For their excellent comments, very special thanks to the editors. Thanks to Andrew Jefferson for sharing his findings on human rights strategies in Nigeria.

the 1990s with the exposure of dreadful prison conditions, and the second period, emerging during the first years of the twenty-first century, is marked by a distinctive global penal politics – human rights penality – that Russia subscribed to with remarkable speed and willingness (Piacentini 2001, 2004c).

After a brief overview of research methods, the chapter comprises three main parts. The first describes the period of penal reform in the 1990s, and explores two areas that made Russia vulnerable to imposed human rights strategies: the ideological vacuum that followed the collapse of the USSR and the physical conditions inside Russia's prisons. The central government's response to the exposure of the scandalous penal system and the role of non-governmental organizations (NGOs) in changing the penal landscape, furthers the discussion.

The second part of the chapter explores the latter phase of penal reform early in the twenty-first century. The central government's reinvigorated authoritarian position provides the background to the communication and dissemination of human rights. The section concludes with the presentation and analysis of interview data on how local actors have interpreted and responded to the discourse of human rights. The third and final part of the chapter locates the research findings in the broader context of globalization and an evolving concept of carceral disgrace.

The Research

The research findings that are presented extend from a major study of post-Soviet penal ideologies and penal practices (Piacentini 2001). Data was gathered from a total of fifteen prison establishments across Russia.

The first phase of fieldwork took place in 1999. It involved an intense period of five months of close-up observation in four penal colonies for men in two geographically disparate regions, one in western Russia (Smolensk), and the other in western Siberia (Omsk). Interviews during this first phase were gathered from 224 respondents (including prisoners, prison officers, and officials).

The second phase of research took place over five weeks in eastern Siberia in May 2003. This later phase provided an opportunity to assess the status of the original research findings four years on. In Omsk two of the penal colonies that participated in the 1999 research were visited again and two more colonies participated. Five rural penal colonies, one remand prison, and one penal colony for drug-addicted prisoners in Kemerovo in eastern Siberia also participated in the research.[2] In total, 25 semi-structured interviews with on-site prison personnel were conducted in this phase (fourteen in Kemerovo, eleven in Omsk). Also interviewed were the Generals who manage each region; the Director of

---

[2] Omsk region is 3,000 km east of Moscow and borders the Russian Republic of Kazakhstan. Kemerovo is 4,000 km east of Moscow, tucked in front of the Altay Mountains which provide a natural border between eastern Russia and Mongolia. Access to the establishments was negotiated directly with the Ministry of Justice in Moscow.

the Moscow Centre for Prison Reform (MCPR); a Moscow politician who campaigns for penal reform; a junior prisons' minister at the central prison authority (GUIN)[3]; and, two EU officials based at the Delegation of the European Commission in Moscow under the European Initiative for Democracy and Human Rights. During this phase, prisoners were not interviewed.[4]

On both research trips all of the interviews were conducted in Russian. The research was qualitative as it aimed to explore the social meanings and concepts shaping the contours of imprisonment in Russia, where the collapse of the USSR has led to, on one level, a more open atmosphere and society, but on another, a massive void in penality at the ideological level. The main methodological approach was ethnographic, with the aim of sharing subjective realities and building rapport (using the local language, socializing with staff, working in the prisons for up to twelve hours each day, and observing).

During the 1999 fieldwork, many obstacles were encountered in obtaining prisoner respondents due to the focus of inquiry (prison work in Russia has a brutal legacy and, in the contemporary system, authorities face many problems with prison work conditions), gender issues, and the uniqueness of the research. Second time round, in 2003, there was very little resistance due to having obtained a stronger foothold in the system. Interviewees were chosen freely and there was less dependence on staff to facilitate the research. The first trip necessitated living inside the regimes. On the second trip, a driver was employed for transportation to the rural colonies.[5]

During the first trip in 1999, the majority of prison officers presented outspoken, thoughtful, and independent views on the complex linkages between crime and punishment amid a turbulent society. Today, the situation could not be more different. The trappings of imprisonment, with its highly visible overcrowding and gruesome conditions, have been exposed to Western 'scrutiny'. Fourteen years after the collapse of the Soviet penal monolith, all discussion is of human rights. An account of this change in interpretation begins with a discussion of the early reforms.

The Early Phase of Reform (1990s)

Russia's penal system has undergone a remarkable and chaotic transition (Piacentini 2004c). Since 1991, there has been an absence of mainstream debate

---

[3] In 2004, the prison system, Chief Administration for the Implementation of Sentences (GUIN), became the Federal Service for the Implementation of Sentences.

[4] In 2003, I was not permitted to interview prisoners. It must be emphasized here that the exclusion of prisoners does not, I believe, weaken the overall focus of the research. It just raises more questions about how imported knowledge of regulation and performance are qualified on the ground by excluding the critical mass of individuals to which that process of regulation principally applies.

[5] An in-depth account of the problems, pitfalls, and the pleasures experienced on both trips can be found in Piacentini (2004c).

about punishment. Consequently the practices and normative structures in prisons have been continually re-stylized by custodians and captives. The turbulent transition has been determined by external inevitabilities (the collapse of the USSR) and internal realities (the material demands of facilitating care and welfare of prisoners amid reduced resources and poor conditions) that created the conditions for the generative force of human rights.

Ideological vulnerability

The collapse of the USSR marked the end of the huge and dreadful logic of Soviet criminal justice, when criminal law was subverted and supplanted to manufacture penal labour on a seemingly infinite scale. Opening the doors of the prison system revealed an overpopulated and inhumane prison environment. Nevertheless, very few officials had any idea of what could fill the void left by the collapse of Marxism/Leninism. Indeed, it was unfashionable at the time to discuss the legacy of the enormous Soviet penal machinery; uttering 'ideology' produced a great deal of anxiety about past atrocities. With worldwide attention focused on conditions in the prisons it was by no means obvious in what direction the prison system would move and what or how change would be achieved. The insecurities and uncertainties over penal doctrine seemed impossible to reconcile. Prison officers have reminisced about how political difficulties in defining the parameters of penal ideology produced emotional obstacles as to how they interpreted the meaning of imprisonment, possibly because the control of the Soviet state had created a degree of stability (albeit authoritarian) that was no longer evident (Piacentini 2004c: 112–14).

Prison conditions and resources

The appalling prison conditions in Russia were (and continue to be) a huge and shocking problem. When the Soviet Union collapsed, rates of TB among the imprisoned were found to be seventeen times higher than in Russian society as a whole, torture was widespread, and human rights violations were constant. That officials claimed the difference in TB testing arose only because of greater testing and diagnosis in prison compared to the general community, was a symptom of the amnesia among officials who at the time played down the scandalous state of the prisons (King and Piacentini 2005). The remand prisons (SIZO) were massively overcrowded (and remain so) in some cities, with large rooms intended for a maximum of twenty prisoners holding more than 60. One toilet was shared between all and less than one square metre of space was available for each prisoner. The cellular prisons in the United Kingdom intended for three persons, would hold thirteen persons in some prisons in Russia (Kresty in St Petersburg, for example) (Rodley 2000). In almost every pre-trial detention centre in Russia, deaths in custody due to lack of oxygen were recorded (MCPR 1996). Prisoners in jails (some with up to 8,000 inmates) often had to queue to obtain a place to sleep. For all prisoners, hygiene facilities were woefully inadequate. Women prisoners also lacked basic sanitary requirements and a general healthcare support system (Moscow Helsinki Group 2003). In the prisons observed as part of the research, dilapidated kitchens made for a depressing sight, with ventilation and water and light supplies not properly established and maintained. Prisoners in the colonies (where most sentenced persons serve their sentences) fared only marginally better. Dormitories were larger and there were more work and education opportunities than in the larger prisons, although comparatively fewer compared with those in the United Kingdom.

Central government response to ideological vulnerability

The ideological vulnerability and conditions inside the regimes illustrate how a penal system in transition is caught somewhere between the past and the future. Past configurations produced particular political, economic, and penological outcomes that were incongruent to Western sensibilities. A modification of policies and practices was therefore necessary. The dismantling of Soviet models began through new legislation, such as the first non-Soviet Penal Code of 1992. This code and the various draft penal codes thereafter recognized that the institutions of justice would operate under a different European rubric, laying the foundation for a new penal sensibility.

Kalinin (2002: 6) states that the early post-1991 prison legislation 'defined new aims, objectives, principles, and directions of the work of corrective colonies, prisons and remand prisons'. Yet looking closely at previous Soviet penal codes, what initially emerged could be criticized as little more than tinkering. The Soviet discourse – the language that named practices and policies as 'Marxist/Leninist' – was replaced by international discourse (human rights, minimum standards, procedures to measure performance, and the concept of prisoners' rights). Without denigrating the positive evocation of human rights, however, there was very little discussion on how Soviet penal sensibilities would evolve. Indeed, at the time a tension emerged between penal reformers and the authorities, with the latter arguing that there was little that could be done with chronic underfunding of the penal system and the collapse of the command economy.

Russian prison authorities were not in a unique situation when faced with the problem of constructing fresh criminal justice frameworks. Research from Northern Ireland and Australia shows clearly how it is possible to reform criminal justice by being creative with the past (for example McEvoy 2003). Yet, in Russia there was a wall of silence about how a modern criminal justice system could be created by the actors administering the system. With alliances forming between local NGOs and powerful reform groups such as Penal Reform International (PRI) and the MCPR, the transformation of criminal justice to extend rights to prisoners gathered momentum ahead of Russia's entry into the Council of Europe (in 1996).

The legacy of the Gulag and the economic meltdown after 1991 created rapidly rising levels of crime (including organized crime), corruption, poverty, and unemployment. All together, this turbulence has contributed to the maintenance of a very high prison population: currently the second highest in the world (611 persons per 100,000 of the population, or 874,000 persons, Walmsley 2003). With a substantial reduction in investment in public services following political and economic crises, authorities faced the colossal task of reforming the prisons and instituting a rule of law amid severe budget cuts. Prisons, alongside schools and hospitals, suffered terribly.

On a global level, because prison conditions deteriorated so severely in the decade when Russia was moving towards integration into the Council of Europe, the problems were deemed to require, and justify, international solutions. The conditions of confinement were to be resolved by improving human rights and central regulation. The former proved initially to be the more successful development. With the loss of an identifiably indigenous discourse, imported norms seemed utterly necessary. The government was committed to penal reform and, with good intentions, reduced the prison population noticeably through amnesties. Other reforms included: a moratorium on the death penalty (which meant that for the first time there were prisoners serving life imprisonment); access to the various EU bulletins for prisoners; improved visiting rights; and another new Penal Code (1997). A system of regional management was also introduced that aimed to alleviate some of the pressure from the centre and to enable a more devolved prison system to emerge.

The role of non-governmental organizations

As indicated above, NGOs played a key role in the process of reform. Their influence was first felt during Gorbachev's programme of Glasnost in the late 1980s when journalists, Helsinki Watch, Amnesty International, and PRI were granted access to Russian prisons. The MCPR, with Western support from the Soros Foundation, also emerged as a forceful voice. For decades, human rights groups had made large-scale efforts to campaign for the release of imprisoned political dissidents from outside the USSR. It was, however, when the doors of the penal system finally opened in 1991 to expose overcrowding, infectious disease, and serious human rights violations that a network of international monitors came to be firmly established inside Russia. The international NGOs were given unprecedented access by GUIN (the central prison authority) to monitor first-hand hundreds of establishments across Russia. Although the emphasis was on 'assisting governments', it is undoubtedly the case that the lobbying work of NGOs in Russia helped to create a climate of greater accountability, putting pressure on the government to manage prisons in line with international standards.

Though undeniably grim, NGO reports documented some positive developments, the most significant of which was that the prison authorities were far more open to monitoring and regulation than might have been expected. In many countries, indigenous NGOs are only now emerging where there is a need for local action. However, in Russia, an active and respected NGO movement participated in government roundtable discussions on penal reform. International NGOs also worked with local NGOs which they monitored for their autonomy before partnerships were forged.

Russian NGOs not only championed human rights. While all international NGOs work with governments and not for governments, the relationship in Russia was one of shared vision: the progress of civil society could be measured by the progress of penal and judicial reform, standardized in European norms. The advocacy role in Russia was politically significant as NGOs became the voice of the Council of Europe, and human rights advocacy was multi-faceted. Fundamentally, it sought recognition and reinforcement of prisoners' rights and improvements in prison conditions. Politically, and on a more abstract level, human rights promised political respectability for a nation that in the past might have been viewed as a global pariah. In a society with enormous prison numbers and which faced continual indictment for violations, the geo-political benefits of human rights were quite profound.

Local response to penal crisis

The chronic underfunding of the penal system in the 1990s, where only 60 per cent of the necessary funds were allocated (at best), alongside the absence of a dominant guiding penal philosophy, left prison staff at the local level in an almost parlous state. The first phase of the research found that the ideological void was eventually overcome, not due to a commitment to *engage with ideology* through official discourse but because the central regulation of the penal system *weakened* further under the then President, Boris Yeltsin, with effects that impacted on the penal apparatus and on prison governors, who began to administer imprisonment quasi-autonomously. It was the devolved management system which eventually led to new, locally developed models of punishment, as resources were increasingly provided through unofficial channels (Piacentini 2004b).

At the local level, prisons were understood as performing a myriad differentiated roles and they began to utilize a range of concepts that were individuated from the central prison authority in Moscow. A traditional, more punitive ideology re-emerged in some areas, while ideas emanating from the West were shaping the contours of imprisonment in regions located nearer Western Europe.

For provisions, staff had to negotiate barter contracts with local businesses, factories, and farmers. Bribery, corruption, and degradation existed everywhere in the penal system. But there was also reciprocal trade with local people and surprisingly welfare-oriented reform strategies based on community partnerships

(Piacentini 2004a). Prisoners were integrated into communities through wheeling and dealing of goods and services, and the prisons themselves assisted lagging communities in rural areas by trade-swaps: from vehicle repairs to offering musical concerts for prisoners. General conditions were poor but staff commitment to reform was real because of their personal vested interest in keeping the prisons operational.

To summarize, by the early twenty-first century the political context was changing, driven by the economic and ideological crisis following the collapse of the USSR. The penal system was struggling to shake off its past, trying to survive and move towards Western models of welfare and care as well as crime and punishment. Amidst all this, a 'Russian' vision of imprisonment was emerging that reflected indigenous/local cultures.

Reform in Twenty-first Century Russia

The current president, Vladimir Putin, came to power in 2000 with a fresh approach to centralized orthodoxy, and one that had widespread appeal, particularly as terrorism was emerging in Russia. There was increased regulation of all spheres of society: the establishment of a tax system, the promotion of legitimate politics, greater accountability, centralization, and reform of regional government. In prisons, regional management was reformed and an extra layer added to create a quasi-devolved prison system. Consequently, many penal practices (psychology booths, barter trade, work with communities) remained outside official, national-level discourse.

Increased centralization and the human rights agenda

A human rights discourse resolved several political predicaments regarding the governance of Russian prisons. It provided a ready-made regulatory model that could be adapted relatively easily to local operations. The development of a human rights agenda was also a politically astute move at a time when Russia was seeking entry into the international community, as its adoption entailed a rejection of Soviet repression. Finally, because human rights were instituted following a period of re-centralization of the management of the prison system and the establishment of criminal and civil procedures, it was associated with a period of standardization, stability, and centralized penal policy that many found familiar.

Human rights as penal ideology follows a decade of transition and blurred demarcation for the penal system. Now the prison system has found a solid script – a 'centralized' penal vision – which officials can present to the international community. This path of development is particularly interesting because it reveals a collision between symbolic global politics and indigenous penal sensibilities. On one side are the fresh approaches that emerged which were based on different knowledges of welfare and care; on the other side are the international conventions that Russia has ratified. There is also an interesting twist to human rights in Russia's prisons: the new orthodoxy is imbued with values that are to be regulated by bodies outside national jurisdictions. Attention has shifted to human rights debates, and the passion with which punishment was administered has been replaced by regimes of central control.

There are numerous mechanisms that diffuse human rights in Russia, but several are directly related to prisons. These are technical support, changes in the roles of staff, changes in the rights of prisoners, and changes in the language of penality and regulation.

Mechanisms for diffusing the human rights agenda

The European Union and the United Nations currently do not offer funds or financial aid to the Russian prison authority to improve prison conditions. Rather, in recent years, the movement towards assistance and harmonization has come in the form of knowledge transfer (technical support, human rights education, and handbooks on how to deliver human rights).

One manifestation of this is the practice of local NGOs bidding for EU contracts. Micro prison projects (small-scale democratization initiatives which are intended to deepen local civil society groups' involvement in the promotion of human rights) are currently being piloted by the European Union Delegation in Moscow. The projects are results-based and involve the NGO establishing how it will meet the objectives. In one example, radio sets were given to prisoners in a pre-trial centre. When that project started, the prison administration told the NGO that the preferred method of assistance would be funds so that they could purchase the radios themselves. Although the prison administration was clear that such direct requests were not possible under EU regulations, anecdotal evidence suggests that personnel were being judged more on whether they could successfully implement the administrative procedures of EU political attitudes channelled via the NGO. The radio sets were given after the end of the project on the basis that the prison had met the NGO's performance indicator of penal reform.

New programmes are also being introduced in Siberian prisons. In the 'Food in Exchange for Progress' initiative, the Red Cross gives colonies meat, butter, beans, vegetables, flour, and rice. The aid was initially marked for prisons where inmates have tuberculosis, but the programme has now extended to other prisons. TACIS, another NGO, has recently begun work within the Federal Ministries and identifies projects, which are then contracted out. TACIS' work is concentrated on the major communicable diseases in prisons (tuberculosis, HIV/AIDS) and health education.

Further mechanisms include international NGOs. The track record of PRI in reforming Russia's penal system has been described by the director of the MCPR as, 'nothing short of outstanding'. Over the last fourteen years, PRI has produced numerous pamphlets, initiatives, and strategies for prison reform, including a book on combating communicable diseases in prisons in Eastern Europe, and exchange programmes between prison personnel in Russia, Northern Ireland, and England. Texts on human rights management and alternatives to custody, as well as work on the social integration of women offenders and their children, have also been produced. Altogether, these programmes are intended to provide practical knowledge and guidance on how to implement international standards. The main point of entry into all these programmes is western expertise. One remarkable development in recent years is that whereas, for decades, the MCPR campaigned for penal reform on the margins, nowadays, MCPR representatives meet government prison officials at the Russian Parliament.

Impact on contemporary practice and local adaptation

In 2002 the position of *pomochnik prava cheloveka*, or 'assistant for human rights' (AHR), was created to assist regional chiefs in administering human rights. In Omsk and Kemerovo, staff who had trained under the Soviet system took up these positions before retirement. One assistant is a former secretary who has worked in the prison system for 25 years. Each prison region employs one AHR (there can be up to 30,000 prisoners and 10,000 staff in a region). It is not yet clear whether the role will extend to the establishments. During interviews, the AHRs expressed mixed views on this possibility with one arguing, 'then we could get carried away with human rights' (author interview).

Other recent changes include the creation of a Prison Ombudsman for the first time in Russian history and prison officer cadets now receive human rights training at prison colleges. There is some human rights training taking place for trainers, education staff, and other professionals who work with offenders in delivering rehabilitation programmes in the prison establishments, but this is limited to a few pilot regions.

Joint partnerships between regional administrations and NGOs channel the rights process into the penal system. The situation of improving rights is far from resolved but there has been an enormous improvement in access to the various EU and UN bulletins and information about prisoners' rights under international law. Interestingly, the EU administrators who were interviewed stated that most of the legal advice requested by prisoners is to do with their rights under international rather than national law. The AHR oversees this process.

The reform of the language of imprisonment in ministerial papers attests to a new criminal justice vernacular through which flows human rights doctrine. There is a kind of missionary zeal in the technocratic, managerial language adopted ('problems', 'assistance', 'pioneering good practice', 'lessons', 'best efforts', and 'progression') that is flowing into national guidelines. At the time of writing, GUIN inspected all prisons annually. The new Federated Regional Administrations are expected to inspect on a more regular basis and then report to GUIN in Moscow. GUIN then reported to the Council of Europe. Inspections by the European Union take place every five years.

Changed ways of seeing and talking about penal reform

Talking with prison officers and observing the day-to-day running of the prison system at local level provides a unique opportunity to gain insight into the ways in which globalized conceptions of human rights are diffused into penal practice.

The data from the second period of fieldwork for this research, in 2003, revealed that prison officers believed that all they were doing was violating human rights because of under-performance. Prison personnel believed that efforts to find fault with the system were accompanied by a raft of targets to meet, performance goals to reach, and bureaucracy, 'devised to manage the extra paperwork generated from the human rights monitoring missions' (author interview). To some, however, human rights talk reached faith-like proportions. Prison officers' narratives were constructed around an assumption that successful prisons were found in nations that believed in human rights. In order to get underneath the words of prison officers it was instructive to ask the following: what does it mean to believe in human rights in Russian prisons? Is it a belief like believing in a faith, or is it a principle? A reading of the interviews with prison officers at all levels of rank shows it to be both, and much more besides. The interpretations of prison officers' views are organized thematically below and the intention is to reveal the inside subjective story of how prison officers see human rights for themselves.[6]

Human rights as an ethic of care

Some respondents understood human rights as having a normative orientation of care. Undertaking assessments of prison conditions was, in the minds of these officers, vitally important for the positive custody of prisoners:

Human rights are important because they are about promoting care and humanity for inmates. Yet we are seeing more control . . . we have to be seen to meet norms because for ten years we did not.

When we get told that progress is being made, I feel good . . . we are getting somewhere.

Human rights as accountability

In the first phase of the research project, prison officers viewed their role as 'punishers', 'custodians', 'carers', and 'responsible for rehabilitation'. Nowadays, however, the majority of respondents viewed human rights as a form-filling exercise to be pushed along desks rather than to be experienced in the cells:

It is about the maintenance of standards. It's about ensuring we meet norms. We get sent EU bulletins now in Russian. We know the outcome that needs to be achieved.

---

[6] All quotations come from interviews with the author.

My job is to check the bulletins to see how many of our prisoners complain.

I am the Human Rights Assistant. My job is to fill in the necessary forms.

Human rights as imperialistic invasion

The above responses certainly revealed an awareness of the terminology under-pinning human rights. Yet when probed, prison officers expressed resentment that human rights were not created by Russian prison authorities for Russian prisoners and that the distinctiveness of Russian practices was submerged under externally derived normative structures:

The westerners come here to tell us how bad our system is and then leave.

What does Europe know? Why should we listen to you? We are in Siberia; we have our own Siberian human rights [laughs].

It's all Europe, Europe, Europe! We're much closer to Europe now and we read pamphlets from the EU.

I am annoyed that these are not our changes. We cannot possibly be like Europe, but I feel the pressure.

Why do our prisoners need the EU? If you look at EU bulletins, it's Britain, France and other countries where more prisoners are reporting grievances. Hardly any prisoners from Russia are mentioned. Our prisoners are fine. I can't stand NGOs. They just say all the negative stuff. They are righteous. They base their reports on an entirely aggressive and negative approach.

The above accounts were typical of those who were interviewed during the 2003 research visit and they reveal the real dilemma facing prison officers whose own lives are in a great state of flux.

Human rights: cynicism, detachment, or acceptance

Cynical responses dominated as respondents found it difficult to explain human rights. These occurred, however, alongside expressions of ambivalence and a growing acceptance:

When I think of human rights, I think of the rights of the prisoners. But I must admit, I don't really know what that means because we never focused on prisoners' rights in our society. Previously, we never listened to other nations. But now we have to listen.

We've got to do better, implement proper practice.

I have forms to fill in every day. Do they have enough water? 'Yes'. Do they have minimum standards? 'Yes'. I cannot answer 'no' to any questions or we are in trouble with the regional chiefs. I see human rights as a list of criteria to meet.

The responses moved from cynicism to detachment and exposed an imbalance between what the prisons could do for themselves to improve human rights and the ongoing need to take note of international pressure:

You ask us whether we think about how we understand punishment in the new post-Soviet society. I never ask myself these questions. I get depressed. We have failed in our punishment. We got it completely wrong and we now have a big mess, a terrible system.

We used to have a principle of imprisonment. It was work and education. We've gone through great change. They tell us that human rights are the most important thing to concentrate on. When we talk or read about prisons we discuss the human rights issues and not much else.

From cynicism and detachment came acceptance. Although human rights norms were a procedural development and obscure in content, the consequences of human rights violations were understood; the legitimacy of the penal system would be questioned:

Ideas? ... they're not important. We must deliver human rights.

Human rights and ambivalence towards the past

The final theme reveals how, as a consequence of the view that human rights discourse is a commodity, some prison officers were found to be jealously guarding their old identities because they felt that the sovereign status of the penal system was under siege. A defiant nostalgia for previous penal policies was evident in the more remote prisons:

It wasn't all that bad in the past. We did have some good work practices. Work was so important for prisoners.

I was born in the Gulag, my father was a prison guard as was his father. I feel that human rights are good for the west but not here. What do you Europeans know about us? We are not European. I can't define human rights because it is not something that we created. The Gulag was ... great. I am a patriot for that penitentiary system.

What can we make of the above discussion? Confronted with the challenge of making their prison system more humane, for many personnel the themes of accountability, imperialism, an ethic of care, and ambivalence towards the past, indicate that human rights are perceived as a Western enforcement mechanism.

Prison officers were emotionally and intellectually cynical about the human rights rhetoric – many simply did not understand what it meant. Similarly, despite the good intentions of NGOs which work tirelessly to improve conditions for prisoners and staff, prison officers believed human rights to be mere window dressing. In analysing the data it was impossible to unpack how Russia has become swallowed up in the European project of political, social, economic, and cultural harmonization. After many years of transition and turbulence, the prisons have succumbed to a notion of good punishment following a period of exposure to globalized penal trends and discourse. Such a development can be found in other societies in transition. Brogden (2003) and Jefferson (2003) argue separately that international model shopping for (respectively) police strategies in the Far East and prison officer training programmes in Nigeria are global movements that have constructed links to penal policy arrangements. Such arrangements, they argue, are contained within the political discourse of integration. Few would disagree with penal reformers that in Russian prisons penal reform was utterly necessary. Yet, the effect is that the forceful impetus to improve the prisons is producing particular – Westernized, Europeanized, regulatory – forms of penal knowledge because the movement from retrogressive to progressive punishments is embedded in global arrangements that fuse together monitoring, regulation, and political integration.

The domestic effects of human rights in Russian prisons expose a paradox: normative questions about humane punishment disappear upon the emergence of a global human rights movement. This is because the strategy of human rights is also feeding into a larger political process of shaming or, as one officer stated to me, 'making them feel bad'. Consequently, the features and logic of human rights doctrine are creating a global penal culture that relies on imported knowledge to construct notions of penal failure and success.

Carceral Disgrace and the Importance of Shame

The data presented in this chapter expose an unexamined Western hegemony over non-western cultures whose prison conditions have been opened up to scrutiny. Is it the case that prisons are humane and therefore 'good' so long as practices are acceptable to the West? And if practices are acceptable to monitors, regulators, and consultants, does this mean that Russian prisons are now 'modern prisons'? In searching for some answers to these questions, some points on how perspectives on punishment are mediated by the geo-political contours of control seem necessary here.

Globalization is in part the process through which, in environments where political communities have collapsed and fallen away from any nationally demarcated territory, national (domestic) policy or sovereignty is no longer the dominant, or preferred, mode of governance. In a world where the contours of political control are blurred, tensions can emerge between national sovereignty and international expansion. The solution is to govern through international rule-making, control, and rule-enforcement. Accordingly, we see an increase in interconnecting international economic phenomena leading to elevated political positions of dominant modes of capitalism (transnational corporations, developments in communications, in transport, and in how production is organized). As Braithwaite and Drahos (2000) argue, this is the epoch of 'information capitalism' where regulatory forms of knowledge depend on complex webs of dependency relations and influence. What is commonly an effect of globalization is the integration of a range of hitherto demarcated activities across state borders. The question I wish to ask here is: how do prisons in transition respond?

Globalization has percolated down to the prisons through human rights strategies. A human rights paradigm raises the profile of inter-governmental and non-state actors that have been involved in assisting international governments (Beeson 2003). However, as this chapter has also shown, local modes of penal activity are being determined by global ideas which are remote and intrusive to Russian prison personnel but which have been appropriated by experts who are setting about civilizing the prison system. For external actors (the global political community) the vacuous state of penality in Russia (the early phase of penal reform) has been sealed off and, consequently, the possible negative effects (high-risk punishments, alienation of cultures, distance and remoteness of rival political economies) are reduced.

Within this context of harmonization and humanity a specific set of global penal arrangements have revealed themselves. First, prison systems come to be premised on human rights and wrongs. A sensibility is thus set for a new global penal politics identified here as *carceral disgrace* whereby those societies that are administering systems of punishment that fail to meet external norms are singled out. The second stage involves importing external standards that are procedurally assessed and monitored. Manuals for best practice replace local and indigenous practices. Thirdly, performance indicators are set to meet the requirements of norms projected outside in. Taken together, notions of disgrace and failure have emerged to govern and direct penal systems in transition. Moreover, carceral disgrace captures some of the conceptual and organizational features characterizing failed penal societies.

Failed penal societies

The recurring anxiety that imprisonment is a failure inheres in the majority of the academic literature that develops a social, political, and cultural critique of imprisonment. Criminological discussion over what we can expect from imprisonment has certainly been enhanced in recent years as more and more light is shed on what is going on inside the prisons in places as far apart as Poland and Pakistan. For example, Jewkes (2002) examines how inmates in English prisons structure relationships utilizing prison-specific adaptive mechanisms such as television; Lowthian (2002) criticizes the barriers to reform in women's prisons in England, while Marchetti (2002) argues that prison accentuates pre-existing social deprivation in cultural, physical, and recreational realms.

When it comes to the anxieties of prisons' failure in societies in transition, however, there are several additional and also more specific difficulties in determining and assessing penality's general effects. In every country in the world there are breaches of international obligations because human rights are difficult to enforce. The US government, for example, approves of a judicial system that sentences people to death, but disapproves of a regime such as that which operated under the Taliban in Afghanistan, which stones women to death. This illustrates that the difficulty of deploying a human rights standard is more than a problem of enforcement: how is it to be characterized as a concept and thus applied in myriad cultural and social settings? This is a problematical question for the political cultures of a range of different countries that operate outside of the group of advanced industrial nations and which have been discredited in the eyes of the international community. While no society in the world can be said to have a perfect penal system, in the majority of the societies with penal systems identified as 'failing', prisons are filthy and overcrowded and they operate outside a rule of law. In some cases observers will acknowledge efforts to reduce overcrowding, which in many countries has improved (Rodley 2000). But it is understood that national standards fall woefully short of international standards and conditions remain intolerable, gruesome even.

The brutalizing spaces and appalling squalor of Russian prisons have shamed the system into making a commitment to penal reform. 'Russia's disgrace' (as it was described to me by one Russian prison worker) has produced a range of emotions. Shame, morality, protocol, and convention lead to confusion, defensiveness, and apology from prison officers. The prison officers' stories revealed that although human rights talk is *de rigeur*, few understood what they were talking about. Indeed, there were some extraordinary claims that human rights offered some sort of carceral respectability in the global political community, as though penal talk of propriety kept the dangers associated with political differences at bay. And the effect? Prison staff are drifting further away from instituting reasons to punish, as the burden of what follows from disgrace looms large. With human rights committees having authority to adjudicate violations that are brought before them, a once-oppressive regime can now be shamed and controlled in ways that were simply not possible during the entire twentieth century.

The ironic loss of normativity

Carceral disgrace is evident in prisons everywhere where all forms of deprivation of liberty raise the question of legitimacy. Yet for prisons in transition the stakes are greater because the path of development of political integration is in part dependent on the success of the indigenous penal system in improving standards. Prison institutions become discredited when they are named as undemocratic, ineffective, and unaccountable to transnational organizations and institutions. Penal regulation by human rights creates the power to name, shame, and punish governments in transition. This is clearly the most powerful aspect of human rights: its enforcement mechanism. The consequences of naming and shaming are that it becomes harder to secure aid and international loans and can lead to political isolation (Zimbabwe, Iraq, and South Africa are some recent examples). It is therefore quite possible that human rights have created a symbolic politics marked by a perception that it is far better to develop a penality of homogeneity than a penality of difference.

Ironically, human rights have not only obscured views on imprisonment, they have also left structural and institutional frameworks intact because the question of why we punish rarely features. In a society where ideology and identities remain hesitant, oscillating, and fleeting, the technocratic and managerialist logic of international norms that are conditioning and predisposing the prison officers to act in certain ways, has become problematic for assessing the normativity of punishment. Against the commitment to introduce human rights training to all cadets training to work in the prison system, there is very little consultation with personnel over that most elementary of questions: what *are* human rights? Without the bearers of the message believing or understanding the message and its basic concepts and dimensions, how can penal reform occur?

Conclusion

While this chapter has contested the progress of penal development in Russia, clearly doing something is better than doing nothing. Improvements in human rights have thrown light on what is going on inside Russia's prisons and this new knowledge opens up closed worlds. Armed with this knowledge, NGOs have reduced the amount of cruelty and unmerited suffering of Russian prisoners. Often national jurisdictions operate prisons at their own discretion, so to impose a system of regulation provides standards against which the national laws can be scrutinized and issues raised on what goes on in prison besides incarceration.

Without such regulation, prisoners would not see their rights judicially recognized. Because of human rights, citizenship rights now extend to inmate populations. As Coyle (2002) notes, there is very little prison research conducted in societies in transition so cataloguing terrible human rights abuses is a contribution in itself and certainly prompts discussion of how prisons can be enhanced. Such an approach, moreover, gives promise for critical penological scholarship as prisoners become sources of knowledge on penal development and are not viewed merely as subjects in the research treadmill.

Critically speaking, the human rights agenda has reconstituted global political difference by demarcating 'successful' from 'failing' prisons. Normalizing standards and standards of conduct are an essential prerequisite for the expansion of global civil society in the broadest sense (Ignatieff 2003). The standards of civilized societies share a common position with the standards of human rights – each seeks to improve society through an authentication of institutions and norms. But political, economic, and social advancement reached through authentication has, this chapter argues, an unfortunate application in penal systems. Authentication is a complex business because it is those states that operate in positions of political dominance that process the authentication of less powerful states and their criminal justice systems. It is succumbing to the process of authentication (styled as 'working together') as much as it is the outcome that is the salient prerequisite for better transnational relations. While it is intended to reduce difference, human rights as penal reform enhances subordinate positions because it is based on liberal power and on the management and regulation of economic, political, and social practices. The operation of human rights as symbolic politics is based on political integration and controlling the threat of political difference. If nations do not meet norms, then they can be kept at a distance (Turkey's delayed accession into the European Union is a good example of how political discrediting arises in part from carceral disgrace). Moreover it is the appearance of making progress, which enhances political legitimacy. So long as nations can demonstrate a commitment to good governance, then change itself becomes secondary. This is particularly complex in prisons, as they remain largely unseen and unfelt institutions. For prisons during transition, change is all the more problematic because the relations of political power that are shaping societies in transition shift constantly.

It was with intellectual fascination that the complex and hidden world of Russian prisons was observed over four years as one that moved from a short-lived phase of local, indigenous philosophies and practices to one marked by checklists of things to do and replication of penal knowledge from western penal systems. It will be interesting to see, for example, how the penal systems of the interim governments of Iraq and Afghanistan evolve in their sensibilities. Penal reform has improved the penal system but it has also served to blur rather than to clarify the most pervading questions about imprisonment around the world: why do we punish and what is effective? Looking ahead, the institution of human rights may create a new actor in the form of the Russian prisoner whose self-awareness may change now that she or he is armed with international rights. So too might prison officers change their view of themselves as members of an internationally recognized profession of guarding.

In the process of becoming mainstreamed into Russian prisons, human rights discourses have become the fighting creed against conflict. The prospect of carceral disgrace of failed penal societies means that there is very little time and space to export knowledge to societies with well-ordered regimes. Is this wise? All forms of power are open to abuse and the power of human rights as a legit-imating force can become exploited by the benefactors as well as by the bene-ficiaries. Questions, therefore, remain on the cross-cultural legitimacy of penalities that exist outside the stable, well-ordered regimes of advanced industrial nations.

7

Lex Vigilatoria—Towards a Control System without a State?[1]

Thomas Mathiesen

Introduction

During the last thirty years or so, we have seeen a massive and accelerating development of various types of transnational information systems pertaining to law enforcement agencies throughout the world. The information systems actually take the form of control or surveillance systems (control and surveillance here taken as synonyms, leaving the question of compliance open). Economic and political change lies at the base of the development, new technology has made it possible. In Europe alone, new concepts flourish – you have:

(1) the Schengen Information System or the SIS, and SIS II;
(2) the SIRENE Exchange;
(3) the Europol Computer Systems or TECS;
(4) the European Asylum System or EURODAC;
(5) the ideas and practices following, more or less, in the wake of the so-called Enfopol papers; and
(6) the Echelon System, which partly goes beyond Europe.

These are only a few of the systems developing in Europe, and if you go further, to the United States, Canada, and elsewhere in the industrial world, you find still another plethora of information systems.

If one aim of this book is to capture the state of punishment at the dawn of a new century, perhaps the most important observation is that the penal sanction is losing its distinction as a response mainly to domestically defined and prosecuted crime, as it melts into a larger global network of identifying presumed threat and monitoring people. New norms are established within the transnational information and surveillance systems, norms emphasizing a future-oriented monitoring of categories of people, thus creating risk profiles of whole groups. Such norms are, in

[1] Part of this chapter will be published in *Essays in Defence of Civil Liberties* (forthcoming, 2006, Spokesman Books). Many thanks to Ben Hayes and Tony Bunyan (Statewatch) for helpful information.

turn, likely to influence our grounds for using penal sanctions, as well as whom we are likely to punish.

The various information systems have been described in detail elsewhere (Mathiesen 2003, 2000, 1999; Hayes 2004; Karanja 2006). Because they are in rapid development and continually expanding, the need for continual updating and revision of descriptions is great.[2] I will here give only a quick outline of the main systems, and go on to a brief presentation of a theoretical idea which may possibly be useful when it comes to a deeper understanding of the systems in question.

The Systems

The police systems in question are transnational, regional (especially, in this chapter, pertaining to the European Union), or even global in character, where vast amounts of information across national borders, within whole world regions, or even globally are entered and/or received. The systems depend heavily on the expanding modern data technology.

The Schengen Information System (SIS), with 878,000 people entered (in addition to about 39,000 aliases and 15 million objects) and 125,000 access terminals (computers) monitoring the system (on a single day in March 2003), is one such system (Hayes 2004). A majority of the persons entered are so-called 'unwanted aliens', entered pursuant to Article 96 of the Schengen Convention.[3] In other words, the Schengen system is to a large extent, but notably not exclusively, a system for border control. The borders between the Schengen countries (virtually all of the EU countries) have been lowered: normally there is no passport control (though notably, exceptions may easily be made on short notice pursuant to Article 2.2 of the Schengen Convention,[4] and though you have to bring your passport for control by airlines and hotels in Schengen states to which you travel). So far, the Schengen arrangement has fifteen member states (thirteen EU states plus Norway and Iceland; the United Kingdom and Ireland are not full members but they participate in the policing aspects of SIS, while Switzerland is on the so-called Mixed Committee), with a central database in Strasbourg and with a database identical to the one in Strasbourg in each of the fifteen participating

---

[2] The civil liberties' organization Statewatch does a great job in this respect. See the Statewatch website <http://www.statewatch.org> and *Statewatch Bulletin*, which is bi-monthly.

[3] Convention of 19 June 1990.

[4] Art 2.2 is not infrequently used. It illustrates how Schengen arrangements have political functions: it is considered important when summits and other major political events take place, to prevent demonstrators crossing national borders. For example, it was used during the World Bank meeting in Oslo, Norway in 2002. The arrangements cover border checks on the basis of Art 2.2 of the Schengen Convention, along with plans to put protestors under surveillance and deny entry to suspected troublemakers, and policies on intrusive surveillance by the use of technologies on biometrics and databases, as well as the controversial EU/US bilateral relations and transfer of Passenger Name Record (PNR) (Apap and Carrera 2003). Apap and Carrera argue that within Schengen, security concerns dominate over the freedom rationale.

countries. After the incorporation of ten new states in the EU, more states will enter the Schengen arrangement. A string of standardized items of information about individuals may be stored in the Schengen database. Data may only be entered according to national legislation, but by the same token, information may also be taken out according to national legislation. Under certain circumstances you may be subjected to 'discreet surveillance' pursuant to Article 99 of the Schengen Convention. Article 99.3, in effect, allows for discreet surveillance of political behaviour – it states that 'a report may be made in accordance with national law, at the request of the authorities responsible for State security' – which means the intelligence services of the various states (Mathiesen 2003: 438–9). A SIS II has long been in the planning and is very soon to be implemented, with a new structure, far greater capacity and a greater number of items of information included, such as biometric information (Hayes 2004; Karanja 2005).[5]

The SIRENE[6] exchange of information is a second system. A so-called 'SIRENE office' is responsible for the administration of the SIS in each participating country. Altogether there are fifteen SIRENE offices throughout Europe. The SIRENE offices may store a vast amount of auxiliary information about individuals registered on the SIS. In Norway, information in national police databases is available to the Norwegian SIRENE office, and may be communicated to other SIRENE offices throughout Europe. The information is extremely comprehensive. A single example from *one part of one Norwegian national police base*, concerning police data on foreigners, includes the following (the information is taken from the relevant police manual in 1999): registration number; registration date; police office code; identification (birth) number; citizenship; passport number; ethnic group; country of origin; sex; name/alias; address; telephone; height; age; bodily features; date of death; hair; language/dialect; spouse (with name and identification number); occupation; position; employer; information about automobiles; information about close acquaintances; other individuals who are closely tied to the person; the person's history ('. . . should provide a brief history of the person's escapades; . . . supplementary information should be entered as time passes . . . '); as well as 'soft info' ('. . . information we don't wish others to see') and other information concerning where the person comes from (this 'in order for us in the future to take out information about a whole nationality'). The operation of the SIRENE system is detailed in a secret manual, which is continuously updated.

Thirdly, there are the Europol Computer Systems (TECS). Europol became operational in 1999, officially with the aim to combat organized crime, terrorism and the like, while in reality and potentially it controls much more widely and diffusely defined categories. Europol has three important computer systems:

(1) A central information system with standardized data about sentenced people and suspects, as well as about possible future offenders within Europol's

---

[5] For further details, see Hayes *op cit.*, Karanja *op cit.*
[6] SIRENE: Supplementary Information Request at the National Entries.

competence. We should notice the diffusely future-oriented character of the system.

(2) Work files for the purposes of analysis: these are special, temporary work files set up for the analysis of specific areas of activity. The work files may contain extensive personal data, not only about persons registered in the central information system, but also about (the following quotes are from the Europol Convention):[7] possible witnesses ('persons who might be called on to testify'); victims or persons whom there is reason to believe could be victims ('...with regard to whom certain facts give reason for believing that they could be victims...'); 'contacts and associates', and informants ('persons who can provide information on the criminal offences under consideration'); in short, a very wide circle of individuals loosely tied to persons who have been sentenced or are under suspicion.

(3) An index system which enables one to find one's way around the vast amount of information.

A bit more about the second of these levels, the work files. The kinds of personal information which may be stored in the work files are not specified in the Convention, only in so-called implementation rules given pursuant to the Convention. As an example of the kinds of personal information for which the work files are designed, mention should be made of a proposal presented in 1996, concerning supplementary information of a highly personal and intimate kind:[8]

It shall be forbidden to collect personal data *solely* on the grounds that they relate to racial origin, religious or other beliefs, sexual life, political opinions or membership of movements or organizations that are not prohibited by law. Such data may be collected, stored and processed only if they supplement other personal data stored in the analysis file and only where they are absolutely necessary, taking into account the purpose of the file in question. (Europol 1996, my emphasis.)

The important word here is 'solely'. It will be seen that the proposal in fact *opens* for inclusion of data about 'racial origin, religious or other beliefs, sexual life, political opinions or membership of movements or organizations that are not prohibited by law' (Europol 1996).

Later, the proposal went through various new editions, following criticism by the European Parliament among others. But the final formulation still allows the inclusion of such intimate personal data. The implementation rules applicable to analysis files state:[9]

Europol shall also specify in this order whether data related to racial origin, religious or other beliefs, political opinions, sexual life or health may be included in the analysis work

---

[7] Convention of 26 July 1995.

[8] Proposal for rules applicable to analysis files, 4 January 1996 4038/96 Europol 2.

[9] Council Act of 3 November 1998 adopting rules applicable to Europol Analysis files: [1999] OJ C26/1, Art 5.2.

file, . . . and why such data are considered to be absolutely necessary for the purpose of the analysis work file concerned. ([1999] OJ C26/1)

With regard to contacts and associates, victims, possible victims, possible witnesses, and informants, such data can only be included after special grounds are given and upon the explicit request from two or more member states. In practice, these limitations are not particularly strict. For other categories of persons, no such limitations are given.

The implementation rules applicable to work files allow the processing of around 70 (at minimum 68) types of 'personal data, including associated administrative data', about persons registered in the central information system. The personal data are grouped in twelve categories, and they are:[10]

   (1) *personal details* (fourteen types of data);
   (2) *physical description* (two types of data);
   (3) *identification means* (five types of data, including forensic information such as fingerprints and DNA evaluation results, though 'without information characterising personality');
   (4) *occupation and skills* (five types of data);
   (5) *economic and financial information* (eight types of data);
   (6) *behavioural data* (eight types of data, including 'life style, such as living above means, and routine', 'danger rating', 'criminal-related traits and profiles', and 'drug abuse');
   (7) *contacts and associates* (subtypes not specified);
   (8) *means of communication used* (a wide range of means given as illustrations);
   (9) *means of transport used* (a wide range of means given as illustrations);
   (10) *information relating to criminal activities* under Europol's competence (eight types of data);
   (11) *references to other data bases in which information on the person is stored* (six types specified, including 'public bodies' and 'private bodies'); and
   (12) *information on legal persons associated with the data referred to* under economic and financial information and information relating to criminal activities (ten types of data) (Europol 1999).

To reiterate, the above-mentioned types of data may not only be included about persons registered in the central information system, but also about possible witnesses, victims, or persons whom there is reason to believe could be victims, contacts and associates, and informants. People working in Europol have immunity within the European Union, and though it is denied by Europol authorities, the Europol police force is said to be rapidly approaching the status of a European FBI. In 2005, Europol had a staff of 536, and 181,000 operational messages exchanged.

---

[10] Council Act of 3 November 1998 adopting rules applicable to Europol Analysis files: [1999] OJ C26/1, Art 6.

A fourth information system is EURODAC – a fingerprint system under the Dublin Convention (1990).[11] The Dublin Convention establishes that only one European state is to be responsible for deciding on an application for asylum, and EURODAC contains fingerprints of all asylum seekers over fourteen years of age. The data are stored for ten years. There are only two exceptions – information about persons who have attained citizenship is to be deleted, and information about persons with formal refugee status, pursuant to the UN Convention relating to the status of refugees, is to be kept for a shorter period and is only to be used for statistical purposes. EURODAC's official goal is, *inter alia*, to avoid asylum seekers seeking asylum in more than one European country. In reality and potentially it is a vast control system for whole categories of ethnic and immigrant groups.

Fifthly, the storage of telecommunications traffic data (telephone, fax, e-mail, internet: traffic data enabling the police to monitor closely who you interact with) is in the making. It began as a collaborative effort between the European Union and the FBI in the early 1990s, and developed into the so-called 'Enfopol papers', originating deep inside the EU structure. The Enfopol papers were made public in the Internet journal *Telepolis*, creating quite a debate. Plans are still moving ahead (Mathiesen 2003).[12], and are now close to finalised within the EU. The London onslaught in July 2005 provided the opportunity. In the panic following this terrorist attack the idea got widespread support. Prime minister Tony Blair quickly made a speech in which he proposed long-term storage of telecommunications traffic data for all British citizens. Critics have pointed out that the masses of data thus stored, will not help, or only help marginally, in catching terrorists. But they will certainly in a massive way threaten civil liberties. This, of course, is an important point, adding to it the more basic question of how far we can go in sacrificing fundamental principles of democracy and the rule of law in our struggle against terrorists. Related proposals were in the making on the EU level, and the final text of a EU directive was issued 3 February 2006 (Council doc. 3677/05, 3.2.06). Under mandatory data retention a record will be kept of *everyone's phone-calls, e-mails, mobile phone calls (including location) and internet usage.* The process of decision making has partly been carried out in secret. A week after the EU directive was adopted, US officials raised the possibility of access to the information with the Council.

A sixth information system is Echelon. This is a regular spy system involving the United States, Britain, Canada, New Zealand, and Australia. Echelon appears to be able to take down vast amounts of telecommunications data from satellites, finding relevant information by means of a system of code words. It is

---

[11] The Dublin Convention of 15 June 1990, to which all EU member states are party, provides a mechanism for determining the state responsible for examining applications for asylum lodged in one of the member states of the EU.

[12] For further details, see generally the very informative Statewatch website <http://www.statewatch.org>.

uncertain how far the technology has come; what is certain is that Echelon exists and that the technology is developing rapidly. A report to the European Parliament by the journalist and researcher Steve Wright may be quoted to indicate the activities of Echelon:

A wide range of bugging and tapping devices have been evolved to record conversations and to intercept telecommunications traffic... However, planting illegal bugs... is yesterday's technology... these bugs and taps pale into insignificance next to the national and international state run interception networks... Modern technology is virtually transparent to the advanced interceptions equipment which can be used to listen in... Within Europe, all email, telephone and fax communications are routinely intercepted by the United States National Security Agency, transferring all target information from the European mainland via the strategic hub of London then by Satellite to Fort Meade in Maryland via the crucial hub in Menwith Hill in the North York Moors of the UK... The ECHELON system works by indiscriminately intercepting very large quantities of communications and then siphoning out what is valuable using artificial intelligence aids like Memox to find key words. Five nations share the results... Each of the five centres supply 'dictionaries' to the other four of key words. Phrases, people and places to 'tag' and the tagged intercept is forwarded straight to the requesting country. (Wright 1998: 18–19)

These are only a few of the systems which are operational or in the making. After 11 September 2001, a large number of new measures and regulations relevant to transnational, regional, and global surveillance have been added. A central point has been the rapid development of a broad and diffuse definition of 'terrorism', making it very clear – if it was not clear before – that the various surveillance systems may be, and are, used politically, far beyond any reasonable definition of terrorism (Mathiesen 2002). In a Statewatch report (February 2005) Tony Bunyan, the editor, summarizes the situation as of today well:

The UK and the EU are facing a defining moment in their response to terrorism. Everyone understands placing suspected terrorists under surveillance and bringing them to court to face charges. But to create new offences of 'preparatory' acts where no crime has been committed and for apology, to employ surveillance techniques which could catch the innocent in the net, and to change the normal rule of law so that defendants will not know the evidence against them or its sources and to imprison or put them under house arrest on this basis tips the balance in favour of security over rights. Where the rights and freedoms of the few are curtailed so too are the rights and freedoms of us all.

Since 11 September 2001 governments, ministers and officials at all levels of the EU have maintained that the swathe of new measures introduced have all been 'balanced' as between the needs of security and respect for fundamental rights. Concerned civil society groups across Europe know differently as do refugees, those stopped and searched or detained and the communities subject to surveillance.

What has been seen as exceptional and draconian becomes the norm. (Bunyan 2005)

Common Features of Information Systems

Two features seem to be basic across the various surveillance systems which are developing:

(1) the integration of systems; and
(2) the weakening of state ties.

Integration of systems

The various information systems are established, as well as operated, by the same, or professionally very similar, organizations and agencies. When Schengen was formally outside the European Union (until the Amsterdam Treaty in 1997, which came into force in 1999), planning was organized so that essentially the same people could discuss Schengen issues in one meeting and other issues in the next. Important example of integration have been mentioned above. It is also possible to be more specific. I select Europol as an example.

The system was clearly planned with a view towards far-reaching integration, *inter alia*, with the Schengen Information System (SIS). For one thing, Article 10.4. No 1–3 in the Europol Convention established a whole range of authorities and bodies within the European Union, from whom Europol could request information: the European Communities and bodies within them governed by public law; other bodies governed by public law established in the framework of the European Union; and bodies based on an agreement between two or more member states within the European Union (also, Article 10.4. No 5–7 established that information could be requested from international organizations and subordinate bodies governed by public law, other bodies governed by public law based on an agreement between two or more states, and Interpol). Clearly, this opened the way for integration with the SIS. As a matter of fact, on 9 April 1997, before Europol was operational, the 'High Level Group on Organized Crime' explicitly recommended that Europol should be given access to the information stored in the SIS.[13] This and other recommendations were on the agenda of the Justice and Home Affairs' Council[14] meeting of 3 to 4 December 1998 in connection with the action plan on establishing a so-called area of freedom, security, and justice, and these recommendations were also discussed in a report of 26 February 1999.[15] The report included a discussion as to whether Europol's authority should be extended to actual searches in the SIS. A Council Decision of 24 February 2005 gives Europol the right to access and search SIS arts 95, 99 and 100. Another decision is required for implementation.

Furthermore, concrete work directed towards facilitating and easing compatibility between Europol, Schengen, and other systems has been going on for a long

---

[13] See document 7421/97 JAI 14.
[14] This comprises Justice and Home Affairs Ministers of EU member states.
[15] 6245/99 Europol 7.

time. The then Norwegian liaison officer in Interpol, Iver Frigaard, outlined a number of the issues, problems, and possible solutions in a lengthy paper as early as 1996 (Frigaard 1996). Frigaard saw Europol, Schengen, and Interpol as three 'mutually interlocking' and 'overlapping' policing initiatives. He discussed their relationship on a systems level and on the level of exchange of information in concrete cases. On the systems level he pointed to the fact that, by 1996, 'only' ten of the 45 states linked to Interpol's information system were also linked to Schengen and Europol. The number of states linking up to all three systems should and could, he argued, be increased. In connection with the exchange of information in concrete cases, he pointed to a lack of harmonization of the various data systems, and discussed, what he viewed as, the great need for compatibility between them as well as how compatibility might be attained technologically. The vigorous tenor of the paper clearly suggested that this was a matter of high priority.

It may be added that, at its meeting on 19 March 1998, the Justice and Home Affairs Council agreed, without debate and as an 'A' point, on rules allowing Europol to request and accept information from non-EU sources (pursuant to Article 10.4. No 4 of the Europol Convention). The report covered the receipt of data from 'third States and third bodies' (a relevant country was Turkey), and included only the most minimal safeguards on data protection. The plans were to be supplemented by a series of 'memorandums of understanding' between Europol and the central services of each of the non-EU states with whom data were to be exchanged.

It may also be added, beyond Europol, that numerous integrating ties exist or are in the planning with respect to the other systems. The EU Commission has recently issued a 'Communication from the Commission to the Council and the European Parliament on improved effectiveness, enhanced interoperability and synergies among European databases in the area of Justice and Home Affairs', COM (2005) 597 final (24 November 2005; the Communication has kindly been provided by Ben Hayes, Statewatch). The Commission Communication is committed to so-called 'interoperability', 'connectivity', 'synergy' and 'principle of availability' of IT systems, focusing specifically on the second generation of Schengen Information System (SIS II, see above), the Visa Information System (VIS), which is to share a 'technical platform' with SIS II, and the European Asylum System (EURODAC). The Commission is also currently working on a proposal to interlink national DNA databases and in the longer term proposes a 'European Criminal Automated Fingerprints Identification System ... combining all fingerprint data currently only available in national criminal AFIS systems'. 'European register(s) for travel documents and identity cards' – *de facto* EU population registers – are also planned along with the 'creation of an entry-exit system ... to ensure that people arriving and departing are examined and to gather information on their immigration and residence status' (information from Ben Hayes, Statewatch). For a critique of the Commission Communication, see European Data Protection Supervisor (EDPS), 'Comments of the Communication of the Commission on interoperability of European databases', Brussels 10 March 2006.

The integration of systems is taking leaps forward.

Weakening of state ties

The second common feature of information systems, is the weakening of ties between ordinary nation-state agencies and the increasingly integrated surveillance systems themselves. There is a development towards a generalized political sphere, above the reach of ordinary nation-state agencies, responsible for the surveillance systems.

National parliament members do not have the time or energy to dig deeply into the heap of documents pertaining to decisions about Schengen, Europol, or other entities. Parliamentary debates become superficial and short, accepting the premises of ministries and even police agencies. In Norway, decisions of Parliament clearly follow the proposals of the government, and the government, in turn, seems to follow the signals and proposals which are central to international police culture and thinking. The mass media, supposedly controllers of it all, are not interested in going into the detail necessary for efficient control. The media, to a large extent a part of the entertainment industry, back off: the dreary details and complexities of the surveillance systems are not in tune with the news criteria of the entertainment industry.

As a consequence, the decision-making persons and groups travelling back and forth between European cities (and especially to Brussels) gain additional discretionary power in relation to key issues. They are hard to compete with if you are closer to the grass roots and outside the higher echelons of power. Presumably, they are knowledgeable experts.

Global Control Without a State?

Are we, then, developing an over-arching, far-reaching integrated global control system existing in and of itself, and also for itself, essentially without a state?

In 1997 Gunther Teubner edited *Global Law Without a State* (Teubner 1997). Among the interesting contributions to the volume is Teubner's own introductory piece 'Global Bukowina: Legal Pluralism in the World Society' (1997: 3–28). Teubner's main concern is the development of *lex mercatoria*, the transnational law of economic transactions, mostly transnational contract law, which he views as 'the most successful example of global law without a state' (1997: 3). Global law, according to Teubner, has some characteristics which are 'significantly different from our experience of the law of the nation-state' (1997: 7):

(1) The boundaries of global law are not formed by maintaining a core territory and possibly expanding from this, but rather by invisible social networks, invisible professional communities, invisible markets which transcend territorial boundaries.

(2) General legislative bodies are less important – global law is produced in self-organized processes of what Teubner calls 'structural coupling' of law with ongoing globalized processes which are very specialized and technical.

(3) Global law exists in a diffuse but close dependence not on the institutional arrangements of nation-states (such as parliaments), but on their respective specialized social fields – in the case of *lex mercatoria*, the whole development of the expanding and global economy.

(4) For nation-building in the past, unity of law was a main political asset. A worldwide unity of law would become a threat to legal culture. It would be important to make sure that a sufficient variety of legal sources exists in a globally unified law.

In my own words, ideal-typically: transnational economic law is developed not by committees and councils established by ministries in nation-states and subsequently given sanction by parliaments, but through the work of the large and expanding professional lawyers' firms, the jet-set lawyers operating on the transnational level, tying vast capital interests together in complex agreements furthering capital interests. As *lex mercatoria* develops, it is not given subsequent primary sanction by national parliaments but is self-referential and self-validating, finding suitable 'landing points' in quasi-legislative institutions (Teubner 1997: 17) such as international chambers of commerce, international law associations, and all sorts of international business associations. It develops as a system of customary law in a diffuse zone around the valid formal law of nation-states, not inside valid formal law but not too far outside it. Eventually it becomes regarded as (equivalent to) valid formal law or at least valid legal interpretation. It develops continuously, one step building on the other, in the end validating a law or a set of legal interpretations far from the law of the nation-states.

The independence of law and legal development is the crux of the matter. There is a great debate going on concerning the independence of global *lex mercatoria* – Teubner calls it a thirty years' war. I will not enter that war here, but simply ask the question: do we, in recent developments in the late twentieth and early twenty-first century, see signs of a developing independent global control system, a kind of frightening *lex vigilatoria* of political and social control? Global control without a state?

The question is complex. There are certainly ties between nation-states and, say, Schengen, the SIRENE exchange, EURODAC, communication control through retention and eventual tapping of telecommunications traffic data, the spy system Echelon, and so on. For one thing, some of them are established or proposed at national level first. The above-mentioned story about how the EU directive on mandatory retention of telecommunications traffic data came about, is an example. Secondly, some of the systems are established through various joint national efforts – some of them complex (meetings and memos over ten years concerning communications control; the lengthy negotiations over Schengen), some of them simpler (framework decisions involving agreements of ministers from the nation-states), some of them very simple (quick common positions cleared by governments). Thirdly, agreements such as partnerships in Schengen, Europol, and EURODAC have to be sanctioned by national parliaments.

At the same time, there are signs suggesting that systems, such as the ones I have discussed, are not only increasingly becoming integrated or 'interlocked', but also increasingly becoming untied or 'de-coupled' from the nation-states. For one thing, as I have mentioned already, the parliamentary nation-state sanctioning of arrangements such as Schengen, Europol, and EURODAC largely takes place without in-depth debates in public space, and, significantly, without parties and members of parliaments really knowing, to any degree of detail, the systems they are sanctioning. Parties and members must necessarily trust the work being done by various sub-committees and so on deep inside the EU structure, over and above agencies of the nation-states. There is neither time nor motive for anything else. An example is the scrutiny of the various *aquis*, enormous heaps of documents drastically reducing transparency for an ordinary parliament member (or even a researcher).

Furthermore, once the various interlocking systems are up and running, they interlock further through informal agreements and arrangements, rapidly expanding their practices – a kind of customary law, again in the diffuse zone of valid formal law. And the systems expand in response to internal sociological forces and logic, far from the control of nation-state institutions. In other words, the systems are increasingly integrated *horizontally*. There are numerous examples of this. There seems to be an important relationship between the *horizontal* integration or interlocking aspects of the various systems, and the *vertical* weakening of ties or de-coupling aspects to nation-state agencies: The more integrated or interlocked the systems become (*horizontal* integration), the more independent of, or de-coupled from, national-state institutions they will be (*vertical* weakening of ties) when the agendas for future developments and operations are set. Integration, interlocking, links the systems together in functional terms. Given moves are therefore simply regarded as 'necessary' or imperative, irrespective of the thinking which might be valid at the nation-state level. Interlocking at the system level also makes particular developments seem imperative from the point of view of the nation-state level. For example, the 'package' consisting of the SIS, Europol, and EURODAC, in which all three systems are increasingly intertwined in terms cooperation and goals, has made it increasingly 'obvious' and 'necessary' for Norway to participate in all three of them – if not without debate, at least with a minimum of debate. The question of Norwegian participation in the first of these, the SIS, created some critical debate. Norwegian participation in Europol and EURODAC hardly reached the newspapers or television at all.

Eventually, the interlockings and de-couplings are taken as *faits accomplis*, simply to be reckoned with. System functionaries – and there are thousands of them – take pride and find legitimacy in such developments. They become part and parcel of their system, defining their system as something they should foster, feeling great satisfaction when they manage to make the system function still better. These are entirely commonplace processes; this is how we all become more or less enveloped by the systems we are working in (Mathiesen 2004). A small example: in a discussion with Norwegian Schengen personnel some years ago, I ventured to guess that their workings were not all that rational after all – they probably took great pride and satisfaction in the computerized technical and complex activities they were involved in and were continuously developing. The response was instant – fumbling with papers, some blushing, some openly agreeing. To be sure, the various interlocking systems have their 'landing points', but, much like *lex mercatoria*, not in responsible parliamentary settings, but in quasi-legislative institutions – in this case especially, branches of the law enforcement agencies with their strongly vested interests.

Conclusion

A cautious conclusion for the time being: the various interlocking systems do not develop quite of their own accord, but with, what I would call, increasingly and strongly *diluted* ties to the institutions of the nation-states. While not global law fully without a state, a dilution of connections with the formal institutions of the nation-state is taking place. Most significantly, the institution of parliamentary sanction has become, at least in several European states, a perfunctory exercise with a silent public as a context.

But perhaps a 'state' is re-entering the scene on a different level? At least as far as the European control systems are concerned, the importance of the institutions of the European Union is enhanced as the nation-state institutions fade. Any state, including a European one, requires certain institutions. One of them is policing (but not necessarily the kind we are witnessing today).

However, the European control systems, though largely emanating from the European Union, also have tentacles far beyond the Union, interlocking horizontally with various systems of control in the United States and other parts of the western world. The EU-FBI attempts, pointed out so clearly by Statewatch, to develop transnational communication control over the last ten years is a case in point.

Are we, then, facing once again a developing, unfinished, expanding global control, if not without a state, at least with increasingly diluted ties to state institutions? A *lex vigilatoria*, if not developing entirely of its own accord, at least with strong internal social forces leading the development, and control measures increasingly out of state control?

If so, we need to understand these social forces better if we are to oppose and contain them. A penetrating and critical research project exactly on this issue would be in order. Such a project could develop into a counter-force. From a critical point of view, it is vital to stem this tide before it is too late.

8

Welfare and Punishment in Comparative Perspective[1]

David Downes and Kirstine Hansen

Introduction

The past two decades of work on the social analysis of punishment have arguably neglected the impact of the commitment to welfare on the scale of imprisonment. This chapter explores several possible reasons for its marginalization and argues the case for its reinstatement as a topic of central importance. The achievement of penal welfarism in *relative* decarceration gains support from the work of Beckett and Western (2001) and from cross-national data on prison numbers and welfare spending. Time series analysis suggests an increasing trade-off between welfare and penal capital, and that the commitment to welfare constitutes a growing constraint on the shift to a more punitive culture of control.

Penal-welfarism or Penality versus Welfare?

Welfare, the 'Welfare State', and allied forms of social provision for human needs were for the first two-thirds of the past century the principal hope of criminologists, penal reformers, and most politicians for the reduction of crime and punishment alike. The high point of that system of beliefs in Britain was arguably reached in the 1950s, with the publication of *Penal Practice in a Changing Society* in 1959 (see especially Bailey 1987, Bottoms and Stevenson 1992, Garland 1985, and Garland and Young 1983). The watershed of the late 1960s and early 1970s saw those hopes dashed, and the principles and assumptions that supported them subject to fundamental challenge. As a result, the last 30 years have seen optimism about welfare in dramatic decline, in relation to crime and punishment, ironically during a period of continued

[1] We would like to express our thanks to Sarah Armstrong, Stephen Machin, Tim Newburn, and Paul Rock for timely help and constructive criticism.

growth in welfare investment and provision. We are now at a point where 'welfare' aims, ideals, and institutions are increasingly and unduly marginalized as key variables in criminal justice policy and practice. The pendulum, as pendulums tend to do, has swung too far away from the view that welfare can or, indeed, should have any real purchase on the character of crime and punishment.

There are several substantial developments that account for so fundamental a shift in criminological perspectives. First, the long and broad reach of the 'Nothing Works' standpoint triggered a vehement reaction against the largely unexamined commitment to rehabilitation as the main aim of punishment. Martinson's widely unread but hugely influential paper (1974) was in many respects a necessary corrective to facile optimism about the aims and methods of rehabilitating offenders. It brought to a head an upsurge of studies which showed little or no beneficial impact being made on young offenders even by 'enriched' forms of residential treatment (see, for example, Bottoms and McClintock 1973, Clarke and Cornish 1975). It did *not* state that nothing could ever work. But it did tend to focus on general rather than specific impacts, so that the extent to which some programmes might work for some groups, but by no means all, was obscured. And its impact did contribute, or even amount to a paradigmatic revolution. The post-Martinson era was bleak indeed for the 'caring' professions of social work, probation and parole in particular, with the heady idealism of the past half century suddenly hitting the buffers of scientific rebuttal. And even when the groundswell of opposition to its pessimism about rehabilitation became the 'What Works?' counter-movement, it was on the changed basis of programmes which had to prove their worth in crime reduction and/or cost terms, rather than that worth simply being assumed, on broad 'help and support' principles. The programmes also tied the hands of practitioners in ways which subtly undermined their professionalism in counselling and claims to expertise in interpersonal skills. Moreover, the gloom about rehabilitation came to be extended to welfare in general. Whatever claims could be made for an increased investment in welfare, they could no longer include any assumptions about reducing crime or punishment. At the same time, the case for disconnecting the process of sentencing from welfare considerations was forcefully mounted by proponents of the 'just deserts' principle (notably by Von Hirsch 1976).

There have, nonetheless, been a plethora of initiatives, programmes, and 'New Deals' mounted by New Labour in Britain over the past nine years of office, some of which, such as the 'Sure Start' (the UK version of the US 'Head Start') programme, derive in part from a strong welfarist tradition. But they remain relatively modest or minimally resourced compared with the core institutions of the 'Welfare State' – the health, education, income maintenance, and social security services which still account for some two-thirds of government expenditure. It is with this basically non-penal structure of the welfare system that this chapter is chiefly concerned.

Secondly, an emerging dominant influence on scholarly thought meant academic research in the area began either to ignore the distinctive importance of welfare, or to see it only for its social control similarities to punishment. If after Martinson the field could never be the same again, how much more so was that the case after the work of Foucault (1979), whose major analytical aim was to connect punishment with post-Enlightenment processes of normalization, regulation, and discipline throughout all social institutions?

Whilst taking issue with key aspects of Foucault's work, in building upon it, Cohen (1985), Garland (1985), and Rose (1980) have tended to view welfare institutions and practices as essentially complementary to, rather than competing with, penality. Two consequences flow from this form of analysis. First, welfare tends too easily to become *little more than* a novel set of bureaucratic and constraining methods: the ends come to be seen as ineluctably subverted by the means. It becomes extremely difficult to accommodate forms of mutual aid and altruism within this model, despite their active development as part of welfare services (see, for example, Titmuss 1974). Secondly, the linking of welfare to penality in Garland's conception of penal-welfarism (1985, 2001) has the effect of welfare becoming subsumed rather than analysed as a variable in its own right.

Garland's path-breaking work (1985) analysed how the re-drawing of the social contract, the enlargement of citizenship, and the intervention of the state into the market for welfare ends, enabled the parallel movement towards a much greater use of community and rehabilitative measures for offenders to be established. And Garland (2001) has in particular linked the waning of penal-welfarism with that of relative decarceration. Yet the concept of penal-welfarism also lends itself to an uncoupling of its two components: penal and welfare capital, as it were. The logic of the formulation points to an inverse relationship between them. Hence the eminently justified warnings that are borne out in a host of changes to welfare 'contracts', and even their liquidation, in the United States, as accompaniments to the rise of mass imprisonment.

Legislation under President Clinton literally and symbolically abolished a welfarist approach to family benefits. The Personal Responsibility and Work Opportunity Reconciliation Act (1996)(PRWORA) created the 'Temporary Assistance for Needy Families' state block grant programme, which replaced the Aid to Families with Dependent Children Act, a founding piece of New Deal legislation that created a not quite unconditional, but still a moral and non-time limited, duty to aid poor families. The replacement of this core commitment with law and policy language, using the words 'work opportunity' and 'temporary', captures the move to a contractarian, time limited, and otherwise heavily conditional approach. It is a historical irony that the less stringent but still clear shift in Britain to this approach is dignified by the term 'New Deal'.

A related development is the ingenious adaptation of the insurance principle to the actuarial character of the newfound 'Risk Society' (Beck 1992, Feeley and Simon 1992). Social insurance as the collective, public, and often, though by no means always, state provided cover against risk, is increasingly deemed archaic. As collective provision is withdrawn to devolve responsibility onto individuals themselves to insure against risk – a trend most pronounced in Britain in the pensions field – new forms of marketization have been developed to bridge the gap between the two. Insofar as the state still has to foot the bill, it demands 'value for money' and older notions of judging public services are replaced by an economistic paradigm of measuring performance in financial management accounting terms. As the 'audit society' (Power 1997) fuses with the 'risk society', means notoriously over-determine ends, so that the very character of health and education provision, for example, come increasingly to be shaped by performance indicators. *In extremis*, the sale of school playing fields and hospital closures to release land for the property market counts as enhanced health and education. This might be so where the resources so released are devoted to better provision of those services. All too often, however, they are used to trim budgets. Insofar as these developments also permeate the areas of criminal justice and penal policy, they have comparable effects, as for example in the 'privatization' of court services and prison management.

However, the fields of crime and punishment can run counter to those of welfare. Budgets for the former have often waxed as those for the latter have waned. Forms of blanket crime prevention coverage proliferate, as in the explosion of electronic surveillance and adolescent curfew, whilst universal provision of welfare is displaced by selective provision or none at all. In sum, the effect of this important stream of work has been arguably to over-emphasize the symmetry between welfare and penal institutions and to underplay their distinctive differences.

Thirdly, the evident failure of welfare provision to prevent rising crime has undoubtedly damaged the case that its proponents can mount for its expansion and even, in some respects, its retention. Scandinavian criminologists, in particular, have been hard-pressed to defend the scale of the commitment to welfare in the teeth of crime rates which, since 1945 in Sweden, for example, have climbed as substantially as in far less welfare conscious societies, though Henrik Tham analysed the evidence to show a steeper rise in crime in England in the Thatcher era of the 1980s and early 1990s, than occurred in Sweden (Tham 1998, cf Smith 1995). A 'double failure' is implicated in one sense: not only has welfare failed to prevent rising crime, but also criminology has failed to predict and explain that failure (Young 1985). But Jock Young could only make that case against a particularly spavined type of criminology, a multi-factorial meliorism. His solution, Left Realism, had its roots in a far more sociologically informed criminology, the tradition of anomie theory which rested on analysing the consequences for deviance of structural inequality. Once welfare provision, however redistributive along social democratic lines, is located within a fundamentally capitalist political economy, its impact is necessarily shaped by the immense inequalities that obtain in almost every sphere of social, cultural, and economic experience. Without substantial welfare provision, it remains the case that far worse forms of criminality than burglary and disorganized street crime would arguably ensue, 'mafiaization' and much higher rates of lethal violence among these (see Currie 1998: 120–57 for a convincing distillation of comparative evidence, especially on the United States; and Rawlinson (1998) and Panasyuk (2000) on the transitional states of Russia and Ukraine respectively).

Moreover, the gradual dawning of the realization that welfare has limited, if any, impact on rising crime rates all too easily gives way to the presentiment that welfare actually makes things worse. In the hands of Charles Murray (1984, 1990), welfare, far from being any kind of solution, becomes the source of the growth of the problem. Murray's widely publicized and corporate think-tank backed thesis runs that generous welfare services promote 'underclass' dependency and illegitimacy, which in turn promote spiralling rates of crime and delinquency. The answer is not more but less welfare and not less but more prison. That the balance of evidence weighs heavily against all parts of this thesis (Jencks and Peterson 1991, NACRO 1995) has done little to deflect Murray from its active propagation. The more recent work of Beckett and Western (2001) in effect amounts to a devastating refutation of Murray. Murray's case, however, is fundamentally immune to refutation, being the tip of the iceberg of what Robert Pinker (1971) memorably termed the 'Spencerian underground': the ideology that state intervention in the 'free market' for welfare ends promotes the survival of the unfittest.

A fourth source of disillusionment with the prospects for welfare provision is the evident failure of social services to deliver the goods in key fields, most lamentably to the most deprived and vulnerable groups. For example, Pat Carlen (1996) has long criticized the 'care' services for amounting to the uncaring services: having been 'in care' is heavily associated with imprisonment. A succession of reports on catastrophic failures in child protection, involving fatalities and sexual abuse, has dented faith in the capacity of the system to do its most fundamental job well. It is worth adding that social workers may be the only profession to be denied any public record of success, for reasons well analysed by Dingwall, Eekelaar, and Murray (1995). By contrast, prison officers 'foil' escape attempts. Police 'swoop' on drug-dealers and 'break' organized crime. Even teachers, a usually maligned group, are allowed occasional success stories. The net result is the public association of the personal social services with failure and neglect rather than successful intervention. Moreover, a long-standing tradition of work in the social policy field has been to discover yet further ways in which the system benefits the more prosperous rather than the most disadvantaged (see Glennerster and Hills 1998, especially 322–4, for a measured overview). This eventually had the unwanted side-effect of discouraging the case for increasing welfare provision as it would only help those who needed it least. The main point of the critics, that welfare provision needed to be far better resourced and shaped to meet the needs of the most disadvantaged, was missed or ignored.

Fifthly, the case against the 'Welfare State' from the neo-marxist left has long been that its development is fundamentally a prop for capitalist exploitation, a spur to false consciousness, and a set of concessions made to the working class to be withdrawn when the going gets tough. Theories of fiscal crisis which, in the 1970s (O'Connor 1973), focused on the growing resistance by the more affluent workers to meet the taxation bills for increased welfare, tend now to be couched in the new 'realities' of globalization. Welfare has become too great a cost to bear in a deregulated world of fast-moving capital and largely immobile labour. The idea that 'welfare' can ever do more than mask punishment, never taken seriously by the radical left, meets even greater resistance in the era of turbo-capitalism.

In combination, and despite their immense differences, these powerful critiques have made it difficult to sustain the view that commitment to welfare continues to offer, indeed has ever offered, a viable alternative to imprisonment and such carceral equivalents as house arrest and electronic tagging. Yet the evidence for the view that welfare capital offers just such a real alternative to penal capital is too substantial to be dismissed or ignored. As Bottoms argued twenty years ago, 'perhaps the very fact that Britain has developed more extensive state welfare provision [than the United States] allows a degree of social control in the informal structures of society such that the formal supervision of offenders – by in effect disciplinary means – becomes less necessary' (1983: 194). Despite the wealth of theory and research since that point was made (see Hudson 2002 for a comprehensive overview) it remains what he termed a 'neglected feature' of contemporary penal systems.

The Poisoning of the Wells

Added to its own merits as a case worth examining, the basis for investment in welfare as distinct from penal capital is now under more severe threat than at any point since 1945. In the past few years, the contrast between the competing political economies of Europe and the United States has become, if anything, even sharper. What one of us then termed the 'macho penal economy' (Downes 2001) has grown in size to surpass the mark of two million prisoners held daily in the United States. Even more deadly, in terms of prospects for the reversal of that trend to mass imprisonment, has been the outcome of the American presidential election of 2000. In the most rigorous assessment of the impact of not only prisoner but felon disenfranchisement on election results in the United States, Uggen and Manza conclude:

In examining presidential elections, we find that the Republican presidential victory of 2000 would have been reversed had felons been allowed to vote, and that the Democratic presidential victory of 1960 may have been jeopardized had contemporary rates of disenfranchisement prevailed at that time. Disenfranchised felons and ex-felons currently make up 2.28 percent of the voting age population, a figure that we project may rise to 3 percent within 10 years . . . Because the margin of victory in 3 of the last 10 presidential elections has been 1.1 percent of the voting age population or less, felon disenfranchisement could be a decisive factor in future presidential races. (Uggen and Manza 2002: 794)

Uggen and Manza go on to summarize felon disenfranchisement as but one of the many factors making for the social exclusion of minority and especially African-American groups, a large majority of whose votes are historically for Democrat rather than Republican candidates, and argue for the restoration of voting rights to ex-felons as a key step in any social inclusion programme. However, it is worth noting an all too evident implication of these findings for the future of American democracy. Whether or not they were aware of it before, the immense political bonus of felon disenfranchisement for the Republican Party will hardly have escaped the attention of its strategists. It is this factor above all which logically constitutes an extraordinary incentive for the Republicans to maintain or even drive up the momentum of their 'war on crime and drugs' penal legislation, locking America in even more permanently to a macho, supermax-ridden system of mass imprisonment. For the Democratic Party, which presided over the doubling of the scale of the prison population in the 1990s, to contest this state of affairs at all vigorously would mean their risking the charge of being 'soft on crime' – the very fear which led Clinton to adopt 'tough on crime' policies in the run-up to the 1992 election and throughout two presidential terms. Yet it is that prospect which any new Democratic Party leadership must face if they are to contest future presidential and state elections, crucial for the composition of the Senate, on anything like an equal footing. Democrats could mount such a challenge on a number of grounds. The denial of the vote to several million citizens makes a mockery of democracy. The vast penal archipelago is also a threat to public health. As Megan Comfort (2003) has shown in convincing detail, the US prison system is a hugely disproportionate source of hepatitis C, HIV, and tuberculosis, by its neglect of basic healthcare among prisoners.

It may well be, of course, that mass imprisonment in the United States comes in time to lose its sway as the automatic answer to problems of crime, drugs, and 'law and order'. It may come about through recession, and the huge budgetary costs of the penal system becoming unsustainable. But the electoral pressures for it to be maintained have increased sharply over the past few years for electoral reasons. What this huge trend represents is a poisoning of the democratic wells. It also means that, albeit indirectly, US criminal justice and penal policy is making an unprecedented impact on global politics. It is, for example, improbable in the extreme that the invasion of Iraq would have been mounted by President Gore.

The same forces are at work in Britain, though to a far less damaging extent. England and Wales in particular, Scotland much less so (see Smith 1999), have since 1992 been ruled in bipartisan fashion by political parties who favour a hybrid version of European and American policies in both social and economic realms. Thus Britain has been characterized famously as a country which prefers European levels of welfare paid for by American levels of taxation. The country has come to adopt a quasi-American winner/loser culture (James 1993) along-side a monarchy and adapted aristocratic forms. New Labour's 'third way' policies have been a complex confusion of reformist and punitive measures, within which are discernible trends towards the 'criminalization of social policy' (Crawford 1998) and indeed the 'criminalization' of criminal justice policy. The first takes as its chief criterion of worth whether or not, and the degree to which, certain social reforms have crime prevention or reduction outcomes, rather than the extent to which they are worth doing in their own right. The second elevates crime reduction to the principal end of the criminal justice system, which one may have thought should be the actual accomplishment of criminal justice. Some 40 years ago Jerome Skolnick (1966) posed the dilemma for all systems of striking the balance between law *versus* order, and Packer (1968) talked of 'due process' and 'crime control' models of law enforcement. That dilemma is increasingly being resolved in favour of the latter, 'tougher', more illiberal, and authoritarian set of options. In Britain, serious erosion of the presumption of innocence, double jeopardy, trial by jury, and other, formerly bedrock, attributes of the rights of defendants are imminent or already enacted.

Exploring the Interaction Between Welfare and Imprisonment

In the most systematic study to date of the links between welfare and imprison-ment, Beckett and Western (2001) view social and penal policy as inextricably linked, both relating to the way policy responds to social marginality. Informed by Esping-Anderson's (1990) concept of 'policy regimes',[2] Beckett and Western argue that regimes (US states in their case) vary according to their commitment to including or excluding marginal groups. Inclusive regimes emphasize the social causes of marginality and aim to integrate the socially marginalized by providing generous welfare programmes. They therefore have less harsh views on crime and are likely to have lower imprisonment rates. Exclusionary regimes, on the other hand, lay responsibility for social problems in the hands of the socially margin-alized. Thus the unemployed are undeserving, deviancy is unjustifiable, and deviants are non-reformable. Such regimes offer less generous welfare provisions, take a harsher stance on crime, and are more likely to favour imprisonment.

Beckett and Western test this idea using data from 32 US states for the years 1975, 1985, and 1995. After controlling for a number of factors which could affect the relationship of primary interest they find a negative relationship between imprisonment and welfare spending. They also find statistically

[2] Defined as the grouping of particular social and economic policies, where each group is characterized by a particular kind of welfare state policy regime.

significant positive associations between imprisonment in a state and the proportion of the population that is black, the percentage of other minority groups such as Hispanic, the poverty rate, and Republican representation in the state. Most of these relationships are found to be stronger in 1995 than in earlier periods and this leads Beckett and Western to suggest that social and penal policy are only closely tied at specific times 'when efforts are made to alter prevailing approaches to social marginality' (2001: 46) as was the case with the Reagan administration. Not only did states with less generous welfare spending have higher imprisonment rates in the 1990s, but this later period also saw states with a higher proportion of blacks, other ethnic minorities, and greater poverty having higher imprisonment rates. Thus Beckett and Western argue 'the more exclusionary approaches to social marginality are especially likely to be adopted by states which house more of those defined in contemporary political discourse as 'trouble makers' (2001: 46).

The major criticism that has been justifiably made of their analysis is that, as Greenberg states, 'implicit in the statistical procedures used by Beckett and Western and all previous analysts of state imprisonment is the assumption that each state formulates its penal policies independently of every other state. This seems unlikely. Governors meet periodically to discuss state policy. It would be surprising if they did not at times attend to policy innovations and outcomes in other states'. (Greenberg 2001: 84). However, the soundness of Greenberg's criticism of the view that each state generates its own 'policy regime' regardless of that in other states, and of the over-arching influence of the national government to promote punitive policies by financial leverage, should not be taken to apply to the reality of the immense variation between states in the delivery of penal pain and its inverse relationship to welfare provision. By the same token, as Newburn (2001) has argued, 'policy transfers' take place between nation-states, often in a highly asymmetrical fashion, as exemplified by the impact of US criminal justice policies on the politics of law and order in Britain. That does not negate the need to look at cross-national as well as inter-state variations on the welfare versus punishment theme.

Comparative Analysis of the Punishment and Welfare Thesis

Cross-country welfare differences

The United States is not the only country where welfare policies are becoming tougher. Such policies in other countries where welfare has traditionally been more encompassing than in the United States, such as Europe, are increasingly incorporating aspects of the United States' market driven approach to welfare (Gilbert 2002). According to Gilbert, this is occurring for a number of reasons, including the fact that an aging population places additional burdens on the welfare state. He also argues that globalization of the economy increasingly means that firms are free to locate where wages and taxes are lower and this has placed pressure on countries with strong welfare states, where wages are generally higher and high levels of taxation are required to fund the welfare provisions.

Despite these trends there remain huge differences in the generosity of welfare provision across different countries. This can be highlighted with reference to two examples. Withstanding recent changes, the Nordic and Scandinavian countries largely continue to provide a generous universal welfare state (Kuhnle *et al* 2000). For example, Sweden provides the most generous paid parental leave, increased child allowances, and increased funding for pre-school and public care. This means that Sweden is a country with high labour market security and, for the most part, low unemployment. A smaller proportion of its workforce are low paid, it has a low incidence of poverty and much less income inequality than seen elsewhere (Freeman and Katz 1995). As Greenberg argues: 'One may thus see the comparative leniency of the Dutch and the Scandinavian criminal justice systems and their low degree of economic inequality (which is substantially a product of their generously funded welfare systems) as manifestations of a high degree of empathic identification and concern for the well-being of others.' (1999: 296–7).

On the other hand, liberal market approaches to the welfare state, typified by the United States, provide minimal welfare provisions for their citizens. Worried about creating a culture of dependency there are strict conditions (that vary by state) for receiving welfare and a time limit on the duration of welfare receipt. Emphasis is very much on getting people into work, rather than preventing poverty. There is less concern with redistribution or equity across the classes, taxes are low[3] and subsequently so too is welfare spending. It is hardly surprising, then, that the United States has a much greater incidence of low pay and earnings dispersion[4] than other countries. For the country that epitomises James' (1993) winner/loser society, inequality among citizens is great, with a small group of high achievers and a long tail of low achievers (Hansen and Vignoles 2005).

It is not difficult to see how differences in welfare state generosity could be related to imprisonment. Not only does a generous welfare state insure citizens against income loss, protecting them from poverty and low pay, it also creates social harmony, and a sense of equality and security for everyone (Atkinson

[3] In 2000 the total tax wedge rate (including employer's social security contributions) for the US was 29.6%. Among OECD countries only Japan and Korea, with 27.1% and 26.1% respectively, had lower rates (OECD 2002). The UK had a rate of 37.4%, while for Sweden, Denmark, and Finland the rates were 54.2%, 48.8%, and 46.9% respectively.

[4] With 24.7% of full-time workers earning less than two-thirds of full-time median earnings, the US has the highest incidence of low pay in 2000 of the 23 countries examined in OECD *Society at a Glance* (2002). In terms of earnings dispersion the US, with a 9th decile to 1st decile earnings ratio of 4.64, has the second largest gap between those at the top of the pay scale and those at the bottom, and is second only to Hungary which has a ratio of 4.92 (*ibid*).

1999). On the other hand, a less generous welfare state is associated with greater inequality among its citizens and the ensuing social problems that this brings.[5] There are clear differences for the citizens of these countries not only in the standard of living, but also in perceptions of fairness, and ultimately in the social cohesion and stability of their society (Kuhnle *et al* 2000). Drawing upon these differences we construct the key hypothesis of this chapter, namely that welfare and imprisonment are inversely related.

Data

This hypothesis is put to the test using comparative data from nineteen countries from the Organisation for Economic Co-operation and Development (OECD). The data on imprisonment refers to the number of individuals held in penal institutions, including pre-trial detainees as well as those convicted and sentenced.[6] From this number an imprisonment rate is calculated as the number of individuals in prison per 100,000 of the adult population in each country.[7] The population figures come from the US 'Bureau of the Census' international database. Welfare expenditure data (which include public expenditure on a range of services)[8] come from the OECD 'Social Expenditure' database (2001), which is published in *Society at a Glance* (OECD 2002). The OECD also provides the source of 'Gross Domestic Product' (GDP) data, which together with the welfare expenditure are used to calculate the percentage of GDP spent on welfare. A range of control variables such as International Labour Organisation (ILO) unemployment rates[9] and international crime rates are also used.[10]

---

[5] Such as a high teenage birth rate. In 1998 the US teenage birth rate was 52.1%, by far the highest of the 28 Countries compared by UNICEF (2001). The UK, which had the next highest rate of 30.8%, looks small in comparison. The comparable rates for Sweden, Denmark, and Finland were 6.5%, 8.1%, and 9.2% respectively.

[6] Published on the UN Criminal Justice Information Network web page <http://www.umcjin.org/Statistics>.

[7] Due to the way the population data was grouped by age, the adult population includes all those over the age of 15. This was done because children are not included in the imprisoned population (the numerator) so including them in the denominator would be misleading. Also Beckett and Western use only the state adult population in their analysis. However, for this reason the numbers are in places marginally different from those published in the World Prison Population List (Home Office 2003) which uses the entire national population as the base group.

[8] These include old-age cash benefits, disability benefits, funding for occupational injury and disease, sickness benefits, services for the elderly and disabled, survivors, family cash benefits, family services, active labour market programmes, unemployment benefits, health, housing, and other contingencies.

[9] ILO unemployment rates include, but are not limited to, individuals claiming unemployment-related benefits. This broader measure is less likely to be correlated with the welfare expenditure variable.

[10] These come from the UN Office of Drugs and Crime <http://www.unodc.org/unodc/en/crime_cicp_surveys.html>.

Table 8.1. Descriptive statistics on imprisonment, GDP, and welfare across countries, 1998

Country	Imprisonment ranking	Imprisonment rate (per 100,000 of the population aged 15+)*	GDP spent on welfare (%)	Welfare score
United States	1	666	14.6	−8.2
Portugal	2	146	18.2	−4.6
New Zealand	3	144	21.0	−1.8
United Kingdom	4	124	20.8	−2.0
Canada	5	115	18.0	−4.8
Spain	6	112	19.7	−3.1
Australia	7	106	17.8	−5.0
Germany	8	95	26.0	3.2
France	9	92	28.8	6.0
Luxemburg	10	92	22.1	−0.7
Italy	11	86	25.1	2.3
Netherlands	12	85	24.5	1.7
Switzerland	13	79	28.1	5.3
Belgium	14	77	24.5	1.7
Denmark	15	63	29.8	7.0
Sweden	16	60	31.0	8.2
Finland	17	54	26.5	3.7
Japan	18	42	14.7	−8.1

Data are from 1998.

* These are the numbers held either as remand prisoners or those convicted and sentenced per 100,000 of the population aged 15 and over. These numbers are slightly different from those published in the World Prison Population list, which gives the imprisonment rate per 100,000 of the entire population. We have excluded young children here, as they are excluded from the imprisoned population.

Descriptive statistics

The basic relationship between imprisonment and welfare spending is examined in Table 8.1, which ranks countries according to their imprisonment rate alongside the percentage of their GDP spent on welfare and their welfare score[11] in 1998.

As Beckett and Western (2001) found using US state-level data, welfare generosity and imprisonment rates appear to be negatively correlated. A simple Spearman rank correlation between the imprisonment rate and the percentage of GDP spent on welfare is −0.56 (with an associated p-value of 0.01). Of the seven countries with the highest imprisonment rates all spend below average proportions of their GDP on welfare, while the eight countries with the lowest imprisonment rates all spend above average proportions of their GDP on welfare, with the exception of Japan.[12] Supporting the earlier discussion, Denmark,

[11] This is measured as the proportion of GDP spent on welfare in a particular country compared to the mean of all countries examined.

[12] Although it should be borne in mind that in Japan at least some of the welfare provision is corporate in nature. This is not accounted for in the data used here.

Sweden, and Finland all spend among the highest proportion of their GDP on welfare and have the lowest imprisonment rates. At the other extreme, the United States spends the smallest proportion of its GDP on welfare and has by far the highest imprisonment rate of the countries examined here.

Table 8.1 is just a snapshot of one point in time[13] and is used to illustrate the basic relationship between imprisonment and social welfare. However, examining data over time, allows us to set these numbers within a wider context of the temporal evolution of imprisonment and welfare spending. This may help to inform us about the determinants or driving forces which lie behind differences in imprisonment rates observed in the cross-sectional data.

This distinction between levels at a point in time and changes over time is important. Over the last ten years or so the imprisonment rate of many countries has been increasing. According to Walmsley (2000), the general trend in imprisonment in the 1990s has been upward, with most countries recording increases of around 20 per cent. Only Sweden and Finland have seen declining imprisonment rates. These increases cannot be accounted for by changes in the crime rates, which in many countries have been stable or even declining. Moreover, the demographic and socio-economic determinants of crime have seen too little change in themselves to explain the large shifts in imprisonment. Instead, Walmsley (2000) argues, much of the rise in prison numbers is attributable to changes in policy which have seen a greater use of custody and the imposition of longer sentences. In the United Kingdom the number of people in prison rose by 50 per cent during the 1990s, fuelled by a 40 per cent increase in the use of custodial sentences and a 10 per cent rise in average sentence lengths (*ibid*). These policy changes were seen as a response to (among other things) a growing fear of crime and loss of confidence in the criminal justice system among the population, which made the general public more favourable towards harsh criminal justice policies. Thus, in certain countries, particularly the United States and to a lesser extent the United Kingdom, public demand for tougher and longer sentences has been met by public policy and election campaigns which have been fought and won on the grounds of the punitiveness of penal policy. In other countries, such as Sweden and Finland, where the government provides greater 'insulation against emotions generated by moral panic and long term cycles of tolerance and intolerance' (Tonry 1999), citizens have been less likely to call for, and support, harsher penal policies and the government has resisted the urge to implement such plans.

Regression analysis

The previous analysis shows a point in time link between lower imprisonment rates and higher welfare spending across countries. This negative association can

---

[13] That time is 1998 and is dictated by the fact that data from 1998 is the latest available for social welfare expenditure (obtainable without paying a fee).

Table 8.2. Percentage of GDP spent on welfare and imprisonment rates across 18 OECD countries, 1998.

	Including the US and Japan			Excluding the US and Japan		
	(1)	(2)	(3)	(4)	(5)	(6)
Percentage of GDP spent on welfare	−29.25*	−24.87*	−46.14*	−2.89***	−3.00***	−3.04***
	(16.78)	(13.77)	(22.12)	(.586)	(.738)	(.789)
ILO unemployment rate		−10.90	3.96		−.809	−.690
		(9.95)	(17.61)		(1.09)	(1.41)
Lagged crime rate (1997)			.058			.000
			(.048)			(.002)
R-squared	.366	.382	.524	.364	.393	.393
Sample size	18	18	18	16	16	16

Robust standard errors in parenthesis

*** >1% significance level, ** 5%, * 10%

be probed and examined more rigorously by carrying out regression analysis. This permits us to consider the role played by other factors correlated with imprisonment (and welfare spending) and to examine whether the negative relationship remains once these additional factors are controlled for.

Table 8.2 shows a number of simple cross-sectional regressions of imprisonment rates on the generosity of welfare spending on imprisonment rates in 1998. The table reports results from six specifications. The first specification in column 1 is the simple regression of imprisonment rates on the proportion of GDP spent on welfare. The second specification (column 2) controls for ILO unemployment to try to proxy for some of the structural differences across countries which may be associated with imprisonment.[14] The third specification (column 3) additionally controls for a lagged measure of the crime rate. It is important to include this measure in the model as we do not want to confound our results with other factors which may be related to the dependent variable.[15]

The first specification, in column 1, simply restates the finding of a negative association between welfare spending and imprisonment, as shown in the descriptive statistics. This is statistically significant at the 10 per cent level, indicating that countries which spend a greater amount on welfare have lower imprisonment rates. The inclusion of controls for ILO unemployment in

[14] As mentioned previously, ILO unemployment should be less correlated with welfare expenditure than claimant count unemployment.

[15] To reduce the endogeneity of including the crime rate as a right hand side variable in a model of imprisonment, the crime rate has been lagged by one year.

specification 2, has little effect on the coefficient of interest, which remains negative and statistically significant at the 10 per cent level. The coefficient on
unemployment itself is statistically no different from zero. When a measure of the
crime rate (one year lagged) is entered into the model in column 3, the coefficient
on the percentage of GDP spent on welfare retains its statistical significance and
increases in magnitude. The coefficients on both the unemployment rate and the
lagged measure of crime remain statistically insignificant. Thus, even after controlling for a number of factors which may be related to imprisonment, there
remains a negative relationship between welfare spending and imprisonment.

These results very much confirm the earlier picture and appear robust even
when crime rates are included in the models. However, the United States and
Japan are very much outliers in the data, the first with an extremely high
imprisonment rate, the second an extremely low one. This is shown in Figure 8.1
below and in Table 8.1 above. Including these observations in the data may not
only be causing the coefficients and standard errors in the analysis to be misleading, but they may in fact be driving the negative relationship found between
welfare expenditure and imprisonment. For this reason, the right hand side of
the table reports specifications 4 to 6 that are identical to 1 to 3 except they
exclude the United States and Japan.

When this is done, the magnitude of the coefficient and the size of the
standard errors are greatly reduced, but the basic tenor of the results remains
unchanged. In all three specifications, countries that spend a greater proportion
of GDP on welfare have lower imprisonment rates. These results are statistically
significant at a greater than 1 per cent significance level, however, when the
United States and Japan are included in the data, the measure of ILO unemployment and the lagged crime rate remain statistically insignificant.

These results suggest the existence of a negative association between welfare
spending and imprisonment across countries. Those countries that spent more of
their GDP on welfare in 1998 had lower imprisonment rates. This relationship is
true whether or not the United States and Japan are included in the data,
although obviously the exclusion of these countries does affect the magnitude of
the relationship.

This evidence supports Beckett and Western's (2001) findings of a negative
relationship between welfare expenditure and imprisonment across US states in
1995. While Beckett and Western found the existence of such a relationship in
1995, they failed to find it in earlier periods. It is possible to see whether this is
also true of the cross-country data analysed here very simply by plotting the
relationship between the two variables in 1998 and in a previous period, 1988.
Thus, Figure 8.1 plots four graphs[16] which all have the proportion of GDP
spent on welfare along their x-axis and the imprisonment rate along their
y-axis. The plotted line is simply the regression coefficient, which is given in

[16] The first two graphs including the US and Japan, the second two excluding these outliers.

Downes and Hansen

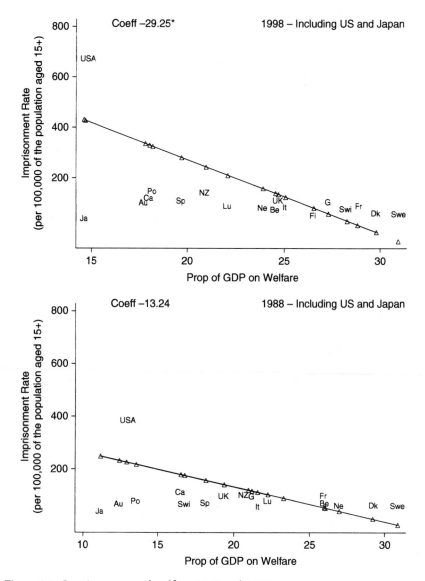

Figure 8.1. Imprisonment and welfare, 1988 and 1998

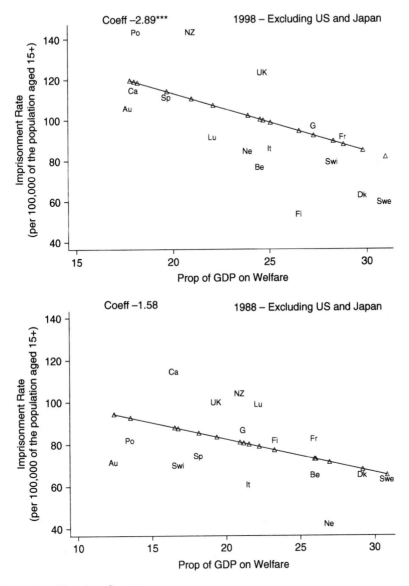

Figure 8.1. (Continued)

the top left of each graph. Examining the graphs it becomes clear that, with or without the outlying countries, the regression slope between welfare expenditure and imprisonment is more negative in 1998, than in 1988. In fact, while the earlier period produces a negative relationship between the two variables of interest, the results remain statistically insignificant. These differences remain even after controlling for unemployment and lagged crime rates.[17]

We actually have data for all years from 1987 to 1998 inclusive. A more flexible way of considering changes over time in the sensitivity of imprisonment rates to welfare spending is either to estimate statistical models year on year, or alternatively to let there be a time trend interaction to pick up shifts in the coefficient over time. When we do this we obtain a statistically significant trend interaction, showing (for the full sample) that the coefficient on welfare spending becomes 1.45 more negative, on average, per year. Thus the coefficient is −10.13 in 1987 and falls to −26.08 by 1998. When the United States and Japan are omitted, the 1987 coefficient is −1.72 and falls by −.16 per year to −3.48 in 1998. Thus, the overall pattern is clear: the association between imprisonment rates and spending becomes more sensitive in the cross-sectional models as the sample progresses over time.[18]

Examining the relationship in changes

Thus, like Beckett and Western's analysis of US states, the cross-country evidence presented herein suggests that the negative relationship between welfare expenditure and imprisonment is evident in the late 1990s, but is not robust when considering earlier time periods. However, while examining the cross-sectional data at two different points in time informs us about the relationship between countries with high and low imprisonment rates and high and low welfare expenditure at two points in time, utilizing national data measured over time allows a different question to be asked–namely what happens to the prison population of a country when the proportion of GDP spent on welfare in that country shifts? This can be examined with data measured across the same countries through time by constructing fixed effects models.[19] By looking at changes within countries through time, fixed effects models are able to control for factors which are constant in countries over the whole sample period (for example being a permanently high imprisonment or welfare spending country).

---

[17] eg, excluding the US and Japan, the coefficient on the full model (equivalent to specification 3, column 6, in Table 8.2) in 1988 is −1.95 (1.33) compared to −3.04 (0.789) in 1998.

[18] When unemployment and the lagged crime rate are controlled for in the full sample (including the US and Japan), the coefficient on welfare spending in 1987 is −24.01. This declines by −1.90 per year, so that in 1998 the coefficient is −44.94. Excluding the US and Japan, but controlling for unemployment and the lagged crime rate, produces an annual decline in the welfare coefficient of −0.18, so that in 1987 the coefficient is −2.05, by 1998 this has declined to −4.03.

[19] This can only be done for a subset of countries for which we have complete data between the years of 1987 and 1998.

Table 8.3. Fixed effects regression of relationship between the imprisonment rate and the percentage of GDP spent on welfare between 1987 and 1998.

	Including US and Japan	Excluding US and Japan		
	(1)	(2)	(3)	(4)
Percent of GDP on welfare	−11.93***	−1.54***	−1.38**	−1.39**
	(3.46)	(.491)	(.544)	(.559)
Control for country unemployment	No	No	No	Yes
Control for lagged country crime rates	No	No	Yes	Yes
Year dummies included	Yes	Yes	Yes	Yes
Excluding US and Japan	No	Yes	Yes	Yes
R-squared	.957	.811	.811	.825
Sample size	216	192	192	192

Robust standard errors in parenthesis

*** >1% significance level, ** 5%, * 10%

Identification of the imprisonment-welfare spending relationship will thus come from studying how changes in welfare spending are associated with changes in imprisonment rates.

Table 8.3 reports the results from fixed effects specifications of the relationship between imprisonment and the proportion of GDP spent on welfare for annual data between 1987 and 1998. The table reports four specifications. The first is a basic model controlling for country and time fixed effects that includes the United States and Japan. The second is the same model but this time excluding these two influential observations. The third specification includes controls for unemployment, while the fourth specification additionally controls for the lagged crime rate.

When the United States and Japan are included in the basic model the coefficient on the change in proportion of GDP spent on welfare attracts a negative, sizable coefficient, which is statistically significant at a greater than 1 per cent significance level. Thus the negative association between imprisonment and welfare spending is also present in these models that investigate the relationship in terms of changes through time. As noted above, this is important since results from these fixed effects models much more closely resemble the conceptually more appropriate question: what happens to imprisonment if welfare spending changes?

One might think that expressing the relationship in changes, so as to net out country fixed effects which show that some countries have permanently higher imprisonment or welfare spending, might eliminate the important influence that the United States and Japan had on the cross-sectional levels results given in Table 8.2 above. However, this is not the case. When these two countries are dropped from the estimation, the coefficient on welfare spending remains statistically significant at a greater than 1 per cent level, but its magnitude is considerably reduced. This suggests two things. First, the United States and Japan are influential observations in terms of changes as well as levels. This may not be surprising when one considers the massive rate of increase in the imprisonment rate that occurred in the United States over the 1990s. Secondly, whilst higher welfare spending is always linked to lower imprisonment, there is a different relationship (in terms of magnitudes) that emerges depending on which countries are studied.

Adding in the control variables does not alter this pattern of results. This is shown in the final two columns of Table 8.2. Inclusion of crime rates and unemployment rates slightly affects the magnitudes of the estimated coefficient on welfare spending, but it remains highly statistically significant. Thus, these results indicate that countries which increased the share of their GDP spent on welfare saw relative declines (or lower rates of increase) in their prison population.

The increased sensitivity of imprisonment to welfare spending over time also emerges in these fixed effects specifications so the welfare spending effect is more negative in 1998.

Letting a time trend interaction pick up shifts in the coefficient over time indicates a statistically significant trend interaction. For the full sample (which includes the United States and Japan) that the coefficient on welfare spending becomes 1.14 more negative, on average, per year. The coefficient is −1.35 in 1987 and falls to −13.89 by 1998. When the United States and Japan are omitted, the 1987 coefficient is −0.610 and falls by −0.17 per year to −2.48 in 1998. As with the cross-sectional results, the association between imprisonment rates and spending in the fixed effects models becomes greater as the sample progresses over time.[20] This finding is extremely important from a policy perspective, as it indicates that a country that increases the amount of its GDP spent on welfare sees a greater decline in its imprisonment rate than in the past.

From the above results we are able to say what happens to the prison population when a country shifts its spending on welfare. Another way to approach the relationship between imprisonment and welfare expenditure is to examine the following counter-factual question: what would the prison population look like today if welfare expenditure, as measured by the proportion of GDP spent on welfare, remained at its initial 1987 level? This can be calculated simply as the coefficient from the full model multiplied by the mean of welfare expenditure in the first period (1987) minus the mean of welfare expenditure in the last period (1998). The results of this calculation (−1.39* (21.53 − 24.17) = 3.67) show that, after controlling for other factors which may

---

[20] When unemployment and the lagged crime rate are controlled for in the full sample (including the US and Japan), the coefficient on welfare spending in 1987 is −1.42. This declines by −1.11 per year, so that in 1998 the coefficient is −13.63. Excluding the US and Japan, but controlling for unemployment and the lagged crime rate produces an annual decline in the welfare coefficient of −0.12, so that in 1987 the coefficient is −0.786, by 1998 this has declined to −2.11.

affect the relationship of interest, there would be four more prisoners per 100,000 of the adult population today if welfare expenditure had stayed at its 1987 level. This may not appear much of a difference, but when we take into account the fact that the average number of prisoners per 100,000 of the adult population was only 75 in 1987 and 95 in 1998, if welfare expenditure had not risen but had remained at its 1987 level there would be 20 per cent more prisoners today than there actually are.[21]

Discussion

The main impetus behind this chapter flowed from the growing sense of pressure exerted on social democratic societies to scale back their commitment to welfare and scale up their backing for punitive penality. We were concerned to explore a little further how far the two sets of choices those tendencies reflect may be linked empirically as well as theoretically. Our findings confirm that variations in welfare provision do relate significantly to penal policy and practice, as measured by the relative scale of incarceration, so that welfare cutbacks do indeed imply penal expansionism. Penal reformers have long sensed this to be the case. They may now have greater confidence that the social policy realm in general does indeed make some impact on the penal estate. Quite how the two interact in policy process terms is a compelling subject for further research. For example, as a quite disproportionate amount of welfare expenditure is devoted to the elderly, who hardly figure at all in terms of either crime or punishment, it is germane to ask what precisely the welfare/punishment relation amounts to? But the elderly represent much that is symbolized in the fear of crime and the quality of care for the most vulnerable is an indirect pointer to the societal balance struck between altruism and self-interest. The links are complex and indirect rather than simple. Richard Wilkinson (2000) has argued convincingly that comparative evidence supports the view that, not only crime and punishment, but also public health and economic prosperity, are causally related to altruism rather than competitive individualism.

The trend towards the marketization of welfare is likely to complicate the already marked problems involved in conducting similar analyses in the future. In Britain, the past few years have seen a coincidence of higher welfare spending and prison population growth. Too much cannot be read into one such combination. But the striking feature of the increased expenditure has been its evident failure to debouch into schools, hospitals, and the caring services in

[21] This is calculated as: (1) the actual rise in imprisonment between 1987 and 1998 = 95 – 75 = 20; (2) the counterfactual rise if welfare spending had remained at its 1987 level = 24; (3) the difference between (1) and (2) in numbers: 24 – 20 = 4; (4) the difference between (1) and (2) as a percentage change: 4/20 = 0.2, 0.2*100 = 20. If the US and Japan are included, the corresponding figures are 11 more prisoners, or a 32% rise had welfare stayed at its 1987 level.

general, at least to the extent expected. New forms of accounting, monitoring, and targeting have greatly complicated resourcing. When huge increases in public service expenditure are in reality financing private sector investment, as seems to be the case with Private Finance Initiatives in the National Health Service, then like is not being compared with like in any time series measure. Future research must cope with the greater complexity such developments harbour.

Conclusions

In conclusion, we would like to emphasize three main points:

(1) We need to reinstate analysis of the Welfare State context in relation to the scale and character of imprisonment, especially as the links are becoming more rather than less significant over the past ten to fifteen years. It is difficult to believe that the consistent finding of an inverse relationship between the commitment to welfare and the scale of imprisonment, both cross-nationally and across the United States, is simply accidental or coincidental.

(2) The nature of the relationship between the two is, nevertheless, still in need of elucidation by further research, and is likely to be highly mediated rather than simple or direct, calling for the use of different methods to explore its complexities (in this regard, see especially Cavadino and Dignan 2006).

(3) The importance of an inclusive Welfare State to liberal Social Democracy remains as vital as ever, more so as it is under threat from the pressures to off-load the costs of welfare provision onto individuals themselves or the market, via privatization, contracting-out, and/or the voluntary sector. Above all, our data imply that a substantial Welfare State is increasingly a principal, if not the main protection against the resort to mass imprisonment in the era of globalization and, what John Gray (1998) termed, the false dawn of the neo-liberal political economy.

9

Sentencing as a Social Practice

Neil Hutton

Introduction

Sentencing is not an area which has received much scholarly attention from sociologists. Most of the scholarly literature has been produced by philosophers who have pursued the normative questions about how to justify punishment in a liberal society (Duff 2000, Von Hirsch 1993) or by legal scholars writing about the legal regulation of sentencing (Ashworth 2000b). In the growing literature on the sociology of punishment there are only occasional references to sentencing (Garland 2001). There is a vast, mostly US, literature on sentencing as public policy (Tonry 1996). However, with a few exceptions, there has been little inquiry into the social character of sentencing.

Little is known about the social practice of sentencing. Sentencers in many jurisdictions enjoy wide discretion in their decision making. While every jurisdiction has complex procedural regulation which much be followed to ensure that sentences are lawful, few have rules which generate the 'correct' sentence from a given set of facts and circumstances. Statistical analyses of sentencing show that sentencing is patterned (Lovegrove 1989). How are these patterns produced through the individual sentencing decisions of judges, given the absence of rules? How do the courts produce an element of consistency in sentencing when judges argue that each case is unique and that they reach sentencing decisions by a process of 'instinctive synthesis' (Freiberg 1995)?

In order to answer these and other questions it is necessary to think about how sentencing can be understood as a social practice as opposed to a legal decision or an exercise in moral philosophy. This essay reviews different approaches to understanding sentencing. These include quantitative sociological approaches which try to analyse the impact of different factors on sentencing outcomes and interpretive sociological approaches which try to understand sentencing from the perspective of the sentencers as a form of rational social action. The chapter argues that the work of Bourdieu, which seeks to understand the cultural and professional frameworks through which law operates, can provide a conceptual framework which is helpful for understanding the sociological distinctiveness of sentencing as a form of legal decision making.

This chapter does not seek to provide a comprehensive 'theory' of sentencing. My starting assumption is that there is no such theory. Nor is there a single yardstick against which these approaches can be measured as being more or less accurate accounts of sentencing. Each of these approaches asks its own questions, adopts its own methodology and generates its own answers. An understanding of these will give us a richer understanding of sentencing. This understanding may in turn help those who would like to change sentencing practices.

The Sociology of Discretion

No one would doubt that UK judges exercise discretion when choosing sentence. There are very few rules which circumscribe their choice of sentence (Hogarth 1971, Hood 1962, Ashworth 1994). The same is true for judges in around half the states in the United States (Reitz 2001) and also in many continental European jurisdictions. US judges in states which have adopted some kind of guideline system, and judges in other continental European jurisdictions, still exercise discretion but the extent of this discretion varies as do the methods used to structure this discretion (Tonry and Frase 2001).

How can this exercise of discretion in sentencing be understood sociologically? Most research efforts, and these have been mostly carried out in the United States, have sought to find evidence for disparity. The null hypothesis to be disproved, has been that like cases are treated alike. A serious methodological problem for this research has been ensuring that 'like' cases are being compared. There is no objective definition of similarity to rely upon. However, setting aside these difficulties, the results of this research effort appear to demonstrate significant inconsistencies in sentencing practice (as well as a considerable element of consistency). Given the absence of rules in sentencing, this finding is hardly unexpected. The problem could usefully be turned on its head. Instead of asking why there are inconsistencies in sentencing (answer: there are no rules), we should be asking how any consistency is achieved in the absence of rules? How do individual decision makers operating in geographically distinct courtrooms, working within local criminal justice cultures, manage collectively to produce a considerable element of consistency in their sentencing decisions? How can we explain this patterned social action? As Hogarth (1971) noted, the fundamental issues are conceptual. We cannot begin to try to measure until we have a clear idea of what it is we are trying to measure and why.

Quantitative Analysis

Modelling the sentencing process

One important way of understanding patterns in sentencing is to look at aggregate sentencing figures and use statistical tools to analyse the patterns that emerge from these. The analysis looks for factors and/or combinations of factors which appear to predict sentencing outcomes with some degree of accuracy. Thus, for example, if one possessed certain information about an offence and about the criminal history of the offender, one could use these analyses to help to predict the sentence that would be passed in a particular court. The most elaborate form of such analyses would produce a 'model' of sentencing which would take into account a wide range of relevant factors and measure the effect which these have on sentencing outcomes. Perhaps the most rigorous and comprehensive attempt to produce a model of sentencing is described in a book published in 1989 by Austin Lovegrove. His central argument is that multi-variate statistical analysis reveals 'the factors determinative of sentence and their relative importance averaged across the data base of cases' (Lovegrove 1989: 47).

His analysis shows that two factors, case seriousness and criminal history, are the best predictors of sentencing outcome. Beyond these two factors, others have much smaller and much less accurately predictable effects on outcome. Nevertheless, Lovegrove's argument is that with more sophisticated conceptual clarification and more comprehensive data collection, a more accurate model of sentencing could be produced.

Lovegrove's use of the term 'determinative' raises the issue of causality. The question is whether Lovegrove intends a 'strong' sense of causality, in the sense drawn from natural science methodology. This implies that his model is able to formulate laws of sentencing behaviour which allow reliable prediction. This, of course, raises the question of how these laws operate and whether they operate independently of any active decision-making processes exercised by judges.

A weaker sense of causality would suggest that the factors play a causal role alongside other factors in producing the outcome. This is important for Love-grove's analysis because he wants to argue that these tools of statistical analysis can be used to predict outcomes from factors. The existence of a statistical correlation between a small number of case factors and sentence outcome does not imply that the former cause the latter. The correlations simply identify the most significant factors governing sentencing. It is hardly surprising that the seriousness of the offence and the criminal record of the offender are the two best predictors of sentence outcome. Taken together, these two factors are likely to narrow down the range of sentencing options very significantly in the vast majority of cases. However, Lovegrove's work does not provide the accurate predictive power that would be necessary for a robust 'model' of sentencing.

Lovegrove's detailed and thorough work has identified patterns of sentencing behaviour. The problem is that this search is based on an unexamined assumption that sentencing is rational and that if one looks hard enough, a model of sentencing can be discovered. This confuses patterns with rationality. The fact that there is a pattern does not imply that there is necessarily a rational model of sentencing being operated unconsciously by sentencers. From an interpretive perspective, sentencers are social actors. They reflexively perceive themselves as making decisions and making choices, albeit within certain boundaries. Scholars working from an interpretive paradigm would argue that these patterns are constructed because judges are reproducing structures of professional knowledge/practice learned through experience. So in order to understand these patterns, we need to investigate the social conditions of sentencing. What are judges trying to achieve? What are the constraints under which they operate? How are their choices made?

Nevertheless, Lovegrove's argument is that these statistical patterns reveal what he calls 'applied' sentencing policy. Even if judges are not able to articulate a sentencing policy, what they actually do in practice constitutes a *de facto* sentencing policy. One can accept that sentencing policy is 'what judges do' but this does not entail accepting that what judges do is therefore systematic or consistent.

The classification and measurement of seriousness

Kathleen Daly (1994) points to another limitation of quantitative approaches to the study of sentencing. This concerns the methods used to classify the variables being counted. Lovegrove's work attempts to discover the extent to which each of a number of variables affects the sentencing outcome in a case. Much of the research into sentencing disparity aims to collect a sample of similar cases and examine the extent to which sentencing outcomes are divergent. In order to do this, categories have to be developed to define what similarity means.[1] However, all of these approaches share the need to develop categories into which 'real' cases can be sorted. As Tamanaha puts it:

... positivism gets off the ground by placing phenomena into categories and then quantifying them. (1997: 62).

In sentencing research, the central problem concerns how to design categories which accurately reflect case 'seriousness'. From the perspective of Lovegrove, the problem is to develop a list of those factors which affect seriousness. These can then be counted and regression analysis applied to measure their relative effect on sentence outcome. Disparity research is concerned to design 'boxes' which contain cases of similar seriousness so that sentencing outcomes can be compared for similar cases. The problem is defining how the contents of one box differ from the contents of the next box: How does one 'level' or 'type' of robbery differ in seriousness from another? This is essentially the same problem as that encountered by those designing sentencing guidelines (Tonry 1996) or information systems (Tata *et al* 1996).

Daly argues that there are an enormous number of factors which may legitimately be taken into account by a sentencer in assessing the seriousness of a case – for example the age of the victim, the nature and extent of the harm caused to the

---

[1] A similar process takes place when numerical sentencing guidelines are being drawn up.

victim, the value of property stolen or damaged, the extent of planning involved, the use of a weapon, the criminal record of the offender, the age of the offender, and so on. Philosophical monographs have been written on how to assess seriousness (Feinberg 1988). A software programme, developed to implement the United States Federal Sentencing Guidelines, calculates a seriousness score for each case, taking into account a formidable range of data (Sentencing Guidelines Council 2004). European jurisdictions have narrative descriptions of the factors which affect seriousness written into sentencing legislation (for Sweden, see von Hirsch and Jareborg 1991; for Italy, see Mannozzi 2002). In England and Wales, David Thomas compiles a huge loose-leaf compendium which can be read as a sprawling jurisprudence of how judges in that jurisdiction have assessed seriousness (Thomas 1999). Morrison has produced a similar encyclopaedia for Scotland (Morrison 2000). More recently in England and Wales, the Sentencing Guidelines Council has issued Final Guidelines on the Overarching Principles of Seriousness <http://www. sentencing-guidelines.gov.uk>.

There are a very large number of factors which may be legitimately taken into account in assessing seriousness. There is considerable disagreement internationally about what these factors are and how they should be taken into account. Some jurisdictions, such as England and Wales, allow judges considerable discretion in assessing seriousness. At the other extreme the Federal Sentencing Guidelines produced by the US Sentencing Commission, have effectively produced an objective definition of seriousness by limiting the range of factors which can be taken into account and quantifying the effect on sentence of these factors. Stith and Cabranes (1998) argue that the Guidelines have produced injustice by treating as uniform cases which are different. They also argue that many judges and academic commentators are unhappy with the Guidelines because the quantitative approach to seriousness fails to take into account important and relevant factors.

A further problem is that of defining categories, there is an assumption that factors relevant to seriousness have the same significance in every context. However, this is not necessarily the case. For example, the age of an offender may be a factor which reduces seriousness in some contexts but makes no difference in other contexts. With reference to drug offences, the US Federal Sentencing Guidelines give considerable weight in the calculation of sentence to the quantity of the drug involved, but much less weight to the extent of involvement of the offender in the business of trafficking the drug. This fixes the significance of drug weight and extent of involvement. Judges, however, argue that in some cases, the extent of involvement is a more important factor in assessing seriousness than the quantity of the drug. The Guidelines do not permit this perception to be reflected in the sentence (Stith and Cabranes 1998: 120).

The problem is that seriousness resists efforts to capture its significance in a purely objective manner. There are so many factors involved and their meaning is so slippery that it is impossible to produce an objective, unambiguous, non-contestable definition. However, in practice, judges make decisions about the relative seriousness of cases every day. It is an unavoidable part of the social practice of sentencing which has real impacts on the lives of sentenced offenders, victims, and their families.

One conclusion from this might be that if seriousness cannot be captured objectively, then there is no point in trying to capture it at all. However, if the assumption of the value of pure objectivity is dropped, this conclusion also disappears. It is difficult to capture seriousness and our ways of trying to do so may have no absolute and objective basis. Nevertheless, it is something which judges do every day, and in our liberal ideals of justice, we give a high value to the aim of treating like cases in a like manner, so we are obliged to find a way of assessing seriousness which we think most helpful to us in pursuing our (unattainable) ideals.

Any categorization of seriousness takes its significance from the meaning used by sentencers themselves, ie meaning is contingent on context and not independent of it (Tamanaha 1997: 70). In other words, when we say that the patterns of sentencing show that case seriousness and criminal record are the best predictors of sentencing outcome, we are not saying that these are the 'real' causes of sentencing outcomes, all we are saying is these seem to be very important factors influencing the outcomes of the social processes of sentencing.

The strength of quantitative studies, such as those conducted by Lovegrove, is that they demonstrate the existence of patterns in sentencing. The main limitation of this work is that it cannot describe how these patterns are produced beyond the important knowledge that two factors, case seriousness and criminal history, make a significant impact. Lovegrove admits that his analysis does not shed light on the judges' 'decision strategy' for combining case facts. In other words, while the statistical analysis might show patterns of sentencing, it does not help us to understand how these patterns are produced by judges.

In the absence of many rules specifying which factors are to be taken into account, how these are to be measured and weighed against each other, and how the resultant 'score' translates into a specific type and amount of punishment, we do not know how judges produce these patterns of sentencing. This is the question that interpretive approaches to sentencing have addressed:

> . . . we need to see logico-scientific and narrative modes of reasoning as poles from which we can glimpse distinctive representational possibilities. In so doing we can think more systematically about narrative and more meaningfully about numbers. (Daly 1994: 265)

Interpretive Analyses

Lovegrove's work demonstrates that there is a considerable element of consistency in sentencing and goes some way to describing the contours of this consistency. The main weakness of his approach is that it does not address the question of how this consistency is produced. Lovegrove seems to be uninterested in the judge as a self-conscious and reflective social actor who is actively engaged in constructing sentencing decisions. These are the concerns of those working in the interpretive tradition in sociology who see the social world as an active production of social action. As Tamanaha puts it:

There are regularities in behaviour because people in a community who are similarly socialized often have shared ideas, beliefs and reasoning patterns and operate under similar constraining conditions...' (1997: 68)

The social field of sentencing

The sociological method of Pierre Bourdieu was intended to avoid what he saw as the false split between subjective and objective approaches in conventional sociological analysis.

A subjective approach draws attention to the ways in which agents perceive themselves as active subjects. It suggests that the social world is an active and ongoing accomplishment of social actors engaged in social practices. An objective approach draws attention to the patterned nature of social life, to the social structures which are reproduced in the social actions of agents.

Agents may think they are employing 'sign systems' but the social world and agency itself is produced by these sign systems. 'Social reality' is produced by the sign systems which we have at our disposal. Meaning is contingent, an idea or object in a sign system only has meaning in relation to other elements of that sign system.

An objective approach can discover the patterns of social life, but cannot explain how these patterns are produced nor how they are transformed. It cannot account for the experience and perceptions agents have of themselves as active, conscious, decision makers.

From Bourdieu's perspective, sentencing decisions can be seen as social actions generated in the social field of sentencing. Bourdieu defines a social field as:

Interaction between institutions, rules and practices, rituals, designations, conventions, appointments and titles which produce and authorize certain discourses and activities. (1977: 21–2)

Hawkins (2003) uses a different conceptual framework to understand the social context for discretionary decision making in law. His concepts of 'surround' and 'field' arguably serve similar functions to Bourdieu's concept of social field. These are the 'external' conditions which shape the exercise of discretion, which include: the broader cultural and political climate of punishment, the representations of sentencing and punishment in the local and national media and judicial perceptions and responses to these, the judicial profession and the system of judicial appointments, the position of sentencing in the series of criminal justice process decisions about cases, the rules governing sentencing, the shared understandings of what constitutes a defensible sentencing decision, and the modes of argument which can be brought to bear to justify these decisions if required. Of course, this field shares much in common with the much broader social field of law, however, sentencing is a distinctive sub-field.

How do these factors generate sentencing practices? Bourdieu uses the concept of 'habitus' to account for the ways in which structural conditions generate social practices. Hawkins uses the concept of 'framing' to understand the processes of interpretation, classification, and justification employed by legal professionals in the exercise of discretion to produce outcomes which are patterned and display an element of consistency.

Habitus

Habitus is 'the durably installed generative principle of regulated improvisations which produce practices' (Bourdieu 1977: 78, quoted in Webb *et al* 2002: 36). Sentencers, like almost all social actors, take their social world for granted – 'he feels at home in the world because the world is also in him' (Bourdieu 2000: 142–3, quoted in Webb *et al* 2002: 25). Webb *et al* describe habitus as a 'feel for the game' (2002: 38). This sits easily with sentencers' own perceptions of sentencing as intuitive and artful (Ashworth 1984). Bourdieu's intention is, however, not to take habitus for granted, but to examine it in context and describe its elements and properties. Habitus is neither natural nor inevitable, but the product of particular social, cultural, and political conditions. It is contingent on these conditions and not essential or transcendent. Habitus is unthinking and unreflective. It can change but is likely to do so slowly in most circumstances.

Judges' sentencing behaviour is patterned because through their education and working experience they have learnt how to think, argue, and make decisions in a judicial way and because they work within the same criminal justice institutions. These social factors both enable sentencing decisions to be made and at the same time set limits on these decisions. Judges have a limited repertoire from which to draw in making their sentencing decisions, but this repertoire can be drawn upon in varied and sometimes novel ways. There is scope for different judges to make different interpretations or evaluations of the same facts. This means that although sentencing is patterned, the pattern is far from uniform, and inconsistencies are found alongside the consistencies. Patterns can and do change. For example, the sentencing of rape and child sexual abuse has changed over the last twenty years as public conceptions and moral evaluations of these offences have changed and, through some means, judges sentencing practices have changed in response to these broader social changes in attitudes.

Social actors think and act strategically. Social practice is improvised and strategic, not behaviour governed by rules. Actors try to use the rules of the game to their advantage. At the same time they are influenced and almost driven by the values and expectations they get from the habitus. They may be conscious of acting strategically but they are unaware that their motives, goals, and aspirations are not spontaneous or natural but are given to them through the habitus:

... the power of the habitus derives from the thoughtlessness of habit and habituation, rather than consciously learned rules and principles. Socially competent performances are produced as a matter of routine, without explicit reference to a body of codified knowledge and without the actors necessarily 'knowing' what they are doing. (Jenkins 1992: 76)

In the context of sentencing, sentencers think that they choose the right sentence. This is done intuitively rather than according to a set of rules. When asked to account for their decision, they do so by reciting facts and circumstances but without explicitly or logically relating these to a calculus of sanctions. Sentencers perceive themselves to be making complex, difficult, and sensitive decisions. They do so by drawing on their experience and professional knowledge but they find it difficult to articulate the elements of these competences:

Judges, we believed, organized their thinking about sentencing not in terms of a series of abstractions but as a series of reactions to particular cases. (Wheeler *et al* 1988: 4, see also Tata 1997)

Using Bordieu's conceptual approach, sentencing decisions emerge from the habitus, the unthinking common sense approach that becomes second nature to experienced judges. From their position within the unreflective habitus, judges can conceive of no other way of making a decision. But what appears to be 'common sense' to them is, for Bourdieu, a socially constructed set of values, motives, methods of analysis, judgemental criteria, assumptions, classifications, and categories which are distinctively the conditions of existence of judges. Take, for example, the judicial perception that offenders who use drugs, have criminal records, chaotic lifestyles, no homes, no jobs, and no appropriate personal relationships etc, are not suitable for community sanctions. This is not inevitable or natural but produced by a discourse which distinguishes between 'real' criminals and 'respectable' people who have made mistakes. Social conditions such as poverty, disadvantage, lack of opportunities, and low social capital which generate persistent young male offenders are translated into the 'sentencing problem' of selecting a sanction which is appropriate for the case at hand.

While the concept of 'habitus' is helpful for understanding the ways in which the taken-for-granted everyday world is unreflectively produced by social actors, the concept has its limitations. De Certeau (1984) criticizes Bourdieu for taking an overdeterministic view of habitus. He argues that agents are more able to reflect on their positions and more culturally literate than Bourdieu allows. Resistance can be almost or completely invisible and take unexpected forms. This is just to argue that habitus is neither completely determining nor completely fixed. Bourdieu sometimes appears to be too deterministic but there may be empirical conditions in which habitus is highly constricting and very difficult to change. Sentencing is an example of a social field where, despite the wide discretion, the opportunities for radical difference are very limited.

Elements of the habitus of sentencing

Populist punitiveness

Commentators have argued that the rise in the prison population which has occurred in many Western jurisdictions over the last twenty years can be at least partly explained by changes in sentencing practice (see also, Downes and Hansen, Chapter 8). Judges appear to be sending more offenders to prison and also sending offenders to prison for longer (Millie *et al* 2003). Unfortunately there is little research which helps us to understand the mechanisms through which this apparent 'punitiveness' changes sentencing practices. The evidence cited for punitiveness is made up of examples of political rhetoric such as 'three strikes' or 'tough on crime, tough on the causes of crime', legislation providing mandatory minimum sentences for anti-social behaviour (Ashworth 2002), and analysis of the representations of crime and punishment in the popular and quality press. Is it true that this punitiveness has had an impact on sentencing practice and if so how has this happened? Garland has argued that this puni-tiveness has been accompanied by a more rational managerial approach to criminal justice 'on the ground', which proceeds without much media attention. In the United Kingdom at least, sentencing has largely escaped the manage-rialism that has transformed other parts of the criminal justice process, for example policing, prosecution, prisons, and criminal justice social work. How has sentencing escaped and what does this tell us about the social practice of sentencing?

Sentencing and the criminal justice process.

Sentencers make decisions about cases which have already been constructed by the work of other agencies and the discretionary decision making of other criminal justice professionals (Hawkins 2003). Their sentencing options are to some extent constrained by decisions made by prosecutors, or negotiated between prosecutors and defence agents, and by reports prepared for the court by probation officials, social workers, and other professionals. Sentencers will also anticipate the way in which their decision will be interpreted by others, most notably the Court of Appeal, but also by the offenders, the victims and their families, and the local and national media. Local court cultures will also generate conditions which affect sentencing decisions. In smaller courts, shared under-standings develop which provide an informal and tacit resource for sentencing decisions.

The judicial profession and legal culture

Judges, at least in the United Kingdom, are drawn from a relatively narrow field. Until recently there were no formal appointment procedures, effectively judges selected themselves. They are likely to have been immersed in a rather narrow section of the legal world for their professional lives. They will have undergone minimal training and professional development in criminal sentencing, and that will have been provided internally by the profession and will have been unlikely to challenge their habits of thought.

I argue below that sentencing presents judges with a problem. Lawyers are trained to analyse facts, find relevant rules, and apply these rules to facts to produce justifiable decisions. Sentencing is different. There are very few rules. How do judges respond to this problem? They do so, I argue, in a way which shares much in common with David Robertson's analysis (1998) of the House of Lords decision making in 'hard' appeal cases. In my view this shows how a broader legal culture permeates and underpins judicial decision making. This helps to understand why UK judges are so resistant to attempts to make sentencing more systematic, rational, and arguably more legal.

Capital

Bourdieu's sociology recognizes the significance of power in social relationships. Power is associated with the possession of 'capital'. This can be economic, social, cultural, or symbolic. Judges have very high levels of all kinds of capital. They are well paid and economically secure. They exercise considerable power and control over their own practices and meanings. Their sentencing decisions are relatively autonomous and not subject to the accounting practices of others beyond their colleagues in the Court of Appeal. They have successfully avoided political interference with sentencing, most notably in the contribution of judges in England and Wales to the criticism of the 1991 Criminal Justice Act. This law attempted to introduce a desert based approach to sentencing in England and Wales and subsequently led to passage of the 1993 Criminal Justice Act. Lawyers have a monopoly over official legal knowledge and method and they therefore have an interest in preserving this intellectual capital. Judges wish to protect their control of sentencing when they perceive their authority being challenged by 'outsiders'.

Cotterrell (1992) argues that because the United Kingdom has no constitution, judges derive their authority from their status. In Weber's terms, their authority is charismatic, based on public perceptions of their political neutrality, experience, and wisdom. Judicial adherence to a pragmatic approach to decision making promotes the perception of judicial wisdom being 'special'. They eschew principles and theory and avoid anything which looks like policy making. Sentencing is done on a case-by-case basis with little reference to principles and no recognition of the existence of any sentencing 'policy'.

Their cultural or symbolic capital derives from their charismatic authority. This aspect of judicial power is perhaps least settled. Survey evidence suggests that the public have limited confidence in the courts, and think that judges are too old and out of touch. There may be a connection between the anachronistic mode of decision making used in sentencing and public perceptions of the judiciary as being 'out of touch'.

Any programme of sentencing reform will involve a political struggle over the distribution of capital within the social field of sentencing. Judges will try to retain as much capital as they can, while those who want to transform sentencing will need to obtain capital to allow change to occur.

Psychological approaches

An interpretive approach can focus on a wide range of contextual factors which have an impact on sentencing. John Hogarth set out to try to understand sentencing from the point of view of magistrates. To that extent his approach is interpretive. However, he also tried to measure the impact of specific factors on sentencing outcomes. These factors are analysed in the context of the other factors. Thus, he is less concerned with measuring the independent effects of factors such as age, political affiliation, penal philosophy, and so on, than with demonstrating how constellations of factors 'fit together'. He uses quantitative methods and statistical analyses but only to support an interpretive picture of how these magistrates operate.

Hogarth's judges adhered to all of the classical justifications of punishment: reformation, general then individual deterrence, incapacitation and punishment. Nearly all claimed to seek to prevent crime. There was, however, a marked inconsistency in their adherence to these principles. For example, a judge may place a high value on reformation but admit that it is not feasible in many cases. The majority of the magistrates believed in the efficacy of the penal measures they apply. Hogarth argues that this is psychologically necessary. Belief in reformation (as opposed to belief in the other penal philosophies) is associated with belief in the efficacy of most penal measures. Hogarth explains this by arguing that judges interpret information in accordance with their beliefs to maximize internal consistency. Where judges conceive of offenders as in need of treatment, they perceive prisons to be places where they will get treatment, conveniently setting aside the high rates of recidivism that they may have heard about. This theory is based on cognition research which shows that people arrange elements of their cognitive system to avoid inconsistency. Carlen's work on Scottish Sheriffs confirms this finding. Judges sent women offenders to prison because they felt that prison was the best place for women to receive medical attention, pre-natal care, drug or alcohol treatment, and other services, whether or not the prison was in fact able to provide these sorts of treatment (Carlen 1983b).

Hogarth found that magistrates perceived themselves as being guided by rules of thumb, such as presumptions for or against probation or for or against imprisonment for cases of different kinds. The seriousness of the offence was felt to be the primary factor leading to custody but magistrates varied in their assessment of seriousness. These decision-making rules of thumb are closely related to the beliefs and attitudes of the sentencer. This is apparent not only in their *post facto* justifications but also in their actual behaviour: 'It seems that justice is a very personal thing' (Hogarth 1971: 82).

Hogarth concluded that judges' beliefs and attitudes had an effect on their sentencing. For example, judges who believed in rehabilitation restricted their use of custody to high risk individuals (Hogarth 1971: 81, Fitzmaurice and Pease 1981). This is not to argue that psychological traits determine sentencing practices. Within the broader social practices of sentencing, variations can be produced by psychological forces.

How do Judges Construct their Decisions?

In an article about the psychology of sentencing, Austin Lovegrove argues that sentencers should be supported by a computerized database which contains both statistical information about past sentencing practices and also a statement of sentencing policy, ie the principles which judges use to analyse these facts and reach a just choice of sentence. Lovegrove argues that the database 'must include a record of the content and sequence of judges' thoughts as they use case facts to determine sentence – how they construe and interrelate the case facts and the concepts they draw on to do this' (Lovegrove 1999: 35). This raises important questions:

(1) Is this an accurate account of the practice of sentencing? This may represent an idealized view of how an über-rational judge might set about providing a justification for a sentencing decision under the system which Lovegrove proposes but there is no evidence that this is an accurate representation of judicial sentencing processes.

(2) How would we go about obtaining such a representation? Asking a judge to verbalize his thought processes may not produce an account of how judges make sentencing decisions but an account of how judges respond to the request of a researcher to verbalize their sentencing. These are not the same sort of account. Judges' public accounts of their sentencing decision making will be different from accounts which they may agree to share anonymously with a researcher and again from accounts which they may share with their colleagues in private (see Tata 2002a).

The search for a 'real' account is mistaken. The choice of a methodology for producing knowledge depends not on a test for objective accuracy but on the purposes for which this knowledge is required, and an assessment of the most valid and reliable way of acquiring this knowledge.

This is really a debate about social science methodology. We need to develop methodological protocols for collecting data in a world where we no longer have faith in any 'pure' theory of objective or value neutral knowledge. The alternative is not pure relativism, but some kind of pragmatism which makes clear the methods used to acquire knowledge and the value assumptions underpinning these.

We should let go of the idea that we can 'know' how sentencing decisions are made or that there is a consistent systematic policy waiting to be uncovered by painstaking scientific research. Instead we should start from what we want to do about and with sentencing (for example make it more rational, more accountable, or more transparent) and ask what we need to find out to allow us to achieve this goal within the limitations outlined above. This is in fact what Lovegrove wants to do, to use judges' reasoning and statistical analysis of case facts to help judges to build a normative policy which can be articulated. The difference between Lovegrove's approach and the approach sketched out in this essay is that the approach sketched here is a political choice, not an objective description.

An interpretive analysis of decision making

Decision making is a part of routine professional practice. It is what judges do every day and what most of them have been doing for many years. Most routine sentencing decisions have to be made quickly with little time for reflection (Hogarth 1971: ch 5). The decision comes first. In all but the hardest cases (and we need to know more about what constitutes a hard case for sentencing) judges 'know' what the right decision is, call this 'instinctive synthesis' (Freiberg 1995) or whatever you like. If required to justify this decision, *post facto* arguments can be constructed. (This is a form of realist argument.) For most routine sentencing decisions in UK jurisdictions at least, judges are not required to justify their decisions in any formal sense. Most will say something from the bench, particularly where the offenders, victim, or victim's family are present, but they are only required to provide a written version of their decision when their decision is appealed, a rare occurrence for most judges. In Scotland, only the Court of Appeal routinely produces public justifications for its decisions.

The important point here is that the decision comes first and the judges work backwards to construct a *post hoc* justification and to demonstrate that the sentence 'fits' the case. Thus, an understanding of sentencing from this perspective is an understanding of the range of legitimate accounts which judges can construct to justify their sentence. This is not an explanation of how a sentence was reached, but of how a plausible account was constructed (Tata 2002b). This speculative theory is intended to refer to the sentencing practices of Scottish sheriffs sentencing criminal cases at first instance. However, the analogy is drawn from Robertson's analysis of the decision making of the House of Lords, the highest court in the United Kingdom. Robertson (1998) argues that his analysis can be applied to a much wider universe of decision making by public officials who make rule-bounded discretionary decisions.

Robertson defines discretion as the requirement of judges (in his case, House of Lords judges) to make a decision about what rule is relevant when there is 'no institutional way that they can be forced to make one rather than another decision' (Robertson 1998: 9).

Robertson argues that the exercise of judicial discretion in these 'hard cases' is a choice which is not 'entailed or enforced' by anything in law:

What we are insisting on is that any case that comes to the House of Lords could be decided either way, and that judges do fully choose the way it will come out, with no important limitations other than those involved in the need to get at least two other Law Lords to agree with them. (1998: 13)

His view is that judges make the decision which they think is 'right' and then deploy argument to justify this decision. The decision is not determined by law, it is a choice made by judges.

What relevance does this argument have for an understanding of sentencing? Discretion is the exercise of choice about which rule is relevant where there is no institutional means of forcing them to make one choice rather than another. If we set aside the very extensive procedural regulation of sentencing, which is usually described as sentencing law, there are few rules governing choice of sentence. Discretion in sentencing, then, is not about deciding which rule is relevant. There are no rules. Moving to the second part. The only institutional check on sentencing decisions is the appeal process. Sentences are only likely to be overturned if they are manifestly unjust or out of line. The Appeal Court mostly describes broad boundaries of acceptability and only in guideline judgements in England and Wales attempts anything more akin to fine tuning.

Sentencing decisions, then, are even more discretionary (ie even less rule bound) than the House of Lords decisions which Robertson analyses. They are thus even more nakedly expressions of value preference or freely exercised choice which are not at all determined by law. In fact one might go so far as to say that they are hardly recognizable as legal decisions at all, which was the point made by Judge Frankel thirty years ago (Frankel 1972). Ashworth argues that judicial arguments defending 'independence' in sentencing amount to little more than assertions of ownership of sentencing (Ashworth 1999).

To pursue this point further it is helpful to examine the way in which judges attempt to justify their sentencing decisions. Take, for example, the reported decisions of the Court of Appeal in Scotland in appeals against sentence. A typical judgement recites the facts and circumstances of the case to display that they have been 'taken into account'. The Court then states an opinion as to whether the original sentence was within the appropriate boundaries or not. Occasionally, the Court will make reference to past cases. Even more rarely, there may be some rehearsal of one or more of the conventional aims of sentencing. However, the judgement never articulates the nature of the relationship between the amount of penalty and the facts and circumstances of the case. 'Instinctive synthesis' is the term coined in a notable Australian judgement to describe how a judgement generates a quantum of sanction from a given set of facts and circumstances (Freiberg 1995).

Sentencing as a legal decision

Robertson (1998) argues that the House of Lords judges are socialized into the very small world of courtroom practitioner lawyers. Since graduation (from a limited number of institutions) they have worked and lived together, fought each other in court, and judged each other for over thirty years. It is not their class position which influences their decision making so much as their membership of this small and relatively closed social group. They learn what it is to make a judicial decision through the development of the skills of advocacy. They operate as individuals and have little experience of working as members of a team, unlike solicitors working in practice. They are also accustomed to generating arguments for either side of a case, and Robertson argues that this facility is transferred, inappropriately, to their duties when they become judges. Robertson argues that their approach to judging is based on a view of what law is supposed to do, sociologists might describe this as the social function of law. Functionalist sociologists might describe this as conflict resolution; civil libertarians might describe law's function as the protection of rights. Roberston argues that his research suggests that House of Lords judges see themselves as problem solvers. His research shows that judges seek a decision that will 'work'. They operate with a tacit 'pragmatic utilitarianism' which Robertson says fits well with Hart's analysis in *The Concept of Law* (Robertson 1998: 20). Of course 'making things work', whether this is fine-tuning welfare state institutions or 'deciding cases according to commercial common sense' cannot be achieved without making value judgements. Robertson's data does not show any particular ideological underpinning, apart from a tendency to behave much like other senior public administrators. He lists the following characteristics of the 'Whitehall view' or the British generalist civil service culture and argues that these characterize the exercise of judicial discretion by House of Lords judges, for whom 'all relevant matters are considered and no irrelevant matters taken into account'; 'decisions are as limited as possible, as consistent with past decisions as possible, as bereft as possible of implications for future decisions'; 'recommendations are justified by comparisons and analogies from the immediate experiences of the decision makers, and the whole matter is treated with virtually no reference to overarching norms or guiding principles' (Robertson 1998: 399). It is administration on a case-by-case basis, heavily dependent on deference to experience on similar committees rather than expertise on the technical matters discussed.

Many aspects of this analysis can be applied to sentencing. Appeal judgements list all factors which should be taken into account, and there is no reference to overarching norms or guideline principles. Sentencer's reports prepared for the Appeal Court thus consist of a list of all of the relevant facts and circumstances of the case but rarely refer to any principles or rules which were 'applied' to these facts to derive a sentencing decision. From a judicial perspective, sentencing works on a case-by-case basis. In that sense the decision is limited in that it is limited to the case at hand and, unless it is a guideline judgement of the Appeal Court, it has very limited implications for future practice, because judges pay little attention to past sentencing patterns and have no access to accurate information about these practices in any case. There is virtually no reference to anything which might be described as 'technical' evidence, for example about past sentencing practice, about the effectiveness of punishment, or about the costs and benefits of sentencing policy. Furthermore, there is little reliance on past practice nor any systematic attempt to be consistent.

Consistency, however, is an important value in sentencing. All judges would accept that it is an important aim of justice that like cases be treated alike. Where does consistency appear in sentencing judgements? Judges do not refer to data about the past sentencing practices of the court (Doob 1990), they only occasionally refer to other decided cases (following precedent in sentencing is quite different from the procedure in civil law). Consistency is alluded to rather than explicitly evoked. Judgements list the relevant factors of a case. On the one hand these factors characterize the case as an individual case, distinctive from other cases, on the other hand some of these features are obviously shared with other cases. Judges do not articulate what makes the case the same and what makes it different. They do not attempt to explain these features to a public audience. Why not?

First, they do not do it because there is no formal requirement for them to do so. However, more importantly, it is an impossible task because there is no systematic structure to which they can refer for help. Their sentencing decision making cannot be explained because there is literally no language which can be used to express it other than the language they use in their judgements. This is something that is part of their professional knowledge. Members of their profession share this knowledge and so there is no need to articulate it in another form. The language of the judgement *is* the way in which judges communicate with one another. It conveys the information which is necessary to account for their decision to the only institution which matters, the Appeal Court. If the judgement is an Appeal Court judgement – there is no higher institution which matters – the Appeal Court is communicating effectively with the profession.

Judges are not explicit about consistency because there is no mechanism to allow them to do this. The structures within which they work do not provide a means of talking about consistency in a legally relevant way. Consistency is an overarching norm or principle and judges are uncomfortable with these. This may partly explain the discomfort felt by the English judiciary with the principle of proportionality underpinning the 1991 Criminal Justice Act. This attempted to impose a principled approach to sentencing which is alien to the English tradition of individualized pragmatic sentencing.

The silence about consistency, which can also be understood as a silence about how to assign similarity and difference to cases, is produced by the general individualized, *ad hoc*, case-by-case, approach to sentencing, which is characteristic not only of sentencing but of a much wider approach to the exercise of discretion by judges. This is part of the habitus of sentencing.

This helps to explain why sentencing has long been regarded as unworthy of scholarly legal attention. The lack of systematic concern for precedent has made the field infertile ground for scholars who want to describe a jurisprudence of sentencing based on an analysis of sentencing decisions. The major works of scholarship in England and Wales and Scotland are encyclopaedias which contain descriptions of the decisions in many cases but which fail to identify any systematic guiding principles (Thomas 1999, Morrison 2000). In civil law scholarship, a common aim of a scholarly text is to accurately describe the law as a relatively closed field; it provides a text to which practitioners can refer to find answers to their problems. This has never really worked in sentencing because there are no rules which can be identified, interpreted, extrapolated, and applied to factual situations. The best that practitioners can hope for is to find a case in the encyclopaedia which shares 'sufficiently similar facts' to be offered as a guide for sentencers. The texts do not provide anything resembling a definition of what 'sufficiently similar facts' might be.

Sentencing does not really provide much for scholarly lawyers to get their teeth into. The kinds of elegant, subtle, and elaborate argument that one finds in civil judgements do not exist in sentencing because of the almost complete absence of rules.

Conclusion: Implications for Sentencing Reform

This chapter has suggested that a range of research techniques are required to understand how sentencing operates as a social practice. These range from an examination of statistical patterns of sentencing, reading, and listening to judicial accounts of sentencing, and an analysis of sentencing as a form of legal decision making. None of these on their own allows us to provide a 'grand theory' of sentencing, nor to build a robust model of sentencing that would enable us to predict sentencing decisions accurately. They can, however, provide an account which helps us to understand the social practice of sentencing and which might help to understand the obstacles to reform of sentencing as well as the mode of reform which has the best chance of working in practice.

Sentencing decisions are not generated by the application of legal rules but through the routine, largely unreflective, day-to-day practices of judges working in a distinctive legal culture and in a local court environment. Habitus offers a useful shorthand term for these processes.

Judicial accounts of sentencing typically relate a narrative of facts and circumstances, from which a sentence emerges through an intuitive process. This discourse of individualized sentencing allows cases to be distinguished from each other as there is an almost limitless range of relevant factors which can be taken into account and no rules which set out with any precision how these factors should affect the calculation of sentence. This discourse recognizes the value of consistency in sentencing, but provides an almost limitless range of ways in which one case can be distinguished from another which effectively means that no rational consideration of consistency is possible.

Most attempts to reform sentencing are efforts to inject a more rational approach to consistency. Where judges resist reform they do so not just to defend their power and social capital, not just because they perceive the reform to threaten the pursuit of justice, but also because the reform attempts represent an alien way of thinking about sentencing. The different approaches to reform, narrative guidelines, numerical guidelines, or sentencing information systems, all attempt to provide a language for addressing the issue of consistency in sentencing. The discourse of individualized sentencing has no such language and is silent on the issue of consistency. Sentencing reform thus needs to challenge the habitus of sentencing. Reformers need to find ways of convincing judges that there is an alternative to individualized sentencing. Inspiration may be sought from judges in the twenty or so US jurisdictions where guidelines operate (Reitz 2001). In most of these jurisdictions, judges exercise discretion within the context of the guidelines and do not feel that their independence or professional judgement is thereby threatened.

10

'Architecture', Criminal Justice, and Control

Richard Jones

Introduction

The aim of this chapter is to show how Lessig's novel concept of 'architecture' offers a useful analytic framework within which to make sense of several aspects of the operation of criminal justice and crime control, including various recent developments involving new technologies.[1] The chapter shows how the explanatory value of this concept is strengthened when combined with Bottoms' (2001) criminological account of compliance. This work by Lessig and Bottoms is synthesized into a larger model of social regulation and compliance, one which integrates and accords due importance to the role of physical space and technological design. This larger theory includes both top-down accounts of regulatory modes and a more bottom-up, or subjective, explanation of the reasons people obey. Finally, the utility of the model is demonstrated by applying it to two particular cases of concern to the sociologies of punishment and social control, namely situational crime prevention and the electronic monitoring of offenders. It is argued that the value of this analytic framework for theoretical work within criminology is that it identifies different fundamental ways in which punishment and social control can be said to operate, including through the use of built space and new technologies, and at the same time contributes to applied criminological research by suggesting a model for understanding why some attempts at obtaining compliance are more successful than others.

'Architecture' and Social Regulation

The starting point for this chapter is Lawrence Lessig's (1999) book entitled, *Code and Other Laws of Cyberspace*. The sections of his book on which I will

[1] I should like to express my gratitude to Sarah Armstrong, Lesley McAra, and Katja Franko for their detailed, insightful, and immensely helpful comments on an earlier version of this chapter.

focus most are those exploring the relationships between law, technology, and social regulation. The starting point of these sections, reflected in the title to Lessig's book, derives from William Mitchell's claim in the influential book *City of Bits* that:

Out there on the electronic frontier, code is the law. The rules governing any computer-constructed microworld – of a video game, your personal computer desktop, a word processor window, an automated teller machine, or a chat room on the network – are precisely and rigorously defined in the text of the program that constructs it on your screen... denizens of the digital world should pay the closest of critical attention to programmed polity. Is it just and humane? Does it protect our privacy, our property, and our freedoms? Does it constrain us unnecessarily or does it allow us to act as we may wish? (*ibid* 1995: 111)

By 'code', Lessig, following Mitchell, is thus referring to the rules that are programmed into any computing system or interface, and that shape our activities and embed certain social and political values.

Left unchecked, certain forces shape our social world

Lessig begins the book by challenging the ideas, sometimes floated in the 1990s, that the internet 'was a place that governments could not control' and that it was somehow socially neutral or inherently liberalizing or even libertarian (1999: 5). Rather, he argues, technology always embeds social and political values. As a constitutional lawyer, Lessig likens the relationship between government and cyberspace to that between government and real societies. For him:

Liberty in cyberspace will not come from the absence of the state. Liberty there, as anywhere, will come from a state of a certain kind. We build a world where freedom can flourish not by removing from society any self-conscious control; we build a world where freedom can flourish by setting it in a place where a particular kind of self-conscious control survives. We build liberty, that is, as our founders did, by setting society upon a certain *constitution*. (1999: 5, emphasis in original)

But, he quickly adds, by 'constitution' he:

... [doesn't] mean a legal text... Rather, as the British understand when they speak of their constitution, I mean an *architecture* – not just a legal text but a way of life – that structures and constrains social and legal power, to the end of protecting fundamental *values* – principles and ideals that reach beyond the compromises of ordinary politics. (1999: 5, emphases in original)

Lessig is thus setting the scene for his argument that: 'Constitutions in this sense are built, they are not found. Foundations get laid, they don't magically appear... There is no reason to believe that the grounding for liberty in cyberspace will simply emerge. In fact, as I will argue, quite the opposite is the case' (1999: 5). Indeed, he suggests that, left unchecked 'the invisible hand of cyberspace is building an architecture that is quite the opposite of what it was at cyberspace's birth', as a result of 'an axis between commerce and the state' (1999:6). Thus, the polity must actively seek to impose its preferred social and political values on such technology if it is to avoid others surreptitiously imposing their own values on the same.

Lessig's key contribution in terms of 'code' is to show how a given computer system or network can be seen to embody, and demand compliance with, certain particular social and political values. The system or network does this through its 'architecture', by which term I understand Lessig to mean any arrangement of physical or virtual elements effectively systematically enabling certain activities while rendering (almost) impossible others. The term 'architecture' obviously alludes to buildings and built architecture, and to the way the properties of buildings shape the social activities taking place within them – we can't walk through walls; placement of doors and windows shapes social usage of space, as do corridors, meeting places, and so on. Similarly, in social planning, street design and layout and design of public spaces both express certain civic values and encourage certain social activities and discourage others. Lessig uses the term 'architecture' in a wide sense, to refer to such wide-ranging phenomena as this built architecture, to the laws of physics insofar as they affect human movement and communications, to computer and network hardware, and to the 'virtual' architecture of software.

Lessig offers a good example of how networks' 'architectures' may differ, and to what social and political effect, in a discussion on the differences between university computing networks requiring user authorization and those permit-ting anonymous unrestricted access to all staff and students (Harvard versus Chicago universities during the 1990s) (1999: 25–9). The former system, he notes, prioritizes (a university's) control over users and discourages improper activity, at the expense of anonymity and hence, possibly, of a certain freedom of speech; the latter system prioritizes anonymity and hence permits a certain freedom of speech, but at the expense of control (including over miscreants). Lessig compares these two technical and value systems with a third – much more restrictive and secure than Harvard's – which he describes as the propri-etary, 'closed' network type. He offers as an example the computer banking network linking ATM units. Thus, to claim that the Internet is 'unregulable' is at best misleading, if not just plain wrong, because: 'If some networks are more regulable than others, this is simply a function of the network's design. The design of an unregulable network could be changed; it could be transformed into a regulable network' (1999: 27). This change could be carried out quite consciously, with the aim of embedding certain values (such as user anonymity, or alternatively, institutional control and security) within the network's technical design. As Lessig notes, the Harvard solution suggests that further layers of control can be *added* to otherwise relatively open networks: '*Architectures of control* could be layered on top of the Net to "correct" or eliminate "imperfections" of control. Architectures of credentials and architectures that label could, in other words, facilitate architectures of control' (1999: 28–9 emphasis in original). In this way, '*even without the government's help*, we will see the Net move to an architecture of control' (1999: 29, emphasis in original).

Developing the argument further, Lessig then explores how code might itself be regulated. He presents examples – some now abandoned or somewhat dated – not just from the internet but also from what today are more mundane information and communications technologies.[2]

Whether left to its own devices or as shaped by legal intervention, (technological) architecture has a systemic, controlling nature. For Lessig this raises the spectre of commercial entities dictating technological systems' formation for their own interests, which could quite possibly run roughshod over important social values: 'Architecture is a kind of law: it determines what people can and cannot do. When commercial interests determine the architecture, they create a kind of privatized law', by which he means a kind of constraining or directing force (1999: 59). Lessig's view is that: 'Choices among values, choices about regulation, about control, choices about the definition of spaces of freedom – all this is the stuff of politics. Code codifies values, and yet, oddly, most people speak as if code were just a question of engineering' (1999: 59).

Lessig's argument to this point is focused on the way in which code (the name given to architecture in the field of the internet) can be seen as having values embedded within it, and how the social and communicative activities this code permits are thus influenced by the code's embedded values. Thus, in a sense, code 'regulates' the internet. For Lessig, this is a problem insofar as the (properly political) decision-making process as to what sort of electronic 'laws' we want is in fact made by corporations, software engineers, marketers, and so on, rather than by governments and polities. His argument is valuable, in that it identifies code, shows how it works, and shows how it can act to 'regulate' the internet.

However, in the next section of the book Lessig modifies his position, and moves away from the suggestion implicit up to this point that the internet is regulated exclusively or even primarily by code. His argument now becomes that while code is important ('We are coming to understand a newly powerful regulator in cyberspace, and we don't yet understand how best to control it'), overall, 'I believe we need a more general understanding of how regulation works. One that focuses on more than the single influence of any one force such as government, norms, or the market, and instead integrates these factors into a single account' (1999: 86).

---

[2] Examples include changes to the architecture of the US digitally-switched telephone network required by a 1994 Act such as to make it easier for law enforcement agencies to carry out authorized wiretaps; copy protection technology in the case of CDs and DAT tapes; or the provisions in the Digital Millennium Copyright Act 1998 making it illegal 'to write and sell software that circumvents copyright management [DRM] schemes' (Lessig 1999: 45, 49).

In order to help to explain his multiple force regulatory model, Lessig invites the reader to consider a 'dot', and to imagine that it represents a person. The dot might be regulated by certain different types of constraints. Taking Lessig's example of smoking, we can imagine the dot to represent a smoker. The dot/smoker may be constrained by laws (relating, for example, to the age at which cigarettes can be purchased, or where it is permitted to smoke). The smoker may also (particularly in America, though increasingly in other countries too) be 'regulated by norms' (1999: 87). Additionally, '[t]he market too is a constraint' (price, quality, supply and demand). Finally, there is the technology of cigarettes (filters, perhaps smokeless, chemicals and drugs added/removed): 'In all of these ways, how the cigarette *is* affects the constraints faced by a smoker. How it is, how it is designed, how it is built – in a word, its *architecture* (1999: 87, emphasis in original):

Thus, four constraints regulate this pathetic dot – the law, social norms, the market, and architecture – and the 'regulation' of this dot is the sum of these four constraints . . . Some constraints will support others; some may undermine others. A complete view, however, should consider them together. (1999: 87)

As we will see in subsequent sections below, while the characterization of the dot as 'pathetic' or passive is useful for the purposes of identifying different modes of regulation, it is inadequate as an account of subjective reasons for (non-)compliance. However, for the time being, let us continue to follow his explication of regulatory modes. Lessig names the four key modes by which his dot, or regulated subject, might be constrained:

(1) by the *market*;
(2) by *law*;
(3) by *norms*; and
(4) by *architecture*.

Each of these distinct modes might constrain singly or in combination:

Each constraint imposes a different kind of cost on the dot for engaging in the relevant behavior . . . The constraints are distinct, yet they are plainly interdependent. Each can support or oppose the others . . . Constraints work together, though they function differently and the effect of each is distinct. Norms constrain through the stigma that a community imposes; markets constrain through the price that they exact; architectures constrain through the physical burdens they impose; and law constrains through the punishment it threatens. (Lessig 1999: 88)

'We can', says Lessig, 'call each constraint a "regulator," and we can think of each as a distinct modality of regulation' (1999: 88). In this book Lessig is, of course, primarily concerned with the impact of these modes of regulation in relation to the internet. In this specific area, Lessig terms the operative version of architecture as 'code': 'an analog for architecture regulates behavior in cyberspace – *code*.

The software and hardware that make cyberspace what it is constitute a set of constraints on how you can behave' (1999: 89). Identifying the techniques used in regulatory 'code', Lessig writes that:

The substance of these constraints may vary, but they are experienced as conditions on your access to cyberspace. In some places . . . you must enter a password before you gain access; in other places you can enter whether identified or not . . . In some places you can choose to speak a language that only the recipient can hear (through encryption); in other places encryption is not an option. The code or software or architecture or protocols set these features; they are features selected by code writers; they constrain some behavior by making other behavior possible, or impossible. The code embeds certain values or makes certain values impossible. In this sense, it too is regulation, just as the architectures of real-space codes are regulations (1999: 89).

From this perspective, the 'code writer, as Ethan Katsh puts it, is the "architect"' (Lessig 1999: 90, see also Katsh 1996).

Giving an example of a type of approach criminology has already termed 'situational crime prevention' (Clarke 1995, Clarke and Homel 1997), Lessig discusses how one might go about reducing car radio theft. Legal penalties for such theft could be increased in an attempt to deter:

But changing the law is not the only possible technique. A second might be to change the radio's architecture. Imagine that radio manufacturers program radios to work only with a single car – a security code that electronically locks the radio to the car, such that if the radio is removed, it will no longer work. This is a *code* constraint on the theft of radios; it makes the radio no longer effective once stolen. (Lessig 1999: 90, emphasis in original)

Other examples of how architecture (in these cases, built architecture) can attempt to regulate social activities, include Louis Napoleon III's role in rede-signing Parisian street layout partly with the aim of making revolution more difficult; and the practice in Washington and elsewhere in relation to the geo-graphical placing of seats of governance, of physically locating the executive and legislature in different parts of town or even different cities in order to reduce the likelihood of direct pressure (or collusion) between one and the other (1999: 91–2). In such cases, argues Lessig, 'a constraint of architecture is changed so as to realize a collective or social end' (1999: 92).

Lessig further argues that instead of being directed at the target 'dot', a mode of regulation may be directed at another mode (with the latter being directed at the 'dot'). In this way, we can see that law, for instance, can function not only directly ('it tells individuals how to behave and threatens punishment if they deviate from that behavior'), but also *indirectly* (in which 'it aims at modifying one of the other structures of constraint') (1999: 95). Lessig terms this kind of regulation, involving one mode of regulation acting on (at least) one other mode of regulation which only then acts on the target, 'indirect regulation'.

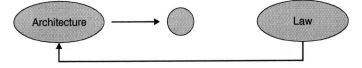

Figure 10.1. Indirect regulation
Source: adapted from Lessig 1999: 93

The diagram in Figure 10.1, derived from one suggested by Lessig (1999: 93), represents law acting on architecture as an indirect way to regulate the target 'dot':

Figure 10.1 represents a scenario in which the law attempts to regulate a target by acting on architecture, which in turn acts on the target. An example of this could be that greater prevalence of wearing car seatbelts might be sought through a legal requirement that car manufacturers connect a car engine immobilizer to a driver's seatbelt sensor, thus forcing drivers to wear them when driving. A similar set of alternatives can be found in relation to the topic of building regulations and disabled persons' access to buildings (1999: 94–5).

The importance of Lessig's overall model should now be becoming apparent. The model he proposes and develops provides us with a way of getting a grasp of design's significance, especially in relation to fast-moving technical developments in areas such as the internet. As new technologies, network protocols, software and hardware facilities and features, are all rolled out to an expectant public, Lessig draws attention to the constraints or limitations that are wittingly or unwittingly embedded in these technologies alongside the features they bring and the practices they enable. In examples ranging from university computer networks, to smoking, to Parisian street layout design, he notes how various political values can and have informed the preferred architectures and policies implemented. Indirect regulation suggests how any mode of regulation, including architecture, may act upon or be acted upon another mode, thus identifying a range of regulatory strategies; yet indirect regulation also introduces an inherent masking effect, meaning that identification of a regulatory strategy at work may be harder to spot, and thus challenge.

The application of Lessig's model, and in particular his concept of 'architecture', to the specific fields of punishment, social control, and crime prevention, will be discussed in detail later in this chapter. However, certain initial points of relevance to criminological topics can already usefully be identified. In terms of punishment, (secure) imprisonment can be seen as an architectural means of depriving a convicted offender of their liberty, while the electronic monitoring of offenders is an architectural solution to the (long-standing) problem of how to police compliance with a home detention curfew order.[3] We can see how architecture can be used in social control and public order strategies, in fields such as

---

[3] I am here referring primarily to the simple 'first generation' electronic 'tags', rather than to 'second generation' GPS satellite 'tracking tags'.

street design, the interior design of buildings such as pubs and shops, and in entertainment complexes (Lessig's perspective offers a new theoretical perspective, for example, for reinterpreting Shearing and Stenning's (1985) classic discussion of Disneyworld). Lastly, from the perspective of Lessig's model, situational crime prevention now can be viewed as a particular application of general features of architectural regulation within the specific area of crime prevention.

I will shortly proceed with an examination of work by Bottoms (1999, 2001) on the topic of individual compliance in the specific context of convicted offenders and the operation of penal sanctions, before suggesting how Lessig's and Bottoms' work can usefully be linked together into a single unified model, emphasizing for the purposes of this present chapter the category of 'architecture'. I will finish the chapter by sketching some of the ways this theoretical model can contribute to various issues within the sociology of punishment. Before turning to Bottoms' work, however, I will briefly suggest some ways I think Lessig's model could be revised.

Ways Lessig's Model Needs to be Developed

Having introduced Lessig's model of social regulation, I will now turn to a discussion of some of the limitations to Lessig's model, and offer some possible improvements.

The first of my suggested amendments to Lessig's model is a very straight-forward one: that we should replace the term 'market' with that of 'economy'. The reason for preferring the latter is that 'market' seems to refer primarily to market forces (price, quantity, supply and demand), whereas it seems desirable to recognize not only these but also government and central bank interventions in markets and indeed in the economy more generally, including (but not limited to) taxation policies, interest rates, and money supply control. In the case of the smoker, for instance, the revised category allows us to recognize the various roles of factors such as cigarette taxation and income tax.

The second point is to note that, as against Lessig's tendency to speak of regulation principally in terms of constraint (whether through constraining something or enabling only certain specific behaviour), it is important to open this up and recognize that 'regulation' always in fact speaks of something that seeks to allow (desirable) activity to continue unfettered while constraining only that which is undesirable. We can also see that regulatory measures are typically targeted at certain groups or behaviours (thus seeking differential impact), and/or adjustable (admittedly albeit with greater or lesser degrees of subtlety and effectiveness) such as to impact in a gradated way on those being regulated (think price, taxation). This duality of enable/constrain appears even more important when we modify Lessig's model to describe the environment in which actors find themselves irre-spective of whether the social forces impacting on them are intentional regulatory strategies or not (see below for further discussion of this point).

The third suggestion is that we should carefully distinguish code, architecture, and technology from one another. (Lessig is mostly very clear in distinguishing these terms, but it is important to maintain these distinctions, first because of the question of intentionality of regulation, and secondly in order to explore the applicability of his model to other areas of social and socio-legal research such as criminology.) While in early parts of *Code* Lessig (1999) makes such claims as 'Code is law', he goes on to develop the four-mode general regulatory model discussed above, in which one of the four modes is 'architecture'. 'Code' in this case is simply the version of architectural regulation we find in the specific fields of the internet and computing. Additionally, it may be helpful to distinguish between architecture and technology. Architecture is social regulation brought about by the physical or virtual properties of objects, systems, or environments. But technology cannot be reduced to architecture. There are two main reasons for this. The first reason is that there appear to be certain features of technology that may not have any identifiable regulatory qualities at all, including colour, aesthetics, ergonomics, and choice of materials, which may be important aspects of its design, use, popularity and commercial success, but which seem at best only marginally related to regulation. The second reason is that it would seem that there is an important difference between intentional and unintentional forms of regulation; we can speak of a technology's physical or virtual properties 'regulating' behaviour in certain ways, but if this is an unintended outcome of the technology, we are using the term 'regulation' in a different sense to that in which these properties were deliberately introduced into a technological design. The outcome may be the same in both cases, but the social and political consequences are different.

Whereas the above point relates to different intentions but similar outcomes, my fourth point relates to the possibility of similar intentions having different outcomes. It seems quite possible that in practice a regulatory measure may not have any particular effect; or that it could have one or more unintended (alternative or additional) consequences, perhaps because of the way it affects other regulatory measures or modes of regulation. A final related possibility is a 'regulatory dissonance', by which I mean the possibility that two (or more) regulatory processes might actually conflict or interfere with one another, leading to failure (or at least sub-optimal regulation) in one or more of the areas. It is an interesting theoretical question as to the circumstances in which these outcomes may result, one that will be addressed in the following sections.

Fifthly, it could be argued that Lessig's model tends to suggest a situation in which society is faced with a social problem which it then considers how to regulate (selecting from one or more of the regulatory modes, whether operating directly or indirectly), yet given the enormous range of regulatory measures in place in modern societies already, Lessig's implicit suggestion that there is always a socially and regulatory 'blank page' on which regulators may write seems implausible (including, already, within the field of internet regulation). Instead, it must be recognized regulation always takes place within a world of regulation.

The sixth and final observation in this section is that it seems worth modifying Lessig's model to take account of the possibility of *resistance* to regulation. There are a number of reasons why it is desirable to incorporate an account of resistance into any regulatory model. A model becomes more powerful analytically if it can account not only for instances of regulatory successes but also of failures. It seems likely that the regulated may not always welcome regulation – a point that is perhaps clearest in the case of convicted offenders being sanctioned, but which may also apply to corporations, drivers, smokers, and many others.

The various above observations and suggested revisions regarding Lessig's model are intended to try to retain the most useful and powerful qualities of his original model while stretching it and attempting to develop it further. In relation specifically to the notion of architecture, what I have tried to caution against in this section is Lessig's occasional tendency (which is entirely under-standable, given his pioneering role in this respect, and his desire to counter the then argument that the internet was unregulable) to characterize architecture primarily in terms of control, prohibition, or disallowance. Instead, the understanding towards which I wish to move is a notion of the regulatory force of architecture as coordination or guidance, and as a powerful force for opening up the possible/not possible, the allowed/not allowed. In this respect, architec-ture may be distinctive and different as compared to law and norms. A mode of regulation structured around the possible/not possible opposition is different to one structured around a right/wrong distinction. It lacks the normative vehe-mence of the latter, and it structures the nature of the response differently. Bearing all of these points in mind, I will now turn to an examination of what might be thought of as the complement of regulatory strategy, namely individual compliance and non-compliance with regulation.

Understanding Why People Comply: Bottoms' Model of Compliance

In the preceding section I examined Lessig's model of regulation which, as we saw, has as its most novel feature the category of 'architecture' as a way of regulating activity. In the context of theorizing 'compliance', and in particular 'the main social and psychological processes that might be involved when an individual complies with legal rules in a given situation', Anthony Bottoms has (quite independently of Lessig) developed a model that appears to share certain characteristics with Lessig's model. Bottoms has a long-standing interest in the issue of compliance by prisoners within prisons, and especially the role of the prison regime and in the quality of staff-prisoner relationships in obtaining such compliance. More recently, in the context of studying the compliance of offenders with community penalties, Bottoms has sought to develop a 'basic

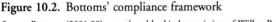

A Instrumental/prudential compliance
  (a) Incentives
  (b) Disincentives
B Normative compliance
  (a) Acceptance of / belief in norm
  (b) Attachment leading to compliance
  (c) Legitimacy
C Constraint-based compliance
  (a) Physical restrictions or requirements on individual leading to compliance
    (i) Natural
    (ii) Imposed
  (b) Restrictions on access to target
  (c) Structural constraints
D Compliance based on habit or routine

Figure 10.2. Bottoms' compliance framework

Source: Bottoms (2001:90) reproduced by kind permission of Willan Publishing.

framework for the understanding of compliant behaviour' (Bottoms 1999: 250ff, see also Bottoms 2001). (In this present chapter I will examine in particular the framework he sets out in his 2001 chapter, as this usefully summarizes his framework and discusses its implications and applications.) As with Lessig's model, Bottoms' has four main dimensions, but whereas in Lessig's the dimensions are of regulatory modes, with Bottoms they are of compliant behaviour (the other side of the coin, as it were). Bottoms identifies four categories of compliance, namely instrumental/prudential ('based on self-interested calculation'), normative ('based on a felt moral obligation, commitment or coercion'), constraint-based ('derived from some form of constraint or coercion'), and compliance based on habit or routine (2001: 90) (Figure 10.2).

These four general types of compliance can be summarized (albeit crudely) respectively in the following colloquial ways: (A) 'it's in my self-interest (not) to do so'; (B) 'I believe I should'; (C) 'I have no choice in the matter'; and (D) 'it's what I usually do'. A certain similarity is apparent as between Bottoms' types and Max Weber's (1968) four types of how social action in general may be 'oriented' (ie that it may be instrumentally rational, value-rational, affectual, or traditional). The most obvious difference between the two models is their third category – Weber identifying 'affect', Bottoms identifying constraint.

As can be seen from Figure 10.2, under the four main headings Bottoms identifies various sub-headings. He discusses the distinctions between these headings and sub-headings from illustrations drawn principally from the topic of community penalties. In relation to instrumental compliance, he writes, two 'simple reasons for compliance may operate', namely incentives (for example 'early termination for good progress in the probation order') and disincentives ('provisions for punishment when the requirements of the order are not fulfilled by the offender') (2001: 91). Normative compliance 'may be of three main sub-types', namely belief in a norm (such as that it is wrong to harm others), social attachment (for example of an offender to their partner and family), or legitimacy (of the authority issuing the law or rule). Constraint-based compliance, the third type of compliance, 'has three sub-types', the first sub-type being physical restrictions ('deriving from the physical characteristics and limitations of the human body. We all need sleep, and when we are asleep we cannot burgle . . . this is Hirschi's [1969] "involvement" '), and which is itself sub-divisible into naturally-occurring limitations and imposed physical restrictions (Bottoms 2001: 92). Bottoms notes that the degree to which such limitations underpin compliance may vary, depending on the fundamental nature of the sanction in question:

It could be said that a central problem for community penalties is that, by their nature, they inevitably find it more difficult to deliver imposed constraint-based physical restrictions on an individual than does the prison. (It is, I believe more helpful to analyse the problem in this manner than through the language of 'toughness'.) But that does not mean that the physical constraints of community penalties are always negligible, a point that is surely becoming increasingly obvious in a context of increasing electronic surveillance, plus the ability to monitor bodily substances by devices such as drug testing or the breathalyzer. (Bottoms 2001: 92–3)

In addition to this type of constraint-based compliance, Bottoms identifies as a second sub-type that 'compliance based on restrictions on one's access to the possible target of non-compliance' (opportunity reduction as found in situational crime prevention), and a third sub-type, 'structural constraint', which Bottoms indicates refers to power or strength-based domination (describing circumstances in which someone is 'cowed into submission' (2001: 93), but under which heading we might also want to include social-structural constraints in general (it is difficult for someone to 'hack' into a bank's computer if, for example, they are illiterate or if they live in a place which does not yet have access to the internet). The fourth and final of Bottoms' main compliance types is 'based upon habit or routine'. Everyday routines may lead to psychological dispositions to do (or not do) certain things, as well as social expectations on the part both of the individual in question as well as others as to what is to happen at certain times on certain days.[4]

Bottoms argues that this analytical framework for thinking about compliance is useful for analysing community penalties in a number of different respects, and offers two specific applications by way of example. The first is a reconsideration of a research study (Sinclair 1971) which had found that the 'failure rates' for offenders 'sentenced to probation orders . . . with a requirement that the first year be spent as a resident in a probation hostel . . . varied markedly by hostel regime, from 14 per cent to 78 per cent', and that an important factor in

---

[4] Bottoms (2001: 93–4) offers the example of family routines accompanying the sending of children off to school each morning, in which the following of the routine becomes largely self-perpetuating after a while.

explaining this wide variation seemed to be probation hostel staff kindness, and their clarity and consistency of rule application (Bottoms 2001: 95–6). Bottoms suggests that the compliance dimension of 'normative attachment' might help to theorize this finding, and that, moreover, it might help to explain another striking finding from the same study, namely that despite the 'marked difference in the in-residence failure rates between hostels, these differences almost completely disappeared when post-hostel reconvictions (in the two subsequent years) were considered' – a phenomenon explicable in terms of the presence (and subsequent absence) of normative attachment (2001: 96).

Bottoms' second example application is an analysis of community penalties policies in the United Kingdom from about 2000–1. He argues that analysis of various distinct policies (including treatment programmes based on cognitive-behavioural psychology, restorative justice programmes, the threat of use of custodial sentences for those failing to comply with a community order, and the electronic monitoring of offenders' compliance with community order requirements) 'shows that they depend upon different anticipated mechanisms of compliance' (2001: 97). For example, restorative justice seems to try to draw upon normative compliance mechanisms, whereas the threat of use of imprisonment for community order breaches seems to be based on deterrence (2001: 97–8). As Bottoms points out, it may be important for policy makers to be more aware than they perhaps are at present of the compliance mechanisms underpinning the different approaches.

Three further significant issues emerge from his compliance model. The first is that the study of compliance necessarily involves attention to the 'individual as subject' (the subjective orientation of the individual whom one is seeking to make compliant). Examples of where such attention is of particular importance include the study of deterrent effectiveness, and the likelihood of prisoners' subjective resentment towards 'very physically restrictive control strategies' adopted by some prison authorities within prisons (2001: 99–100). The second issue is that of legitimacy. Research has seemed to suggest that (perceived) procedural fairness, the manner in which the rule-appliers apply the rules and, in the context of prisons (though one might also predict similar results elsewhere in the criminal justice system), prisoners' perceptions of the quality of staff-offender relationships (Bottoms 2001: 101–4). The third issue emerging from the compliance model is what Bottoms terms the possibility of interaction effects between different compliance mechanisms. As an example of what is meant by this he cites the proposition, which seems to have support in empirical research, that:

... deterrence works best for those persons who have strong ties of attachment to familial or social groups or institutions, in a context where those groups or institutions clearly disapprove normatively of the behaviour at which the deterrent sanction is aimed. (Bottoms 2001: 104, emphasis removed)

Bottoms cites Sherman's research on the effects on subsequent domestic violence offending behaviour by differential police responses to domestic violence offenders, noting that instrumental measures may succeed in having deterrent effects 'because of what he [the potential offender] fears he will lose':

But what the subject has to lose, from what Sherman interestingly calls 'the *social* consequences of arrest' (emphasis added), arises from the facts that (i) he regards himself as having a significant attachment to the family/social group/social institution in question (the group is important to him), and (ii) that the members of that family/social group/ social institution have certain normative expectations about how people should behave [see von Hirsch *et al* 1999: 40], and may censure the subject if he breaches those expectations. Where such normative factors are not present, instrumental compliance is weaker. (Bottoms 2001: 105–6)

As Bottoms notes, this example suggests that one might want to explore both how interaction effects operate at a general level (for example between normative and instrumental compliance mechanisms in general), but also how they operate differently for different individuals (in the context, perhaps, of the persons' particular histories, personalities, and present relationships). These three issues identified by Bottoms help to identify what is particularly distinctive about his contribution, namely the focus on the question as to *why* people do or do not comply, given their subjective perspective of *how* regulation is *experienced* – an area that it is essential to understand if we are to understand why it is that certain policies designed to achieve compliance succeed while others fail.

In a final example reflecting on the role of compliance mechanisms within criminal justice generally, Bottoms discusses a visit he made to Texas in 1999 during which he witnessed an extreme example of a constraint-based compliance system. In the 'Adseg 3' maximum restrictiveness section at one particular prison, used to deal with the most difficult prisoners:

... prisoners are completely confined to their cells, except for very short periods of exercise (three half-hour periods per week), such exercise being taken in tiny exercise 'cages', each housing only one prisoner. Food is provided to prisoners by pushing trays through slots in their cell doors. The transition from cell to exercise cage is managed by shackling the prisoner to a guard on each side, with handcuffs and leg-irons. It is the closest thing to attempted total physical constraint-based compliance that I have ever seen (Bottoms 2001: 111).

Bottoms notes that he and others in his visiting group were shocked to learn that there was no system of preparation for release back into the community for such prisoners, involving a stepped diminution in security level and/or degree of physical restraint over the years and months prior to a prisoner's release, but instead the prisoners were simply released straight back into the community. It is perhaps noteworthy from the perspective of Lessig's 'architecture' that two things may be particularly problematic about the Adseg 3. First, it is not that the architecture is ineffective in obtaining (short-term) compliance, but precisely that it *is* so unremittingly effective, suggesting that as was noted above, systems of architecture always both constrain and enable, and it may be that the political and social acceptability of a given measure may depend on where this balance between the two is struck. Secondly, it could be said that the aspect of the Adseg 3 practice which is objectionable (to some eyes, at least) is the values embedded in the architecture. However, these two reasons also alert us contrarily to the possibility that the extreme example of the Adseg 3 unit should not tempt us to condemn architectural or physical constraint approaches *per se*, but rather to recognize that any genre of regulation has the possibility for being draconian (in intent or effect), and that there may be nothing intrinsic to architectural regulation that is more objectionable than any other possible approach.

In his work on compliance, Bottoms offers a number of significant insights relating, in particular, to the role of constraint-based physical restrictions within imprisonment and, to a lesser extent, community penalties, to the 'interaction effects' between different types of compliance, to the subjective dimension of compliance, and to the importance of dimensions such as legitimacy and attachment. In the next section of this chapter, I will sketch how Lessig's and Bottoms' models can be synthesized into a general model of regulation and compliance, before finishing the chapter by suggesting two applications of this model.

Synthesizing Lessig's and Bottoms' Models

Although originating in very different areas and with different concerns in mind, both Lessig's and Bottoms' models are notable for their shared emphasis on architecture/constraint-based compliance, and for their recognition that this dimension, important though it is, needs to be incorporated within a wider model also featuring other factors. Both models seek to characterize not only different types of regulatory approach but also to suggest why such measures may or may not be effective in achieving compliance. However, Lessig's model is more explicit in its identification of the possible modes of regulation, while Bottoms' model, with its analysis of the principal reasons why someone might be compliant, and its implicit favouring of an analysis exploring the subjective dimension, seems better placed to account for how regulation is experienced by individuals. Following on from this, we can use the two models as the bases for two elements of the regulatory model: Lessig's as the basis for a 'top-down' or 'objective' regulatory perspective, and Bottoms' for a 'bottom-up' or 'subjective' approach. Having isolated these two elements, we can also see how they can readily be combined into a single model. Since both elements incorporate the dimension of architecture/physical constraints, consequently not only is the resulting model able to include this aspect, but it will also be able to help identify

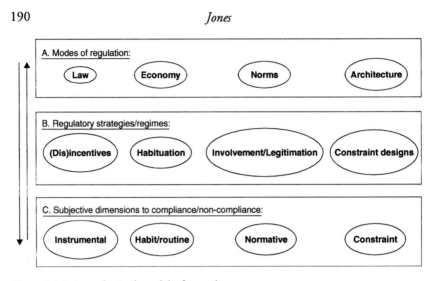

Figure 10.3 A synthesized model of compliance

some of the potential reasons and mechanisms by which Lessig's architecture may wholly or partly fail to obtain compliance. In Figure 10.3 I suggest a way in which Bottoms' and Lessig's approaches might be incorporated (not such a difficult task, given their obvious similarities and overlaps).

The figure is intended to represent ways in which a regulatory measure based upon one of the core modes of regulation (A), might be filtered through a regulatory mechanism (B), and the main ways in which this will be subjectively experienced (C) by a given individual. (And vice versa, from (C) to (A)). *The model does not attempt to predict whether an individual will or will not comply with a given measure.* Rather, the elements in the bubbles are conceptual building-blocks. Using these elements, empirical mechanisms of actual compliance or non-compliance can be analysed, or theoretical future compliance or non-compliance can be hypothesized.

The filtering process by which a regulatory measure is pursued (by a government, company, or institution), and its eventual reception by an individual, is represented by the downward arrow. The upward arrow represents instead the situation where the individual is the starting-point of analysis.

Rows A and C derive from Lessig's and Bottoms' original models respectively, while Row B derives primarily from sub-categories of Bottoms' model, though also (to a certain extent) from Lessig's discussion of different ways in which his modes of regulation might operate. In the synthesized model, as represented in Figure 10.3 above, Lessig's modes of regulation are cast in terms so as to represent the broad genres by which regulation can be pursued, while Bottoms' 'principal mechanisms underpinning compliant behaviour' are cast in terms of their being some primary subjective dimensions of compliance or non-compliance. The significance of Row B, regulatory mechanisms, is that it seeks to identify some of the different strategies or tactics that regulators may employ in respect of a mode of regulation, or that might be seen to be at work, and hence to represent some of the different ways in which modes or genres of regulation may be employed with the aim of seeking compliance.

There are three key features to the above regulatory model worth emphasizing. The first is that while from a regulatory perspective there may appear to be certain more obvious regulatory 'paths' from rows A to B to C (for example, law may employ an incentives/disincentives strategy designed to appeal to individuals' instrumental orientations), *other paths or combinations may also be possible*. For example, the architectural mode may be employed, with the regulators adopting the obvious strategy of designing a system of constraints exploiting certain architectural features, but it is possible, in theory at least, that even if such a regulatory approach is effective in obtaining compliance it is not because these constraint designs are in practice particularly effective but because the (limited) constraint has become part of people's habit or routine, or because they believe in the normative values embedded in the architecture and the resulting social practices which it supports. In this way, one can see that there are many potential possible ways in which the elements in the various columns could be combined or re-combined. The second key point of the model is that it can potentially be used either by regulators in order to consider different possible regulatory strategies and to hypothesize as to the mechanisms by which such regulation might work (and to alert them as to possible ways in which it might not), or by sociologists seeking a preliminary framework within which to model the (possibly intricate) ways in which new and existing regulatory frameworks and social forces might interact, including how different regulatory mechanisms (intended and unintended) might be at work and how subjective orientations of individuals might relate to compliance effectiveness.[5] A third feature of the model is that it neither presumes regulatory success nor its failure, but rather seeks to model the social forces potentially at play. In these three ways, among others, the model attempts to address some of the potential shortcomings identified with Lessig's (and to a lesser extent Bottoms') original models (for instance, the model is able to model issues relating to regulatory intentionality, and to unintended consequences).

Applying the Model to the Sociology of Punishment

In this, the penultimate section of this chapter, I will very briefly discuss two applications of the above synthesized regulatory model relating respectively to

---

[5] One can imagine, eg, ways in which James Coleman's (1990) work on the possible instrumental reasons underpinning norm-compliance might feature in a given sociological explanation of compliance or non-compliance.

situational crime prevention and to the electronic monitoring of offenders, by way of illustrating potential applications of the model.

Architecture and situational crime prevention

My first example application is in relation to situational crime prevention. Situational crime prevention would seem to be a particularly striking example of an approach based primarily upon 'architectural' constraints. Clarke's classic typology of situational crime prevention identifies three principal types of approach, involving three different crime prevention (law compliance) mechanisms, namely increasing the risk of getting caught, reducing the rewards, and increasing the effort. Each of these three typically involve exploiting architectural, physical-world properties of materials, mechanics, systems, barriers, locks and so on, with the aim of invoking one or more of these three mechanisms. For instance, increasing the risk of getting caught may involve using materials that are noisy when broken; increasing the optical visibility of a particular place; or installing alarm systems. Reward reduction may involve switching from coin-based to electronic funds-based retailing; the use of electronic immobilizers; or ways of disabling stolen devices so as to reduce their sell-on value to thieves. Lastly, criminal activities can be made more of an effort for potential offenders by the use of stronger materials in doors, containers, and windows; the use of more complex and secure locking devices; or exploiting aspects of the physical world such as geographical remoteness, height off the ground, or weight or bulk of the target object.

From the perspective of the synthesized model sketched out in the previous section, a number of points about situational crime prevention can be made. First, Clarke is careful to couch his typology in terms of increases or reductions (for instance of reward) rather than suggest, as Lessig is wont to do, that architectural methods are intrinsically likely to succeed. Instead, Clarke argues that measures only work if they are well designed and thought out, and reflect a good understanding of the mechanisms by which a particular offence in a particular setting has previously been carried out; moreover, even a 'successful' measure may not be wholly successful, but rather may be successful insofar as it is effective in respect of most of the people, most of the time. Dedicated offenders may still devise ways of circumventing any given preventive measure if they are sufficiently and unusually motivated so to do. In this respect, the synthetic model seems better placed to map onto Clarke's understanding of the operation of situational crime prevention measures than Lessig's model alone, despite their evident relationship.

Secondly, Clarke's model is based on a particular psychological model of offending, taking as its starting point the offending situation (setting, environment, features, social dynamics), in which offenders, just like anyone else, are seen partly as self-interested and utility-maximizing, partly as opportunistic, and partly as subject to habits, routines, and social norms (although their offending behaviour may also rely on their exploiting others' practices or beliefs in these respects). Famously, rather than seek to change potential offenders, situational crime prevention seeks to change the crime setting, and thus to influence offending behaviour. From the perspective of my synthetic model, situational crime prevention could therefore be read as taking the subjective dimensions of compliance as given, seeking to employ architecture and constraint design strategies in order to appeal to one or more of these dimensions. The most obvious and central one of these in terms of situational crime prevention is, of course, constraint, but it is not the only one; it also appeals to social norms that seem to inhibit offending behaviour in many people in situations where they believe they are being watched. In this respect, my regulatory model both helps make apparent and helps explain what is otherwise a slight anomaly in Clarke's typology, namely that measures seeking to increase visibility of offending behaviour as a mechanism to self-inhibit potential offenders *do* seem to be 'architectural' (they rely on optics) but *do not* seem to be a type of *physical* constraint (there is nothing physically to stop an offender from offending).

Thirdly, a central but often overlooked dimension to situational crime prevention, is that on reflection it is clearly an approach based on analyzing offence mechanisms in order to constrain undesirable behaviour while allowing desirable, law-abiding practices to continue as uninhibited as possible. (Indeed, this may be one of the reasons it sometimes attracts the ire of the political left, because the practices it leaves remaining enabled are often commercial or property-related activities of one sort or another, meaning that it can seem politically conservative.) As such, situational crime prevention simultaneously constrains and enables; a situational crime prevention measure that overly constrains all activity is unlikely to be favoured by users in general, and hence may even be subverted by them – as in the case of overly noisy or laborious mechanical security doors which regular users simply leave unlocked or even permanently jammed ajar. The enabling dimension of situational crime prevention is significant in one other respect; it may be that practices that overly constrain have greater potential for being perceived subjectively as being punitive (even if this involves a misattribution of regulators' intentionality), and it may be that it is precisely the avoidance of such a perception that has driven situational crime prevention, or customers so voting with their feet or money, towards its most successful implementations, those in which it is simultaneously powerful yet minimally intrusive.

One final comment is also worth making regarding situational crime prevention and punishment. As Wortley (2002) has shown, situational crime prevention has various possible applications within prisons, though as Bottoms' (1999) and Sparks, Bottoms and Hay's (1996) research suggests, and as Bosworth (2003) has argued, we should be wary of according too great a role to it within prisons, partly because of the importance of the quality of staff-prisoner relationships and inter-personal dynamics within prisons, and partly and relatedly because the temptation within prisons may be to use more restrictive situational measures, possibly in response to the perception of the characteristics of the potential offending group, but which could quite possibly have counter-productive effects.

Architecture and the electronic monitoring of offenders

My second application relates to the electronic monitoring of offenders. Where in the first example we found an example of architecture used as constraint but to preventive rather than punitive ends, in this second example we find an instance of architecture used in relation to punishment, but where neither is the architecture one of constraint (at least not in a simple, physical way) nor is it directly punitive. Electronic monitoring, or 'tagging', involves attaching a small device to a convicted offender (typically to the ankle), with the aim of monitoring certain aspects of their whereabouts. In England and Wales the two main offender groups presently constituting the majority of persons monitored, are offenders sentenced to a home curfew order (as the whole or part of their community sentence), and qualifying offenders permitted early release from a prison sentence under the Home Detention Curfew scheme, who may serve the final part of their sentence at home subject to their agreeing to be electronically monitored and to respect certain home curfew conditions (such prisoners are released under licence and are thus subject to recall to prison should they breach their curfew conditions or re-offend).

Electronic tag technology can be divided into two types, the 'first generation' tags capable only of monitoring compliance with a home curfew order, and 'second generation' 'tracking' tags, capable of tracking an offender's whereabouts. First generation tags are simply low power radio devices emitting an intermittent identifying signal. A base unit (connected to a dedicated telephone line) listens out for this signal during specified curfew hours. Since the tag is a low power device it has a limited signal range, and if the offender strays more than 50 metres or so from the base unit it cannot detect the signal, and during curfew hours automatically telephones a central monitoring station to notify a curfew breach. This is thus a good example of the properties (otherwise seen as limitations) of a technology (in this case the tag's signal range) being exploited to useful effect. The role of the tag is thus, formally speaking anyhow, simply to monitor compliance with a curfew order, not to 'punish' by virtue of being tagged – although it may well be that for some or many individuals the experience of being tagged is nevertheless itself experienced as being punitive.[6] A tag could subjectively be experienced by an

---

[6] There may be an analogy between electronic tags used to monitor curfew order compliance and traffic speed cameras used to monitor driver compliance with speed limits. In the UK at present, certain driver lobby groups and Conservative politicians are opposed to speed cameras which they view as overly restrictive or even 'punitive', but the cameras are merely policing compliance with present, often long-standing, legal speed limits.

offender as punitive in one or more of three ways: first, that the physical attachment of the tag to the body is an unwanted inconvenience; secondly, that it is symbolic punishment; and thirdly, because that which it enforces (the curfew order, and all its social limitations and implications) is experienced as punitive, a punitiveness that is metonymically attributed to the tag. Electronic tagging in this case is an architectural solution not to a punitive problem but to a compliance-monitoring problem; home curfew orders long pre-date electronic monitoring technologies, but a problem with them has always been how to monitor compliance. It can also be seen that, in Lessig's terms, the electronic tag (architecture) is being used here in connection with law (the curfew order is a legal order, and typically has as a sanction for non-compliance the possibility that the offender will instead be imprisoned) and with norms (curfew orders seem to be founded in part on traditional normative beliefs as to home and family life, family-time, work-time, and time-discipline). Technical monitoring failures aside, if an offender breaches their curfew order, it is properly a breach of the order rather than a 'failure' of electronic tagging (on the contrary, insofar as it correctly detects the breach, the technology has 'worked'). Second-generation 'tracking tags', which seem likely to be introduced shortly in the United Kingdom, are based on a combination of satellite-based global positioning system (GPS) and mobile (cellular) telephone technologies, involve a quite different technology, having an extended and different range of applications (potentially including monitoring compliance with multiple attendance orders and exclusion orders, at various times and dates) whose social and political implications have yet to be fully explored in the United Kingdom. However, in terms of the fundamental role of the monitoring technology from the perspective of modes of regulation (the Lessig half of the regulatory model), they would seem to have a very similar role to that of first generation tags.

From the perspective of the subjective reasons for (non-)compliance, the reasons are again likely to be similar in both cases, namely that offender compliance is likely to be determined by instrumental reasons (in this case, primarily the disincentive threat of imprisonment for order breach, as against the incentive of experiencing the comparative benefits of a community sentence); normative reasons (whether the offender believes in the norms expressed in the order, has familial or other attachments leading to compliance, and regards such an order as legitimate); and, whether their ingrained habits and routines, especially in terms of time-keeping and place-attendance, are compatible with the order requirements. It seems possible that for some offenders it is the last of these that could prove most problematic, and lead to their re-imprisonment; it is also possible that for many offenders, for reasons similar to those explained by Bottoms in relation to the probation hostel recidivism research, the compliance effects of curfew orders for many offenders so sentenced are relatively short-lived beyond the completion of the order.

Conclusion

Compliance lies at the very heart of punishment. Enforcement of the state's demand that sentenced offenders undergo unpleasant experiences and/or comply with treatment or welfare programmes on which many would probably prefer not to spend their time, can be sought by a variety of approaches, four primary genres of which are identified by Lessig (albeit originally in a very different context). Among these, architecture has a long, and in many respects dark, history within punishment. Capital punishment, torture, branding, and transportation are all examples of how properties of the physical world and of the human body – of 'architecture' – have been exploited to inflict suffering on convicted offenders. Prisons, their walls, cells, locked doors, architectural designs, and sequestration from public view, similarly are 'architecture' at work. Michel Foucault's (1979) classic study of the emergence of the modern prison now re-appears prescient in its identification of the centrality of architecture (*avant la lettre*) to punishment, yet naive in the degree to which it privileges architecture (in both senses) above all else.

By synthesizing research by Lessig and by Bottoms, I have sought to develop a provisional model that identifies, is able to account for, and helps to analyse the dimension of 'architecture' within criminal justice, but which locates this dimension as just one element within a wider analytic framework. By attending both to 'objective' regulatory and 'subjective' compliance perspectives, I have sought to develop a model that could assist in the theoretical and empirical exploration and study of the operations of sanctions at a number of levels. Like all analytic models, the various models discussed above are simplifications. The elements, simple as they are, nevertheless permit a certain complexity of re-combination and interaction. The existing and possible roles of architecture and constraint-based compliance within criminal justice sanctions are apparent from Bottoms' work, and further possible lines of enquiry have been suggested in this present chapter. However, as was shown in the situational crime prevention example, not only is punishment not always centrally based on architecture alone, neither is architecture always punitive in nature. Architecture always enables to some degree as well as constrains, and it may be that in exploring how this balance can better be achieved is Lessig's lasting, albeit unintentional, contribution to the sociology of punishment.

11

Power, Social Control, and Psychiatry: Some Critical Reflections

Andrew Scull

Introduction

This chapter will examine some developments in the study of social control during the past quarter century or so through a particular prism, my own intellectual evolution over that period. It will thus combine autobiographical elements with reflections on larger scholarly themes. In keeping with the focus of my work, though I shall pay some attention to the study of punishment and the penal system, for the most part my attention will be focused elsewhere: on psychiatry and its role in social control. Too often, in my view, social scientists have obfuscated or ignored the ideological and institutional differences that characterize these two realms, the punitive and the psychiatric. To be sure, the two interpenetrate and overlap: the mental health ethos has frequently penetrated adult and juvenile correctional institutions, and mental hospitals have most certainly served to incarcerate as well as, perhaps, to treat. Moreover, our understandings of social control in modern societies can only benefit from comparing and contrasting the operations of power and the shifting foundations of social control across institutional sectors. Yet to do so effectively requires that we first grasp what is distinctive about institutional practice and its unfolding development in a particular arena, in this case the empire of 'asylumdom' and its modern-day dispersed and de-institutionalized successors.

To speak of psychiatry as a form of 'social control' was quite common in the 1970s and 1980s, but became increasingly unfashionable in the last decade or so. In recent years, historians of psychiatry, in particular, have shied away from such language, and have adopted a more benign perspective on the psychiatric profession and its institutions. Intentionally or not, they thus echo in their scholarship, what have long been, the reactions of the psychiatric profession itself to critics who have questioned its benevolence or doubted its devotion to the interests of those who serve as the objects of its attentions. Anxious to be seen as being in the business of helping and healing, psychiatrists can be (and have been) provoked to paroxysms of anger by the suggestion that they act as agents of social control, for such language conjures up images of coercion and constraint, if not the intentional infliction of hurt and harm. Such connotations are all very well in the overtly punitive realm of the criminal justice system, for retribution is an acknowledged and, within limits that vary in time and space, an acceptable face of punishment. But they consort uneasily with the pretensions of a profession supposedly solely devoted to the interests of their nominal clients, the patients, and bent on curing them.

I shall suggest that some of the objections raised by the new generations of historians, to an earlier historiography that stressed social control, are well-taken. It will not do to adopt an unduly reductionist view that treats psychiatry as *only* a form of social control; and an earlier generation of scholarship, my own included, tended to focus too narrowly on a state-centred view of social control and to downplay issues of agency and resistance. But I shall conclude by arguing that issues of power and social control, broadly conceived, are indeed central, and necessarily so, to any balanced understanding of the psychiatric realm.

A Personal Odyssey

In the past quarter century, the academic study of punishment and other forms of social control has continued to generate a great deal of creative scholarship. In important ways, naturally enough, the field has moved on from the pre-occupations that were so evident among the contributions to two seminal volumes from the early 1980s that helped to define the state of the field in that period, *Social Control and the State*, which I edited with Stanley Cohen (1984), and *The Power to Punish*, edited by David Garland and Peter Young (1983), to which both Cohen and I contributed. If the preoccupations of the field have changed, so too have those of the contributors, most of whom, two decades ago, were still nearer the beginning than the end of their academic careers. And yet, on another level, I suspect that the fundamental problematics that engaged the otherwise diverse group of us who wrote for those two collections continue to fascinate us all: the common concerns with, as Garland's and Young's title proclaimed, power and punishment; the underlying fascination with the bases of social order and the containment of challenges to it; the shared commitment to endeavouring to explain, as well as describe, shifts in social control styles and practices; and (in varying degrees, to be sure – though that was as true twenty years ago as now) the consciousness of the political dimensions of our own scholarship, associated as that has necessarily been, with an interest in reflecting upon the possible connections between our ivory-tower analyses and the larger social universe within which we find ourselves embedded.

The two books were influential in substantial measure because they brought together authors who had something significant to say, and did so at a moment when the critical analysis of penality had become an increasingly fashionable topic in social theory. During the 1970s, in Britain, in France, in North America, the analysis of social control had been reconnected to the study of power and the political order. Revisionist scholars in history, in criminology, in socio-legal studies, and in sociology, were seizing upon crime and punishment, madness and its confinement, poverty and its management as intellectually exciting topics, worthy of examining as something more than a problem of administration or a tale of linear progress.

My own intellectual interest in power and punishment had emerged only indirectly. Interested when I entered graduate school in joining together sociological and historical analysis, and combining those interests with a deep concern with issues of political power and process, I became fascinated with one aspect of what is surely the central question for sociologists, the problem of social order. Specifically, and it must be said largely serendipitously at the outset, I found myself increasingly drawn to the question of the changing structures and techniques of social control in the era of the 'Great Transformation', seeking both to grasp what the central characteristics of those changes had been, and to begin to account for their unfolding development.

In principle, these concerns might have led me in a variety of directions. I might have examined, for example, as Michael Ignatieff (1980) proceeded to do at just that time, the nexus of crime and punishment. Or I might have focused on the crucial issue of poverty and its containment, as Frances Piven and Richard Cloward (1971) had begun to do a few years earlier. Revisionist studies of schools as vehicles for the control of children had begun to appear (Katz 1968, Tyack 1974), as had studies of emerging systems for controlling children already gone bad (Platt 1969, Schlossman 1977),[1] and perhaps I could have added to their number. Here, too, there would have been a clearer path forward to a concern with modern penality.

Instead, I elected first to focus upon the issues surrounding craziness and its treatment. It was the nineteenth-century asylums, those monuments of moral architecture I was to dub 'museums of madness', and the proto-professionals who ran them, the variously titled mad-doctors/alienists/psychiatrists that first attracted my gaze, and to which and to whom I devoted much of the first decade of my career as scholar – more than that, it would turn out, but that is a topic to which I shall return later on in this Chapter. This intellectual focus on the management of the mad in part reflected some of my reading at that time: Michel Foucault's *Madness and Civilization* (1971), David Rothman's *Discovery of the Asylum* (1971), and Erving Goffman's *Asylums* (1961). But it also derived from my conviction that the empire of 'asylumdom' and its nominal rulers were a strategically crucial site for investigating larger themes.

---

[1] A more recent contribution is Sutton (1988).

As I saw and still see it, there were a number of key elements distinguishing deviance and its control in modern societies from the shapes which such phenomena assume elsewhere. In British (and to some extent American) society, from the eighteenth century forward, one observed a substantial and growing involvement of the state, and the emergence of a highly rationalized, centrally administered and directed, social control apparatus. Increasingly, the treatment of many types of deviance in institutions provided a large measure of segregation from the surrounding community. It also provided a steady differentiation of different sorts of deviance, and the consignment of each variety to its own set of institutions; and, as a corollary of this process of differentiation (and in part produced by it), the parallel emergence of professional and semi-professional occupations laying claim to expertise in the management of crime, delinquency, poverty, craziness, mental handicap, and so forth. From this perspective, the differentiation of the insane, the rise of a state-supported asylum system, and the emergence of the psychiatric profession can be seen to represent no more than a particular, though very important, example of this much more general series of changes in the social organization of deviance. This is interesting not least because, even though psychiatry for much of its history has been an isolated and stigmatized branch of the medical profession, its claims to ground its expertise in the neutral, value-free foundation of 'science' have been accorded more credibility and respect than less developed claims by those operating in other sectors of the social control apparatus. The dramatic and radical changes in the typical societal responses to the deranged between 1750 and 1850 were thus the focus of my first major scholarly research, which examined the metamorphosis at the level of both ideas and social practices.

The Discovery of the Asylum

Whereas in the eighteenth century, only the violent and destructive among those now labelled insane would have been segregated and confined apart from the rest of the community, with the achievement of what was widely portrayed as a major social reform, symbolized by the passage of the Asylums Act in 1845, the asylum was endorsed as the sole officially approved response to the problems posed by mental illness. In the process, and equally important, the boundaries of who was to be classified as mad, and thus liable to incarceration, were themselves transformed. One needs to understand how, then, over the course of a century and more, the crystallization of this new ensemble of social practices and moral meanings came about, and to make sense of their striking and significant embodiment in new physical forms that constitute such a notable example of the moral architecture of the nineteenth century. And in analysing these developments, it is vital simultaneously to attend to the reciprocal constitution of new forms of expertise and knowledge alongside, and in intimate relationship with, this new institutional apparatus, to pay attention to the development of new theoretical codes and technologies of intervention, and to explore the way in which the boundaries were redrawn between the normal and the pathological. Institutions and knowledge, theory and practice, and the constitution and the capture of particular sorts of problem populations do not develop in some linear, sequential fashion, with one side of these equations preceding and producing the other. They are, on the contrary, mutually reinforcing and deeply inter-dependent, the development of the one deriving from, and simultaneously advancing, the maturation of the other.

My work on 'lunacy reform' in nineteenth-century England in one important respect paralleled the influential reinterpretation of the rise of the asylum in the United States that David Rothman had offered a few years earlier, for Rothman, too, interpreted the rise of segregative responses to insanity through the lens of social control. But Rothman's perspective was in most respects very different from mine. His vision of society and its dynamics; his relative lack of interest in trying to tease out connections between changing social and political structures and the rise of asylums; and his treatment of developments in the United States in isolation from parallel changes elsewhere, all combined to produce a very different portrait of the *sources* of institutional change, even if both of us took sharp issue with the Whiggish histories that had hitherto dominated the field and concurred, for the most part, in our assessments of the *outcome* of 'reform'.[2] We did share, however, one other point of theoretical convergence. Heavily influenced by his reading of Goffman, as his use of the term 'asylum' as a synonym for 'total institution' made clear to any sociologist encountering his work, Rothman saw the rise of the lunatic asylum as co-extensive with, and only understandable within the context of, a broader shift towards institutionally-based modes of responding to deviance, just as he argued that the subsequent history of penitentiaries, poor houses, and asylums displayed some fundamental similarities.[3]

This was a position with which I had considerable, indeed perhaps at that time too much sympathy, for I have subsequently come to feel that one must be careful about the analytic dangers that flow from eliding the distinctiveness of institutions directed at crime, poverty, madness, and so forth. That is not to suggest that there are no points of convergence or structural similarity, or to deny that to some degree changes in all these sectors may respond to a similar underlying set of factors. But it is to acknowledge that there are risks and dangers in neglecting the distinctiveness of each of these realms, and the separate logics that may and frequently do inform developments in each of them. This is a point

[2] For a more extensive discussion of these differences, and a critique of Rothman's analytic stance, see Scull (1989a: ch 2).

[3] For anyone inclined to doubt the intellectual genealogy, Rothman subsequently acknowledged it in a Canadian interview (Chunn and Smandych 1982).

David Garland has also forcibly made in his critique of Foucault's work on the penal system:

When [Foucault] says that the prison is 'just like' the factory, or the school, or the monastery [or, we might add, the asylum], he is referring only to its internal practices, and not to the social meanings through which it is publicly understood. And while there are clear technical homologies linking what is done within these various institutions, their social usage and significance are altogether different. (Garland 1991: 111)

Alongside my continuing interest in the empire of 'asylumdom', in the mid-1970s, I had become interested in the contemporary drive towards dein-stitutionalization, and had begun the research that led to the publication of my book, *Decarceration* (Scull 1977).

In many respects, that period represented the high tide of the dein-stitutionalization movement, at least on the ideological level. The drive towards community corrections for both adult and juvenile offenders was widely por-trayed as a far-reaching reform, as was the contemporaneous effort to replace the traditional mental hospital with a community-based mental health system. Moreover, the ideology that underpinned the changes, or apparent changes in all these sectors, shared much in common, being premised on a shared assumption that the rise of the penitentiary, the reformatory, and the lunatic asylum had formed part of a common Enlightenment project that had proved to be a colossal mistake.

Gary Wills (1975) vividly made the case for the bankruptcy of the traditional reliance on the prison. The penitentiary was, he asserted, a classic 'failed experiment' that had somehow lingered on for almost two centuries:

...the most disastrous survivor of the Enlightenment still grasping at a death-like life. [In] our culture's human sewer, clogged and unworkable with human waste...the criminal is sequestered with other criminals, in conditions exacerbating the lowest drives of lonely and stranded men, men deprived of loved ones, of dignifying work, of pacifying amenities...Smuggling, bullying, theft, drug traffic, homosexual menace, are ways of life. Guards, themselves brutalized by the experience of prison, have to ignore most of the crimes inflicted on inmates, even when they do not connive at them, or incite them. [As a result,] prisons teach crime, instil crime, inure men to it, trap men in it as a way of life. (Wills 1975)

Studies of the mental hospital echoed the theme. American psychiatrists expressed the fear that 'the patients are infantile...because we infantilize them' (Redlich 1958). British psychiatrists wrote of the dangers of 'institutionalism', and one of their number coined a new diagnostic category for this iatrogenic disorder: 'institutional neurosis' (Barton 1965, Wing and Brown 1970). Sociologists were still fiercer in their criticisms. One could not help concluding, one of them suggested, that 'in the long run the abandonment of the state hospitals might be one of the greatest humanitarian reforms and the greatest financial economy ever achieved' (Belknap 1956: 212). The bins we had inherited from the Victorian age were, in Erving Goffman's words:

... hopeless storage dumps trimmed in psychiatric paper. They have served to remove the patient from the scene of his symptomatic behavior, ... but this function has been performed by fences, not doctors. And the price that the patient has had to pay for this service has been considerable: dislocation from civil life, alienation from loved ones who arranged the commitment, mortification due to hospital regimentation and surveillance, permanent post-hospital stigmatization. This has not merely been a bad deal; it has been a grotesque one. (Goffman 1971)

Sociological critics of the total institution were for a time convinced that prisons, reformatories, and mental hospitals deformed and destroyed the human raw materials they processed for fundamentally similar structural reasons. In the 1970s, their account of the virtues of their preferred alternative, community care or community corrections, used the same rhetoric and arguments about these two very different domains. Just as David Rothman's nineteenth-century reformers had touted the nineteenth-century asylum as a model of sociability for the larger society, so their contemporary equivalents boasted of the larger value of their chosen panacea:

... the destination is a degree of community participation and effectiveness which has all but departed our lives as people living together. Part of the powerlessness and frustration which some may sense at this juncture will be resolved in this trend, to the benefit not only of inmates or clients or patients or criminals now in institutions – but of the community as a whole. (Alper 1973: viii)

Living in the United States that boasts one of the highest rates of imprisonment in the world, and in a state whose prison system was alone spared the budgetary axe in the midst of desperate manoeuvring to paper over a $35 billion dollar deficit, it is difficult to recall how different the picture looked in the mid-1970s, when, for a decade, state and federal prison populations had been static or declining, albeit slowly, and where a state like Massachusetts had just, with much fanfare, shut its juvenile reformatories (Miller 1973). In an era of three strikes laws, moral panics about juvenile crime, and popular pressure to try children as adults, the notion of a stable, let alone a declining prison population, seems a pipedream. Yet the apparent match of rhetoric and reality in the penal sector in 1975, and the even sharper fall-off in mental hospital censuses, made it all too easy to conclude that the changes that were under way were fundamentally similar in character across this whole array of institutions. The Goffmanian vision, which lumped together prisons, reformatories, nunneries, boot camps, concentration camps, and mental hospitals seemed to have been embraced by politicians and policy makers, and the flight seemed to be on from these disabling, custodial institutions.

But only *seemed* to be so, and for a very few years at that. To be sure, the abandonment of the asylum has continued apace. The brooding presence of the barracks asylum, which for so many years dominated both the physical and the symbolic landscape of madness, has largely been superseded by the sidewalk psychotics who are now so familiar a feature of our urban landscape. But matters are far different with respect to crime and punishment, for the penal apparatus has remained heavily wedded to imprisonment as a dominant response to the criminal. Ideologically, even in the 1970s, there was a strong conservative backlash against anything smacking of leniency towards crime and criminals, and where mental hospital populations have declined remorselessly and at an accelerating pace, the opposite has been true for the penitentiary. If 'community treatment' of the mentally ill has in reality mostly corresponded to a policy of neglect and abandonment of the chronically crazy, 'community corrections' in its various manifestations has more commonly consisted of a widening of the net of social control, what Stan Cohen (1979, 1985) early on identified as a substantial growth of the crime control apparatus. Criminals and delinquents, as Chan and Ericson would have it, 'are not diverted *from*, but *into* and within the system' (Chan and Ericson 1981: 55, see also Blomberg 1977).

Social Control and the Net-widening Thesis

To study social control is, as we all must have reflected from time to time, to enter a Kafkaesque universe rife with ironies. Here is one of them: the very fact that the measures designed to dispose of the disoriented and the senile are ostensibly undertaken from a benevolent and humanitarian concern for their welfare has facilitated their casual dumping. If it is concluded that traditional approaches to the management of the gravely mentally ill, centred around their confinement in large asylums, are destructive and anti-therapeutic, then non-intervention, dressed up as community treatment, and promoted in the name of the very virtues once attributed to the asylum, can be advocated on the grounds of its advantages to the client. Coupled with the claim that a revolutionary breakthrough has occurred in the technological capacities of the professionals to whose charge they are entrusted, in the form of the miracle of modern psychopharmacology, and the fact that many of the chronically disturbed can be isolated and contained while being neglected (their very infirmity limiting the threat they pose), and one understands why, in the words of Sir Roy Griffiths, a skeletonized community care can persist like the proverbial pernicious 'poor relation: everybody's distant relative, but nobody's baby' (Griffiths 1988).

By contrast, as David Garland has emphasized, 'the punitive, condemnatory sign throws a long shadow over everything the penal system does' (1991: 111). Foucault famously sought to assimilate penal practices and the rationalities they employ to the administrative normalization of modern societies, claiming to trace the transformation of punishment 'from being a morally-charged and emotive set of ritual practices into an increasingly passionless and professionalized instrumental process' (Garland 1991: 97). Such assertions capture important dimensions of the evolution of the power to punish, but as Garland rightly contends, as a global portrait of modern penality, they are clearly inadequate, for they neglect the persistent presence of passionate moral condemnation and of retributive sentiments in the criminal justice arena, those vengeful emotions that Durkheim (1983) insisted continue to lie at the heart of our collective response to crime.

'Radical non-interventionism' thus had few supporters beyond the professoriate as a crime control strategy. On the contrary, the fear of crime is a political issue capable of mobilizing powerful if somewhat confused pressures for 'action' among an otherwise fractured and fragmented public. As James Jacobs suggested two decades ago, and as the popularity of California's misguided, fiscally irrational, and yet immensely popular three strikes law has more recently confirmed, here is an issue that transcends standard ideological divisions to provide 'strong support for a fundamental change in punishment policy – one that pushes toward greater severity and more frequent use of incarceration' (Jacobs 1983).

Neglect has still other disadvantages as a response to crime and many forms of delinquency. To the extent that crime represents a 'rational' form of activity, the perceived erosion of sanctions threatens to elicit more of it. If criminals are able to violate the law with something approaching impunity, the incentives to conform are significantly weakened, and public outrage is all but certain. And a social and political order that is seen to permit such developments will suffer an insidious but powerful loss of legitimacy. It should thus come as no surprise to learn that, quite apart from the striking increases in prison populations I have already referred to, there is substantial evidence that the development of so-called 'diversionary' programmes leads instead to 'a more voracious processing of deviant populations, albeit in new settings and by professionals with different names' (Cohen 1979: 350). Adding still further weight to these pressures to broaden the scope of the crime control apparatus, the fate of the crime control bureaucracy, unlike that of the profession of psychiatry, is inextricably bound up with the state sector. Police and prison officers operate in a severely restricted market, and the sorts of professional 'convenience' that David Rothman (1980) identified as serving to shape the character of such Progressive Era reforms as the introduction of probation and parole, add yet a further layer of pressure towards a policy of greater intervention and further expansion of their own empires. In California, for instance, the three strikes law, the massive expansion of the prison system, and the inexorable rise in spending on incarceration owe much to the carefully calculated financial contributions of the prison officers' union, and to the pressing need of our politicians, from the governor on down, to secure the money they need for their campaigns and the politically potent endorsements that signal that they are 'tough on crime and criminals'.

Towards a More Complex Understanding of Coercive Institutions

Andrew Abbott (1988) has defined the capture, defence, and expansion of professional jurisdictions as a key feature of the growing role of expertise in modern societies, and the associated struggle by increasingly organized occupational groups to achieve some degree of market closure in the struggle for a privileged place in the social division of labour. And just as one can trace such efforts on the part of the police and the correctional bureaucracy, so, even more clearly, one can see them in the psychiatric realm. Since the mid-1980s, the mental health sector has again become the major focus of my own researches, and the changing role and scope of the psychiatric profession in the regulation of social life has been one of the central themes I have sought to explore.

It has to be said that among the profession itself, and even among many of the scholars examining the mental health sector, any attempt to speak of social control has become unpopular, even anathema. Referring to a profession and its associated institutions, whose public persona is one of benevolence and therapy, as instances of social control is a rhetorical move almost bound to provoke paroxysms of rage from the professionals, and those who identify with them. But in the past decade or so, a new generation of scholars who fail to fit into either camp have also increasingly abandoned such language.

To some extent, I think such a move reflects a weariness with an older set of debates on the subject. The positions of the combatants on each side of the question had tended to become fixed and somewhat predictable, and the arguments familiar.[4] There was a natural desire to open up new avenues of inquiry, and to push research in different directions, both topically and temporally. But that is not the whole story. In reaction against the earlier revisionist historiography, a younger generation of scholars has moved to embrace what the historian Joseph Melling (1999) has called a late-Whiggish position on the nineteenth-century asylum. Rather than viewing Victorian bins as cemeteries for the still-breathing, an array of hidden repositories for society's unhinged and unwanted, a more benign role has been posited for these institutions.[5]

---

[4] On the one side, see Roth (1973), Grob (1977, 1990), and Quen (1974). For contrary views, see Rothman (1976, 1984), Scull (1991).

[5] In my view, this more positive view of the asylum in the last third of the 19th century and the first half of the 20th century, is largely mistaken. The malign neglect that has masqueraded as 'community care' in recent decades has encouraged a nostalgia for traditional mental hospitals that relies upon a rose-tinted, and deeply distorted, view of what they were like. Victorian bins and their 20th century counterparts were, for the most part, truly awful places that systematically dehumanized their patients and, very often, those who presided over them as well. The comparisons some well-informed observers made in the 1940s, between American state hospitals and Nazi concentration camps, were not hyperbole. See, eg, Deutsch (1948), Maisel (1946), Orlans (1947), and Wright (1947). Wright's volume, based on the experiences of conscientious objectors sent to work in mental hospitals to punish them for their pacifism, deliberately omitted the most serious abuses

One element in this revised portrait has been the observation, well-established by now, that there was considerably more traffic across the boundary between asylum and community than the first generation of revisionist studies had allowed.[6] Even in the late nineteenth century, a substantial fraction of those who entered an asylum in any twelve-month period could expect to be discharged within a year, and a handful more over the next twelve months – perhaps a third or two-fifths of the intake. Adding to this the ten to eighteen per cent of patients who died within a year of admission, and the repeated finding that the median length of stay for a new asylum inmate in the last third of the nineteenth century hovered between a year and a year and a half seems wholly unsurprising, if at odds with a previous insistence on the custodial character of the Victorian bins.

For some, this trafficking to and fro across the margins of the madhouse sector, the existence of patients who were 'brought back' into society after being previously 'cast out,'[7] was sufficient by itself to refute the image of the asylum as an instrument of social control, and to revive its credentials as a therapeutic institution. Such arguments, however, strike me as profoundly mistaken. First, to assert that mental hospitals serve vital social control functions is not by any means to assert that this is the *only* social role they play. Therapy and social control may be intertwined and complementary aspects of the asylum system, not contradictory and binary opposites. Secondly, even temporary incarceration may serve important social control goals, whether viewed from the perspective of the patient's immediate family, of the local community, or of the larger society. And thirdly, it will not do to replace a one-sided view of the late nineteenth-century asylum as a storage dump, a repository of dead souls, with an equally one-sided portrait of it as a benevolent and therapeutic institution.

For, notwithstanding the restoration of a significant fraction of its intake to the larger society, every year a very substantial fraction of asylum admissions remained behind to swell the population of chronic, long-stay patients, and as the size of public asylums grew relentlessly, annual admissions formed a smaller and smaller fraction of the whole. In the mammoth bins that were scattered across the *fin-de-siècle* landscape, a large and growing proportion of the asylum population quickly came to be composed of chronic, long-stay patients, for those who did not leave within twelve or twenty-four months seldom exited, save in a pine box. And it was this spectre of chronicity, this horde of the hopeless, which

these men had observed, lest they seemed too outlandish and cast doubt on the lesser parade of horrors they *did* include! If the situation was not always and everywhere this bad, it was dreadful enough in all conscience. For a case study of how the profound power imbalances inherent in the relationship between certified lunatics and their captors could license literally deadly treatment, see Scull (2005).

  [6] The pioneering study here was Ray (1981).

  [7] I echo here the title of John Walton's seminal paper, 'Casting Out and Bringing Back in Victorian England: Pauper Lunatics, 1840–1870' (1985).

was to haunt the popular imagination, to constitute the public identity of the asylums, and to dominate late nineteenth- and early twentieth-century psychiatric theorizing and practice.[8]

Central in other respects to the renewed attempt to reassert the humanitarian credentials of the asylum, and thus at least implicitly to contest both Foucault's broad-ranging assault on the Enlightenment project and the arguments put forward in the first generation of Anglo-American revisionist historiography, has been a growing move away from the macro-sociological level of analysis. As the more global analyses of the rise of the asylum have become unfashionable in recent years, so too there has been something of a retreat from efforts to connect the rise of 'asylumdom' to the larger social and political context – to the dynamics of class society, for example, or to the growing commercialization of existence in the eighteenth and nineteenth centuries.[9] By no means does such a shift in analytic focus *determine* a move away from questions of this sort. For example, my recent collaborative work with Jonathan Andrews, on the eighteenth-century trade in lunacy, and the patrons and customers of its most famous mad-doctor, John Monro, places such concerns at the heart of its analysis (Andrews and Scull 2001: 2003). Yet an examination of a series of individual cases certainly encourages an emphasis on the particularities of person, institution, and place. And in the celebration of what is idiosyncratic about a certain setting and the articulation of the complexities of an individual example, there is a natural tendency to criticize and shy away from global generalizations, rather than refining and extending them.

The risk, of course, is the construction of meticulously detailed individual accounts that overlook or underweight larger structural and organizational imperatives, and lapse into telling stories of incremental change that retreat back into a sort of neo-solipsism. That is not to deny the value of confronting general models with detailed empirical analyses. Only in this way can we hope to develop a more subtle and sophisticated understanding of the phenomena under study and expose the limitations of previous generalizations. But it is to emphasize that it is equally vital that we acknowledge that we can only achieve this larger aim if we consciously seek to show the more general significance of a given set of phenomena and transcend the peculiarities of person and place. A mindless empiricism, a view of social reality as just one damn thing after another, is a stance that avoids the intellectual risks and inevitable pitfalls of a more vaunting ambition, but at the heavy price of embracing a constricted vision that flattens and distorts our sense of perspective, and leaves in obscurity aspects of historical reality that acquire meaning only when placed in a larger contextual frame (Scull 1999).

---

[8] See the extended discussion of these points in Scull (1993).

[9] For a sensitive exploration of this body of recent scholarship by a sympathetic participant, see Melling (1999).

Regrettably, the division between those focusing on the micro-politics of insanity and those continuing to insist on the importance of a broader scholarly perspective, corresponds to some considerable extent with disciplinary boundaries and loyalties. I say regrettably, because I have long argued that the distinction between sociology and history is an artificial and unfortunate one. To be sure, it is a distinction that has become entrenched over the years in institutional structures and professional organizations, but it is a foolish and distorting division, one that mirrors and reinforces the parochialism of much contemporary academic life. That remains the case no matter how skillfully the separation is rationalized by the self-interests of academic guilds, and no matter how fiercely it is defended by the border guards who spend their days on the prowl, looking out for intellectual interlopers to shoot at (Scull 1989b).

In turning to the micro-politics of insanity, however, historians have also been engaged in a more laudable task. The late Roy Porter once wittily remarked that asylums shut up their inmates in a double sense, and for a long time, historians and sociologists tended to follow suit. In David Ingleby's words, the history of psychiatry resembled nothing so much as 'the histories of colonial wars[: it told] us more about the relations between the imperial powers than about the "third world" of the mental patients themselves' (Ingleby 1983: 142). But this is a criticism that no longer holds good, for a variety of historians have made it their business to try to recover the patients' voices and perspectives, and those of their families.[10]

The task is by no means easy and the dangers of romanticization great. Almost by definition, the experiences and consciousness of most of the seriously mad are largely inaccessible and difficult to recover, and the difficulty is further compounded by the predominance of the poor and illiterate or quasi-literate among their ranks, at least into the twentieth century. Generally, the surviving evidence is fragmentary, not representative (whatever that might mean in this context), and often filtered through the case notes and sensibilities of their confidants and captors. For the middle and upper classes the situation is a little better, not least because the power and privileges accruing to the well-to-do generally accorded them greater levels of individual attention, thus making it somewhat more likely that relevant evidence (correspondence, diaries, first hand reports) will have survived. This is especially true if one widens one's focus from the inmate him or herself to encompass the immediate family, for the impact of insanity on the domestic circle, almost inevitably, was so great as to prompt commentary and discussion among the patient's intimates, often in written form.

The emerging interest in recovering the perspectives of mental patients and their families forms part, of course, of a wider interest on the part of professional

---

[10] One of the pioneering examples of this approach is Tomes (1984). Roy Porter (1987) soon followed suit, and a whole array of scholars followed in their footsteps over the past decade, including Andrews and Scull (2003).

historians in constructing a 'history from below'. Rather than viewing those who ended up in asylums (and their nearest and dearest) as mere ciphers, passive victims whose fortunes and fates are wholly at the disposal of those funding and running the institutions, a sustained effort is now under way to give voice to the voiceless, and to provide a more nuanced, less one-sided account of the inter-action of magistrates, Poor Law officials, alienists, families, and patients. Fam-ilies, it is now fashionable to argue, were not just put-upon, submissive pawns pushed about by a Leviathan state and its minions, but actively used and manipulated the asylum system for their own ends.[11] Recent scholarship has suggested, for instance, that it was not so much the judgments of asylum superintendents, but rather the ability and willingness of patients' families to absorb particular individuals back into the household, regardless of continuing mental disturbances and infirmities, that must be seen as the central determi-nants of decisions over discharge or retention within the confines of the asylum (Wright 1999). On some accounts, too, patients are to be accorded a measure of agency. If not quite the masters or mistresses of their fates, neither, the new orthodoxy would have it, were they wholly incapable of resistance and of influencing the terms of their confinement (cf Jackson 2000).

Yet it is easy to push these arguments too far. For there are gross imbalances of power and resources at work here, for families and, even more clearly, for patients, where the problems of social subordination and economic power-lessness are compounded to an extraordinary degree by the impact of the label of insanity. For the lunatic, the madman, the psychotic, the schizophrenic, call them what you will, suffers a sort of social and moral death. Their wishes and will, their very status as moral actors, as agents capable of expressing valid pre-ferences and exercising autonomous choice, are deeply suspect in the light of their presumed pathology, as the often dark history of their treatment under confinement abundantly shows. Erving Goffman's essays on the 'moral career of the mental patient' and the 'under-life' of the total institution (1961: ch 2 and 3) long ago pointed to acts of distancing and resistance employed by inmates. But the pathetic and self-defeating qualities of the 'make-dos' he describes, which serve only to reinforce others' sense of them as pathologically different and inferior, are powerful reminders of the profound power imbalances that structure the over-matched inmates' lives, and of their moral and political insignificance in the larger equation.

In the regulation of madness, accredited experts, families, their soon-to-be excluded members, and the larger civil society all enter into the picture. We must acknowledge that the analytic model of the all-powerful state coercing entirely helpless individuals (patients and their families) has been shown to be hopelessly simplistic, however great its ideological appeal in some quarters.

---

[11] Perhaps the best discussion of the interaction of family and institution is Forsythe *et al* (1996). See also Walsh (1999), Wright (1998), and Michael (2003).

The same may be said of the way the concept of social control has at times been applied to the study of punishment, where again there is a risk of narrowing one's focus too much. Two decades ago, writing of revisionist work on the prison and penitentiary, and including his own work in the criticism, Michael Ignatieff confessed that the new generation of scholarship had overstated the importance of the state. It had fostered, he suggested, the misconceptions 'that the state enjoys a monopoly over punitive regulation of behaviour in society, that its moral authority and practical power are the binding sources of social order, and that all social relations can be described in the language of subordination' (Ignatieff 1984: 77). But to acknowledge the importance of this broader array of actors, and to reject a simple reductionism that would equate the psychiatric (or the punitive) enterprise with nothing more than a relentless effort to control a particular class of deviants – one which adopts the Szaszian line, for instance, that psychiatrists are merely concentration camp guards in disguise (Szasz 1970) – is not at all the same thing as accepting the claim, made by many in the profession and their apologists, that theirs is a purely therapeutic and humanitarian intervention. As Goffman noted in an obscure and little-cited paper, mental illness is all about havoc and disarray, and efforts to contain and mitigate the problems that flow from that disorder and threat (Goffman 1971). Bringing family, community, profession, and patient back into the picture does not alter that reality, or, in my judgment, make the issue of social control any less central to a balanced assessment of the psychiatric enterprise.

Likewise, I remain as convinced as I was two decades ago, of the centrality of psychiatry and of psychiatric ideologies and technologies to the study of social control in modern societies. Indeed, over the past century or so, their centrality has surely grown. Many astute analysts of the punitive sphere, as we have seen, have been struck by the broadening and net-widening impact of 'reforms' in this sector. One can readily observe a parallel extension and expansion of psychiatric forms of social control into new social settings and institutional domains. Traditionally a profession structurally hamstrung by the extraordinary weakness of its claims to possess special knowledge and capacities, and thus compelled to hold on tightly to the reassuring social power that derived from its autocratic control over 'asylumdom', psychiatry in the second and third decades of the twentieth century, substantially assisted by the epidemic of shell-shock in the 'war to end all wars,' ventured forth to capture an ever wider sphere for its ministrations and interventions (Scull 1991). The psychiatric casualties of war (Stone 1985a), the management of infancy and childhood (and particularly of delinquent childhood) (Horn 1989, Rose 1985, Ingleby 1973), alcoholism and other forms of intemperance and excess (Conrad and Schneider 1980), marital disharmony and divorce (Donzelot 1979, Lasch 1977), the alienation of the industrial workforce (Stone 1985b), the translation of these and other moral problems and disturbances not readily susceptible to legal sanctions and intervention into technical, medicalized conditions, provided psychiatry with a greatly expanded territory within which to practice.[12] A widening array of forms of deviance was thus systematized within an orderly framework, and in reducing them to a medical paradigm, an attempt was made to reconstitute them as conditions 'completely emptied of moral significance' (Ingleby 1983).[13]

Helpless, hopeless, and highly stigmatized, the institutionalized population that presumably remained at the core of psychiatry's claims to expertise, proved an increasing embarrassment, one which the more 'progressive' segments of the profession were anxious to leave behind. The suffocating constraints and frustrations of attempting to cope with the recalcitrant, increasingly senile occupants of the mental hospital (Grob 1983, Goldhammer and Marshall 1953) stood in ever starker contrast with the attractions of new worlds to conquer. A paroxysm of experimentation among institutional psychiatrists with various forms of physical therapy – surgical evisceration (Scull 1987), malaria and other forms of fever therapy, metrazol-induced seizures, insulin comas, electroshock treatment, and crude surgical assaults on the brain itself (Valenstein 1986, Pressman 1986, Grob 1983) – provided no relief, indeed, may well have contributed its quota to the dilapidated denizens of the back wards. And the upshot was the desertion of the professional elite, followed by a decisive shift in the profession's centre of gravity away from the dismal, despised, and depressing institutional sector.[14]

The marginalization of the seriously deranged as targets of professional intervention and concern, and the attempted reconceptualization of a variety of other social problems as medical conditions in need of treatment, were thus symbiotic processes which marked a crucial transition in the development of the psychiatric profession.[15] What is generally termed the rise of the therapeutic state constituted a potentially massive expansion of psychiatry's role in the processes of social control, particularly since the 'thrust of the expansion of the application of medical labels has been toward addressing (and controlling) the *serious* forms of deviance, leaving to the other institutions [traditionally involved in social control, law and medicine,] a residue of essentially trivial and narrowly defined technical offences' (Freidson 1970: 249, emphasis in the original). Under the appealing banner of *parens patriae*, the profession laid claim to the right to intervene in an ever-widening range of spheres of social life, defining for others what was in their own best interests, and offering the benign reassurance

[12] For general discussions of these developments, see Miller (1980), Castel *et al* (1982), and D. Armstrong (1980).

[13] For an early discussion of the growing role of medicine in the enforcement of moral norms, cf Zola (1972).

[14] Gerald Grob (1983) has traced this abandonment of the chronic in considerable detail for the US, in the years leading up to the Second World War. Raw numbers tell the tale: by 1956, only 17% of the members of the American Psychiatric Association were employed in state hospitals or Veterans Administration facilities (Grob 1983: 287).

[15] For a general discussion of the US case, see Abbott (1988: 280–314).

that, like a good substitute parent, psychiatry always had benevolence and rationality on its side.

Constraints and Resistances to Psychiatric Power

In stressing the substantial expansion that has taken place in psychiatry's jurisdiction, and the even greater potential for intervention in daily life that is implicit in the therapeutic approach, I do not want to minimize the countervailing forces which have to some extent held these tendencies in check. Clearly, one source of difficulty for psychiatry and its allied professions has been the continuing intellectual vulnerability of their cognitive claims, and the practical deficiencies of the 'remedies' on offer to consumers of its services. The opposite concern – the persistent disquiet aroused in many quarters on contemplating the implications of an approach which threatens to equate any deviation from conventional moral and social standards with illness, and to impose compulsory treatment – has also placed significant constraints on psychiatric expansionism. (The polemical assaults of such figures as Thomas Szasz (1970) and Nicholas Kittrie (1972) on the dangers of the therapeutic state are only the most recent manifestations of a long history of spasms of public anxiety on this score.) Finally, psychiatry operates within a larger matrix of contending professions, each jealous of any attempt to seize portions of its jurisdiction. Lawyers, in particular, have a highly developed sense of turf, and the social power and cultural authority to offer a vigorous defence of their territory. Psychiatrists, pushing their deterministic universe of discourse to its limits, have on occasion been rash enough to extend their imperial claims to encompass all forms of criminality, threatening to substitute pathology for sin, determinism for free will, treatment for punishment. Such efforts have tended to provoke sharply adversarial responses from the legal profession, whose traditional mandate to control crime has the advantage of being rooted in a common sense schema wherein will or intention and the voluntary basis of action, assume a central place. Discretion being the better part of valour, and neither principle of social regulation being capable of fully vanquishing the other, both professions have more usually adopted a policy of conceding each other's heartland, with jurisdictional disputes only occurring at the margin – where they generally take on a ritualized, if symbolically charged, character.[16]

The expanding role for psychiatry, in the United States in particular, was facilitated in part by the rise of psychoanalysis to a position of temporary dominance in the years after the war with Hitler and Hirohito. But the invention

---

[16] For a sophisticated examination of perhaps the most prominent arena in which such jurisdictional issues are fought out, the seemingly irreconcilable debate over insanity and criminal responsibility, see Smith (1981).

and embrace of psychotherapeutic treatment techniques and of psychodynamic accounts of functional 'mental illness', vital as they were as weapons in the struggle for professional jurisdiction, were not unproblematic in their implications. Most seriously, of course, there was the question of why a branch of the medical profession was uniquely qualified (indeed, qualified at all) to diagnose and treat, if the aetiology and therapeutics of these conditions were primarily *psychological*.[17] Unsurprisingly, a number of different professional disciplines – most notably clinical psychology and social work – now emerged to invade psychiatry's turf and, at least temporarily, to contest its dominance.[18]

The contest, however, rapidly proved to be one-sided. Psychologists and social workers largely lacked independent control of the institutions within which they worked. Their bureaucratic subordination to psychiatrists in such settings as outpatient and child guidance clinics, even though the psychiatrist-director often attended the clinic only part-time (cf Abbott 1988) limited their autonomy from one direction. Their aspirations to independence were further thwarted by medical monopolization of the psychoanalytical training institutes, an organizational source of domination which was of great strategic value, given the insistence within psychoanalysis on the centrality of training analyses for the therapists themselves (Abbott 1988). Social work, in particular, lacked any independent intellectual basis for its claims to jurisdiction and quickly surrendered any aspirations to autonomy, its subordination overtly acknowledged with the adoption of the term *psychiatric* social work.[19] Psychology gained somewhat more leeway from its independent control over the technology of mental testing (Stone 1985b), but despite the usefulness of these techniques to corporations and in schools, they provided the basis for only a limited degree of separate authority. Necessarily, therefore, psychologists for the most part also submitted to a submissive relationship with their medical rivals,[20] and, notwithstanding occasional outbreaks of 'fratricidal strife . . . , a practical division of labour was established within the psychiatric units, hospitals and clinics' (Rose 1986: 79).[21] One suspects that one source of the relatively unproblematic subordination that

[17] Alienists had repeatedly expressed precisely these concerns throughout the 19th century, persistently tying their mandate to treat to a metaphysical embrace of the body: an incessantly reiterated insistence on the somatic basis of insanity, and an equally fierce rejection of psychological approaches to mental disorder (Scull 1975, Jacyna 1982, Dowbiggin 1985, Clark, 1981).

[18] On the tactics employed by organized psychiatry as it sought 'to retain a dominant position in the mental health professions', cf Grob (1983: ch 10).

[19] The American Association of Psychiatric Social Workers even went so far as to treat supervision by psychiatrists as a central qualification for membership in the organization (Abbott 1988: 307). For discussions of psychiatric social work, see Lubove (1965), and Timms (1964). The demography of social work – its position as an almost exclusively female specialty – presented a further obstacle to any attempt to escape medical dominance (cf Grob 1983).

[20] On the initial conflicts and tensions between psychology and psychiatry in the US, cf Grob (1983: 260–4).

[21] Jurisdictional settlements of this sort were made easier by the fact that psychiatry, lacking the manpower to service the expanding territory it laid claim to, had room to cede the marginal and less desirable portions to subordinate groups of specialists.

ensued was the predominantly feminized character of both social work and clinical psychology, for, notwithstanding ideological proclamations about gender equality, the fundamentally unequal place of the two sexes in the workplace remains, not totally impervious, yet still remarkably resistant to change.

In the years since the Second World War, psychiatry has thus been able to view with relative detachment the sharp curtailment (though not quite the total demise) of the institutional sector that formerly constituted its heartland. The rapid rundown of mental hospital populations, the de-institutionalization of even the chronically crazy, has simply marked a further step in the profession's retreat from socially contaminating contact with an impoverished and clinically hopeless clientele.[22] The 'miracles' of modern psychopharmacology – the phenothiazines, lithium, and the burgeoning variety of anti-depressants – clearly played a subordinate role in bringing about these mass discharges (Scull 1984, Lerman 1982, Gronfein 1984). But, notwithstanding their far from miraculous therapeutic properties, for the profession they have been a virtually unmitigated blessing.[23]

Pills have replaced talk as the dominant response to disturbances of emotion, cognition, and behaviour. Pharmaceutical corporations have underwritten the revolution, and have rushed to create and exploit a burgeoning market for an ever broader array of drugs aimed at treating some of the hundreds of 'diseases' psychiatrists claim to be able to identify (Healy 1997).[24] And patients and their families have learned to attribute their travails to biochemical disturbances, to faulty neurotransmitters, and to genetic defects, and to look to their doctors for the magic potions that will produce better living through chemistry. Spurred on by the neo-Kraepelinean revolution embodied in DSM III and its revisions, psychiatry has embraced a conceptualization of mental illnesses as specific, identifiably different diseases, each allegedly amenable to treatment with different drugs or 'magic bullets', though the whole conceptual edifice rests upon the shakiest of foundations, and the treatments themselves are decidedly less efficacious than the public relations flacks for the industry would have us believe. Meanwhile, at the level of language, both the profession of psychiatry and popular culture have become saturated with biological talk, though, as David Healy has wisely remarked, 'it can reasonably be asked whether biological language offers more in the line of marketing copy than it offers in terms of

---

[22] On the scope and sources of the mental hospital's demise, cf Scull (1984).

[23] For the patients, however, given the serious and often irreversible iatrogenic 'side-effects' the treatments produce, the picture is distinctly more mixed. For some references to the relevant literature, see Scull (1995). Cf, as well, the recent controversies about the heightened susceptibility to suicide of depressed children treated with anti-depressants, and the emerging evidence that drug companies have deliberately suppressed data that would have harmed their profits, allowing the continued distribution of products that harmed or killed many of those who took them.

[24] Healy records that 'DSM-IV has over 350 [illness categories], where DSM-IIIR had only 292 and DSM-II had 180'. More remarkably still, 'Today's classification systems make it possible to have many different illnesses at the same time – something that happens nowhere else in medicine' (Healy 1997: 175).

clinical meaning' (Healy 1997: 5). Most certainly, though, psychopharmacology has reinforced the notion that the behavioural and emotional problems its weapons are trained upon are purely intra-individual and biological in character. They thus provide a neutral 'scientific' justification and technique for the control of the wayward, one their relations (and very often the deviants themselves) embrace with avidity. For pills and a biological aetiology reduce or eliminate problems of morality, guilt, and blame, and suggest the existence of technical remedies for life's troubles.

Simultaneously, the advent of the new science has meant that psychiatric involvement with the unrewarding cases, which used to throng mental hospital wards, can now be reduced to the occasional prescription of psychoactive drugs, preferably to be dispensed by others – a thin veneer of continuing medical attention in which profession and public can, nonetheless, take comfort. On a wider canvas, alongside, and increasingly instead of, the psychotherapeutic techniques that first allowed the spread of its jurisdiction beyond the asylum, psychiatry now can proffer a new treatment technology, adaptable without strain to the general hospital, the outpatient clinic, the private consulting room. And since psychopharmacology is a form of treatment which is unambiguously and indisputably the monopoly of the medically trained, it provides a decisive means of re-cementing the profession's jurisdictional claims to the value-free realm of medical science.

Conclusion

In rationalizing the maintenance of social order, psychiatry can lay claim, more plausibly than potential competitors, to a foundation 'laid firmly on the ground of the natural sciences' (Mayer-Gross *et al* 1960). In reality a moral enterprise, actively engaged in the creation and application of social meanings to particular segments of everyday life, it masked (and masks) the necessarily evaluative dimension of its activities behind a screen of scientific objectivity and neutrality. Moreover, its explanatory schema locates the source of the pathology it identifies in intra-individual forces, and, in principle, can allow the redefinition of all protest and deviation from the dominant social order in individualistic and pathological terms. It was and is, therefore, of great potential value in legitimizing and de-politicizing efforts to regulate social life and to keep the socially disruptive in line: the more so since, so far from appearing as merely a repressive or negative force, psychiatry can often direct its interventions at willing subjects, 'those who have come to identify their own distress in psychiatric terms, believe that psychiatric expertise will help them, and are thankful for the attention they receive' (Rose 1986: 83). Perhaps, when all is said and done, the power to exercise social control is most effectively exercised when it does not appear to constitute punishment.

12

Origins of Actuarial Justice[1]

Malcolm Feeley

Introduction

A decade ago, Jonathan Simon and I published a pair of articles that introduced the idea of the 'new penology' and 'actuarial justice' into criminology (Feeley and Simon 1992, 1994). Our arguments struck a chord just as concern with 'risk' was being embraced in the social sciences more generally. We have been edified by the reception. Our articles have taken on something of a life of their own, and risk analysis is now commonplace in criminal law and criminal justice scholarship. I suppose that Simon and I should take some credit or at least share some blame for this development.

There are, however, three criticisms of the new penology that we – or at least, I – take issue with. It is not that I am so irritated that I feel obliged to set the record straight. Indeed, I believe that once launched my scholarly work heads directly for a black hole, and so am edified when someone pays attention to it, even if they sometimes get it wrong. However, I think it may be useful to address some of these criticisms, and then turn to recount my – and I emphasize my and not our – involvement in the concern with risk. If nothing else it provides me with an opportunity to reflect on one aspect of my increasingly long career. More generally, it might be instructive to reveal how ideas take root, can stay with one, transmuted, and be joined with still other ideas. At any rate this is the spirit in which I offer my comments. But first it will be useful to begin this account with my reaction to some (very mild and generally insightful) criticisms of the new penology. They set the scene for the discussion that follows.

The first criticism, is that there is 'nothing new' about the 'new' penology; it is little more than old wine in new bottles. Second, despite new language and even some new actuarial technologies, practices remain more or less the same. Third, the 'technology' implicit in the new penology was a non-starter; just as risk

---

[1] This chapter began as a paper prepared for the Scottish Criminology Conference (Edinburgh 2003), and retains something of the informality of the event. I wish to express my deep appreciation to Sarah Armstrong for having invited me to the conference, making insightful comments at the time, and pressing me to prepare this piece for publication.

technocrats appeared on the scene, a resurgence of a primitive politics of vengeance established the dominance of a crude and crushing version of retribution. The first criticism suggests that the only thing that is 'new' about the new penology is postmodern jargon. The second maintains that the new penology reifies decision making and neglects agency, substituting abstract 'forces' for flesh-and-blood officials who bring their own understanding of the law and their own objectives to bear on their decision making. The third criticism points to the new 'culture of control' that fosters repression, not risk management. All three arguments have been advanced to challenge our theory, and to suggest that at worst the 'new penology' is little more than wordplay, and that at most it reveals little more than the fact that officials have adopted some of the language and techniques of modern management. Admittedly, the criminal process is complex, so the new is not wholly new, nor does the old disappear entirely. And certainly agency has not suddenly evaporated. If we implied any of this, we misspoke. What we meant to suggest is that a new and powerful way of characterizing the criminal process has emerged and taken root. This new way of thinking is important even if it is not faithfully or fully executed. It provides a new way of framing issues, a new set of purposes, and it invites establishment of new institutions with new objectives. That they are no more successful nor fully realized than most other new policies does not negate their importance.

In taking exception to these criticisms, I want to point out the concrete consequences and permanent new arrangements that have been fostered by the new penology. But first, and on a not-very-interesting personal note, I should declare myself decidedly un-postmodern. I cannot tell you the differences between postmodernism spelled with large and small case 'p' and 'm,' or with or without a hyphen or a space. And upon the rare occasions when I cite their works, I must check and double check the spelling of the names of even the most *au courant* thinkers. Indeed, I am not even very far into the 'cultural turn'. I remain anchored in grubby empiricism and institutionalism. I have spent most of my scholarly career unearthing details that challenge conventional wisdom and dissecting organizational pathologies, and suspect I have more affinity with the Chicago School of sociology of the 1920s and 1930s than with the postmodernism and deconstructionism of the latter part of the century. Second and more generally, the interest that initially led towards the new penology emerged from field work and attention to practical criminal justice reforms. For a period of nearly 30 years, from the mid-1960s to the early 1990s, I witnessed, at times at close range, a series of reforms in the pretrial release process that has had a profound effect on the American criminal justice system. When I first started writing about these decisions in the 1970s, I juxtaposed what I called an 'administrative strategy' against a 'rights-based strategy' whose erosion I was witnessing first hand. Some time later when I moved to Berkeley, first in conversations with my new colleague the late Caleb Foote, and then in conversations with my colleague Shelly Messinger, also deceased and my then-student and now-collaborator and colleague, Jonathan Simon, we worked through these and other closely related ideas and began to generalize. Shelly, Jonathan, and I – and particularly Jonathan – began exploring new developments in sentencing, parole, career criminals, selective incapacitation, and the like and looking at them through the lens of risk. Actuarial justice was the result.

But the origins of my involvement with these ideas go back to the mid-1960s, and are rooted in the vantage point from which I observed close up and over a long period of time the destruction of the *ideal* of the *right* to bail, and the construction and institutionalization of preventive detention. This transformation was – and remains – all the more poignant to me because it was orchestrated not by retrograde conservatives or proponents of a 'crime control model', but by my friends, colleagues, and heroes, all well-meaning liberal reformers. It was this experience that led me to reflect on at least one of the twin challenges of social change, one animated by the power of vision and mission – rather than ideology and politics – and that suggests that we can become prisoners of our paradigms of thought. A new technology invites a new way of thinking and a new way of framing – and hence solving – problems. Once this new technology caught the imagination of reformers, it took on a life of its own.[2] I beg your indulgence as I take you through something of a biographical journey. My purpose is not to reveal too much of myself – I'm not very interesting – but to show how ideas originate, stay with us, and can be transmuted.

Stumbling into a New Idea

In the fall of 1972, I took a leave from New York University where I was teaching political science, and moved 75 miles north to New Haven, Connecticut, to take a postdoctoral position at the Yale Law School. I was fortunate; the Russell Sage Foundation was generously funding post docs to pursue 'law and the behavioral sciences'. I was doubly fortunate because over the past few months in New York I had been unsuccessful in securing cooperation for an in-depth study of the operations of Manhattan's criminal courts. Legal Aid lawyers had given me the cold shoulder, prosecutors had agreed only if I would conduct statistical research that would refute the findings of a study introduced in a lawsuit against them, and judges never returned my telephone calls. I was happy to be moving to New Haven;

---

[2] It is interesting to note that bail and bail reform are treated at greatest length by the Task Force on Science and Technology in the 1968 reports of the President's Crime Commission. The report of this Task Force stands out from the several other reports issued by the Commission. The other reports were all anchored in a vision of penal welfarism, and sought to strengthen and reinforce the adversary system. In contrast, the Science and Technology report is informed by operations research and systems analysis and enamoured by the idea of constructing a 'unified' criminal justice system. This is but one indicator that the ideas Simon and I point to are new, at least when applied to the criminal process.

city officials were amenable to social science research,[3] the Law School was providing me with resources to allow me do my own work, and its dean, a notable criminal scholar, was particularly supportive of my project. In short order I was wandering the halls of the Court of Common Pleas talking to criminal defendants, prosecutors, public defenders, bail bondsmen, and bailiffs, watching cases in the overheated courtroom, and sitting in '[Judge] Mancini's Bargain Basement' where plea negotiations took place. During the early mornings at the law school, I was also sitting in on Guido Calabresi's class on torts, a course I had selected precisely because I knew next to nothing about accident law and because of Calabresi's reputation as a superb teacher.

Within a few weeks these two activities intersected in ways I could never have imagined. My research in the misdemeanor court led me to develop what I came to call the 'pretrial process model', which holds that the most meaningful sanctions the court dispensed were the process costs it extracted from those who had been dragged into it – a few nights in jail awaiting a hearing, the bail bondsman's commission, docked wages from missed work, repeated trips to the public defender's office and court. I found that this understanding was widely intuited by the accused as well as by almost everyone else who occupied an official role in the courthouse. Together they organized operations so as to try to minimize some of these costs. Adjudicating guilt and pronouncing sentence, although not quite afterthoughts, were nevertheless usually not the most salient decisions in this process. Rather, managing the process in a way that rendered a rough form of substantive justice was the object of their actions.

This 'pretrial process' model was at odds with the then dominant framework. Herbert Packer's (1968) famous contrast between the 'Due Process Model' and the 'Crime Control Model.' Indeed, I recall having spirited discussions with various colleagues, who admonished me to interpret my observations in the light of this well-known dichotomy. Some of them regarded my refusal to do so as something close to heresy. In retrospect, I can see this refusal as just one small step away from the influence of Packer and one small step towards an 'administrative' model and still later the model of the new penology.[4]

The pretrial process, and in particular pretrial release (ie remand decisions), loomed large in my administrative model. New Haven had adopted a release on your own recognizance (ROR) programme closely modelled after the one that the Vera Institute had established in New York City a few years earlier.[5] I was familiar with the Vera programme and was keen on learning how its progeny was

---

[3] Next to Chicago, New Haven may be the most studied city in America, owing in large part to Robert Dahl (1961) and his colleagues who used the city as a 'laboratory' to explore many of their ideas.

[4] My work was eventually published as *The Process Is the Punishment* (1979).

[5] There are several published accounts of this well-known project, which initially was known as the Manhattan Bail Project. The best account is Ares *et al* (1963), a lengthy account written by the project's director and two colleagues. Although this research is flawed in some respects (see Feeley 1983), it does provide a rationale for the project, as well as a description of its origins and operations.

faring. However, my fortuitous choice of classes at the Yale Law School allowed me to see these things in a new light.

The connection between my observations of the criminal process and tort law was two-fold. Formally, I discovered, tort law was a lot like criminal law; and indeed I learned that criminal law emerged from tort law in the late medieval period. Calabresi instructed us in the principles of classical tort law which required that those morally responsible for an accident are liable for the consequences. He parsed the issues of intent, negligence, causation, necessity, and deterrence, all of which are basic ingredients of criminal law as well. He also taught us modern tort law: torts as public policy, a system for 'managing' accidents in a fair and efficient manner. He brought us right up to date by assigning his just-published book, *The Cost of Accidents* (Calabresi 1970), which advanced the newest of the new theories. In it he argued that accident law has no deterrent effects, that the cost of determining who is at fault swamps the cost of the damage itself, and that a fair and efficient tort system had to set these issues aside and 'manage' accidents, that it should not aspire to deter or to hold people morally responsible. He went on to argue that the courts and other policy makers had intuitively begun to streamline the 'tort system' in ways consistent with these principles – through expanded strict liability, no-fault rules, and the like – but the time was ripe for a new theory that recognized and rationalized these developments, and in so doing would provide the impetus for extending them still further. One – but by no means the only – factor that drove this sea change, he argued, was the widespread availability of *insurance*. If transaction costs for the parties and the courts had not driven morality out of tort law, he continued, insurance certainly had. Insurance companies are neither interested in morality nor deterrence. They are interested in money, in minimizing information and transaction costs, in spreading the costs of accidents, and in actuarial predictability.

Confronting Calabresi's arguments during the fall of 1972 was exciting. I read and reread the book, and reviewed it for the *American Political Science Review*. It was illuminating, not because it presented torts in a new and exciting way, which it did, but because it unwittingly invited me to think of the criminal process in a new way. The insights on torts which I gleaned from eight to nine o'clock every morning, Monday through Thursday, shaped my thinking about the criminal process which I immersed myself in later those same mornings. Calabresi had unwittingly provided me with a new lens through which to observe this process: minor criminal offences were much like fender benders: both are 'problems' to be *managed*, not moral lapses for which one is to be held accountable. Nor is the response understood by anyone to be aimed at deterrence. Events happen; the task is to manage the aftermath effectively and efficiently. What through the lenses of legalism could appear outrageous, took on a certain compelling logic through the perspective of the new tort law. Indeed, at times the accident/crime distinction was reversed for me. 'Points' added to one's driving record after an accident often impose much more substantial costs than a criminal conviction and fine. At the time a typical fine in the Court of Common Pleas was $50 or $100; an increase in insurance premiums after an accident might be twice or three times these amounts, and imposed not just once but each year for three to five years. When costs are so diffuse and ancillary to determination of guilt, the logic of efficient management and the quest for substantive situational justice has an appeal that a regime of rights may not.

If the entire criminal process, at least in lower courts, began to take on the actuarial characteristics of the new tort law that I was learning about in Professor Calabresi's torts class, this way of thinking loomed especially large in the pretrial release process that I was watching. With the support of foundations in New York and progressive faculty members at the Yale Law School, New Haven in the 1950s and 1960s had experimented with social reforms in public housing, urban renewal, welfare, and legal services that all later served as prototypes for President Johnson's Great Society programmes. Among them was pretrial release reform.

In the early 1960s, Herbert Sturz, a young social worker and staff writer for *Boy's Life* magazine in New York City examined the plight of young men and women who had been arrested for petty offences and remained in jail for pro- longed periods – far in excess of what their sentences would have been – because of an inability to post bail of $500 or so, or even scrape together 10 per cent of that amount for a bail bondsman's commission. His solution: get rid of bail, at least for some people. Those with strong ties to the community, he reasoned, were good risks for reappearance, and thus – if the court could learn who they were – were good candidates for release on their own recognizance (ROR). A superb entrepreneur and publicist, Sturz interested philanthropist Louis Schweitzer in 'grub-staking' his idea, convinced city officials of its merit, and recruited volunteers – law students from NYU – to staff it. The Vera Institute – named after Schweitzer's late wife – was born. Volunteers interviewed arrestees shortly before their initial appearance in court and determined if they had strong ties to the community, measured by such things as having an apartment lease, a telephone or public utilities account in their name, a steady job, and the like – and if so, recommended to the court that they were good candidates for ROR rather than money bail. The experiment caught the attention of some early architects of the Great Society. New York's Mayor Wagner praised it and created a line item in the City's budget for it. The Ford Foundation promoted it. Early on it also caught the imaginations of two young criminal justice reformers in the Department of Justice, Daniel Freed and Patricia Weld, who incorporated its spirit in their important monograph, *Bail in the United States* (1964), and their draft bail reform legislation that eventually became the Bail Reform Act of 1966. US Attorney General and later New York Senator Bobby Kennedy promoted it. It was also highlighted in the President's Crime Commission report (1968) as one of the most promising criminal justice innovations. The Vera Institute's original ROR programme in New York later received a second high-profile evaluation by legendary social researchers, Hans Zeisel at the University of

Chicago and Paul Lazarsfeld (1974) at Columbia University, which gave it high marks. It was clearly an idea whose time had come. Through connections in the foundation world and the New York criminal justice system, the faculty of the Yale Law School worked with officials in New Haven to replicate the programme there. New Haven quickly became the second city to implement a community ties-based pretrial release system. By the mid-1970s dozens if not hundreds of cities across the country from Long Island to San Francisco had pretrial release programmes modelled after New York's and New Haven's pioneering work.

One prominent scholar of bail reform, however, was not impressed. In 1955, University of Pennsylvania law professor Caleb Foote (later my colleague at Berkeley) had written what he hoped would be a prophetic law review article, 'The Coming Constitutional Crisis in Bail'. Anticipating its far-reaching implications, Foote recognized that *Brown v Board of Education* (1954), the US Supreme Court decision that had proclaimed an end to segregation in the public schools, was likely to precipitate a 'rights revolution'. He hoped that it would awake interest in breathing meaning into the Eighth Amendment's prohibition against excessive bail, a provision in the US Constitution that had all but lain dormant since it had been adopted without comment in 1789. Foote's campaign was doomed even before it got off the ground. It was doomed not because law and order conservatives sought to suppress it, but because the Vera Institute's community ties ROR model captured the liberals' imaginations. Rather than treating bail as a *right*, and pressing to invest it with substance, liberal bail reformers almost to a person ignored Foote's call for a rights-based approach and embraced an 'administrative' approach, advocating the establishment of what came to be called 'pretrial service agencies' which developed and administered schemes for predicting appearance at trial based upon community ties. Although some scholars eventually joined Foote in questioning this administrative approach to bail reform (for example Dill 1972), the community ties predictive model was enthusiastically promoted by the media-savvy founder of the first programme and his colleagues (Ares *et al* 1963), the Ford Foundation, and later the President's Crime Commission, the national media, prominent social researchers (Lazarsfeld 1974), the bar, and leading politicians and criminal justice officials in New York and Washington, DC. A rights model did not have a chance against the support of this phalanx. Indeed, Foote's proposal never even secured a real hearing.

Although there were few – and nothing has changed in this regard – if any first-rate evaluations of community ties-based ROR programmes (for a history of bail reform and an assessment of the social science scholarship of it, see Feeley 1983), nevertheless the model took off. It came to be heavily promoted by the federal Law Enforcement Assistance Administration (LEAA) and the National Institute of Justice, which also funded it liberally and heavily. Since the Vera Institute established the first such programme in 1961, it has remained entrenched as the primary model of bail reform. (For an account of the development of programmes created in Vera's wake, written by proponents of the idea, see Mahoney *et al* 1997, and Clark and Henry 2003.) Although its fortunes have varied as funding has waxed and waned, the basic approach has held steadfast. The administrative model is now *the* model.[6] On the federal level, legislation has mandated that each federal district court have its own 'Pretrial Services Agency' whose primary purpose is to assist the court in 'administering' pretrial release. Throughout the United States, most major cities and some states support programmes that help to 'administer' a prediction-driven pretrial release programme (for an overview, see Henry and Clark 1999, Clark and Henry 2003).

However, the purpose to which this administrative model was to be put to use was soon transformed, and indeed turned upside down. Imbued with the liberal and optimistic spirit of the 1960s, the administrative model of pretrial release sought to put modern technology to good liberal use, using predictive models to determine who would be good risks to release pretrial without having to impose money bond.[7] Faith in science, technology, and the idea of an integrated criminal justice 'system' were compelling, accepted with virtually no dissent. (I can think of only one prominent dissenter to these views who was deeply involved with the Crime Commission. George Kelling, later of 'Broken Windows' fame, in 1968 penned a strong challenge to some of the new group-think views, arguing that the adversary process had purposefully constructed something of an obstacle course as a means of fragmenting power and protecting rights.) Some time later, but at best only on the fringes of the enterprise, I joined the ranks of dissenters.[8] Having surveyed the research on the subject, I found most flawed in major ways. More important, I questioned the logic of the 'administrative' model. The claim to be able to predict who will and will not appear at trial was, I and others warned, just a small step away from claiming to be able to predict dangerousness, who will commit offences while awaiting trial and thus be appropriately subject to detention.

Our warnings were prescient. The administrative model for bail reform emerged in full bloom just as the liberal moment in criminal justice began to dim. There is no doubt about the liberal intentions of the architects of this model – they were intent on relieving unnecessary harshness in the criminal process. But the model they created and then institutionalized had a life of its

---

[6] For a period in the mid-1970s, the Vera Institute had a branch office in London, collaborating with the Home Office on 'technology transfer'. One of the transfers was its community ties model of ROR. So far as I know, the history and consequences, if any, of the Vera Institute's collaboration with the Home Office have not been the object of anyone's study.

[7] This sprit of optimism pervades the Task Force reports of the President's Crime Commission, and nowhere so enthusiastically as in the Report of the Task Force on Science and Technology, where interestingly enough the discussion of pretrial release takes place (as opposed to another report that focuses on defendants' rights).

[8] In the early 1970s, I was a consultant to New Haven's pretrial release programme and other related activities, and also took part in an on-going seminar at the Yale Law School that worked closely with the Vera Institute on pretrial release, pretrial diversion, and related projects based on the 'system' idea.

own. As I wrote in the early 1980s, 'Advocates of pretrial release programs usually avoid the issue of whether their elaborate information systems and predictive techniques should be used for purposes of preventive detention' (Feeley 1983: 72). Although at the time, there was one statute explicitly authorizing pretrial detention, it applied only to the District of Columbia and had never been used.[9] Still, the election of Richard Nixon in 1968 and the replacement of Earl Warren with the law-and-order focused Warren Burger as Chief Justice of the Supreme Court symbolized the end of liberal criminal justice administration. The reports of the President's Crime Commission in 1968 represent both the high-water mark of liberal influence and its last hurrah. Writing over a decade later, I noted the lost opportunity to have developed a liberal rights-based approach to bail reform, observing that 'Caleb Foote's hope that a crisis in bail would be resolved through constitutional law reform has not been fulfilled . . .' and continuing, '[p]erhaps [these failures] have been conditioned by the conservative tenor of the Burger Court, but they may also be due to a sense of complacency about the administrative approach to bail reform as reflected in pretrial release programs [which are the handiwork of liberal reformers]' (Feeley 1983: 77). That is, I warned, there is 'great reason to believe that the façade of science will be used to justify increased harsh treatment of allegedly dangerous people. This may be one of the lasting, if unwitting, consequences of the administrative and scientific approach to bail reform' (*ibid:* 75).

At the same time, I noted that other liberal reforms had the potential to be easily put to uses quite different from those intended by their creators. Legislation ostensibly designed to breathe meaning into the US Constitution's Sixth Amendment guarantee of a criminal defendant's 'right' to speedy trial was quickly embraced by prosecutors as one more device to pressure defendants into pleading guilty. Pretrial diversion, a programme whose origins are traceable to liberal criminology's labelling theory, came to be used as a way of imposing sanctions in petty cases without having to secure conviction first (see generally, Feeley 1983: 80–113). And, of course, liberal supporters of determinate sentencing were co-opted by conservatives and ushered in the era of draconian sentencing.

However, what I only dimly perceived in the late 1970s and could only speculate about in 1983 soon materialized with a vengeance. Congress enacted the Bail Reform Act of 1984, a law that embraced preventive detention for the entire federal system. The administrative approach to bail reform had been implemented just as the tide was turning, and political conservatives consolidated their hold on government and certainly their hold on the imaginations of criminal justice policy makers. Their agenda: to dismantle the tattered shreds

---

[9] This statute was adopted in 1969 after having been introduced by the new Nixon Administration. Because of questions about its constitutionality, Congress limited its jurisdiction to the District of Columbia rather than the federal system more generally. However, as of the early 1980s, it had never been invoked or challenged in court, so its constitutionality was still in doubt. For a discussion of it, see Feeley (1983).

of penal welfarism; turn back the advances of the due process revolution; and impose harsher penalties. They made inroads in all of these areas, often with the help of liberals. They seized upon Robert Martinson's (1974) rhetorical question, 'What Works?' (in offender rehabilitation) and answered it, 'Nothing!', and co-opted liberals who had joined them to work to replace indeterminate sentencing schemes with determinate – and much longer – sentences. And they intensified the campaign to roll back the Warren Court's liberal rulings on criminal procedure. The consequences of this campaign are all too familiar – the emergence of the 'culture of control' in Garland's (2001) apt phrase that doubled and then re-doubled America's prison population as well as the number of those on probation or parole, a trend that only now, in the early 2000s, shows some small signs of abating.

In my view, the single most rapid and dramatic change of course was the turnabout in the aims of bail reform. Within the space of just a few years, policy shifted from the liberal aspiration of maximizing pretrial release to the draconian provisions for preventive detention. The transformation was rapid and thorough; states quickly followed the federal cues. One reason for this sudden and successful about-face was that the community ties-prediction model put in place by the liberals was easily adaptable for use with the new objectives. Agencies that had been charged with predicting risk of flight based upon the strength of community ties were now charged with predicting risk to public safety. If they could do one, they could do the other. Indeed, staff advocates welcomed the challenge, and viewed this new charge as a validation of their technology and professionalism. In short order the mission of the pretrial service agencies was transformed from predicting appearance at trial to predicting dangerousness for purposes of preventive detention, and from reminding releasees of their pending appearances in court to engaging in surveillance of lower risk releasees.

The Triumph of Actuarial Reasoning in the Pretrial Process

In 1974, provision for pilot 'Pretrial Service Agencies' in ten federal districts was slipped into the Speedy Trial Act of 1974. According to Yale Law Professor Daniel Freed, who drafted the Act and had included this provision, it was to be a first quiet step towards institutionalizing the administrative model for bail reform nationwide. His ambition was soon fully realized. With the passage of still another Freed-drafted law, the Pretrial Services Act of 1982, Congress expanded the ten district pilot programme to all 94 federal district courts. The idea quickly caught on in the states as well, and soon there were dozens if not hundreds of pretrial service agencies in major cities across the country. However, this growth took place just as the new law and order regime was consolidating its hold on the public discourse about crime and punishment. Almost from the outset, these new agencies used the administrative approach to facilitate preventive detention and surveillance of those released, and not the bail reformer's goal of release on the 'least restrictive conditions' possible. Below I chart the expansion and evolution of the preventive detention functions of these federal pretrial services agencies, and outline the parallel developments that have taken place in the states.[10]

The central logic of the new Pretrial Service Agencies was to establish a neutral third party in the criminal process which could 'provide sufficient accurate and objective information regarding the defendant, his background, the offense and all other evidence that relates to the question of whether he will appear for trial' (Mahoney *et al* 2001: 6).[11] To this end, the Act provided for agency staff to collect information on new arrestees prior to court appearance in order to undertake a risk assessment to determine likelihood of appearance at trial, a process modelled after the Vera Institute's community ties index. In so doing, the Act *institutionalized* a process that largely bypassed a rights-based adversarial process and instead employed expert third parties to present 'objective' evidence about risk. This constituted a sharp break with past ideals (practice is another matter) as well as a sharp break with the traditional responsibility accorded prosecution and defence counsel in the adversarial process. Although this new administrative system has never operated in any 'pure' form, its establishment has helped to foster a new and quite different understanding about the nature of the criminal process.[12] With it, 'administration' in the oft-used phrase, the *administration of criminal justice*, took on a new and a more concrete significance.

[10] It is important to emphasize that there are over 50 separate jurisdictions in the US, a federal court system which handles only a tiny fraction of the country's trial business, 50 state legal systems that handle the vast bulk of all cases, and a handful of other jurisdictions – the District of Columbia, Puerto Rico, and other territorial systems. Within the states there is considerable variation. For instance: 35 states permit the death penalty; 15 forbid it; the incarceration rate per 100,000 for Louisiana is over 800, while the rate for Minnesota is 150, and the rate for the other states ranges between these two figures. Accordingly, it is difficult to generalize about 'American' practices. Still, almost all states have embraced preventive detention, and pretrial service agencies or their functional equivalents have been established in the courts of virtually every major city across the country. For discussions of variation among the states and the challenges of generalizing about the US, see Rubin and Feeley (1994) and Feeley and Rubin (1998: 149–203). For a thoughtful analysis that examines substantial variations in criminal sentencing and the response to crime, see Barker (2006).

[11] Testimony of Judge Gerald B. Tjoflat, Chairman of the Committee on the Administration of the Probation System of the Judicial Conference of the United States.

[12] There is a vast amount of research on pretrial service agencies. Most of it is internally generated and self-serving. But the most systematic of this work, from whatever sources, acknowledges that the agencies fall far short of their more expansive claims to be able to offer accurate and reliable predictions. False positives and false negatives abound. So too does incomplete data, and inept administration. The product of these efforts has enough flaws of all sorts to warrant the label, pseudo-science. When such programmes have been challenged, however, the courts have upheld them. Courts have granted them the traditional deference accorded to administrative decision making, and in so doing have not scrutinized them as arrangements that might violate the *rights* of the criminally accused. Administration has trumped rights. For analysis of the failure to consider the problems with these institutions in terms of criminal justice rights analysis, see Klein (1997: 281).

Pretrial Service Agencies grew by leaps and bounds between the time the first ten pilot programmes were established in 1972 and the turn of the century. As of 2003, there were at least 337 state and local jurisdictions that had pretrial services programmes (Clark and Henry 2003). In addition, several states – Connecticut, Delaware, Kentucky, Virginia – operate state-wide programmes (Clark and Henry 2003: 2). Although their financing remains precarious – the dominant troika of judge, prosecution, and public defender continue to receive the lion's share of funding – these newer appendages nevertheless have found a niche in the criminal process. They are here to stay, complete with a sense of professionalism, a set of professional 'standards,' a national organization (National Association of Pretrial Service Agencies, or NAPSA), and an annual meeting. And like all bureaucracies they have become adept at making themselves indispensable.

In their infancy in New York, New Haven, and a few other cities, their sole task was to help the court to decide if particular arrestees were good risks for pretrial release. But as noted above, their functions quickly expanded and shifted. According to one recent and authoritative survey of their functions, two-fifths of them have delegated authority to release arrestees on their own without having to wait for the review and approval of a judge (Clark and Henry 2003: 8). While this certainly facilitates early release, it also underscores their administrative nature. But their functions quickly expanded beyond this, a fact that is reflected in the name change they underwent early on in their development. Originally called 'pretrial release agencies', by the time the federal legislation was being considered, they had come to call themselves 'pretrial *service* agencies', an acknowledgement that they performed many more services than advising the court on likelihood of appearance at trial. Early on many of them were charged with contacting and 'reminding' defendants on release of their upcoming court dates. At times this meant requiring 'clients' to check in periodically, and to accept home visits by staff. In some places, staff gained peace officer status, allowing them to detain and forcibly return no-shows to court.

With this expanding capacity to follow-up and monitor those released prior to trial, it was all but inevitable that courts would begin to attach conditions to pretrial release. In addition to requiring them to show up at trial (which historically has been the function of bail), judges began conditioning pretrial release on payment of child support, attendance at school, maintaining employment, avoiding contact with undesirables, and the like. That is, pretrial release became a sort of pretrial probation. In good bureaucratic form, pretrial agencies expanded the range of services they offered. For instance NAPSA standards state that pretrial service agencies should monitor pretrial releasees and provide information to the court that is relevant for the *pre-sentence* investigation, and one survey reports that over 80 per cent of pretrial programmes 'comply' with this standard (Clark and Henry 2003: 19). Other functions they have added include providing pretrial diversion services, screening defendants for indigency to determine eligibility for public defenders, conducting classification services for local jails, and providing mediation services for defendants and victims (*ibid*). However, what few of the programmes have is a validated instrument for assessing risk (Clark and Henry 2003: 24). By their own admission, almost all of them operate by the seat-of-their pants without even a pretence at systematic, scientific, or objective decision making.

Some of these new agencies are especially problematic. Many of them have been charged with special responsibilities dealing with arrestees thought to have mental health problems, others deal with juveniles charged as adults or those involved in domestic violence. These pose special challenges. For instance, over 80 per cent of all pretrial service agencies systematically collect information in interviews to screen for indicators of mental illness. Despite laws requiring informed consent and protecting privacy of informants, these agencies routinely fail to advise 'clients' of their rights in this regard and routinely pass on acquired information to third parties – jailers, judges, prosecutors, probation officials (Clark and Henry 2003: 32–3). Many agencies have special responsibilities when dealing with juveniles charged as adults, and aid the court in devising pretrial release or detention plans that are age appropriate. And in cases involving charges of domestic violence, many agencies try to balance their concern for the alleged victim, which usually means delaying release or recommending restrictive conditions for release.

That many of these conditions are similar to conditions of probation imposed at sentencing is not surprising. Many pretrial release agencies are in fact operated by probation departments. They appear to believe that a person in need of supervision is a person in need of supervision, regardless of whether or not they have been a convicted criminal.

It may appear that I have strayed far from my concern with the new penology. So, let me connect this discussion of pretrial release to the argument that I laid at the outset about the rise of actuarial justice. The concept might be thought of as having two components, one weak and one strong. The strong component focuses on the capacity to offer risk assessment and the ability to make valid and reliable predictions. This, as I have suggested, has certainly not been fulfilled by the pretrial services agencies. Indeed, it has rarely even been tried. So, one might conclude, as some have, that the new penology is little more than a figment of our imaginations, a half-baked idea that to date has not led to very much.

But the weak conception has had enormous impact. Although it too envisions an institution that can predict behaviour, this institution's real power is not that it really can make such predictions. Rather it is the fact that this aspiration has led to the establishment of a new organization with new aims, new authority, and new responsibilities. Once an organization was established to predict appearance at trial, it was but a small step to ask it to predict dangerousness. As suggested, it can do neither of these things yet, but once the aspiration was legitimized, it was authorized to engage in a host of activities that would not be permitted under a more traditional rights regime. This weak conception of the new penology is certainly alive and well in the pretrial process in the United States.

It may appear that I am making a mountain out of a molehill by reading so much significance into the expanded activities of the pretrial service agencies. However, the problems with the logic of pretrial service agencies loom large when we look at the functions that have been grafted onto them and that fit comfortably within their rationale. Two developments in particular stand out. First is the moment in 1969 when Congress adopted the preventive detention statute. Even though the law's coverage was limited to the District of Columbia out of concerns about its constitutionality, once it had withstood a challenge at this level, Congress rolled out the law nationally. The Bail Reform Act of 1986 represents a sea change in American criminal justice. Secondly, its embrace of preventive detention occurred just as Congress was escalating the 'war on drugs', enacting a series of laws that required harsh mandatory minimum sentences for drug-related offences.

It was probably inevitable that these two concerns – preventive detention and the war on drugs – would be joined. And it was probably inevitable that the newly established pretrial services agencies would be drawn into combat. Indeed, they were well-poised to contribute to both. If they could predict appearance at trial, as they claimed to do, they should be able to predict dangerousness. The objectives are similar, the models much the same. This new responsibility precipitated an expanded set of duties. First the agencies assumed responsibilities for assessing dangerousness. This new-found responsibility immediately involved them with drugs. Drug use, conventional wisdom holds, is highly correlated with criminal violence, and thus is a good predictor of dangerous behaviour and criminal activity. So too are contextual factors – who do you hang out with, are you employed, and so on. Accordingly, pretrial services agencies began systematically collecting data about these factors as well.

However, drug use and contextual circumstances can change rapidly. Inquiry into these issues invites not one-shot questioning, but continuous monitoring. The consequence: pretrial service agencies got involved in the drug testing and surveillance business (Bureau of Justice Assistance 1989, 1999; Alan and Clark 1999, Rhodes *et al* 1996). High risk defendants were, of course, recommended for preventive detention, but mid- and low-level risks might receive conditional release. Conditions could include a requirement to stay away from old associates; curfews; rules about maintaining employment; and submitting to electronic surveillance and drug testing. To effect these conditions, pretrial agencies were charged with monitoring the activities of their 'clients'. But monitoring soon expanded into supervision. Pretrial service agencies eventually came to be running diversion programmes, drug testing programmes, drug treatment programmes, electronic monitoring programmes, and developing 'partnerships with other entities involved in initiatives focused on community crime problems – including the police, probation, and community organizations – to enhance the prospects for effective community-based supervision' (Goldkamp and White 1998:159–60).

This is the nutshell history of the consequences of the bail reform project of the mid 1960s.[13] The great vision for bail reform advanced by a pantheon of liberal reformers is now firmly ensconced in a regime of preventive detention and drowning in a sea of urine. Pretrial services programmes have recreated – and significantly extended – the panoply of options traditionally associated with probation. The one striking difference, of course, is that the first group of people, those subjected to pretrial probation, have not been convicted of any crime.

Conclusion

I have offered this brief and incomplete account of bail reform and its consequences – told largely from my ring-side seat over the years – for several reasons. First and foremost I wanted to emphasize the unintended consequences of reforms. But more particularly I wanted to reveal how a new idea – based on actuarial principles – took root and grew. Admittedly this new institution does not operate in a 'strong' sense; it does not employ fine-tuned statistical analysis. But it would be wrong to conclude that actuarial principles are unimportant. The weak version of actuarial organization is still powerful enough. The patina of science, technology, and prediction has legitimized a practice that historically was alien to the Anglo-American criminal jurisprudence. It has led to new objectives, new techniques, and new institutions. These have had real and far-reaching consequences.

I have chosen to concentrate on the one area of actuarial development I know best. But it is not the only area with such developments. A similar story could be told – and to some extent has been told – about the emergence of selective incapacitation in sentencing and its many more modest variations such as 'three strikes' laws, career criminals, sentencing guidelines, and the increasing use of civil commitment for sexual predators. Risk analysis, or at least what I termed above the 'weak version' of it, is emerging and being recognized in any number of other areas of the criminal process. In recent years there have been important assessments of its influence in criminal law doctrine (Mathiesen 1998, Robinson 2001), and post-conviction civil commitment (Monahan 2006, forthcoming). In the future, I think, these several separate concerns will be brought together and form a new unified actuarial 'system' that will completely transform the criminal process into an administrative system.

Indeed, that future may already be near at hand. The State of Virginia has enacted a comprehensive statute charging a state-wide pretrial services agency with responsibility for developing models of risk prediction and administering a

---

[13] A full institutional history akin to Jonathan Simon's wonderful book, *Poor Discipline* (1990), cries out to be written. One hopes that some enterprising graduate student will pick up this idea and run with it.

scheme of preventive detention and pretrial monitoring based upon these models (Ostrom *et al* 2002, Virginia Pretrial Risk Assessment Instrument 2003). It has also enacted a comprehensive statute establishing selective incapacitation as its guiding principle for sentencing, and established a state sentencing council to develop predictive models and monitor this process. In many respects the aims and range of activities of the pretrial and the sentencing councils are indistinguishable; both are anchored in the same framework of actuarial justice. Interestingly, Virginia also has the highest rate of executions and the fastest pace of executions of any state in the United States. This may all be coincidence, but then again, we may be witnessing the emergence of the first true 'system' of criminal justice in the United States, and thus a preview of a more general future. To examine this, I hope someone soon writes a dissertation: Virginia and its System of Actuarial Justice. Whatever the case, actuarial justice is now firmly entrenched in the American criminal process.

Bibliography

Abbott, A. (1988). *The System of Professions: An Essay in the Division of Expert Labor.* Chicago: University of Chicago Press.

Adams, L. and McLaughlin, M. (2004). 'Revealed: the True Facts about Crime', *The Herald* 26 August (www.theherald.co.uk).

Agamben, G. (1998). *Homo Sacer. Sovereignty and Bare Life.* Stanford: Stanford University Press.

—— (2005). *State of Exception.* Chicago: University of Chicago Press.

Allen, F. (1981). *The Decline of the Rehabilitative Ideal: Penal Policy and Social Purpose.* New Haven: Yale University Press.

Allen, H. E. and Abril, J. C. (1997). 'The New Chain Gang: Corrections in the Next Century'. *American Journal of Criminal Justice* 22: 1–12.

Alper, B. (1973). 'Foreword', in Y. Bakal (ed), *Closing Correctional Institutions.* Lexington, Mass: D.C. Heath.

American Law Institute (1962). *Model Penal Code: Official Draft and Explanatory Notes: Complete Text of Model Penal Code As Adopted at the 1962 Annual Meeting of the American Law Institute.* Washington, DC: American Law Institute and American Bar Association.

Anderson, B. (1983). *Imagined Communities: Reflections on the Origin and Spread of Nationalism.* London: Verso.

Anderson, D. (1995). *Crime and the Politics of Hysteria.* New York: Times Books.

Andrews, J. and Scull, A. (2001). *Undertaker of the Mind: John Monro and Mad-Doctoring in Eighteenth Century England.* Berkeley: University of California Press.

—— —— (2003). *Customers and Patrons of the Mad Trade: The Management of Lunacy in Eighteenth Century London.* Berkeley: University of California Press.

Apap, J. and Carrera, S. (2003). 'Maintaining Security Within Borders: Towards a Permanent State of Emergency in the EU?' Available online at: http://www.eliseconsortium.org/article.php3?id_article = 104.

Appadurai, A. (1990). 'Disjuncture and Difference in the Global Cultural Economy', *Theory, Culture and Society* 7(2–3): 295–310.

—— (1996). *Modernity at Large: Cultural Dimensions of Modernity.* London and Minneapolis: University of Minnesota Press.

—— (2001). 'Grassroots Globalization and the Research Imagination', in A. Appadurai (ed), *Globalization.* Durham: Duke University Press.

Ares, C. E., Rankin, A., and Sturz, H. (1963). 'The Manhattan Bail Project: An Interim Report on the Use of Pre-trial Parole', *New York University Law Review*, 38: 67–95.

Armstrong, D. (1980). 'Madness and Coping'. *Sociology of Health and Illness* 2: 293–316.

Armstrong, S. (2003). 'Bureaucracy, Private Prisons, and the Future of Penal Reform', *Buffalo Criminal Law Review* 7(1): 275–306.

Ashworth, A. (1975). 'Self-Defence and the Right to Life', *Cambridge Law Journal* 34: 282.

Ashworth, A. (1984). *The English Criminal Process: A Review of Empirical Research.* Oxford: University of Oxford Centre for Criminological Research.

——(1994). *The Criminal Process.* Oxford: Clarendon.

——(1999). *Principles of Criminal Law.* Oxford: Oxford University Press.

——(2000a). 'Victims' Rights, Defendants' Rights and Criminal Procedure', in A. Crawford and J. Goodey (eds), *Integrating a Victim Perspective within Criminal Justice.* Aldershot: Ashgate, 185–204.

——(2000b). *Sentencing and Criminal Justice* (3rd edn). London: Butterworths.

——(2002). 'Sentencing', in M. Maguire, R. Morgan, and R. Reiner (eds), *The Oxford Handbook of Criminology* (3rd edn). Oxford, Oxford University Press.

——(2004). 'Social Control and "Anti-Social Behaviour": The Subversion of Human Rights?', *Law Quarterly Review* 120: 263–91.

Atkinson, A. B. (1999). *The Economic Consequences of Rolling Back the Welfare State.* Cambridge, Mass: MIT Press.

Auerhahn, K. (2003). *Selective Incapacitation and Public Policy.* Albany, NY: SUNY Press.

Baier, A. (2001). *Trust.* Princeton, NJ: Princeton University Press.

Bailey, J. (2000). 'Some Meanings of "the Private" in Sociological Thought', *Sociology* 34(3): 381–401.

Bailey, V. (1987). *Delinquency and Citizenship: Reclaiming the Young Offender 1914–1948.* Oxford: Clarendon Press.

Balibar, E., Chemillier-Gendreau, M., Costa-Lascoux, J. and Terray, E. (1999). *Sans-papiers, l'archaïsme fatal.* Paris: Editions La Découverte.

Barker, V. (2006). 'The politics of punishing: Building a state governance theory of American imprisonment variation', *Punishment and Society* 8(1): 5–32.

Barton, R. (1965). *Institutional Neurosis* (2nd edn). Bristol: Wright.

Baudrillard, J. (1993). *Symbolic Exchange and Death.* London: Sage.

Bauman, Z. (1989). *Modernity and the Holocaust.* Cambridge: Polity Press.

——(1993). *Postmodern Ethics.* Oxford: Blackwell.

——(1998). *Globalization: the Human Consequences.* Cambridge: Polity Press.

——(2000). 'Social Issues of Law and Order', in D. Garland and R. Sparks (eds). *Criminology and Social Theory.* Oxford: Oxford University Press.

——(2002). *Society Under Siege.* Cambridge: Polity Press.

——(2004). *Identity.* Cambridge: Polity Press.

Beaud, S. and Pialoux, M. (1999). *Retour sur la classe ouvrière.* Paris: Fayard.

Beck, U. (1992). *Risk Society.* London: Sage.

Beckett, K. (1997). *Making Crime Pay.* Oxford: Oxford University Press.

—— and Western, B. (2001). 'Governing Social Marginality', in D. Garland (ed), *Mass Imprisonment: Social Causes and Consequences.* London: Sage, 35–50.

Beeson, M. (2003). 'Sovereignty Under Siege: Globalisation and the State in the Southeast Asia', *Third World Quarterly* 24(2): 357–74.

Belknap, I. (1956). *Human Problems of a State Mental Hospital.* New York: McGraw-Hill.

Benhabib, S. (1999). 'Citizens, Residents, and Aliens in a Changing World: Political Membership in the Global Era', *Social Research* 66: 709–44.

Bennington, J. (1994). *Local Democracy and the European Union: The Impact of Europeanisation on Local Governance.* London: Municipal Journal/Commission for Local Government.

Bigo, D. (1992). *L'Europe des polices et la sécurité intérieure*. Brussels: Editions Complexe.

—— (2005). *Les nouveaux enjeux de l'(in)sécurité en Europe : terrorisme, guerre, sécurité intérieure, sécurité extérieure*. Paris: L'Harmattan.

Billig, M. (1995). *Banal Nationalism*. London: Sage Publications.

Blackstone, W. (1966 [1765–9]). *Commentaries on the Laws of England* (reprint) Chicago: Chicago UP, 1966.

Blinken, A. (2001). 'The false crisis over the Atlantic: with friends like this', *Foreign Affairs* 80: 35–49.

Blomberg, T. (1977). 'Diversion and Accelerated Social Control', *Journal of Criminal Law and Criminology* 68: 274–82.

—— Cohen, S. (eds) (1995). *Punishment and Social Control*. Hawthorne, NY: Aldine de Gruyter.

Bogard, W. (1996). *The Simulation of Surveillance: Hypercontrol in Telematic Societies*. Cambridge, Cambridge University Press.

Boltanski, L. (1999). *Distant Suffering: Morality, Media and Politics*. Cambridge: Cambridge University Press.

Bosworth, M. (1999). *Engendering Resistance: Agency and Power in Women's Prisons*. Aldershot: Ashgate.

—— (2003). 'Book Review of Situational Prison Control: Crime Prevention In Correctional Institutions, by Richard Wortley; Prison Architecture: Policy, Design and Experience, edited by Leslie Fairweather and Sean McConville', *British Journal of Criminology* 43(3): 634–5.

Bottoms, A. E. (1980). 'An Introduction to the Coming Crisis', in A. E. Bottoms and R. Preston, (eds) *The Coming Penal Crisis: a Criminological and Theological Exploration*. Edinburgh: Scottish Academic Press.

—— (1983). 'Neglected Features of Contemporary Penal Systems', in D. Garland and P. Young (eds) *The Power to Punish*. London: Heinemann, 166–202.

—— (1995). 'The philosophy and politics of punishment and sentencing', in C. Clarkson and R. Morgan (eds) *The Politics of Sentencing Reform*. Oxford: Clarendon Press.

—— (1999). 'Interpersonal Violence and Social Order in Prisons', in M. Tonry and J. Petersilia (eds), *Crime and Justice: A Review of Research, Volume 26: Prisons*. London: University of Chicago Press.

—— (2001). 'Compliance and Community Penalties', in A. E. Bottoms, L. Gelsthorpe, and S. Rex (eds), *Community Penalties: Change and Challenges*. Cullompton, Devon: Willan Publishing.

—— and McClintock, F. H. (1973). *Criminals Coming of Age*. London: Heinemann.

—— and Stevenson, S. (1992). 'What Went Wrong? Criminal Justice Policy in England and Wales 1945–1970', in D. Downes (ed) *Unravelling Criminal Justice*. Basingstoke: Macmillan, 1–45.

Bourdieu, P. (1977). *Outline of a Theory of Practice*. Cambridge, Cambridge University Press.

—— (1984). *Distinction: A Social Critique of the Judgement of Taste*. London: Routledge & Kegan Paul.

—— (1987). 'The Force of Law', *Hastings Law Review* 38: 805–53.

—— (1991). 'Rites of Institution'. *In Language and Symbolic Power*. Cambridge, Mass: Harvard University Press.

Bourdieu, P. (1998). *Acts of Resistance: Against the Tyranny of the Market*. Cambridge: Polity Press.

—— (1999). *The Weight of the World: Social Suffering in Contemporary Society*. Cambridge: Polity Press.

—— (2000). *Pascalian Meditations*. Cambridge: Polity Press.

Boutellier, H. (2001). 'The Convergence of Social Policy and Criminal Justice'. *European Journal on Criminal Policy and Research* 9: 361–80.

Braithwaite, J. (2000). 'The New Regulatory State and the Transformation of Criminology', *British Journal of Criminology* 40(2): 222–38.

—— and Drahos, P. (2000) *Global Business Regulation*. Cambridge: Cambridge University Press.

Brennan, M. (2000). 'Towards a Sociology of (Public) Mourning?', *Sociology* 35(1): 205–12.

Brion, F. (1996). 'Chiffrer, déchiffrer: Incarcération des étrangers et construction sociale de la criminalité des immigrés en Belgique', in S. Palidda (ed) *Délit d'immigration/ immigrant delinquency*. Brussels: European Commission, 163–223.

Brogden, M. (2003). 'Community Policing in Transitional Society'. Paper presented at The British Criminology Society, 2003, Proceedings held at University of Wales, Bangor.

Brookes, D. (2004). 'Restorative Justice in Scotland's Youth Justice System', in J. McGhee, M. Mellon, and B. Whyte (eds) *Addressing Deeds: Working with Young People Who Offend*. London: NCH.

Brudner, A. (1993). 'Agency and Welfare in the Criminal Law', in S. Shute, J. Gardner, and J. Horder (eds) *Action and Value in the Criminal Law*. Oxford: Clarendon Press.

Bunyan, T. (2005). 'Crossing the Rubicon: The Emerging Counter-terrorism Regime'. *Statewatch Report*. London: Statewatch.

Bureau of Justice Assistance (1989). *Estimating the Costs of Drug Testing for a Pretrial Services Program*. Washington, DC: US Department of Justice, Office of Justice Programs.

—— (1999). *Integrating Drug Testing into a Pretrial Services System: 1999 Update*. Washington, DC: US Department of Justice, Office of Justice Programs.

Calabresi, G. (1970). *The Costs of Accidents: A Legal and Economic Analysis*. New Haven: Yale University Press.

Canovan, M. (2000). 'Taking Politics to the People: Populism as the Ideology of Democracy', paper presented to conference on Populism and Democratic Theory, European University Institute, Florence, January.

Carlen, P. (1983a). 'On Rights and Powers: Some Notes on Penal Politics', in D. Garland and P. Young (eds) *The Power to Punish. Contemporary Penality and Social Analysis*. London: Heinemann, 203–16.

—— (1983b). *Women's Imprisonment: A Study in Social Control*. London: Routledge & Kegan Paul.

—— (1985). *Criminal Women: Autobiographical Accounts*. Cambridge: Polity Press.

—— (1996). *Jigsaw: A Political Criminology of Youth Homelessness*. Buckingham: Open University Press.

Carter, C. and Smith, A. (2004). 'Conceptualising Multi-level Orders of Scottish Fish and Bordeaux Wine: The Role of Territory and Political Assignment', paper given at the *Colloque Internationale Université de Rennes*, 4–5 March.

Cashmore, E. and McLaughlin, E. (eds) (1991). *Out of Order? Policing Black People.* London: Routledge.

Castel, F., Castel, R., and Lovell, A. (1982). *The Psychiatric Society.* New York: Columbia University Press.

Castells, M. (1997). *The Power of Identity.* Oxford: Blackwell.

Cavadino, M., and Dignan J. (2006). *Penal Systems: A Comparative Approach.* London: Sage.

Cebrian, J. L. (1999). 'The Media and European Identity', *New Perspectives Quarterly* 16(3): 39–42.

Chan, J. and Ericson, R. C. (1981). *Decarceration and the Economy of Penal Reform.* Toronto: University of Toronto Centre of Criminology.

Christie, N. (1977). 'Conflicts as Property', *British Journal of Criminology* 17(1): 1–15.

—— (1993). *Crime Control as Industry.* London: Routledge.

Chunn, D. and Smandych, R. (1982). 'An Interview with David Rothman'. *Canadian Criminology Forum* 4: 152–62.

Cid, J. and Larrauri, E. (1998). 'Prison and Alternatives to Prison in Spain', in V. Ruggiero, N. South, and I. Taylor (eds) *The New European Criminology.* London: Routledge, 146–55.

Clark, J. and Henry, D. A. (2003). *Pretrial Services Programming at the Start of the 21st Century: A Survey of Pretrial Services Programs.* Washington, DC: Bureau of Justice Assistance, National Institute of Justice.

Clark, M. (1981). 'The Rejection of Psychological Approaches to Mental Disorder in Late Nineteenth Century British Psychiatry', in A. Scull (ed) *Madhouses, Mad-Doctors, and Madmen: The Social History of Psychiatry in the Victorian Era.* Philadelphia: University of Pennsylvania Press, 271–312.

Clarke, J. (2002). 'Reinventing Community? Governing in Contested Spaces', paper delivered at Spacing for Social Work Conference, Bielefeld, 14–16 November 2002.

Clarke, R. V. G. (1995). 'Situational Crime Prevention', in M. Tonry and D. Farrington (eds), *Building a Safer Society: Crime and Justice: A Review of Research, Volume 19.* Chicago: University of Chicago Press.

—— and Cornish, D. (1975). *Residential Treatment and its Effects on Delinquency.* London: HMSO.

—— and Homel, R. (1997). 'A Revised Classification of Situational Crime Prevention Techniques', in S. P. Lab (ed) *Crime Prevention at the Crossroads.* Cincinnati, Ohio: Anderson.

Clifford, J. (1998). 'Mixed Feelings', in P. Cheah and B. Robbins (eds) *Cosmopolitics: Thinking and Feeling Beyond the Nation.* Minneapolis: University of Minnesota Press.

Coates, N. (1992). *Ecstacity*, Exhibition Catalogue, Nigel Coates, Introductions by Brian Hatton and John Thackara, London: Architectural Association Publications.

Cohen, S. (1972). *Folk Devils and Moral Panics.* Harmondsworth: Penguin

—— (1979). 'The Punitive City: Notes on the Dispersal of Social Control'. *Contemporary Crises* 3: 339–63.

—— (1983). 'Social Control Talk: Telling Stories About Correctional Change', in D. Garland and P. Young (eds) *The Power to Punish: Contemporary Penality and Social Analysis.* London: Heinemann, 101–29.

—— (1985). *Visions of Social Control: Crime, Punishment and Classification.* Cambridge: Polity Press in association with Basil Blackwell.

Cohen, S. (1993). 'Human Rights and Crimes of the State: The Culture of Denial', *Australian and New Zealand Journal of Criminology* 17: 347–57.

—— (2001). *States of Denial*. Cambridge: Polity Press.

—— and Scull, A. (eds) (1984). *Social Control and the State: Historical and Comparative Essays*. Cambridge: Polity Press.

Cole, A. (2005). *Beyond Devolution and Decentralisation: Building Regional Capacity in Wales and Brittany*. Manchester: Manchester University Press.

Coleman, J. (1990). *Foundations of Social Theory*. London: Harvard University Press (The Belknap Press).

Comfort, M. (2003). 'United States: Sentenced to Sickness', *Le Monde Diplomatique*, August (2003).

Conrad, P. and Schneider, J. (1980). *Deviance and Medicalization: From Badness to Sickness*. St. Louis: Mosby.

Cotterrell, R. (1992). *Sociology of Law: an Introduction*. London: Butterworth.

Council of Europe (1987) *The European Prison Rules*. Strasbourg: Council of Europe

—— (1999). *Europe: A Death Penalty Free Continent*. Report by the Committee on Legal Affairs and Human Rights, Doc No 8340.

—— (2001). *Abolition of the Death Penalty in Council of Europe Observer States*. Report by the Committee on Legal Affairs and Human Rights, Doc No 9115.

Coyle, A. (2002) *Managing Prisons in a Time of Change*. London: International Centre for Prison Studies.

Crawford, A. (1997). *The Local Governance of Crime*. Oxford: Clarendon

—— (1998). *Crime Prevention and Community Safety: Politics, Policies and Practices*. Harlow: Longman.

Currie, E. (1998). *Crime and Punishment in America*. New York: Holt.

Dahl, R. (1961). *Who Governs?* New Haven: Yale University Press.

Dal Lago, A. (1999). *Non-Persone. L'esclusione dei migranti in una società globale*. Milano: Feltrinelli.

—— (ed) (1998). *Lo straniero e il nemico*. Genoa: Costa e Nolan.

Daly, K. (1994). *Gender, Crime and Punishment*. Newhaven: Yale University Press.

de Certeau, M. (1984). *The Practice of Everyday Life*. London: University of California Press.

De Stoop, C. (1996). *Vite, rentrez le linge. L'Europe et l'expulsion des 'sans-papiers'*. Arles: Solin/Actes Sud.

Delanty, G. (1995). *Inventing Europe: Idea, Identity, Reality*. London: Macmillan.

—— (2002). 'Models of European Identity: Reconciling Universalism and Particular-ism'. Paper Presented to the 13th International Conference of Europeanists 'Europe in the New Millennium: Enlarging, Experimenting, Evolving'. Chicago, 14–16 March.

Deleuze, G. (2001). *Pure Immanence: Essays on A Life* (Translator: Boyman, Anne). Zone Books: New York.

Deutsch, A. (1948). *The Shame of the States*. New York: Harcourt Brace.

Dill, F. (1972). 'Bail and Bail Reform: A Sociological Study', unpublished doctoral thesis, Berkeley, California: University of California at Berkeley.

Dingwall R., Eekelaar J., and Murray, T. (1995). *The Protection of Children: State Intervention and Family Life*. Aldershot: Avebury.

Ditton, J. and Short, E. (1999), 'Yes It Works – No It Doesn't: Comparing the Effects of Open-Street CCTV in Two Adjacent Town Centres', *Crime Prevention Studies* 10: 201–23.

Doak, J. (2003). 'The Victim and the Criminal Process: An analysis of recent trends in regional and international tribunals', *Legal Studies* 23(1): 1–32.

Donzelot, J. (1979). *The Policing of Families*. New York: Pantheon.

Doob, A. (1990). *Evaluation of a Computerized Sentencing Aid*. Select committee of experts on sentencing, European committee on crime problems. Strasbourg: Council of Europe.

Douglas, M. (1992). *Risk and Blame: Essays in Cultural Theory*. London: Routledge.

Dowbiggin, I. (1985). 'Degeneration and Hereditarianism in French Mental Medicine 1840–90: Psychiatric Theory as Ideological Adaptation' in W. F. Bynum, R. Porter, and M. Shepherd (eds) *The Anatomy of Madness*, Vol 1. London: Tavistock, 188–232.

Downes, D. (1988). *Contrasts in Tolerance: Post-war Penal Policy in the Netherlands and England and Wales*. Oxford: Clarendon Press.

—— (2001). 'The Macho Penal Economy: Mass Incarceration in the US–A European Perspective', *Punishment and Society* 3(1): 61–80.

Dubber, M. D. (2002). *Victims in the War Against Crime. The Use and Abuse of Victims' Rights*. New York: New York University Press.

—— (2003). 'Criminal Justice Process and the War on Crime', in C. Sumner (ed) *The Blackwell Companion to Criminology*. Oxford: Blackwell.

—— (2004). *The Police Power: Patriarchy and the Foundations of Criminal Law*. New York: Columbia University Press.

Dudziak, M. (2000). 'Giving Capital Offense', *Civilization* 7(5): 50–4.

Duff, R. A. (2000). *Punishment, Communication and Community*. New York, Oxford University Press.

Durkheim, E. (1964). *The Rules of Sociological Method*. New York, Free Press.

—— (1983). 'Two Laws of Penal Evolution' in S. Lukes and S. Scull (eds) *Durkheim and the Law*. New York: St. Martin's Press.

Eder, K. (2000). 'Zur Transformation nationalstaatlicher Offentlichkeit in Europa', *Berliner Journal für Soziologie* 10 (2): 167–84.

—— (2001). 'Integration through Culture? The Paradox of the Search for a European Identity', in K. Eder and B. Giesen (eds) *European Citizenship: National Legacies and Postnational Projects*. Oxford: Oxford University Press.

—— and Giesen, B. (eds) (2001). *European Citizenship. National Legacies and Postnational Projects*. Oxford: Oxford University Press.

Ekirch, A. R. (1987). *Bound for America: The Transportation of British Convicts to the Colonies, 1718–1775*. Oxford: Clarendon Press.

Ellison, L. (2001). *The Adversarial Process and the Vulnerable Witness*. Oxford: Oxford University Press.

Engbersen, G. (1995). 'The Unknown City'. *Berkeley Journal of Sociology* 40: 87–112.

—— (1997). *In de schaduw van morgen: Stedelijke marginaliteit in Nederland*. Amsterdam: Boom.

—— and van der Leun, J. (1999). 'Illegality and Criminality: The Differential Opportunity Structure of Undocumented Immigrants', in K. Koser and H. Lutz (eds) *The New Migration in Europe: Social Constructions and Social Realities*. London: Palgrave Macmillan, 199–223.

Ericson, R. V., Baranek, P., and Chan, J. (1991). *Representing Order*. Buckingham: Open University Press

—— and Haggerty, K. (1997). *Policing the Risk Society*. Oxford: Oxford University Press.

Esping-Anderson, G. (1990). *The Three Worlds of Welfare Capitalism*. New Jersey: Princeton University Press.

European Council of Ministers Council Framework Decision 2001/220/JHA. *On the Standing of Victims in Criminal Proceedings: New Rights for Victims of Crime in Europe*.

European Union (General Affairs Council) (1998). *Guidelines: EU Policy towards Third Countries on the Death Penalty*. Luxembourg: 29 June 1998. Available online at:http://europa.eu.int/comm/external_relations/human_rights/adp/guide_en.htm.

Faber, J. (2000). *Les Indésirables. L'intégration à la française*. Paris: Grasset.

Faugeron, C. (1994). 'Légitimité du pénal et ordre social'. *Carrefour* 16, Special Issue on 'Ethique, démocratie et droit pénal': 64–89.

Feeley, M. (1979). *The Process Is the Punishment*. New York: Sage Foundation.

—— (1983). *Court Reform on Trial: Why Simple Solutions Fail*. New York: Basic Books.

—— and Rubin, E. (1998). *Judicial Policymaking and the Modern State: How Courts Reformed America's Prisons*. Cambridge: Cambridge University Press.

—— and Simon, J. (1992). 'The New Penology: Notes on the Emerging Strategy of Corrections and Its Implications', *Criminology* 30(4): 449–74.

—— —— (1994). 'Actuarial Justice: The Emerging New Criminal Law', in D. Nelken (ed) *The Futures of Criminology*. London: Sage.

Feinberg, J. (1988). *The Moral Limits of the Criminal Law* (4 volumes). New York: Oxford University Press.

Fine, G. A. (1997). 'Scandals, Social Conditions and the Creation of Public Attention', *Social Problems* 44: 297–323.

Fitzmaurice, C. and Pease, K. (1986). *The Psychology of Judicial Sentencing*. Manchester: Manchester University Press.

Fleishman, J. (2000, August 20). 'Italians Fight U.S. Use of Death Penalty', *Philadelphia Inquirer*.

Fletcher, G. (1978). *Rethinking Criminal Law*. Boston: Little, Brown & Co.

—— (1988) *A Crime of Self Defense. Bernard Goetz and the Law on Trial*. New York: Free Press.

—— (1995). *With Justice for Some. Protecting Victims' Rights in Criminal Trials*. Reading, Mass: Addison-Wesley.

Fontaine, P. (1993). *A Citizen's Europe* (2nd edn). Luxenburg: OOPEC.

Foote, C. (1954). 'Compelling Appearance in Court: Administration of Bail in Philadelphia', *University of Pennsylvania Law Review* 102: 1031–79.

—— (1965). 'The Coming Constitutional Crisis in Bail: I', *The University of Pennsylvania Law Review*. 113: 959–1185.

Forsythe, B., Melling, J., and Adair, R. (1996). 'The New Poor Law and the County Pauper Lunatic Asylum – The Devon Experience, 1834–84', *Social History of Medicine* 9: 335–56.

Foucault, M. (1971). *Madness and Civilization: A History of Insanity in the Age of Reason*. London: Tavistock.

—— (1978). *The History of Sexuality vol. 1: The Will to Knowledge*. Harmondsworth: Penguin.

—— (1979). *Discipline and Punish: The Birth of the Prison*. Hammondsworth: Penguin.

—— (2003). *Society Must be Defended*. London: Allen Lane.

Frankel, M. (1972). *Criminal Sentences: Law Without Order*. New York: Hill and Wang.

Freed, D. J. and Wald, P. M. (1964). *Bail in the United States*. Washington, DC: US Department of Justice and Vera Foundation.

Freeman, R. B. and Katz, L. F. (1995). *Differences and Changes in Wage Structures*. National Bureau of Economic Research, Comparative Labour Markets Series. Chicago: University of Chicago Press.

Freiberg, A. (1995). 'Sentencing Reform in Victoria: A Case Study', in C. Clarkson and R. Morgan (eds) *The Politics of Sentencing Reform*. Oxford: Clarendon Press.

Freidson, E. (1970). *The Profession of Medicine: A Study in the Sociology of Applied Knowledge*. New York: Dodd, Mead.

Frigaard, I. (1996). 'Police Cooperation: Current Problems and Suggestions for Solutions in Interstate Police Co-operation in Europe. Paper delivered at the Fourth Schengen Colloquium of the European Institute of Public Administration: *Schengen and the Third Pillar of Maastricht*. Maastricht, 1–2 February.

Furedi, F. (2004). *Therapy Culture. Cultivating Vulnerability in an Uncertain Age*. London: Routledge.

Gailliègue, G. (2000). *La Prison des étrangers, clandestins et delinquents*. Paris: Imago.

Gamble, A. and Wright, T. (eds) (1999). *The New Social Democracy*. Oxford: Blackwell.

Garfinkel, H. (1956). 'Conditions of Successful Degradation Ceremonies', *The American Journal of Sociology* 61(5): 420–4.

Garland, D. (1985). *Punishment and Welfare: A History of Penal Strategies*. Aldershot: Gower.

—— (1990). *Punishment and Modern Society: a Study in Social Theory*. Oxford: Clarendon Press.

—— (1991). 'The Rationalization of Punishment', in H. Pihlajamäki (ed) *Theatres of Power: Social Control and Criminality in Historical Perspective*. Helsinki: Matthias Calonius Society.

—— (1994). 'Of Crimes and Criminals: The Development of Criminology in Britain', in M. Maguire, R. Morgan, and R. Reiner (eds) *The Oxford Handbook of Criminology* (1st edn). Oxford: Clarendon Press.

—— (1996). 'The Limits of the Sovereign State. Strategies of Crime Control in Contemporary Society', *British Journal of Criminology* 36(4): 445–71.

—— (1999). 'The Commonplace and the Catastrophic: Interpretations of Crime in Late Modernity', *Theoretical Criminology* 3: 353–64.

—— (2000). 'The Culture of High Crime Societies'. *British Journal of Criminology* 40: 347–75.

—— (2001). *The Culture of Control: Crime and Social Order in Contemporary Society*. Oxford: Oxford University Press.

—— (2002). 'The Cultural Uses of Capital Punishment', *Punishment and Society* 4(4): 459–87.

—— and Young, P. (1983). 'Towards a Social Analysis of Penality', in D. Garland and P. Young (eds) *The Power to Punish. Contemporary Penality and Social Analysis*. London: Heinemann.

Garland, D. and Young, P. (eds) (1983). *The Power to Punish: Contemporary Penality and Social Analysis.* London: Heinemann Educational.

Geddes, A. P. (2000). *Immigration and European Integration: Towards Fortress Europe?.* Manchester: Manchester University Press.

Geissler, R. and Marissen, N. (1990). 'Kriminalität und Kriminalisierung junger Ausländer: Die tickende soziale Zeitbombe – Ein Artefakt der Kriminalstatistik'. *Kölner Zeitschrift für Soziologie und Sozialpsychologie* 42: 663–87.

Gellner, E. (1983). *Nations and Nationalism.* Oxford: Blackwell.

Gelsthorpe, L. (1997). 'Feminism and Criminology', in M. Maguire, R. Morgan, and R. Reiner (eds) *The Oxford Handbook of Criminology* (2nd edn). Oxford: Clarendon Press.

Gendreau, P. and Ross, R. (1980), 'Effective Correctional Treatment: Bibliotherapy for Cynics', in R. Ross and P. Gendreau (eds) *Effective Correctional Treatment*, Toronto: Butterworths.

Getzler, J. (2006). 'Property, personality, and violence', in T. Endicott, J. Getzler, and E. Peel (eds) *Properties of Law: Essays in Honour of James W. Harris.* Oxford: Oxford University Press.

Giddens, A. (1979). *New Rules of Sociological Method.* London: Hutchinson

——(1984). *The Constitution of Society: Outline of the Theory of Structuration.* Cambridge: Polity Press.

——(1990). *The Consequences of Modernity.* Stanford, Cal: Stanford University Press.

——(1991). *Modernity and Self-Identity.* Cambridge: Polity Press.

——(1998). *The Third Way: The Renewal of Social Democracy.* Cambridge: Polity Press.

Gilbert, N. (2002). *Transformation of the Welfare State: The Silent Surrender of Public Responsibility.* Oxford: Oxford University Press.

Gilroy, P. (1987). 'Lesser Breeds Without the Law', in P. Gilroy (ed) *'There Ain't No Black in the Union Jack': The Cultural Politics of Race and Nation.* Chicago, Ill: University of Chicago Press, 72–113.

Girling, E. (2002). 'We, on Death Row: Death Penalty in the US under the European Gaze', in C. Boulanger, V. Heyes, and P. Hanfling (eds) *Zur Aktualitaet der Todesstrafe. Interdisziplinaere und globale Perspektiven.* Berlin: Arno Spitz.

——(2004). '"Looking death in the face": The Benetton Death Penalty Campaign', *Punishment and Society* 6(3): 271–87.

——(2005). 'European Identity and the Mission against the Death Penalty in the US', in A. Sarat and C. Boulanger (eds) *The Cultural Lives of Capital Punishment.* Stanford: Stanford University Press.

——Loader, I., and Sparks, R. (2000). *Crime, Law and Social Change in Middle England: Questions of Order in an English Town.* London: Routledge.

Glennerster, H., and Hills, J. (eds) (1998). *The State of Welfare: The Economics of Social Spending* (2nd edn). Oxford: Oxford University Press.

Goffman, E. (1961). *Asylums: Essays on the Social Situation of Mental Patients and Other Inmates.* New York: Doubleday.

——(1971). 'Appendix: The insanity of place', in *Relations in Public: Micro studies of the Public Order.* New York: Basic Books, 335–90.

Goldhammer, H. and Marshall, A. (1953). *Psychosis and Civilization: Two Studies in the Frequency of Mental Disease.* Glencoe, Ill: Free Press.

Goldkamp, J. S. (1979). *Two Classes of Accused: A Study of Bail and Detention in America.* Cambridge: Ballinger.

—— and White, M. D. (1998). *Restoring Accountability in Pretrial Release: The Philadelphia Pretrial Release Supervision Experiments.* Philadelphia: Crime and Justice Research Institute.

Grant, S. (1998). 'A Dialogue of the Deaf? New International Attitudes and the Death Penalty', *Criminal Justice Ethics* 17(2): 19–32.

Gray, J. (1998). *False Dawn: The Delusions of Global Capitalism.* Cambridge: Granta.

Gready, P. and Kagalema, L. (2003). 'Magistrates under Apartheid: A Case Study of the Politicisation of Justice and Complicity in Human Rights Abuse', *South African Journal on Human Rights* 19(2): 141–88.

Green, S. P. (1999). 'Castles and Carjackers: Proportionality and the Use of Deadly Force in Defense of Dwellings and Vehicles', *University of Illinois Law Review* 1: 1–42.

Greenberg, D. F. (1999). 'Punishment, Division of Labor, and Social Solidarity', in S. Laufer and F. Adler (eds) *The Criminology of Criminal Law. Advances in Criminological Theory*, vol 8. Somerset, NJ: Transaction Publishers.

—— (2001). '*Novus ordo saeclorum*? A commentary on Downes, and on Beckett and Western', in D. Garland (ed) *Mass Imprisonment: Social Causes and Consequences.* London: Sage, 70–81.

Griffiths, Sir R. (1988). *Community Care: Agenda for Action: A Report to the Secretary of State.* London: HMSO.

Grob, G. (1977). 'Rediscovering Asylums: The Unhistorical History of the Mental Hospital', *Hastings Center Report* 7: 33–41.

—— (1983). *Mental Illness and American Society, 1875–1940.* Princeton: Princeton University Press.

—— (1990). 'Marxian Analysis and Mental Illness'. *History of Psychiatry, Volume, 1*: 223–32.

Gronfein, W. (1984). 'From Madhouse to Main Street: The Changing Place of Mental Illness in Post World War II America'. Unpublished PhD dissertation, State University of New York at Stony Brook.

Guardian, The (2000). 'In His Own Words: Tony Martin's Story', *The Guardian*, 26 April.

—— (2004). 'Tony Martin Bill Blocked', *The Guardian*, 30 April.

Gwin, P. (2000). ' "End Execution" Campaign', *Europe: Magazine of the European Union* 401: 10–12.

Habermas, J. (1987). *The Theory of Communicative Action*, volume 2. Cambridge: Polity Press in association with Basil Blackwell.

Hall, S. and Winlow, S. (2003). 'Rehabilitating Leviathan: Reflections on the State, Economic Regulation, and Violence Reduction', *Theoretical Criminology* 7(2): 139–62.

—— , Clarke, J., Critcher, C., Jefferson, T., and Roberts, B. (1978). *Policing the Crisis.* London: Macmillan.

Hannah-Moffat, K. (2005), 'Criminogenic Needs and the Transformative Risk Subject – Hybridizations of Risk/Need in Penality', *Punishment & Society* 7(1): 29–51.

Hannerz, U. (1990). 'Cosmopolitans and Locals in World Culture', in M. Featherstone (ed) *Global Culture*, London: Sage.

Hansen, K. and Vignoles, A. (2005). 'The UK Education System: An International Perspective', in S. Machin, A. Vignoles, and G. Conlon (eds) *Economics of Education in the UK*. New Jersey: Princeton University Press.

Harnden, T. (2001) 'Bush Team Angry over EU Pressure on Death Penalty', *Daily Telegraph*: 8 March.

Hart, H. L. A. (1968). *Punishment and Responsibility*. Oxford: Clarendon.

Hastings, A. (1997). *The Construction of Nationhood: Ethnicity, Religion and Nationalism*. Cambridge: Cambridge University Press.

Hathaway, O. (2002). 'Do Human Rights Treaties Make a Difference?', *The Yale Law Journal* 111(8): 1935–2042.

Hawkins K. (2003). 'Order, Rationality and Silence: Some Reflections on Criminal Justice Decision Making', in Gelsthorpe, L. and Padfield, N. (eds) *Exercising Discretion Decision Making in the Criminal Justice System and Beyond*. Cullompton, Devon: Willan Publishing.

Hayes, B. (2004). 'From the Schengen Information System to SIS II and the Visa Information (VIS): The Proposals Explained'. *Statewatch Report*. London: Statewatch.

Hayward, K. (2004). *City Limits: Crime, Consumerism and the Urban Experience*. London: GlassHouse Press.

Hayward, R. and Sharp, C. (2005). *Young People, Crime and Anti-social Behaviour: Findings from the 2003 Crime and Justice Survey*, Home Office Research Findings No 245.

Healy, D. (1997). *The Antidepressant Era*, Cambridge, Mass: Harvard University Press.

Held, D. (2000). 'The Changing Contours of Political Community', in B. Holden (ed) *Global Democracy: Key Debates*. London: Routledge.

——, McGrew, A. G., Goldblatt, D., and Perraton, J. (1999). *Global Transformations: Politics, Economics and Culture*. Cambridge: Polity Press.

Henry, D. A. and Clark, J. (1999). *Pretrial Drug Testing: An Overview of Issue and Practices*. Washington, DC: Bureau of Justice Assistance.

Hernández, G. Imaz, E., Martín, T., Naredo, M., Pernas, B., Tandogan, A., and Wagman, D. (2001). *Mujer gitanas y sistema penal*. Madrid: Ediciones Metyel.

Hier, S. (2003). 'Risk and Panic in Late Modernity: Implications of the Converging Sites of Social Anxiety', *The British Journal of Sociology* 54(1): 3–20.

Hirschi, T. (1969). *Causes of Delinquency*. Berkeley: University of California Press.

Hobbes, T. (1968 [1651]). *Leviathan*. Harmondsworth: Penguin.

Hobsbawm, E. (1990). *Myths and Nationalism since 1780: Programme, Myth and Reality*. Cambridge: Cambridge University Press.

Hodgkinson, P. and Rutherford, A. (1996). *Capital Punishment: Global Issues and Prospects*. Winchester: Waterside Press.

Hogarth, J. (1971). *Sentencing as Human Process*. Toronto: University of Toronto Press.

Home Office (2003). World Prison Population List (4th edn). *Research Findings 188*. London: HMSO.

Hood, R. (1962). *Sentencing in Magistrates' Courts*. London: Tavistock.

—— (1993). *Race and Sentencing*. Oxford: Oxford University Press.

—— (1996). *The Death Penalty: A Worldwide Perspective* (2nd edn). Oxford: Clarendon Press.

—— and Koralev, S. (2001). *The Death Penalty: Abolition in Europe*. Strasbourg: Council of Europe Publishing.

Hope, T. (2004). 'Pretend it Works: Evidence and Governance in the Evaluation of the Reducing Burglary Initiative', *Criminal Justice* 4: 287–308.

Horder, J. (1992). *Provocation and Responsibility*. Oxford: Oxford University Press.

Horn, M. (1989). *Before It's Too Late: The Child Guidance Movement in the United States*. Philadelphia: Temple University Press.

Howe, A. (1994). Punish and Critique: Towards a Feminist Analysis of Penality. London: Routledge.

Hudson, B. (2002) 'Punishment and Control', in M. Maguire, R. Morgan, and R. Reiner (eds) *The Oxford Handbook of Criminology*. Oxford: Oxford University Press (3rd edn). 233–63.

Hughes, G. (2004). 'Straddling Adaptation and Denial: Crime and Disorder Reduction Partnerships in England and Wales', *Cambrian Law Review* 25: 1–23.

Hume, D. (1884). *Commentaries on the Law of Scotland respecting Crimes* (4th edn). Edinburgh: Bell & Bradfute.

Huntingdon, S. (1996). *The Clash of Civilizations*. New York: Simon & Schuster.

Husak, D. (2002). 'Limitations on Criminalization and the General Part of the Criminal Law', in S. Shute and A. Simester (eds) *Criminal Law Theory: Doctrines of the General Part*. Oxford: Oxford University Press.

Ignatieff, M. (1980). *A Just Measure of Pain: The Penitentiary in the Industrial Revolution, 1750–1850*. New York: Columbia University Press.

——(1984). 'State, Civil Society and Total Institutions: A Critique of Recent Social Histories of Punishment', in S. Cohen and A. Scull (eds) *Social Control and the State: Historical and Comparative Essays*. Cambridge: Polity Press, 75–105.

——(1998) 'Identity Parades', *Prospect* 29.

——(2003) *Human Rights as Politics and Idolatry*. Princeton: Princeton University Press.

Ingleby, D. (1973). 'The Psychology of Child Psychology'. *The Human Context* 5: 557–68.

——(1983). 'Mental Health and Social Order', in S. Cohen and A. Scull (eds) *Social Control and the State: Historical and Comparative Essays*. Oxford: Martin Robertson.

Jackson, M. (2000). *The Borderland of Imbecility: Medicine, Society, and the Fabrication of the Feeble Mind in Late Victorian and Edwardian England*. Manchester: Manchester University Press.

Jackson, R. (1999). 'Introduction: Sovereignty at the Millennium', *Political Studies* XLV11: 423–30.

Jacobs, J. B. (1983). 'The Politics of Prison Construction', in *New Perspectives on Prisons and Imprisonment*. Ithaca, NY: Cornell University Press.

Jacyna, S. (1982). 'Somatic Theories of Mind and the Interests of Medicine in Britain, 1850–1879', *Medical History* 26: 233–58.

James O. (1993) *Juvenile Violence in a Winner/Loser Culture*. London: Free Association Press.

Jamieson, L. (1998). *Intimacy: Personal Relationships in Modern Societies*. Cambridge: Polity Press.

Jefferson, A. M. (2003) 'Reforming Prisons in Democratic, Developing Countries Questioning a Global(ising) Agenda', paper presented at Euro Group (UK)/Edge Hill organised conference Tough on Crime . . . Tough on Freedoms, Chester UK, 22–24 April.

Jencks, C. and Peterson, P. (eds) (1991). *The Urban Underclass*. Washington DC: Brookings.

Jenkins, R. (1992). *Pierre Bourdieu*. London: Routledge.

Jewkes, Y. (2002) *Captive Audience: Media, Masculinity and Power in Prisons*. Cullompton, Devon: Willan Publishing.

Johnston, L. (1996). 'What is Vigilantism?' *British Journal of Criminology* 36(2): 220–36.

Jones, T. and Christie, M. (2003). *Criminal Law* (3rd edn). Edinburgh: W. Green & Son.

Junger, M. (1988). 'Racial Discrimination in Criminal Justice in the Netherlands'. *Sociology and Social Research* 72: 211–16.

Junger-Tas, J. (1997). 'Ethnic Minorities and Criminal Justice in the Netherlands', in M. Tonry (ed) *Ethnicity, Crime, and Immigration: Comparative and Cross-National Perspectives. Crime and Justice: A Review of Research*, vol. 21. Chicago: University of Chicago Press, 257–310.

Kaldor, M. (1999). *New and Old Wars: Organised Violence in a Global Era*. Cambridge: Polity Press.

Kalinin, Y. I. (2002) *The Russian Penal System: Past, Present and Future*. London: International Centre for Prison Studies, King's College, London.

Kames, Lord (Henry Home). (1792). *Historical Law Tracts* (4th edn). Edinburgh: Bell & Bradfute.

Kapteyn, P. (1991). ' "Civilization under Negotiation": National Civilizations and European Integration – The Treaty of Schengen'. *Archives Européennes de Sociologie* 32: 363–80.

Karanja, Stephen K. (2005) 'SIS II Legislative Proposals 2005: Gains and Losses!' *Yulex*, Norwegian Research Center for Computers and Law.

—— (2006). *Schengen Information System and Border Control Cooperation: A Transparency and Proportionality Evaluation*. Faculty of Law, University of Oslo, PhD dissertation.

Katsh, E. (1996). 'Software Worlds and the First Amendment: Virtual Doorkeepers in Cyberspace', *University of Chicago Legal Forum*, 335–60.

Katz, M. (1968). *The Irony of Early School Reform: Educational Innovation in Mid-Nineteenth Century Massachusetts*. Cambridge, Mass: Harvard University Press.

Kaufman-Osborne, T. (2002). *From Noose to Needle: Capital Punishment and the Late Liberal State*. Ann Arbor, MI: University of Michigan Press.

King, R. D. (1999). 'The Rise and Rise of Supermax: An American Solution in Search of a Problem?', *Punishment & Society* 1(2): 163–86.

—— and Piacentini, L. (2005). 'The Russian Correctional System during the Transition', in W. A. Pridemore (ed) *Ruling Russia: Law, Crime and Justice in a Changing Society*. Rowman and Littlefield Publishers Inc.

Kittrie, N. (1972). *The Right to be Different: Deviance and Enforced Therapy*. Baltimore: Johns Hopkins University Press.

Klapp, O. (1954). 'Heroes, Villains and Fools as Agents of Social Control', *American Sociological Review* 19: 56–62.

Klein, D. J. (1997). 'The Pretrial Detention "Crisis": The Causes and the Cure', *Journal of Urban and Contemporary Law* 52: 281–305.

Kraidy, M. and Goeddertz T. (2002). 'Transnational Advertising and International Relations: US Press Discourses on the Benetton "We on Death Row" Campaign', *Media, Culture and Society* 25(2): 147–65.

Krause, A. (2000). 'Life versus Death', *Europe: Magazine of the European Union*, 401: 6–10.

Kubink, M. (1993). *Verständnis und Bedeutung von Ausländerkriminalität: Eine Analyse der Konstitution sozialer Probleme*. Pfaffenweiler: Centaurus.

Kuhn, A. (1998). 'Populations carcérales: Combien? Pourquoi? Que faire?' *Archives de politique criminelle* 20: 47–99.

——, Tournier, P., and Walmsley, R. (2000). *Le Surpeuplement des prisons et l'inflation carcérale*. Strasbourg: Editions du Conseil de l'Europe.

Kuhnle, S., Hatland, A., and Hort, S. (2000). *A Work-Friendly Welfare State: Lessons from Europe*. Report prepared for the World Bank.

Lacey, N., Wells, C., and Quick, D. (2003). *Reconstructing Criminal Law. Cases and Materials* (3rd edn). London: Butterworths.

Lacorne, D. (2001). 'The Barbaric Americans'. *Wilson Quarterly* 25: 51–4.

Landreville, P. (2002). 'Va-t-on vers une américanisation des politiques de sécurité en Europe?', in L. Mucchielli and P. Robert (eds) *Crime et sécurité. L'état des saviors*. Paris: Editions La Découverte, 424–33.

Lanham, D. (1966). 'Defence of Property in the Criminal Law'. *Criminal Law Review* (July): 368–79 (Part I), (August): 426–35 (Part II).

Lasch, C. (1977). *Haven in a Heartless World: The Family Besieged*. New York: Basic Books.

Law, J. and Urry, J. (2004). 'Enacting the Social', *Economy and Society* 33(3): 390–410.

Lawrence, P. (2000). ' "Un flot d'agitateurs politiques, de fauteurs de désordre et de criminals": Adverse Perceptions of Immigrants in France between the Wars', *French History* 14: 201–21.

Lazarsfeld, P. (1974). *An Evaluation of the Pretrial Services Agency of the Vera Institute of Justice*. New York: Vera Institute of Justice.

Lea, J. and Young, J. (1984). *What is to be Done about Law and Order?* Harmondsworth: Penguin.

Leonard, M. (1998). 'Europe; a Continent in Search of a Mission', *New Statesman* 127: 20–2.

Lerch, M. and Schwellnus, G. (2006). 'Normative by Nature? The Role of Coherence in justifying EU's External Human Rights Policy', *Journal of European Public Policy* 13(2): 304–21.

Lerman, P. (1982). *Deinstitutionalization and the Welfare State*. New Brunswick: Rutgers University Press.

Lesser, I., Hoffman, B., Arquilla, J., Ronfeldt, D., Zanini, M., and Jenkins, B. M. (1999). *Countering the New Terrorism*. Santa Monica, Cal: RAND.

Lessig, L. (1999). *Code and Other Laws of Cyberspace*. New York: Basic Books.

Leverick, F. (2002a). 'Is English Self-Defence Law Incompatible with Article 2 of the ECHR?' *Criminal Law Review* (May): 347–62.

—— (2002b). 'The Use of Force in Public and Private Defence and Article 2: A Reply to Professor Sir John Smith'. *Criminal Law Review* (December): 963–7.

Lianos, M. with Douglas, M. (2000). 'Dangerization and the End of Deviance: The Institutional Environment', *British Journal of Criminology* 40(2): 261–78.

Lichtenstein, A. (1996). *Twice the Work of Free Labor: The Political Economy of Convict Labor in the New South*. London: Verso.

Loader, I. and Sparks, R. (2002). 'Contemporary Landscapes of Crime, Order, and Control: Governance, Risk, and Globalization', in M. Maguire, R. Morgan, and R. Reiner (eds) *The Oxford Handbook of Criminology* (2nd edn). Oxford: Oxford University Press.

————(2004). 'For an Historical Sociology of Crime Policy in England and Wales since 1968', *Critical Review of International Social and Political Philosophy* 7(2): 5–32.

Lovegrove, A. (1989). *Judicial Decision Making, Sentencing Policy, and Numerical Guidance.* New York: Springer-Verlag.

——(1999). 'Statistical Information Systems as a Means to Consistency and Rationality in Sentencing', *International Journal of Law and Information Technology* 7: 31–72.

Lowman, J. Menzies, R., and Palys, T. (eds) *Transcarceration: Essays on the Sociology of Control, Cambridge Studies in Criminology.* Cambridge: Gower.

Lowthian, J. (2002) 'Women's Prisons in England: Barriers to Reform', in P. Carlen (ed) *Women and Punishment: The Struggle for Justice.* Cullompton: Willan.

Lubove, R. (1965). *The Professional Altruist.* New York: Atheneum.

Lyon, D. (1994). *The Electronic Eye: The Rise of Surveillance Society.* Cambridge, Polity.

Magnette, P. (2003). 'European Governance and Civic Participation: Beyond Elitist Citizenship', *Political Studies* 51(1): 144–60.

Mahoney, B., Beaudin, B. D., Carver, J. A., Ryan, D. B., and Hoffman, R. B. (2001). *Pretrial Services Programs: Responsibilities and Potential.* NCJ 181939. Washington, DC: National Institute of Justice.

Maisel, A. Q. (1946). 'Bedlam 1946: Most U.S. Mental Hospitals are a Shame and a Disgrace', *Life* 20: 102–3.

Major, C. (2005). 'Europeanisation and Foreign and Security Policy – Undermining or Rescuing the Nation State' *Politics* 25(3): 175–90.

Manners, I. (2002). 'Normative Power Europe: A Contradiction in Terms?', *Journal of Common Market Studies* 40(2): 235–58.

——and Whitman, R. (2003). 'The "difference engine": Constructing and Representing the International Identity of the European Union', *Journal of European Public Policy* 10(3): 380–404.

Mannozzi, G. (2002). 'Are Guided Sentencing and Sentence Bargaining Incompatible? Perspectives of Reform in the Italian Legal System', in Hutton, N. and Tata, C. (eds) *Sentencing and Society: International Perspectives.* Aldershot, Ashgate.

Marchetti, A.M, Nice, R (Trans), Wacquant, L (Trans) (2002) 'Carceral Impoverishment: Class Inequality in the French Penitentiary Ethnography', *Ethnography* 3(4): 416–34.

Marshall, J. (2000). 'Death in Venice: Europe's Death-penalty Elitism', *The New Republic,* 31 July.

Martinson, R. (1974). 'What Works ? Questions and Answers about Prison Reform', *The Public Interest* 35: 22–54.

Mathiesen, T. (1998). 'Selective Incapacitation Revisited', *Law and Human Behavior* 22: 455–76.

——(1999). *On Globalization of Control: Towards an Integrated Surveillance System in Europe.* London: Statewatch.

——(2000). 'On the Globalization of Control: Towards an Integrated Surveillance System in Europe', in P. Green and A. Rutherford (eds) *Criminal Policy in Transition.* Oxford – Portland: Hart Publishing, 167–92.

—— (2002). 'Expanding the Concept of Terrorism?', in P. Scraton (ed) *Beyond September 11. An Anthology of Dissent*. London: Pluto Press, 84–93.

—— (2003). 'The Rise of the Surveillant State in Times of Globalization', in C. Sumner (ed) *The Blackwell Companion to Criminology*. Maiden, Oxford, Victoria, and Berlin: Blackwell Publishing, 437–51.

—— (2004). *Silently Silenced. Essays on the Creation of Acquiescence in Modern Society*. Winchester: Waterside Press.

Mayer-Gross, W., Slater, E., and Roth, M. (1960). *Clinical Psychiatry*. London: Cassell, 1960.

McAra, L., (2005). 'Modelling Penal Transformation', *Punishment and Society* 7(3): 277–302.

—— and McVie, S. (2005). 'The Usual Suspects? Street-life, Young Offenders and the Police', *Criminal Justice* 5(1): 5–36.

McEvoy, K. (2003) 'Beyond the Metaphor: Political Violence, Human Rights and "New" Peacemaking Criminology', *Theoretical Criminology* 7(3): 319–46.

McGuire, J. (ed) (1995). *What Works Reducing Offending: Guidelines from Research and Practice*. Chichester: Wiley.

McKibbin, R. (2006). 'The Destruction of the Public Sphere', *London Review of Books* 28(1): 3–8.

Melling, J. (1999). 'Accommodating Madness: New Research in the Social History of Insanity and Institutions', in J. Melling and B. Forsythe (eds) *Insanity, Institutions and Society, 1800–1914*. London: Routledge, 1–30.

Melossi, D. (2001). 'The Cultural Embeddedness of Social Control: Reflections on the Comparison of Italian and North-American Cultures Concerning Punishment', in *Theoretical Criminology* 5: 403–25.

Mermaz, L. (2001). *Les Geôles de la République*. Paris: Editions Stock.

Merton, R. K. (1968). 'The Self-Fulfilling Prophecy'. In *Social Theory and Social Structure* (3rd edn). New York: The Free Press, 475–90.

Michael, P. (2003). *Care and Treatment of the Mentally Ill in North Wales 1800–2000*. Cardiff: University of Wales Press.

Miers, D. (2000). 'Taking the Law into their Own Hands: Victims as Offenders', in Crawford, A. and Goodey, J. (eds) *Integrating a Victim Perspective within Criminal Justice*, Aldershot: Ashgate.

—— (2004). 'Situating and researching restorative justice in Great Britain', *Punishment and Society* 6: 23–46.

Miles, R. (1993). 'The Articulation of Racism and Nationalism: Reflections on European History', in J. Wrench and J. Solomos (eds) *Racism and Migration in Western Europe*. Oxford: Berg, 35–52.

Miller, J. (1973). 'The Politics of Change: Correctional Reform', in Y. Bakal (ed) *Closing Correctional Institutions*. Lexington, Mass: DC Heath.

Miller, P. (1980). 'The Territory of the Psychiatrist'. *Ideology and Consciousness* 7: 63–106.

Millie, A. Jacobson, J. and Hough, M. (2003). 'Understanding the Growth in the Prison Population in England and Wales'. *Criminal Justice* 3(4): 369–87.

Modood, T., Berthoud, R., Lakey, J., Nazroo, J., Smith, P., Virdee, S., and Beishon. S. (1997). *Ethnic Minorities in Britain: Diversity and Disadvantage*. London: Policy Studies Institute.

Moisi, D. (2001). 'The Real Crisis Over the Atlantic', *Foreign Affairs* 80 (July/August): 149–54.

Monahan, J. (forthcoming 2006). 'A Jurisprudence of Risk Assessment: Forecasting Harm among Prisoners, Predators, and Patients', *Virginia Law Review*.

Moore, M. H., Estrich, S. R., McGillis, D., and Spelman, W. (1984). *Dangerous Offenders: The Elusive Target of Justice*. Cambridge: Harvard University Press.

Moravcsik, A. (2001). 'The New Abolitionism: Why Does the U.S. Practice the Death Penalty while Europe Does Not?' *Council of European Studies Newsletter*. Available online at: http://www.europanet.org/past_newsletters/200109/default.htm.

Morrison, N. (ed) (2000). *Sentencing Practice*. Edinburgh: W. Green.

Morrison, W. (1994). 'Criminology, Modernity and the "Truth" of the Human Condition: Reflections on the Melancholy of Postmodernism', in D. Nelken (ed) *The Futures of Criminology*, London: Sage.

Moscow Centre for Prison Reform (MCPR) (1996). *Human Being in Prison*. Moscow: Moscow Centre for Prison Reform.

Moscow Helsinki Group (2003). *The Situation of Prisoners in Contemporary Russia*. Moscow Helsinki Group.

Muncie, J., (2002). 'Policy Transfers and What Works: Some Reflections on Comparative Youth Justice', *Youth Justice* 1(3): 27–35.

Murray, C. (1984). *Losing Ground: American Social Policy 1950–1980*. New York: Basic Books.

—— (1990). *The Emerging British Underclass*. London: Institute for Economic Affairs.

Mythen, G. and Walklate, S. (2005). 'Criminology and Terrorism', *British Journal of Criminology*, Advance Access, published on 28 July.

NACRO (1995). *Crime and Social Policy: A Report of the Crime and Social Policy Committee*. London: NACRO.

Naffine, N. (ed) (1995). *Gender, Crime and Feminism*, Aldershot: Dartmouth.

Nellis, M. (2004). ' "Into the Field of Corrections": The End of English Probation in the Early 21st Century?', *Cambrian Law Review* 25: 115–33.

Newburn, T. (2001). *'Atlantic Crossings' Inaugural Lecture*. London: Goldsmiths College.

—— (2003). *Crime and Criminal Justice Policy* (2nd edn). Harlow: Longman.

Newmann, I. B. (1998). 'European Identity, EU Expansion and the Integration/Exclusion Nexus', *Alternatives: Social Transformation and Humane Governance* 23: 397–417.

—— (1999). *Uses of the Other: The East in European Identity Formation*. Manchester: Manchester University Press.

Norko, M. A. and Barnaoski, M. V. (2005). 'The State of Contemporary Risk Assessment Research', *Canadian Journal of Psychiatry* (January): 18–26.

Norris, C., Moran, J., and Armstrong, G. (1998). 'Algorithmic Surveillance – the Future of Automated Visual Surveillance' in C. Norris, J. Moran, and G. Armstrong (eds) *Surveillance, Closed Circuit Television and Social Control*. Aldershot: Ashgate.

O'Connor, J. (1973). *The Fiscal Crisis of the State*. New York: St. Martin's Press.

OECD (2002) *Society at a Glance*.

O'Malley, P. (2003). 'Review of Crime and Modernity', *Theoretical Criminology* 7(4): 508–10.

Orlans, H. (1947). 'An American Death Camp'. *Politics* 5: 162–8.

Oshinsky, D. M. (1996). *Worse Than Slavery: Parchman Farm and the Ordeal of Jim Crow Justice*. New York: Free Press.

Ostrom, B. J., Kleinman, M., Cheeseman, F., Hansen, R., and Kauder, N. B. (2002). *Offender Risk Assessment in Virginia: A Three Stage Evaluation*. Washington, DC: National Institute of Justice.

Ozimek, N. A. (1997). 'Reinstitution of the Chain Gang: A Historical and Constitutional Analysis'. *Boston University Public and International Law Journal*, 6: 753–57.

Packer, H. L. (1968). *The Limits of the Criminal Sanction*. Stanford: Stanford University Press.

Palidda, S. (1996). 'La construction sociale de la déviance et de la criminalité parmi les immigrés: le cas italien', in S. Palidda (ed) *Délit d'immigration/immigrant delinquency*. Brussels: European Commission, 231–66.

Panasyuk, N. (2000). *Concepts of Social Tolerance and Social Policy: A Case Study of Crime and Penal Practice in the Transitional Period in Ukraine*. PhD thesis (unpublished). London: London School of Economics.

Pattie, C., Seyd, P., and Whiteley, P. (2003). 'Citizenship and Civic Engagement: Attitudes and Behaviour in Britain', *Political Studies* 51(3): 443–68.

Piacentini, L. (2001). 'Work to Live: The Function of Prison Labour in the Russian Prisons System'. Unpublished PhD thesis. Bangor: University of Wales.

—— (2004a) 'Barter in Russian Prisons', *European Criminology* 1(1): 17–45.

—— (2004b) 'Penal Identities in Russian Prisons Colonies', *Punishment & Society* 6(2): 131–47.

—— (2004c) *Surviving Russian Prisons: Punishment, Economy and Politics in Transition*. Cullompton, Devon: Willan Publishing.

Pinker, R. (1971). *Social Theory and Social Policy*. London: Heinemann.

Piven, F. and Cloward, R. (1971). *Regulating the Poor: The Functions of Public Welfare*. New York: Pantheon.

Platt, A. (1969). *The Child Savers: The Invention of Delinquency*. Chicago: University of Chicago Press.

Porter. R. (1987). *A Social History of Madness: Stories of the Insane*. London: Weidenfeld and Nicolson.

Portes, A. and Böröcz, J. (1987). 'Contemporary Immigration: Theoretical Perspectives on its Determinants and Modes of Incorporation'. *International Migration Review*, 23: 606–30.

Power, M. (1997). *The Audit Society: Rituals of Verification*. Oxford: Oxford University Press.

Pratt, J. (2001). 'Beyond "Gulags Western Style"? A Reconsideration of Nils Christie's Crime Control as Industry', *Theoretical Criminology*, 5(3): 283–314.

—— (2002). *Punishment and Civilization: Penal Tolerance and Intolerance in Modern Society*. London: Sage.

President's Commission on Law Enforcement and Administration of Justice (1967). *The Challenge of Crime in a Free Society*. Washington, DC: US Government. Printing Office.

Pressman, J. (1986). 'Uncertain Promise: Psychosurgery and the Development of Scientific Psychiatry in America, 1935 to 1955'. PhD dissertation (unpublished). Philadelphia, PA: University of Pennsylvania.

Prodi, R. (2000). *Europe as I See It*. Cambridge: Polity Press.

Prokhovnuik, R. (1999). 'The State of Liberal Sovereignty', *British Journal of Politics and International Relations* 1(1): 1–63.

Quen, J. (1974). 'Review of The Discovery of the Asylum by David Rothman', *Journal of Psychiatry and the Law* 2: 119–20.

Rawlinson, M. P. (1998). *Hunting the Chameleon: The Problems of Identifying Russian Organised Crime.* PhD thesis (unpublished). London: London School of Economics.

Ray, L. (1981). 'Models of Madness in Victorian Asylum Practice'. *European Journal of Sociology* 22: 229–64.

Redlich, F. C. (1958). 'Preface', in W. Caudill, *The Psychiatric Hospital as a Small Society.* Cambridge, Mass: Harvard University Press.

Reitz, K. (2001). 'The Disassembly and Reassembly of US Sentencing Practice', in Tonry, M. and Frase, R. (eds) *Sentencing and Sanction Systems in Western Countries.* New York: Oxford University Press.

Rhodes, W., Hyatt, R., and Scheiman, P. (1996). *Predicting Pretrial Misconduct with Drug Tests of Arrestees: Evidence from Six Sites.* Washington, DC: US Department of Justice, Office of Justice Programs, National Institute of Justice.

Ricoeur, P. (1970). *Freud and Philosophy.* New Haven: Yale University Press.

Rivera Beiras, I. (ed) (1999). *La Cárcel en España en el Fin del Milenio.* Barcelona: Editorial M.J. Bosch.

Robertson, D. (1998). *Judicial Discretion in the House of Lords.* Oxford: Clarendon Press.

Robertson, R. (1992). *Globalization: Social Theory and Global Culture.* London: Sage.

Robinson, P. H. (2001). 'Punishing Dangerousness: Cloaking Preventive Detention as Criminal Justice', *Harvard Law Review* 114: 1429–56.

Rodley, N. (2000). *The Treatment of Prisoners under International Law.* New York: Oxford University Press.

Rose, N. (1980). 'Sociology and Social Policy: the Problem of Inequality', *Politics and Power* 2.

—— (1985). *The Psychological Complex: Psychology, Politics, and Society in England 1869– 1939.* London: Routledge and Kegan Paul.

—— (1986). 'Psychiatry: The Discipline of Mental Health', in P. Miller and N. Rose (eds) *The Power of Psychiatry.* Oxford: Polity Press.

—— (2000). 'Government and Control', in D. Garland and R. Sparks (eds) *Criminology and Social Theory.* Oxford: Oxford University Press.

Rosenau, J. N. (1997) *Along the Domestic-Foreign Frontier: Exploring Governance in a Turbulent World.* Cambridge: Cambridge University Press.

Roth, Sir M. (1973). 'Psychiatry and Its Critics'. *British Journal of Psychiatry,* 122: 374–402.

Rothman, D. (1971). *The Discovery of the Asylum: Social Order and Disorder in the New Republic.* Boston: Little, Brown.

—— (1976). 'Review of "Mental Institutions in America" by Gerald Grob'. *Journal of Interdisciplinary History* 7: 534.

—— (1980). *Conscience and Convenience: The Asylum and Its Alternatives in Progressive America.* Boston: Little, Brown.

—— (1984). 'Social Control: The Uses and Abuses of the Concept in the History of Incarceration', in S. Cohen and A. Scull (eds) *Social Control and the State: Historical and Comparative Essays.* Cambridge: Polity Press.

Rumford, C. (2003). 'European Civil Society or Transnational Social Space?', *European Journal of Social Theory* 6(1): 22–43.

Rubin, E. and Feeley, M. (1994). 'Federalism: Some Notes on a National Neurosis', *UCLA Law Review* 41: 903–51.

Runciman, D. (2004). 'The Precautionary Principle', *London Review of Books* 26(7).

Rusche, G. and Kirchheimer, O. (1934). *Punishment and Social Structure*, New York: Russell and Russell.

Sachs, W. (2001). 'Rio + 10 and the North-South Divide', *World Summit Papers of the Heinrich Böll Foundation: No. 8*. Berlin: Germany.

Santel, B. (1995). *Migration in und nach Europa. Erfahrangen, Strukturen, Politik.* Leverkusen: Leske und Budrich.

Santos, B. de S. (2002). *Toward a New Legal Common Sense*. London: Butterworths LexisNexis.

Sarat, A. (2001). *When the State Kills: Capital Punishment and the American Condition.* Princeton: Princeton University Press.

—— (ed) (1999). *The Killing State*. Oxford: Oxford University Press.

Sasson, T. (1995). *Crime Talk: How Citizens Construct a Social Problem*. New York: Aldine de Gruyter

Sayad, A. (1991). *L'Immigration ou les paradoxes de l'altérité*. Brussels: DeBoeck Université.

—— (1999). *La Double Absence. Des illusions de l'émigré aux souffrances de l'immigré.* Paris: Editions du Seuil.

Schabas, W. (1997). *The Abolition of the Death Penalty In International Law*. Cambridge: Cambridge University Press.

Schlesinger, P. (1987) 'On National Identity; Some Conceptions and Misconceptions Criticized', *Social Science Information* 26(2): 219–64.

—— (1999). 'Collective Identities, Friends, Enemies'. *Innovation: The European Journal of Social Sciences* 12(4): 461–70.

Schlossman, S. (1977). *Love and the American Delinquent: The Theory and Practice of 'Progressive' Juvenile Justice 1825–1920*. Chicago: University of Chicago Press.

Scull, A. (1975). 'From Madness to Mental Illness: Medical Men as Moral Entrepreneurs'. *European Journal of Sociology* 16: 219–61.

—— (1977). *Decarceration: Community Treatment and the Deviant – A Radical View.* Englewood Cliffs, NJ: Prentice-Hall.

—— (1984). *Decarceration: Community Treatment and the Deviant – A Radical View* (2nd edn). Cambridge: Polity Press.

—— (1987). 'Desperate Remedies: A Gothic Tale of Madness and Modern Medicine'. *Psychological Medicine* 17: 561–77.

—— (1989a). *Social Order/Mental Disorder: Anglo-American Psychiatry in Historical Perspective*. Berkeley: University of California Press.

—— (1989b). 'Reflections on the Historical Sociology of Psychiatry', in *Social Order/ Mental Disorder: Anglo-American Psychiatry in Historical Perspective*. Berkeley: University of California Press, 1–30.

—— (1991). 'Psychiatry and Social Control in the Nineteenth and Twentieth Centuries'. *History of Psychiatry* 2: 149–69.

—— (1993). *The Most Solitary of Afflictions: Madness and Society in Britain, 1700–1900.* London and New Haven: Yale University Press.

—— (1995). 'Psychiatrists and Historical "Facts," Part One: The Historiography of Somatic Treatments'. *History of Psychiatry* 6: 225–41.

—— (1999). 'Rethinking the History of Asylumdom', in J. Melling and B. Forsythe (eds) *Insanity, Institutions and Society, 1800–1914*. London: Routledge, 295–315.

Scull, A. (2005). *Desperate Remedies: A Gothic Tale of Madness and Modern Medicine*. London and New Haven: Yale University Press.

Sennett, R. (1998). *The Corrosion of Character*. New York: Norton.

Sentencing Guidelines Council (SGC) (2004). *Overarching Principles: Seriousness. Guideline*. Accessed online at: http://www.sentencing-guidelines.gov.uk/docs/Seriousness_guideline.pdf.

Serrano, M. M. (1993). 'Los efectos sociales de la política inmigratoria'. *Política y Sociedad* 12: 37–43;

Shearing, C. and Stenning, P. (1985). 'From the Panopticon to Disneyworld: the Development of Discipline', in A. N. Doob and E. L. Greenspan (eds), *Perspectives in Criminal Law*. Aurora: Canada Law Book Co.

Shore, C. (2000). *Building Europe: the Cultural Politics of European Integration*. London: Routledge.

Short, J. (1984) 'The Social Fabric at Risk: Toward the Social Transformation of Risk

Simester, A. and Sullivan, R. (2003). *Criminal Law: Theory and Doctrine* (2nd edn). Abingdon: Hart Publishing.

Simon, J. (1990). *Poor Discipline*. Chicago: University of Chicago Press.

—— (1997). 'Governing through Crime', in G. Fisher and L. Friedman (eds) *The Crime Conundrum*. Boulder, Colorado: Westview Press.

—— (2001). 'Entitlement to Cruelty: Neo-Liberalism and the Punitive Mentality in the United States', in K. Stenson and R. Sullivan (eds) *Crime, Risk and Justice*. Cullompton, Devon: Willan Publishing.

—— (2002). 'Governing through Crime Metaphors', *Brooklyn Law Review* 67(4): 1035–70.

Sjoberg, G., Gill, E., and Williams, N. (2001). 'A Sociology of Human Rights', *Social Problems* 48(1): 11–47.

Skolnick, J. H. (1966). *Justice without Trial: Law Enforcement in Democratic Society*. New York: Wiley.

Smith, A. D. (1998). *Nationalism and Modernism*. London: Routledge.

Smith, D. J. (1995). 'Youth Crime and Conduct Disorders', in M. Rutter and D. J. Smith (eds) *Psychosocial Disorders in Young People: Time Trends and their Causes*, Chichester: Wiley.

—— (1997). 'Ethnic Origins, Crime and Criminal Justice', in M. Maguire, R. Morgan, and R. Reiner (eds) *The Oxford Handbook of Criminology* (2nd edn). Oxford: Oxford University Press.

—— (1999). 'Less Crime Without More Punishment', *Edinburgh Law Review* 3: 294–316.

Smith, J. C. (2002). 'The Use of Force in Public or Private Defence and Article 2', *Criminal Law Review* (December): 958–62.

Smith, R. (1981). *Trial by Medicine: Insanity and Responsibility in Victorian Trials*. Edinburgh: Edinburgh University Press.

Snacken, S., Beyens, K., and Tubex, H. (1995). 'Changing Prison Populations in Western Countries: Fate or Policy?', *European Journal of Crime, Criminal Law and Criminal Justice* 3: 18–53

Sparks, R. (1991). 'Reason and Unreason in Left Realism: Some Problems in the Constitution of the Fear of Crime', in R. Matthews and J. Young (eds) *Issues in Realist Criminology*. London: Sage.

—— (1992). *Television and the Drama of Crime*. Maidenhead: Open University Press.

—— (1997). 'Recent Social Theory and the Study of Crime and Punishment', in M. Maguire R. Morgan and R. Reiner (eds) *The Oxford Handbook of Criminology* (2nd edn). Oxford: Clarendon Press.

—— (2000). ' "Bringin' it all back home": Populism, Media Coverage and the Dynamics of Locality and Globality in the Politics of Crime Control', in K. Stenson and R. Sullivan (eds) *Crime, Risk and Justice*. Cullompton, Devon: Willan Publishing.

—— (2003). 'Punishment, Populism and Political Culture in Late Modernity', in S. McConville (ed) *The Use of Punishment*. Cullompton, Devon: Willan Publishing.

—— Bottoms, A. and Hay, W. (1996). *Prisons and the Problem of Order*. Oxford: Clarendon Press.

—— Girling, E. and Loader, I. (2001). 'Fear and Everyday Urban Lives', *Urban Studies* 38(5–6): 885–98.

Spicer, M. (2004). 'Public Administration, the History of Ideas, and the Reinventing Government Movement', *Public Administration Review* 64(3): 353–62.

Stellars, K. (2002). *The Rise and Rise of Human Rights*. Stroud: Sutton.

Stevenson, N. (1999). *The Transformation of the Media: Globalisation, Morality and Ethics*. London: Longman.

Stith, K. and Cabranes, J. A. (1998). *Fear of Judging: Sentencing Guidelines in the Federal Courts*. Chicago: University of Chicago Press.

Stolcke, V. (1995). 'Talking Culture: New Boundaries, New Rhetorics of Exclusion in Europe', *Current Anthropology* 36: 1–13.

Stone, M. (1985a). 'Shellshock and the Psychologists', in W. F. Bynum, R. Porter, and M. Shepherd (eds) *The Anatomy of Madness*, Vol 2. London: Tavistock, 242–71.

—— (1985b). 'The Military and Industrial Roots of Clinical Psychology in Britain, 1900–1945'. Unpublished PhD dissertation, London School of Economics and Political Science.

Strath, B. (2000a). 'A European Identity: To the Historical Limits of the Concept', *European Journal of Social Theory* 5(4): 387–401.

—— (2000b). 'EU efforts at creating a European Identity: 1973 and beyond'. Florence: RSCAS-EUI IDNET Conference Paper EUR/72.

Sutton, J. (1988). *Stubborn Children: Controlling Delinquency in the United States 1640–1981*. Berkeley: University of California Press.

Szasz, T. (1970). *The Manufacture of Madness*. New York: Harper and Row.

Tamanaha, B. Z. (1997). *Realistic Socio-Legal Theory*. Oxford: Clarendon Press.

Tata, C. (1997) 'Conceptions and Representations of the Sentencing Decision Process', *Journal of Law and Society* 24(3): 395–420.

—— (2002a). 'So What Does "and Society" Mean?', in C. Tata and N. Hutton, (eds) *Sentencing and Society, International Perspectives*. Aldershot: Ashgate.

—— (2002b). 'Accountability for the Sentencing Decision Process – Towards a New Understanding', in N. Hutton, and C. Tata (eds) *Sentencing and Society. International Perspectives*. Aldershot: Ashgate.

—— Hutton, N., Wilson, J., and Paterson, A. (1996). 'Sentencing and Computerised Information Systems: The Process and Progress of the Scottish Prototype', *The Juridical Review* (January): 486–503.

Taylor, L. (1997). 'Crime, Anxieties and Locality: Responding to the "Conditions of England" at the End of the Century', *Theoretical Criminology* 1(1): 53–75.

Teubner, G. (ed) (1997). *Global Law without a State*. Aldershot: Dartmouth Publishing.

Tham, H. (1998). 'Crime and the Welfare State: The Case of the United Kingdom and Sweden', in V. Ruggiero, N. South, and I. Taylor (eds) *The New European Criminology: Crime and Social Order in Europe*. London: Routledge, 368–94.

Thomas, D. A. (1999). *Current Sentencing Practice*. London: Sweet and Maxwell.

Thompson, J. (1996). *The Media and Modernity*. Cambridge: Polity Press.

Timms, N. (1964). *Psychiatric Social Work in Great Britain 1939–1962*. London: Routledge.

Titmuss, R. M. (1974). *The Gift Relationship: Human Blood and Social Policy*. London: Allen and Unwin.

Tomes, N. (1984). *A Generous Confidence: Thomas Story Kirkbride and the Art of Asylum Keeping, 1840–1883*. Cambridge: Cambridge University Press.

Tomlinson, J. (1999). *Globalization and Culture*. Cambridge: Polity Press.

—— (2000). 'Proximity Politics', *Information, Communication and Society* 3(3): 402–14.

Tonry, M. (1996). *Sentencing Matters*. Oxford: Oxford University Press.

—— (1999). 'Why are US Incarceration Rates so High?', *Crime and Delinquency*, 45: 419–37.

—— (2001). 'Symbol, Substance and Severity in Western Penal Policies', *Punishment and Society* 3(4): 517–26.

—— and Frase, R. (eds) (2001). *Sentencing and Sanction Systems in Western Countries*. New York: Oxford University Press.

Tournier, P. (1996). 'La délinquance des étrangers en France: analyse des statistiques pénales', in S. Palidda (ed) *Délit d'immigration/immigrant delinquency*. Brussels: European Commission.

—— (2002). *Statistique pénale annuelle du Conseil de l'Europe, Enquête 2001*. Strasbourg: Editions du Conseil de l'Europe.

Tripier, M. (1990). *L'Immigration dans la classe ouvrière en France*. Paris: CIEMI and L'Harmattan.

Tulkens, F. (2002) 'Vers une justice pénale européenne?', in L. Mucchielli and P. Robert (eds) *Crime et sécurité: L'état des saviors*. Paris: Editions La Découverte, 414–23.

Tyack, D. (1974). *The One Best System: A History of American Urban Education*. Cambridge, Mass: Harvard University Press.

Uggen, C. and Manza, J. (2002). 'Democratic Contraction? The Political Consequences of Felon Disenfranchisement in the United States', *American Sociological Review* 67(6): 777–803.

Uniacke, S. (1994). *Permissible Killing. The Self Defence Justification of Homicide*. Cambridge: Cambridge University Press.

UNICEF (2001). *A League Table of Teenage Births in Rich Nations*.

United Nations (1955). *The United Nations Standard Minimum Rules for the Treatment of Prisoners*. New York: The United Nations.

Urry, J. (1998). *'Globalisation and Citizenship'* , paper stored online at Department of Sociology, Lancaster University, Lancaster LA1 4YN, UK, available online at: http://www.comp.lancs.ac.uk/sociology/papers/Urry-Globalisation-and-Citizenship.pdf

—— (2000). 'The global media and cosmopolitanism' paper stored online at Department of Sociology, Lancaster University, Lancaster LA1 4YN, UK, available online at: http://www.comp.lancs.ac.uk/sociology/soc065ju.html.

Valenstein, E. (1986). *Great and Desperate Cures: The Rise and Decline of Psychosurgery and Other Radical Treatments for Mental Illness*. New York: Basic Books.

Van de Steeg, M. (2002). 'Rethinking the Conditions for a Public Sphere in the European Union', *European Journal of Social Theory* 5(4): 499–519.

Van Ham, P. (2000). *European Integration and the Postmodern Condition: Governance, Democracy, Identity*. London: Routledge.

Van Houtoum, H. and Van Naerssen, T. (2002). 'Bordering, Ordering and Othering', *Tijdschrift voor Economische en Sociale Geografie* 95(2): 125–36.

Van Nostrand, M. (2003). *Assessing Risk Among Pretrial Defendants in Virginia: The Virginia Pretrial Risk Assessment Instrument*. Richmond, Va: Virginia Department of Criminal Justice Services.

van Zyl Smit, D. and van der Spuy, E. (2004) 'Importing Criminological Ideas in a New Democracy: Recent South African Experiences', in T. Newburn and R. Sparks (eds), *Criminal Justice and Political Cultures: Exploring National and International Dimensions of Crime Control*. Cullompton, Devon: Willan Publishing.

Vanpaeschen, L. (1998). *Les Barbelés de la honte*. Brussels: Luc Pire.

Von Hirsch, A (1993). *Censure and Sanction*. Oxford: Clarendon Press.

—— (1976). *Doing Justice*. New York: Hill and Wang.

—— and Jareborg, N. (1991) 'Gauging Criminal Harm: A Living Standard Analyisis', *Oxford Journal of Legal Studies* 11: 1–38.

Wacquant, L. (2000). 'The New "Peculiar Institution": On the Prison as Surrogate Ghetto', *Theoretical Criminology* 4(3): 377–89.

—— (2005). 'Race as Civic Felony'. *International Social Science Journal* 181: 127–42.

—— (2006). *Deadly Symbiosis: Race and the Rise of Neoliberal Penality*. Cambridge: Polity Press.

—— (2007). *Punishing the Poor: The New Government of Social Insecurity*. Durham NC: Duke University Press.

Walker, M. A. (1989). 'The Court Disposal and Remands of White, Afro-Caribbean, and Asian Men in London', *British Journal of Criminology* 28: 353–67.

Walker, R. B. J. (1997). 'The Subject of Security', in K. Krause and M. C. Williams (eds) *Critical Security Studies: Concepts and Cases*. Minneapolis: University of Minnesota Press.

Walmsley, R. (2000). *Prison Population Size: Problems and Solutions*. Paper presented at a Council of Europe Seminar.

—— (2003). *World Prison Brief 2003*. London: Home Office. Accessed online at: http://www.kcl.ac.uk/depsta/rel/icps/worldprisonbrief.

Walsh, O. (1999). ' "The Designs of Providence": Race, Religion and Irish Insanity', in J. Melling and B. Forsythe (eds) *Insanity, Institutions and Society, 1800–1914*. London: Routledge, 223–42.

Walter, M. and Kubink, M. (1993). 'Ausländerkriminalität: Phänomen oder Phantom der (Kriminal-)Politik?' *Monatsschrift für Kriminologie und Strafrechtsreform*, 76: 306–17.

Walton, J. (1985) 'Casting Out and Bringing Back in Victorian England: Pauper Lunatics, 1840–1870', in W. F. Bynum, R. Porter, and M. Shepherd (eds) *The Anatomy of Madness*, Vol 2. London: Tavistock, 132–46.

Walzer, M. (1983). *Spheres of Justice. A Defence of Pluralism and Equality*. New York: Basic Books.

Walzer, M. (1994). *Thick and Thin: Moral Argument at Home and Abroad*. Notre Dame: Notre Dame University Press.

Webb, J., Schirato, T., and Danaher, G. (2002). *Understanding Bourdieu*. Crows Nest: Allen and Unwin.

Weber, M. (1968). *Economy and Society*. Berkeley: University of California Press.

Wheeler, S., Mann, K., and Sarat, A. (1988). *Sitting in Judgment: The Sentencing of White Collar Criminals*. New Haven: Yale University Press.

Wilkinson, R. (2000). *Mind the Gap: Hierarchies, Health and Human Evolution*. London: Weidenfeld and Nicolson.

Wills, G. (1975). 'The Human Sewer'. *New York Review of Books* 22: 3–8.

Wilson, W. (2002). *Central Issues in Criminal Law Theory*. Abingdon: Hart Publishing.

Windlesham, D. (1998). *Politics, Punishment and Populism*. Oxford: Oxford University Press.

Wing, J. K. and Brown, G. W. (1970). *Institutionalism and Schizophrenia*. Cambridge: Cambridge University Press.

Wortley, R. (2002). *Situational Prison Control: Crime Prevention in Correctional Institutions*. Cambridge: Cambridge University Press.

Wrench, J., Rea, A., and Ouali, N. (eds) (1999). *Migrants, Ethnic Minorities, and the Labour Market: Integration and Exclusion in Europe*. London: Palgrave Macmillan.

Wright, D. (1998). 'Family Strategies and the Institutional Commitment of Idiots in Victorian England'. *Journal of Family History* 23: 189–208.

—— (1999). 'The Discharge of Pauper Lunatics from County Asylums in Mid-Victorian England: The Case of Buckinghamshire, 1853–1872', in J. Melling and B. Forsythe (eds) *Insanity, Institutions and Society, 1800–1914*. London: Routledge, 93–112.

Wright, F. Jr (ed) (1947). *Out of Sight, Out of Mind*. Philadelphia: National Mental Health Foundation.

Wright, S. (1998). *An Appraisal of Technologies of Political Control*. Luxemburg: European Parliament, Directorate General for Research, PE 166.499. Available online at: http://cryptome.org/stoa-atpc.htm.

Wuthnow, R., Hunter, J., Bergesen, A., and Kurzweil, E. (1984). *Cultural Analysis*, London: Routledge.

Young, A. (1996). *Imagining Crime*. London: Sage.

Young, J. (1971). 'Deviancy Amplification in Industrial Societies', in S. Cohen, S. (ed) *Images of Deviance*, London: Pelican.

—— (1985). 'The Failure of Criminology', in R. Matthews and J. Young (eds) *Confronting Crime*. London: Sage.

—— (1999). *The Exclusive Society*. London: Sage.

—— (2003). 'Merton with Energy, Katz with Structure: The Sociology of Vindictiveness and the Criminology of Transgression', *Theoretical Criminology* 7(3): 388–414.

Young, R. (2000). 'Integrating a Multi-Victim Perspective into Criminal Justice through Restorative Justice Conferences', in A. Crawford and J. Goodey (eds) *Integrating a Victim Perspective within Criminal Justice*. Aldershot: Ashgate.

Zauberman, R. (2000). 'Victims as Consumers of the Criminal Justice System?', in A. Crawford and J. Goodey, (eds) *Integrating a Victim Perspective within Criminal Justice*. Aldershot: Ashgate.

Zedner, L. (2002). 'Victims', in M. Maguire, R. Morgan, and R. Reiner (eds) *The Oxford Handbook of Criminology* (3rd edn). Oxford: Oxford University Press.

—— (2003a). 'The Concept of Security: An Agenda for Comparative Analysis', *Legal Studies* 23(1): 153–76.

—— (2003b). 'Too Much Security?' *International Journal of the Sociology of Law* 31(3): 155–84.

Zimring, F. (2003). *The Contradictions of American Capital Punishment.* Oxford: Oxford University Press.

Zola, I. K. (1972). 'Medicine as an Institution of Social Control'. *The Sociological Review* 20: 487–504.

INDEX